UQ HOLDER!

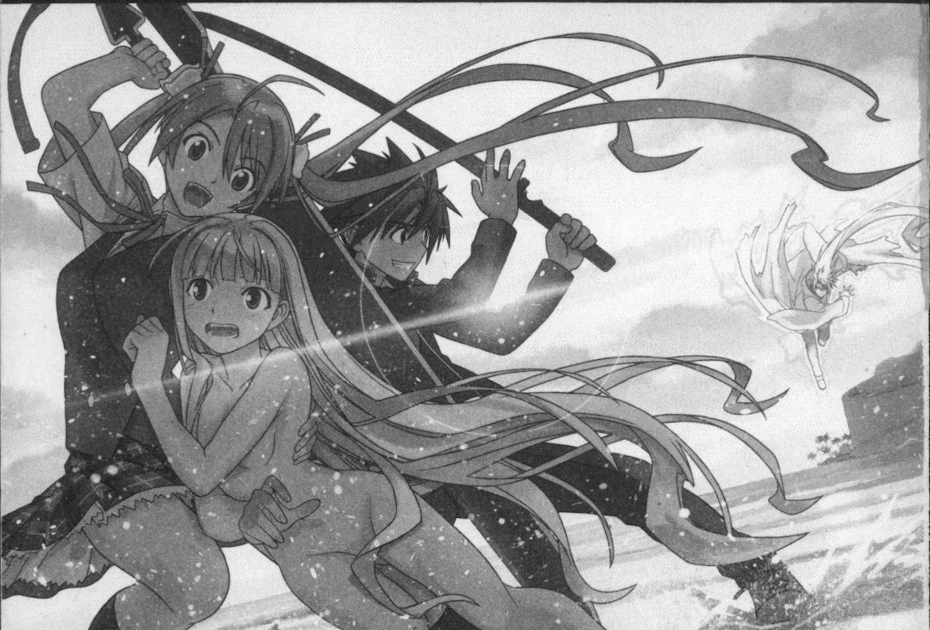

KEN AKAMATSU

vol.13

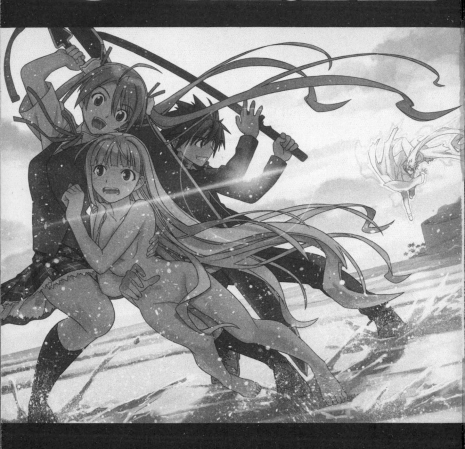

CONTENTS

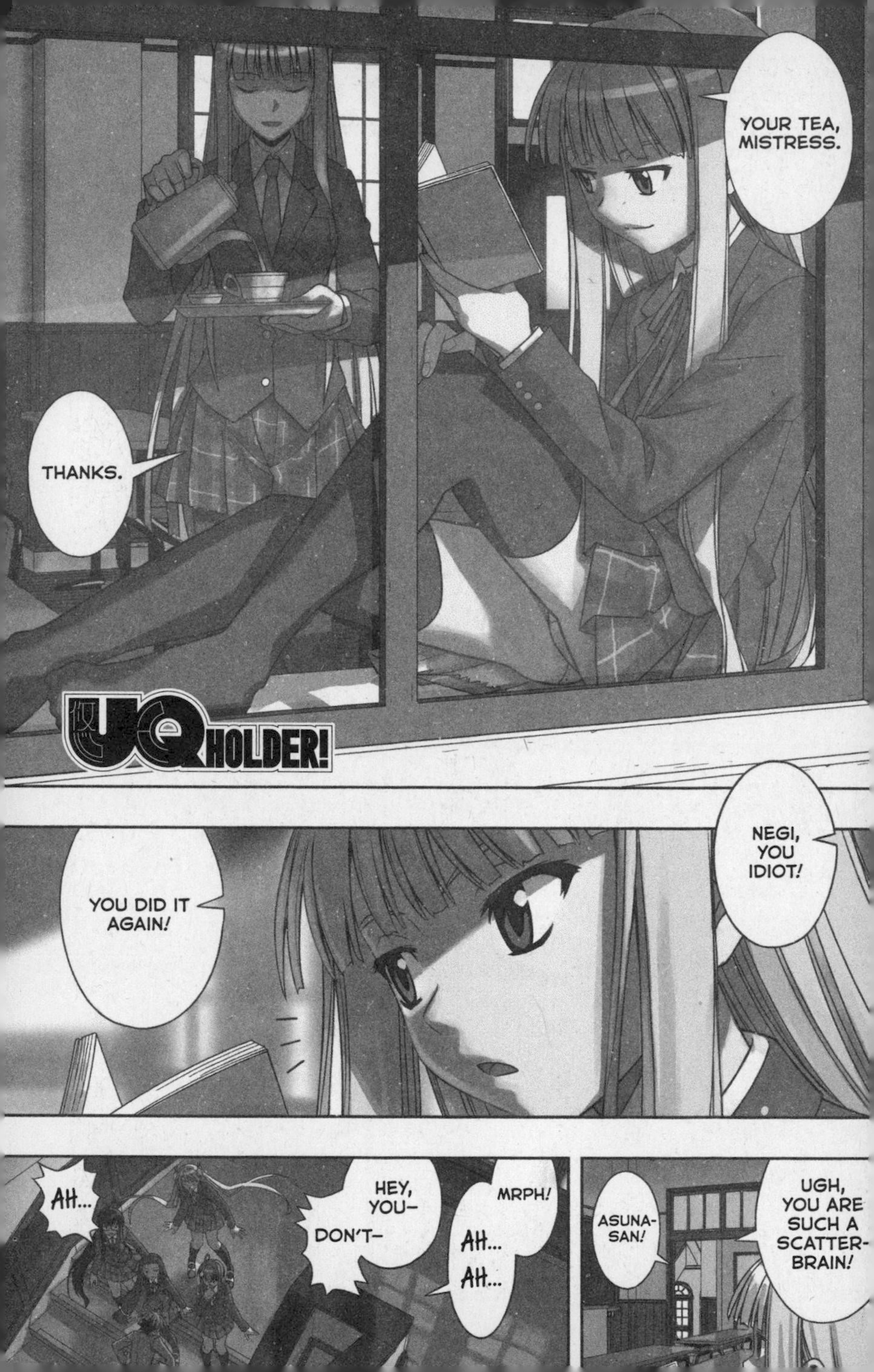
YOUR TEA, MISTRESS.
THANKS.
NEGI, YOU IDIOT!
YOU DID IT AGAIN!
UGH, YOU ARE SUCH A SCATTER-BRAIN!
ASUNA-SAN!
MRPH!
AH... AH...
HEY, YOU—
DON'T—
AH...

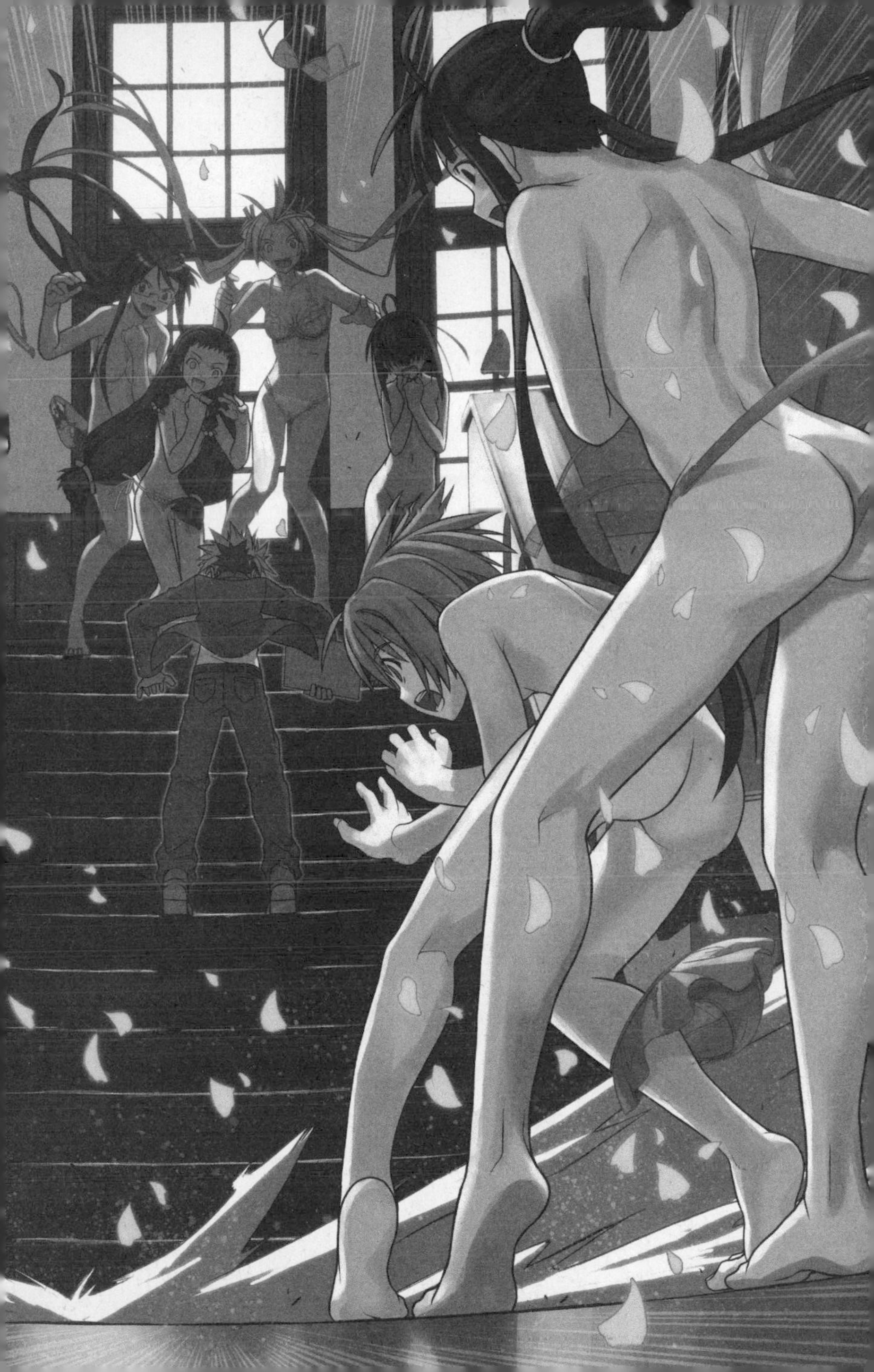

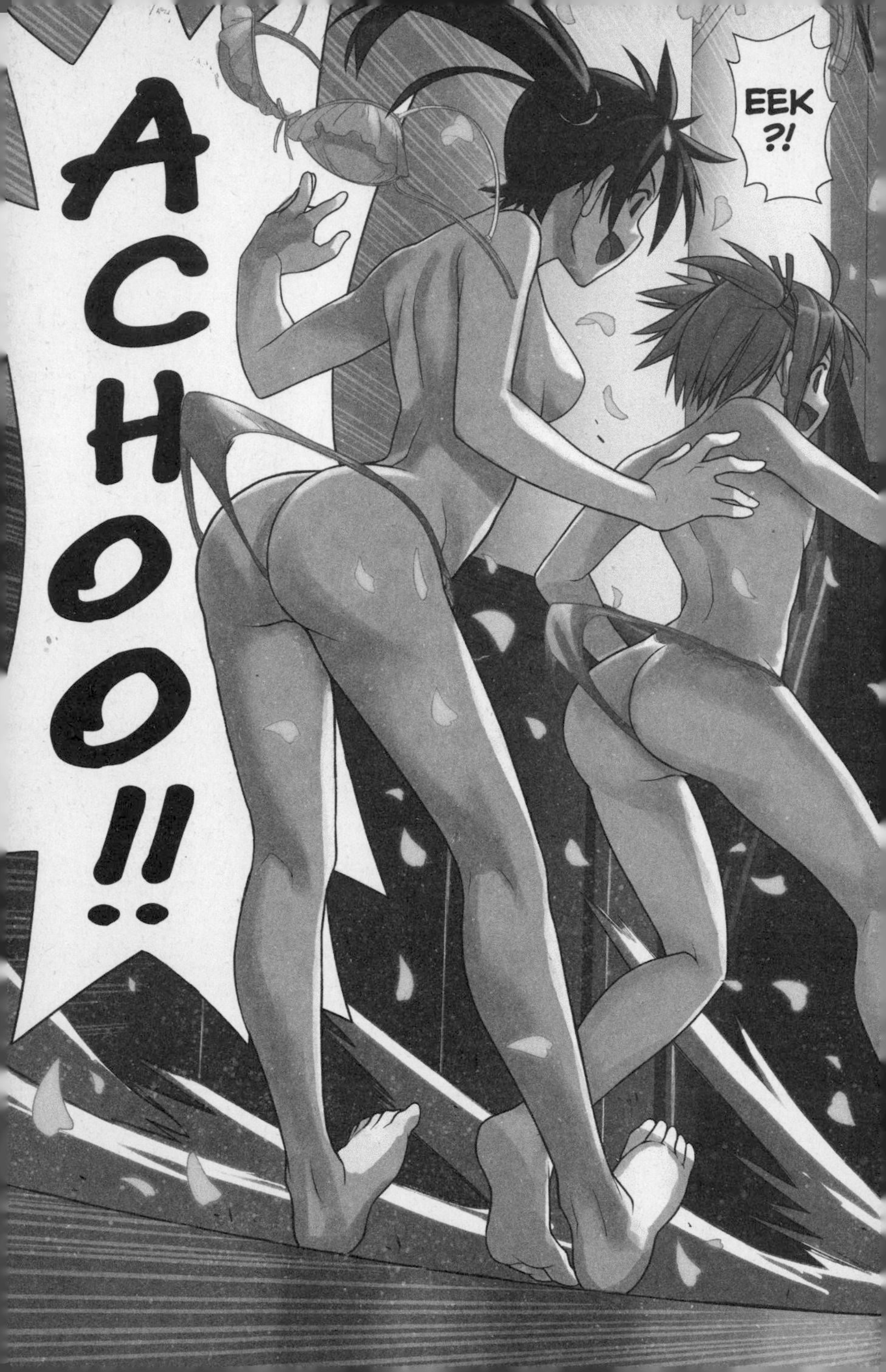
EEK ?!
ACHOOO!!

UQ HOLDER!

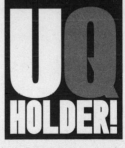

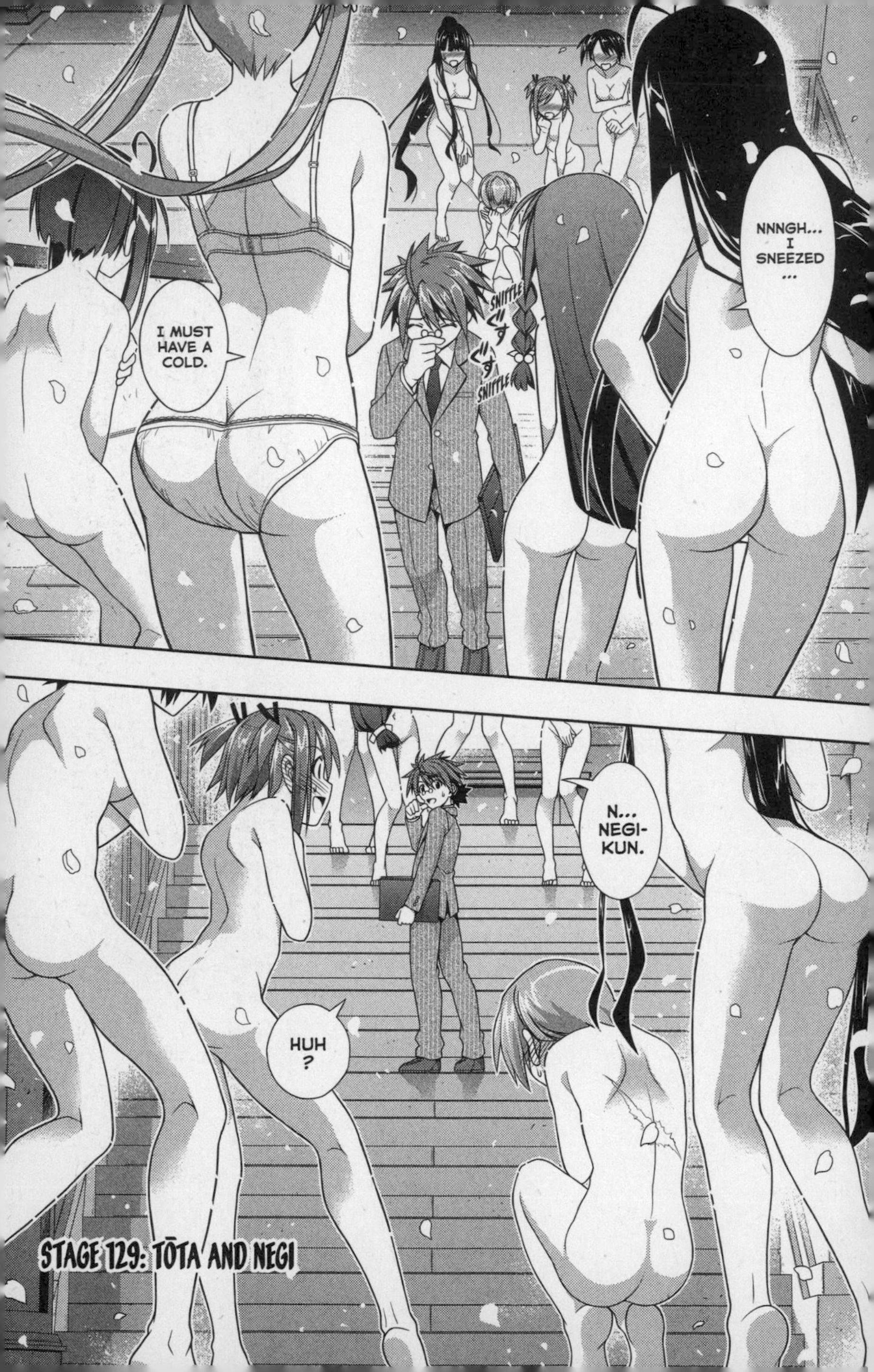
NNNGH... I SNEEZED ...
SNIFFLE ぐす
ぐす SNIFFLE
I MUST HAVE A COLD.
N... NEGI-KUN.
HUH ?

STAGE 129: TŌTA AND NEGI

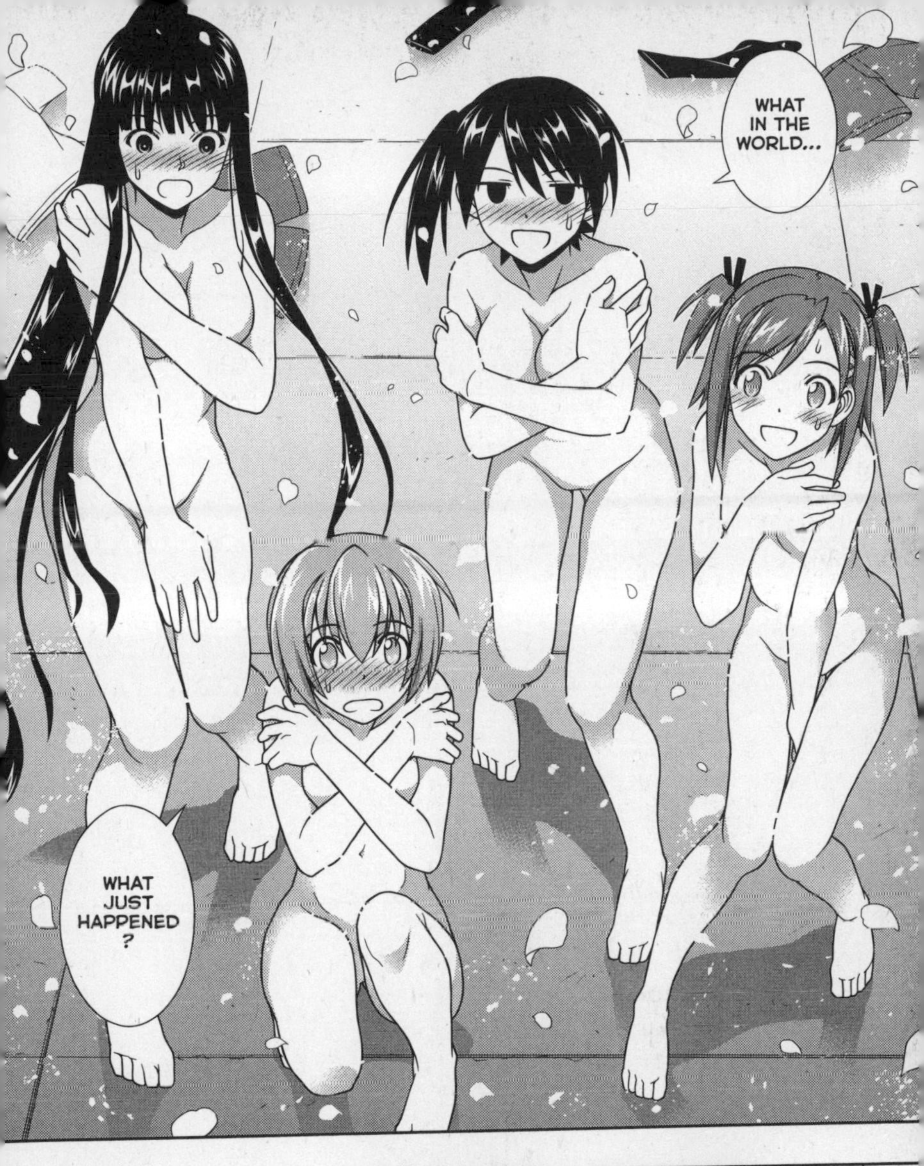
WHAT IN THE WORLD...
WHAT JUST HAPPENED?
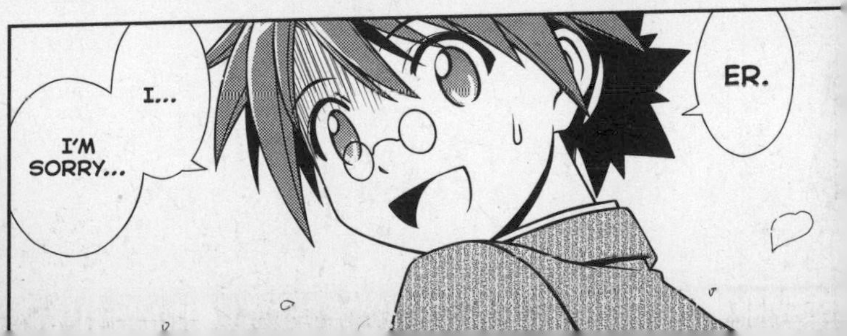
ER.
I...
I'M SORRY...
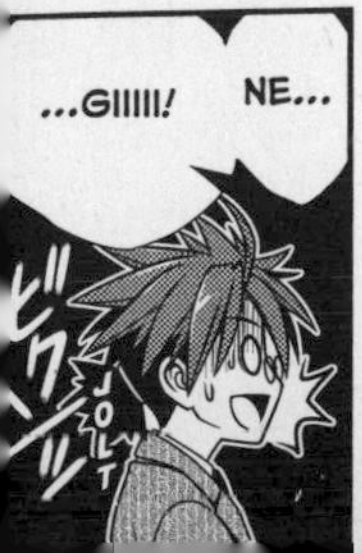
NE...
...GIIIII!
JOLT

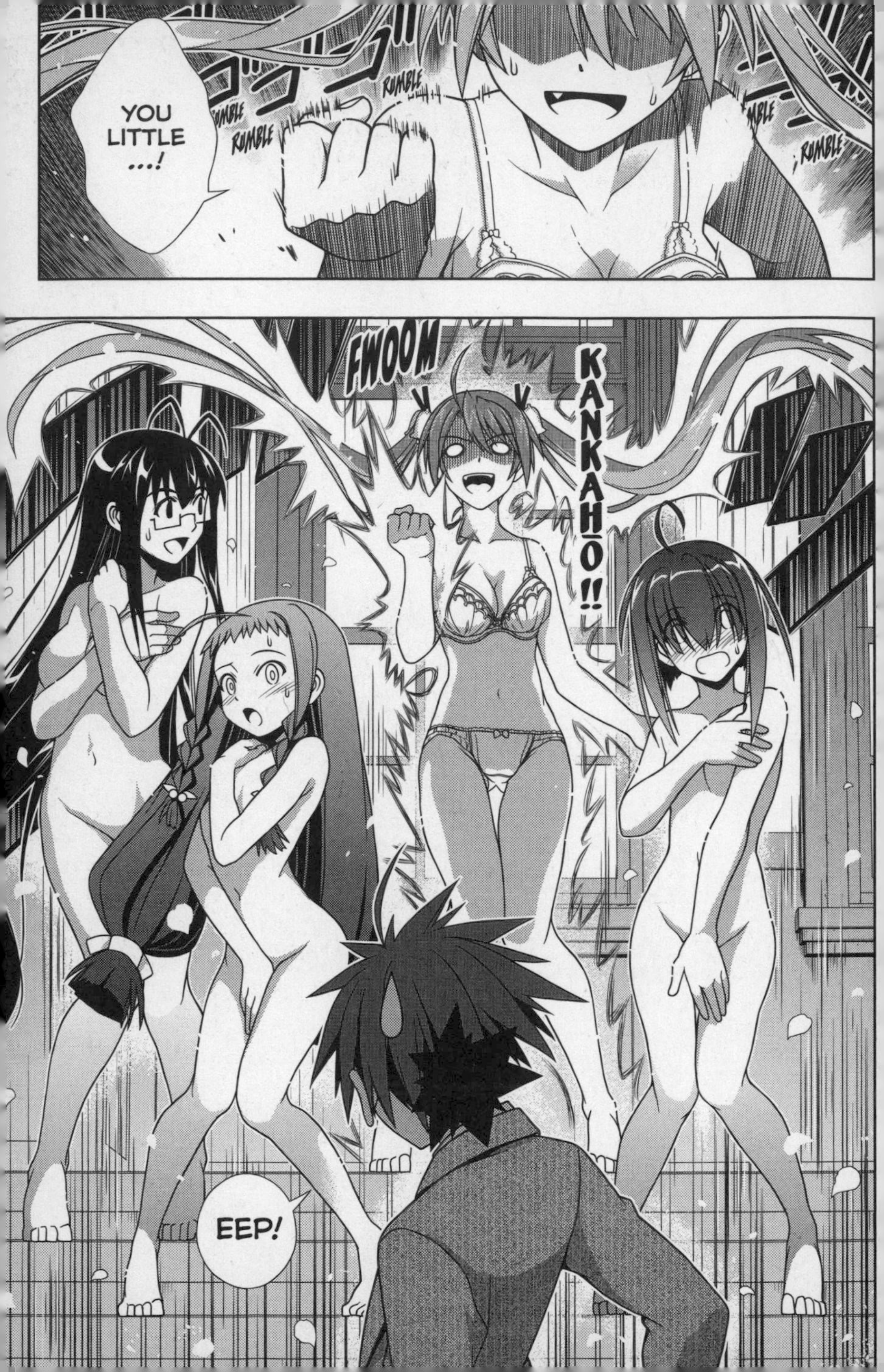
RUMBLE
RUMBLE
RUMBLE
RUMBLE
RUMBLE
YOU LITTLE ...!
KANKAHŌ!!
FWOOM
EEP!

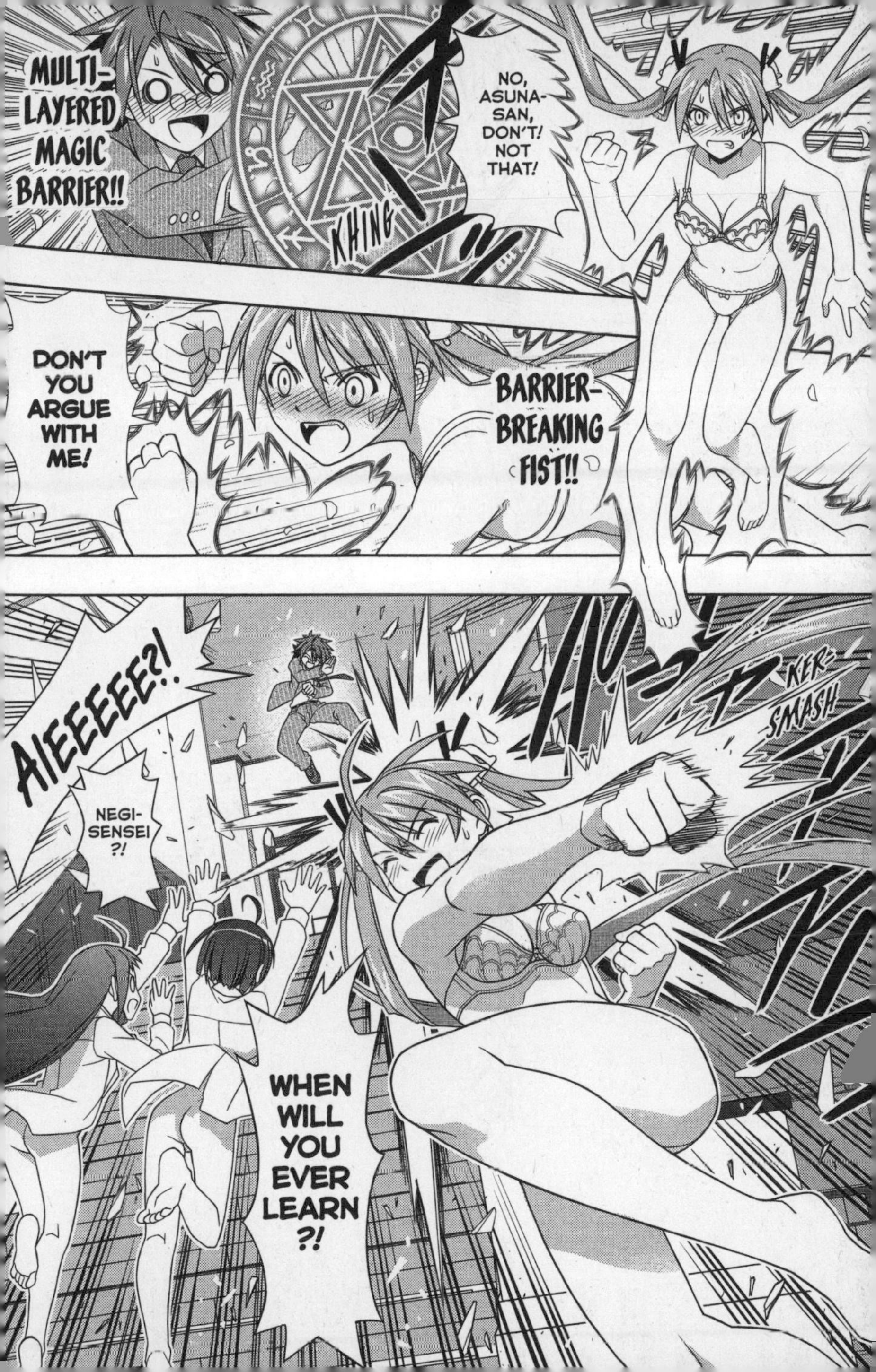
NO, ASUNA-SAN, DON'T! NOT THAT!
KHING
MULTI-LAYERED MAGIC BARRIER!!
BARRIER-BREAKING FIST!!
DON'T YOU ARGUE WITH ME!
KER-SMASH
AIEEEEE?!
NEGI-SENSEI ?!
WHEN WILL YOU EVER LEARN ?!

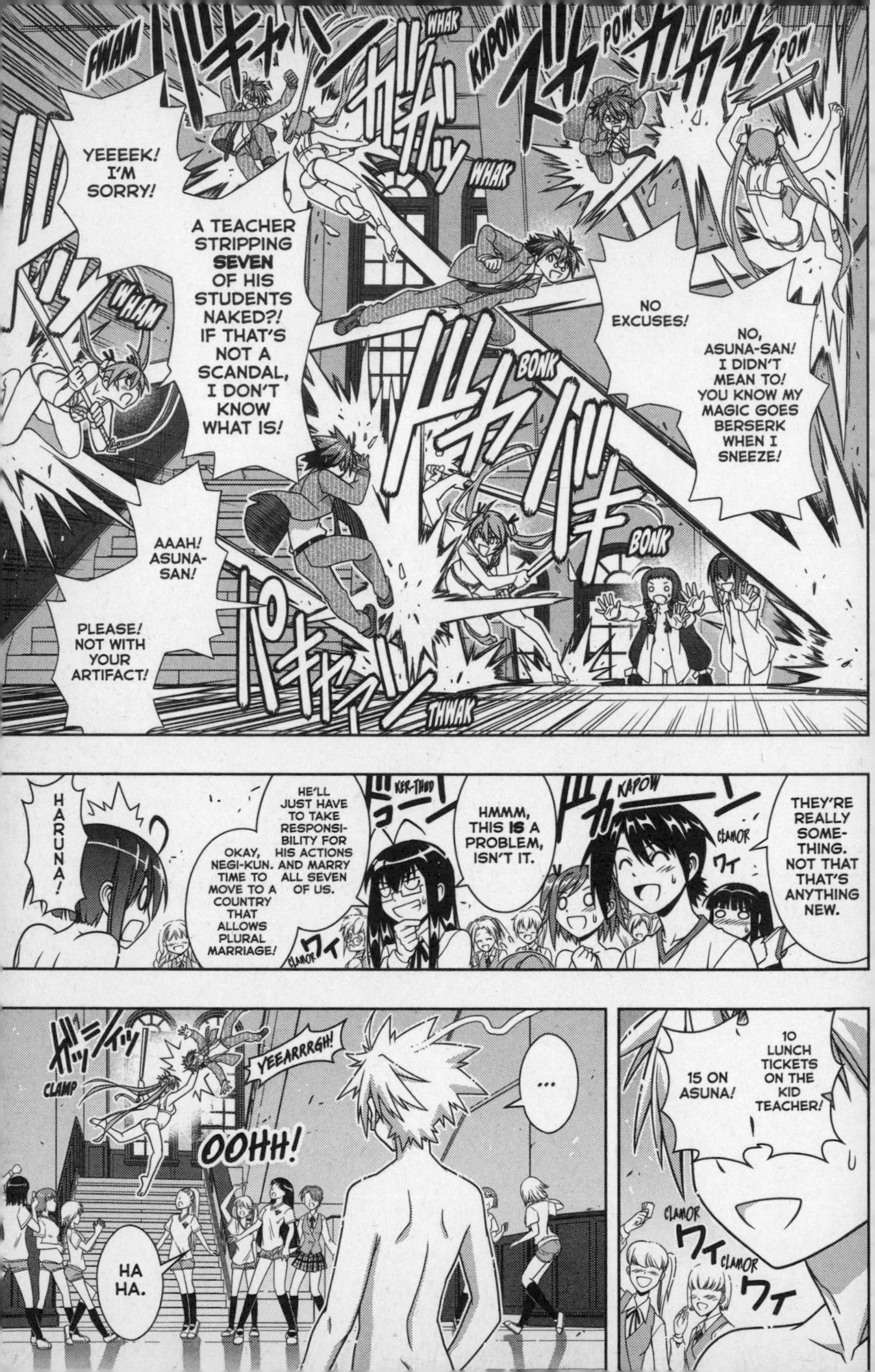

POW
POW
POW
KAPOW
WHAK
WHAK
FWAM
NO, ASUNA-SAN! I DIDN'T MEAN TO! YOU KNOW MY MAGIC GOES BERSERK WHEN I SNEEZE!
NO EXCUSES!
YEEEEK! I'M SORRY!
A TEACHER STRIPPING SEVEN OF HIS STUDENTS NAKED?! IF THAT'S NOT A SCANDAL, I DON'T KNOW WHAT IS!
WHAM
BONK
BONK
AAAH! ASUNA-SAN!
PLEASE! NOT WITH YOUR ARTIFACT!
THWAK
THEY'RE REALLY SOMETHING. NOT THAT THAT'S ANYTHING NEW.
CLAMOR
KAPOW
HMMM, THIS IS A PROBLEM, ISN'T IT.
KER-THUD
HE'LL JUST HAVE TO TAKE RESPONSIBILITY FOR HIS ACTIONS AND MARRY ALL SEVEN OF US.
OKAY, NEGI-KUN. TIME TO MOVE TO A COUNTRY THAT ALLOWS PLURAL MARRIAGE!
CLAMOR
HARUNA!
10 LUNCH TICKETS ON THE KID TEACHER!
15 ON ASUNA!
CLAMOR
CLAMOR
...
YEEARRRGH!
CLAMP
OOHH!
HA HA.

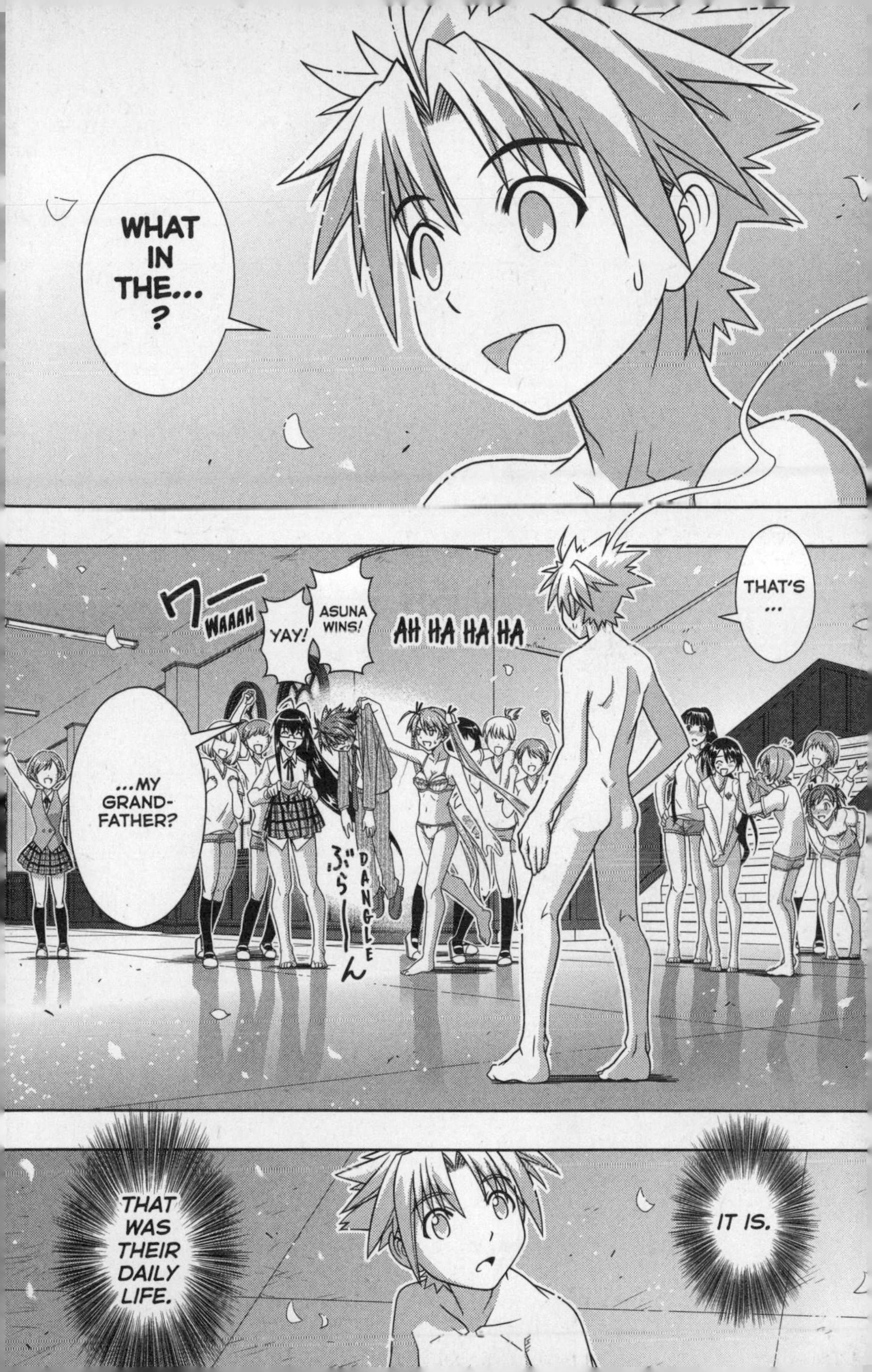
WHAT IN THE...?
THAT'S ...
AH HA HA HA
ASUNA WINS!
YAY!
ワー WAAAH
...MY GRAND-FATHER?
ぶらーん DANGLE
IT IS.
THAT WAS THEIR DAILY LIFE.

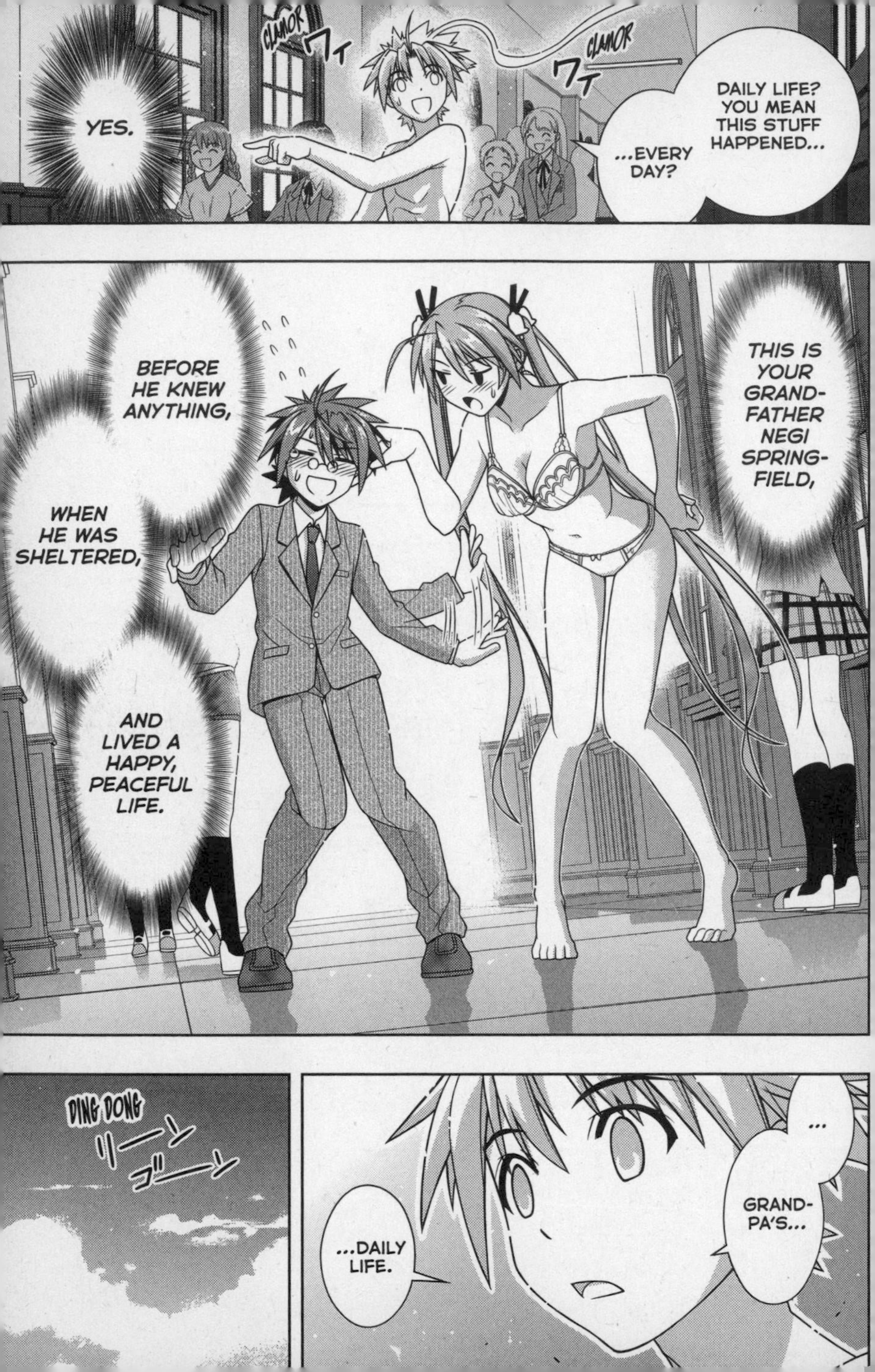
CLAMOR
ワァ
DAILY LIFE? YOU MEAN THIS STUFF HAPPENED...
...EVERY DAY?
CLAMOR
ワァ
YES.
THIS IS YOUR GRANDFATHER NEGI SPRINGFIELD,
BEFORE HE KNEW ANYTHING,
WHEN HE WAS SHELTERED,
AND LIVED A HAPPY, PEACEFUL LIFE.
...
GRANDPA'S...
...DAILY LIFE.
DING DONG
リーンゴーン

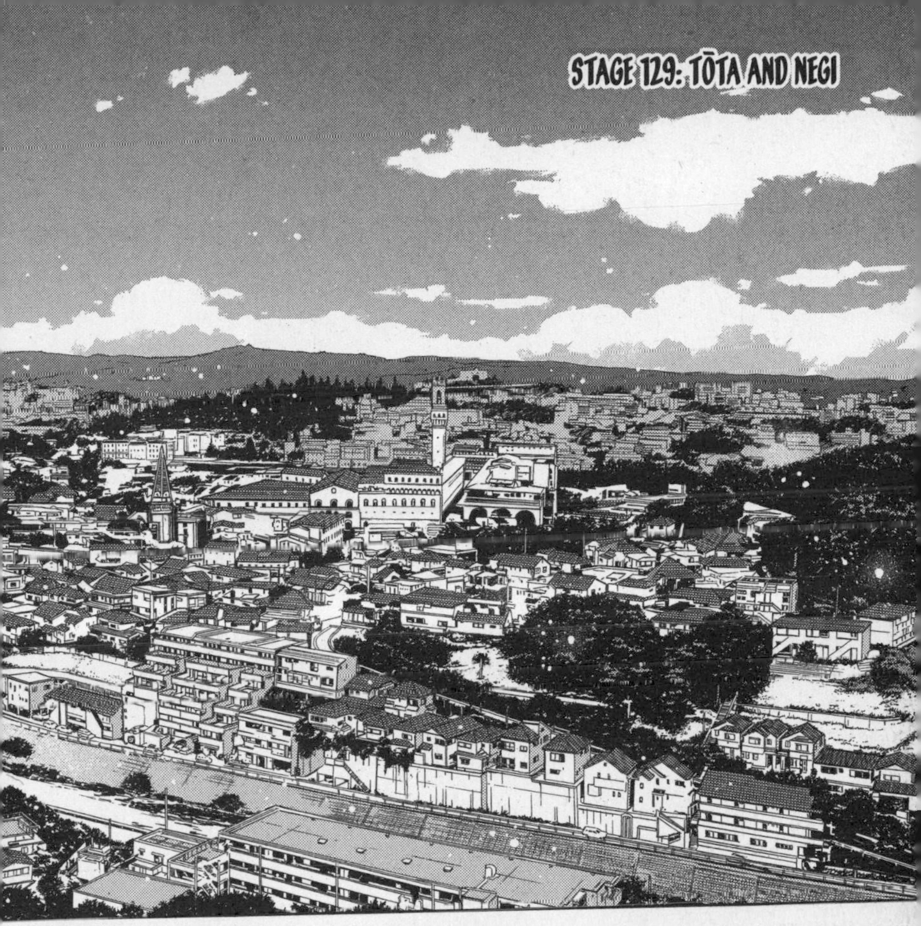
STAGE 129: TŌTA AND NEGI

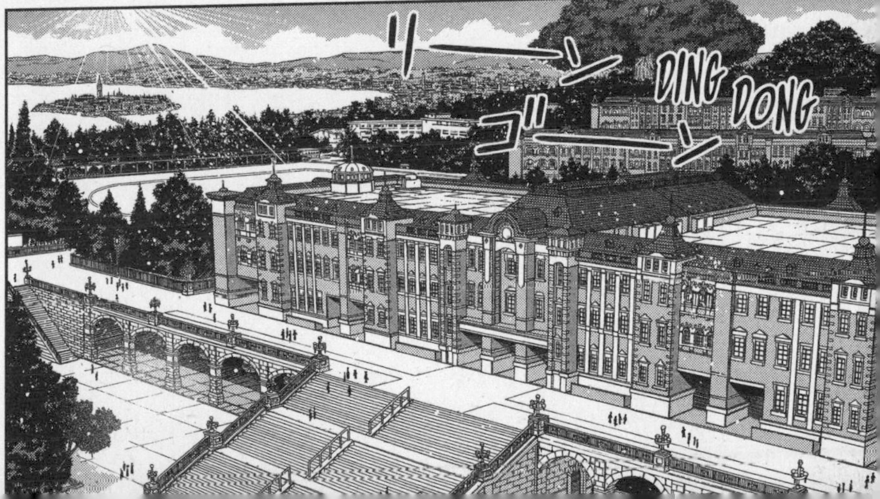
リーーン
ゴーーン
DING DONG

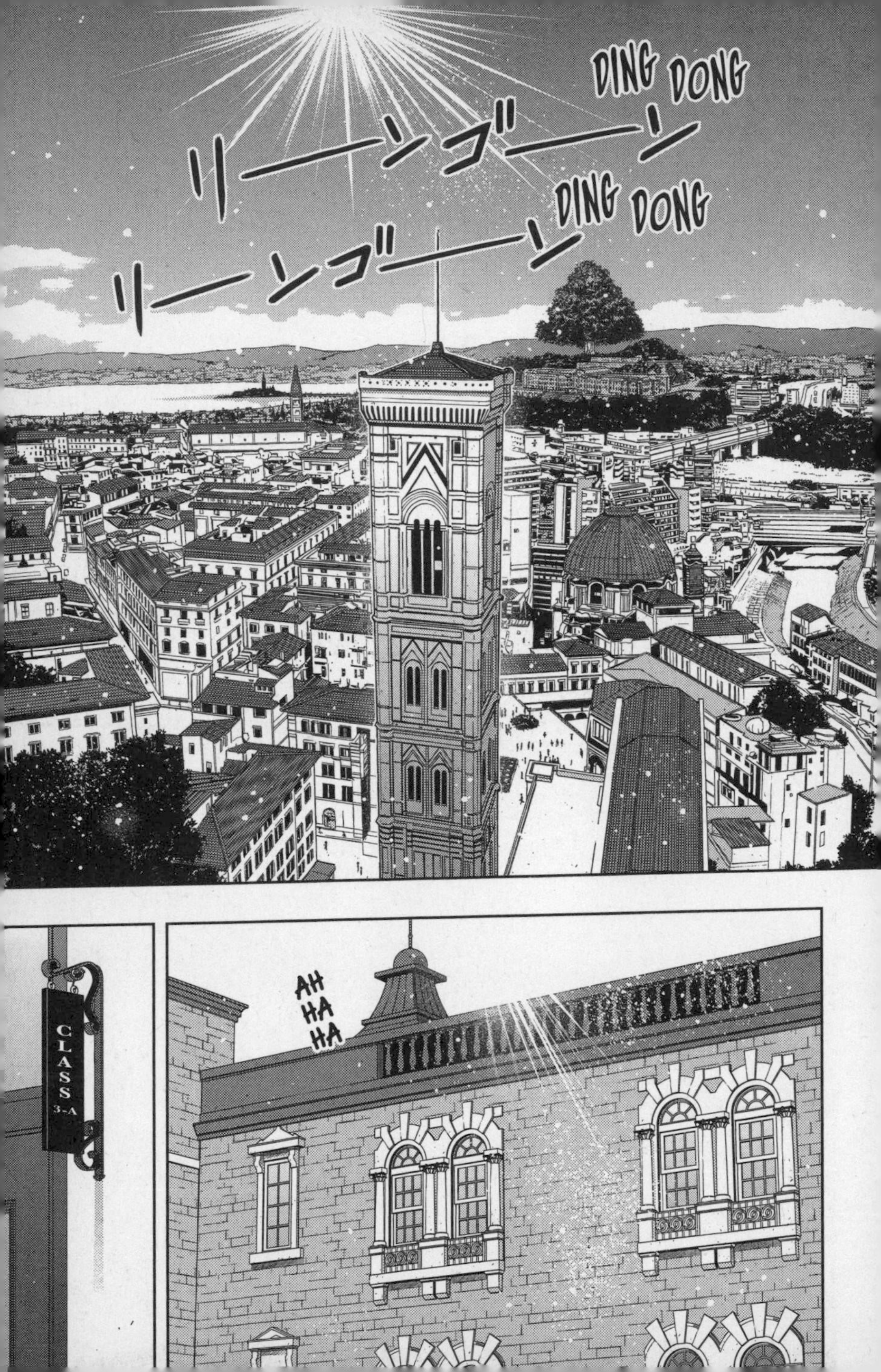
リーンゴーン
DING DONG
リーンゴーン
DING DONG
AH HA HA
CLASS 3-A

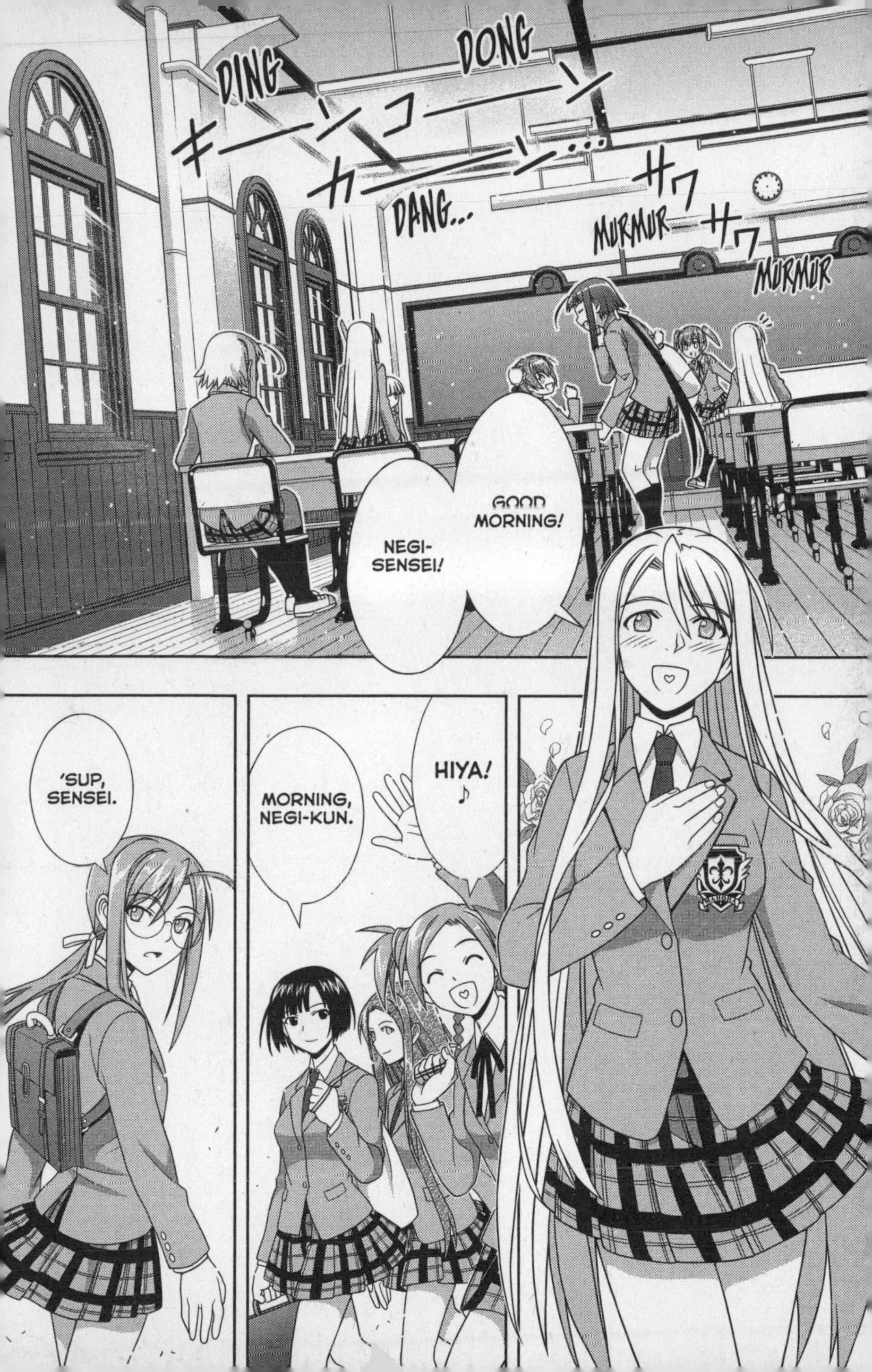
DING
キーンコーン
DONG
カーン…
DANG...
サワ
MURMUR
サワ
MURMUR
GOOD MORNING! NEGI-SENSEI!
HIYA! ♪
MORNING, NEGI-KUN.
'SUP, SENSEI.

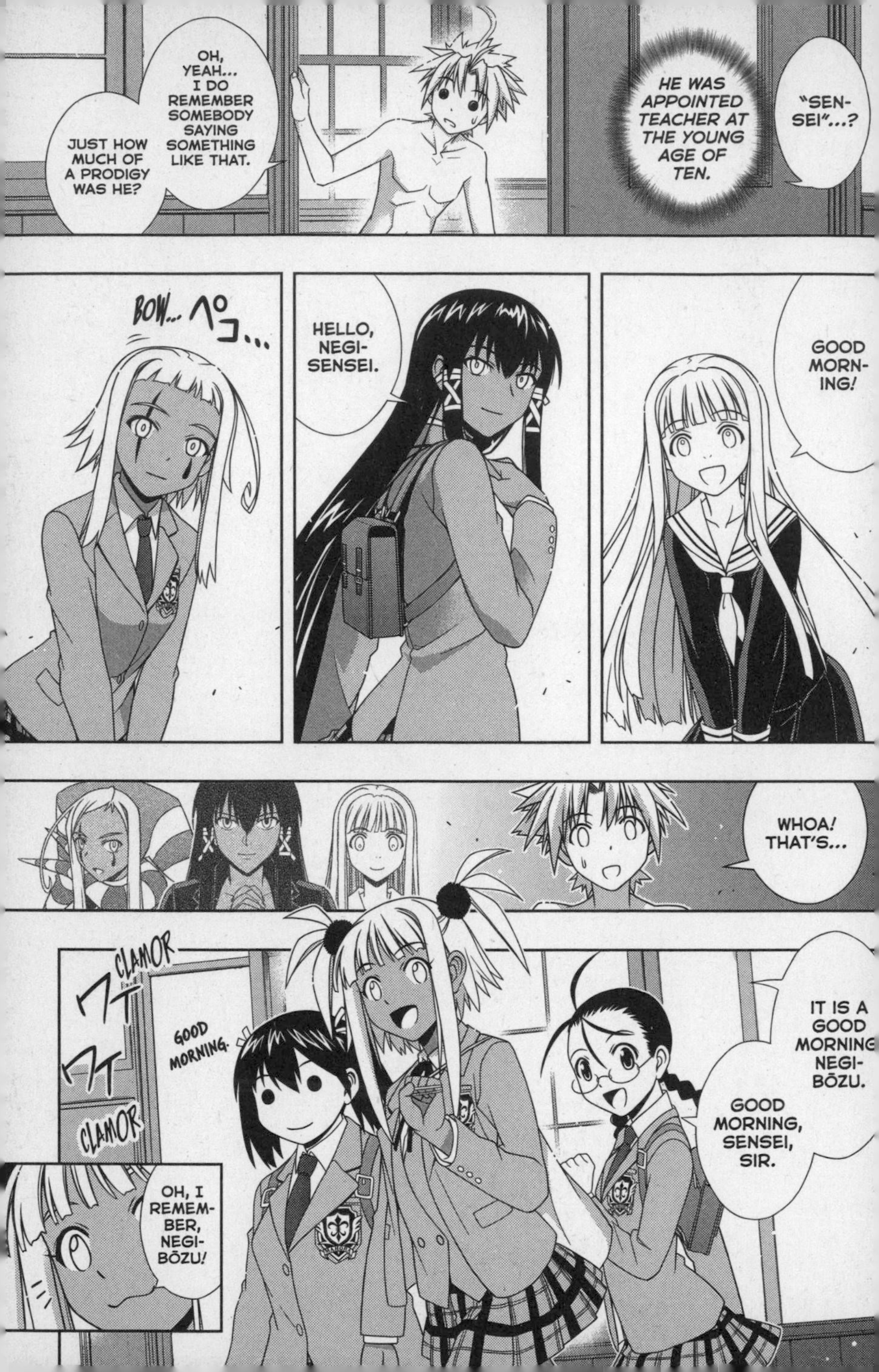
"SEN-SEI"...?
HE WAS APPOINTED TEACHER AT THE YOUNG AGE OF TEN.
OH, YEAH... I DO REMEMBER SOMEBODY SAYING SOMETHING LIKE THAT.
JUST HOW MUCH OF A PRODIGY WAS HE?
GOOD MORNING!
HELLO, NEGI-SENSEI.
BOW... ペコ...
WHOA! THAT'S...
IT IS A GOOD MORNING NEGI-BŌZU.
GOOD MORNING, SENSEI, SIR.
GOOD MORNING.
CLAMOR
ワイ
ワイ
CLAMOR
OH, I REMEMBER, NEGI-BŌZU!

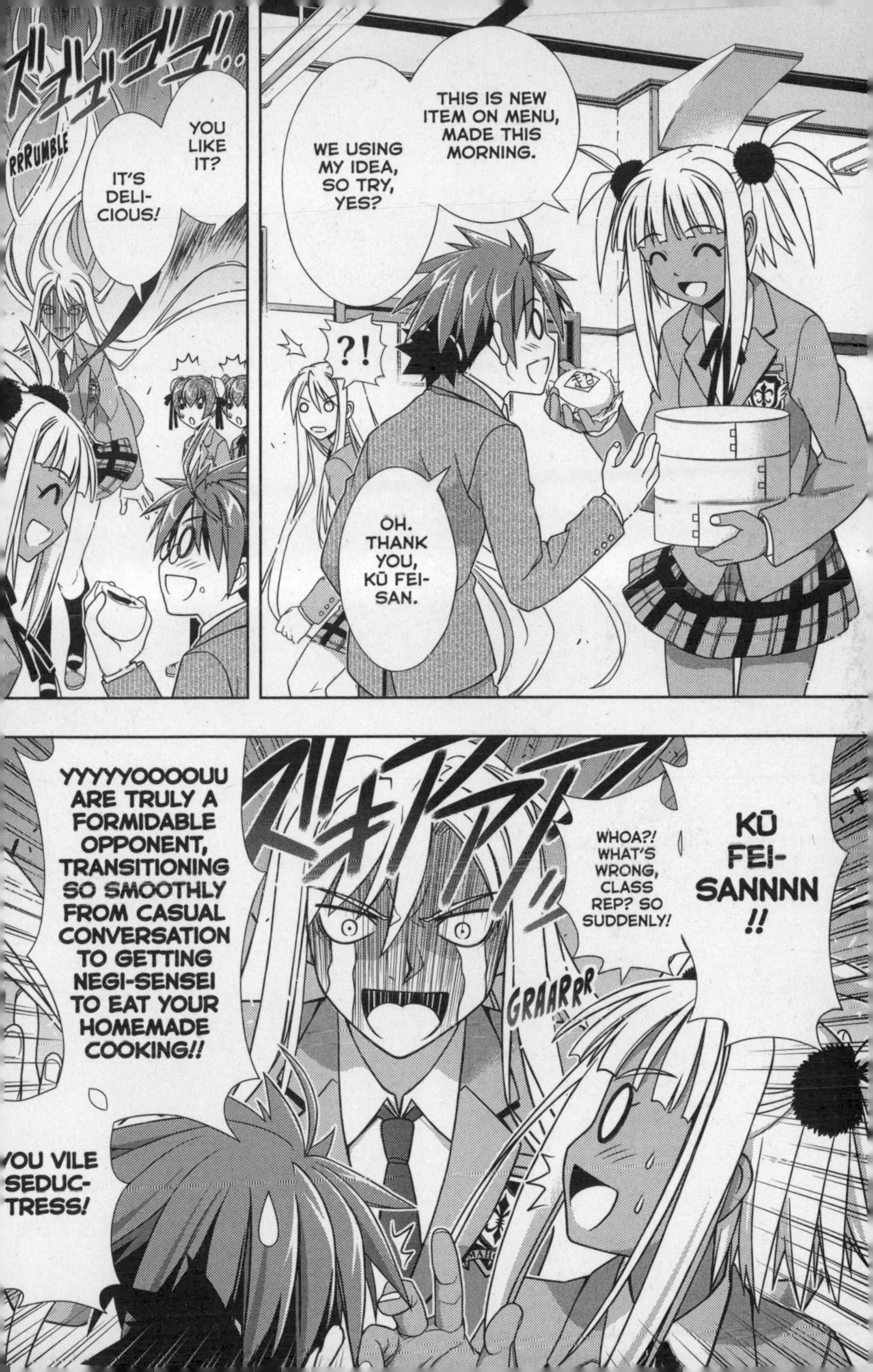
THIS IS NEW ITEM ON MENU, MADE THIS MORNING.
WE USING MY IDEA, SO TRY, YES?
?!
OH. THANK YOU, KŪ FEI-SAN.
RRRUMBLE
YOU LIKE IT?
IT'S DELICIOUS!
KŪ FEI-SANNNN!!
WHOA?! WHAT'S WRONG, CLASS REP? SO SUDDENLY!
GRAARRR
YYYYYOOOOUU ARE TRULY A FORMIDABLE OPPONENT, TRANSITIONING SO SMOOTHLY FROM CASUAL CONVERSATION TO GETTING NEGI-SENSEI TO EAT YOUR HOMEMADE COOKING!!
YOU VILE SEDUC-TRESS!

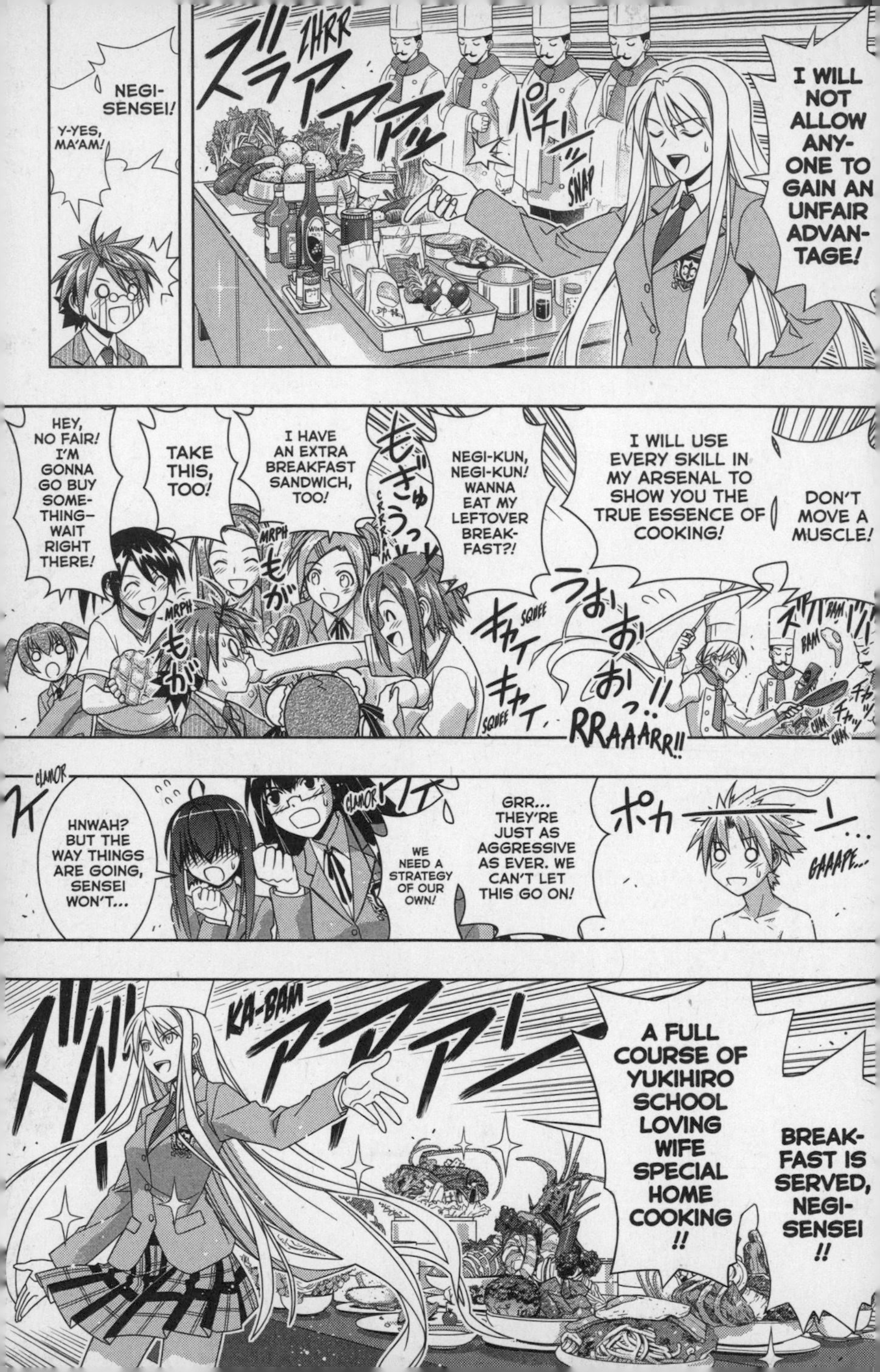

I WILL NOT ALLOW ANY-ONE TO GAIN AN UNFAIR ADVAN-TAGE!
SNAP
ZHRR
NEGI-SENSEI!
Y-YES, MA'AM!
DON'T MOVE A MUSCLE!
BAM
BAM
CHAK
CHAK
I WILL USE EVERY SKILL IN MY ARSENAL TO SHOW YOU THE TRUE ESSENCE OF COOKING!
RRAAARR!!
NEGI-KUN, NEGI-KUN! WANNA EAT MY LEFTOVER BREAK-FAST?!
SQUEE
SQUEE
I HAVE AN EXTRA BREAKFAST SANDWICH, TOO!
CRRRRK
TAKE THIS, TOO!
MRPH
MRPH
HEY, NO FAIR! I'M GONNA GO BUY SOME-THING—WAIT RIGHT THERE!
GAAAPE...
GRR... THEY'RE JUST AS AGGRESSIVE AS EVER. WE CAN'T LET THIS GO ON!
WE NEED A STRATEGY OF OUR OWN!
CLAMOR
HNWAH? BUT THE WAY THINGS ARE GOING, SENSEI WON'T...
CLAMOR
BREAK-FAST IS SERVED, NEGI-SENSEI!!
A FULL COURSE OF YUKIHIRO SCHOOL LOVING WIFE SPECIAL HOME COOKING!!
KA-BAM

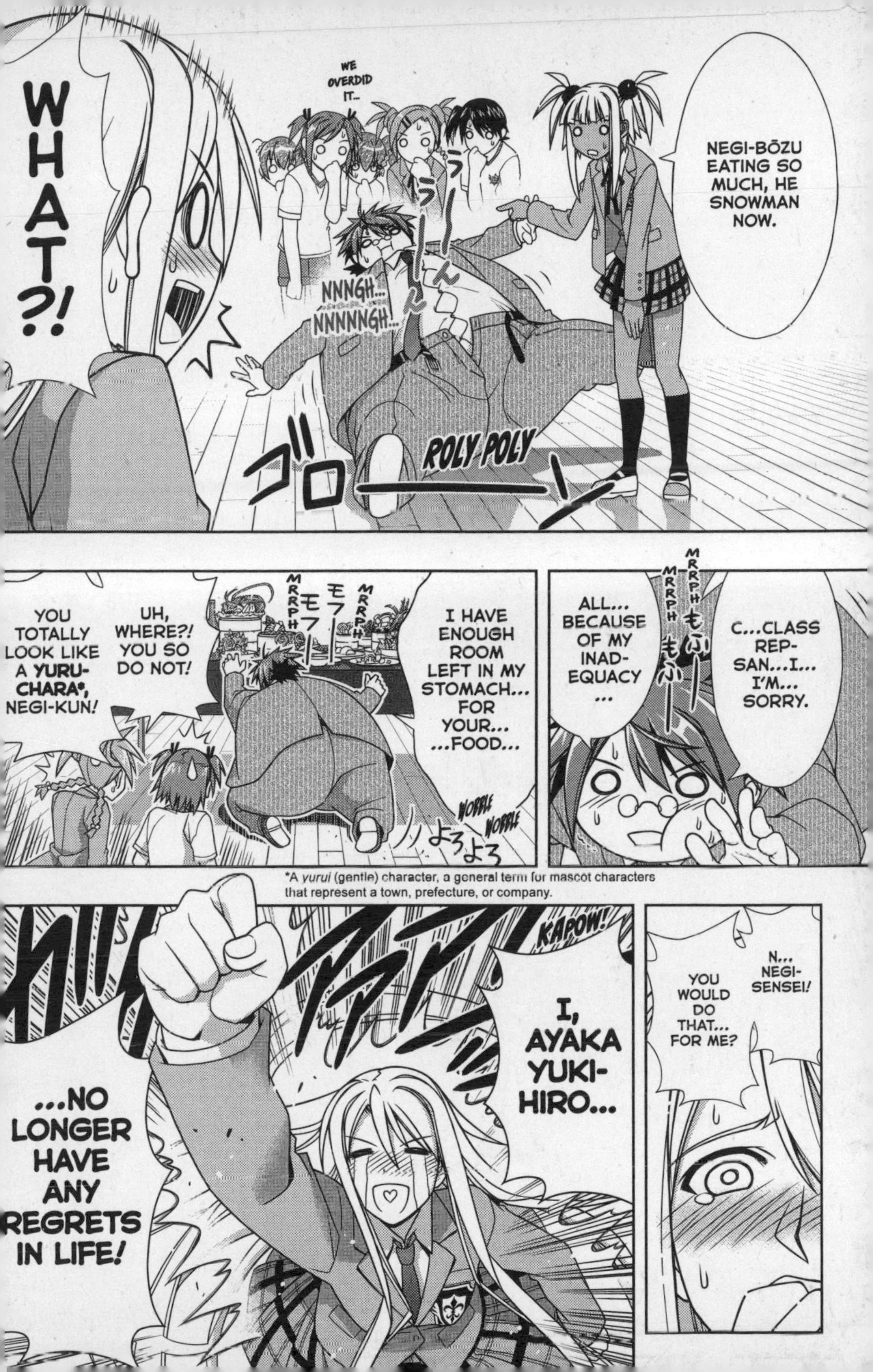
NEGI-BŌZU EATING SO MUCH, HE SNOWMAN NOW.
WE OVERDID IT...
NNNGH... NNNNNGH...
WHAT?!
ROLY POLY
C...CLASS REP-SAN...I... I'M... SORRY.
ALL... BECAUSE OF MY INAD-EQUACY...
MRRPH MRRPH
I HAVE ENOUGH ROOM LEFT IN MY STOMACH... FOR YOUR... ...FOOD...
MRRPH MRRPH
UH, WHERE?! YOU SO DO NOT!
YOU TOTALLY LOOK LIKE A YURU-CHARA*, NEGI-KUN!
WOBBLE WOBBLE
N... NEGI-SENSEI!
YOU WOULD DO THAT... FOR ME?
KAPOW!
I, AYAKA YUKI-HIRO...
...NO LONGER HAVE ANY REGRETS IN LIFE!

*A *yurui* (gentle) character, a general term for mascot characters that represent a town, prefecture, or company.

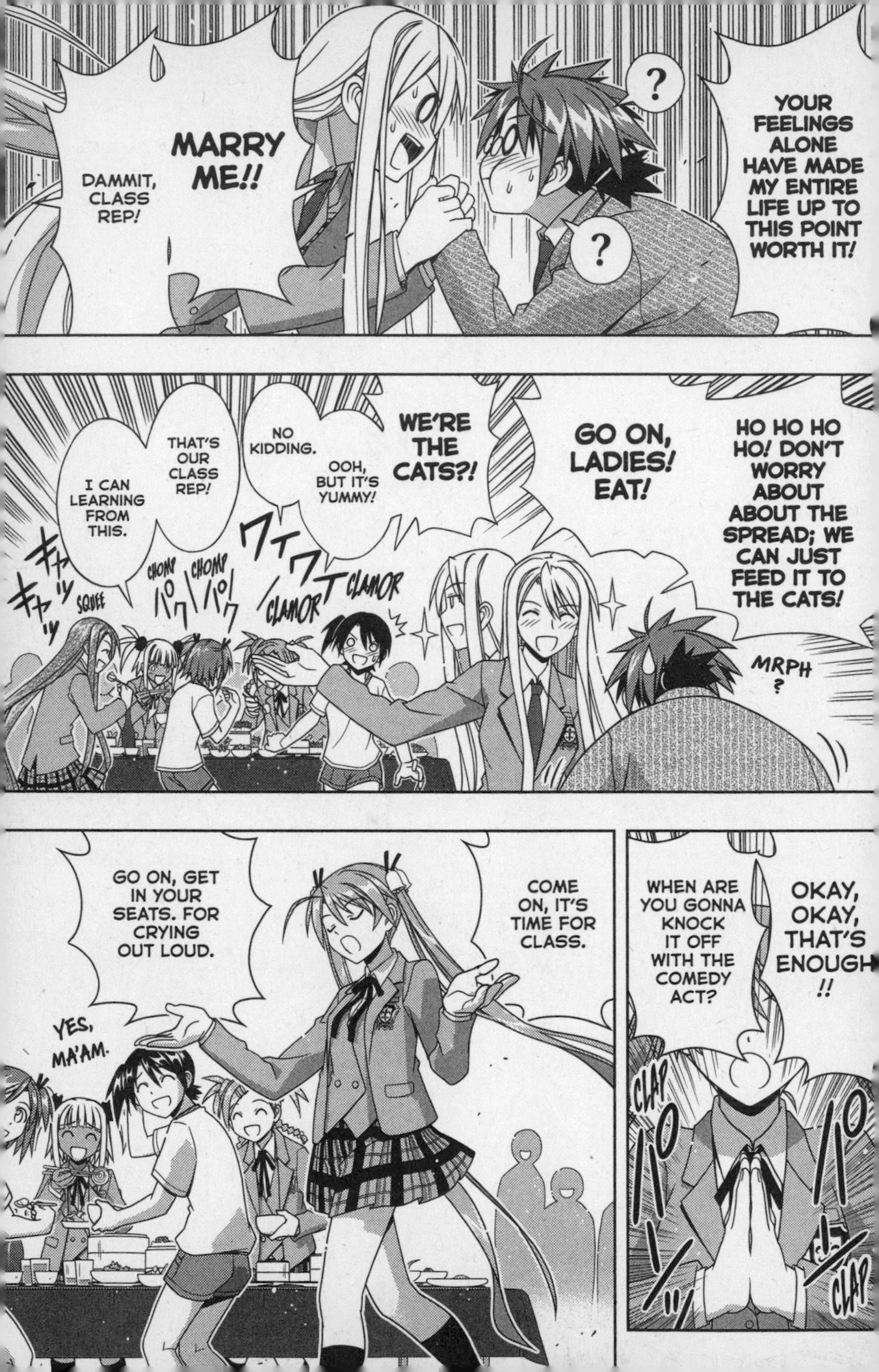
YOUR FEELINGS ALONE HAVE MADE MY ENTIRE LIFE UP TO THIS POINT WORTH IT!
?
?
MARRY ME!!
DAMMIT, CLASS REP!
HO HO HO HO! DON'T WORRY ABOUT ABOUT THE SPREAD; WE CAN JUST FEED IT TO THE CATS!
MRPH ?
GO ON, LADIES! EAT!
WE'RE THE CATS?!
OOH, BUT IT'S YUMMY!
NO KIDDING.
CLAMOR
CLAMOR
THAT'S OUR CLASS REP!
CHOMP
CHOMP
I CAN LEARNING FROM THIS.
SQUEE
OKAY, OKAY, THAT'S ENOUGH!!
WHEN ARE YOU GONNA KNOCK IT OFF WITH THE COMEDY ACT?
CLAP
CLAP
COME ON, IT'S TIME FOR CLASS.
GO ON, GET IN YOUR SEATS. FOR CRYING OUT LOUD.
YES, MA'AM.

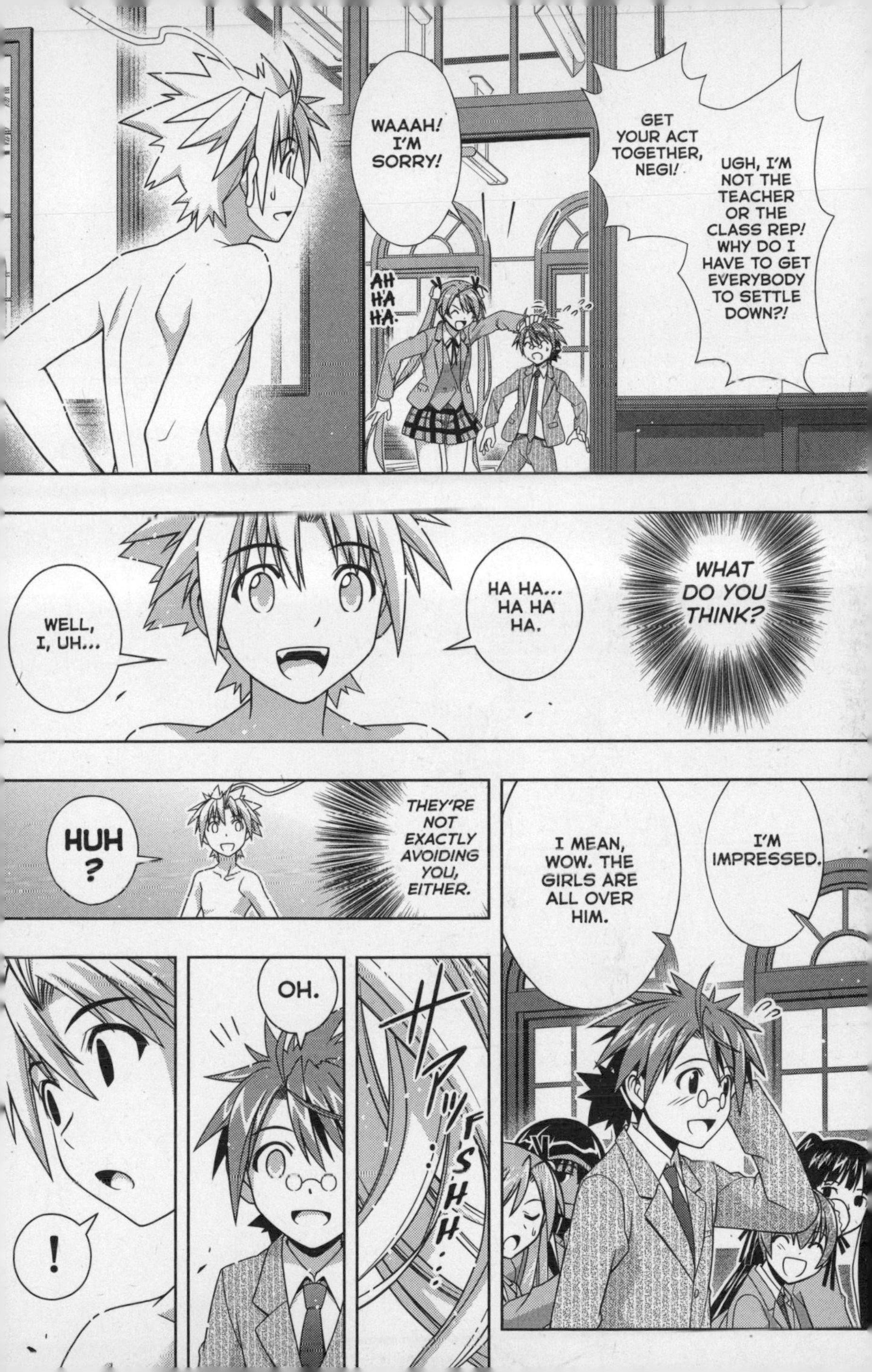
GET YOUR ACT TOGETHER, NEGI!
UGH, I'M NOT THE TEACHER OR THE CLASS REP! WHY DO I HAVE TO GET EVERYBODY TO SETTLE DOWN?!
WAAAH! I'M SORRY!
AH HA HA HA.
WHAT DO YOU THINK?
HA HA... HA HA HA.
WELL, I, UH...
I'M IMPRESSED.
I MEAN, WOW. THE GIRLS ARE ALL OVER HIM.
THEY'RE NOT EXACTLY AVOIDING YOU, EITHER.
HUH?
FSHH...
OH.
!

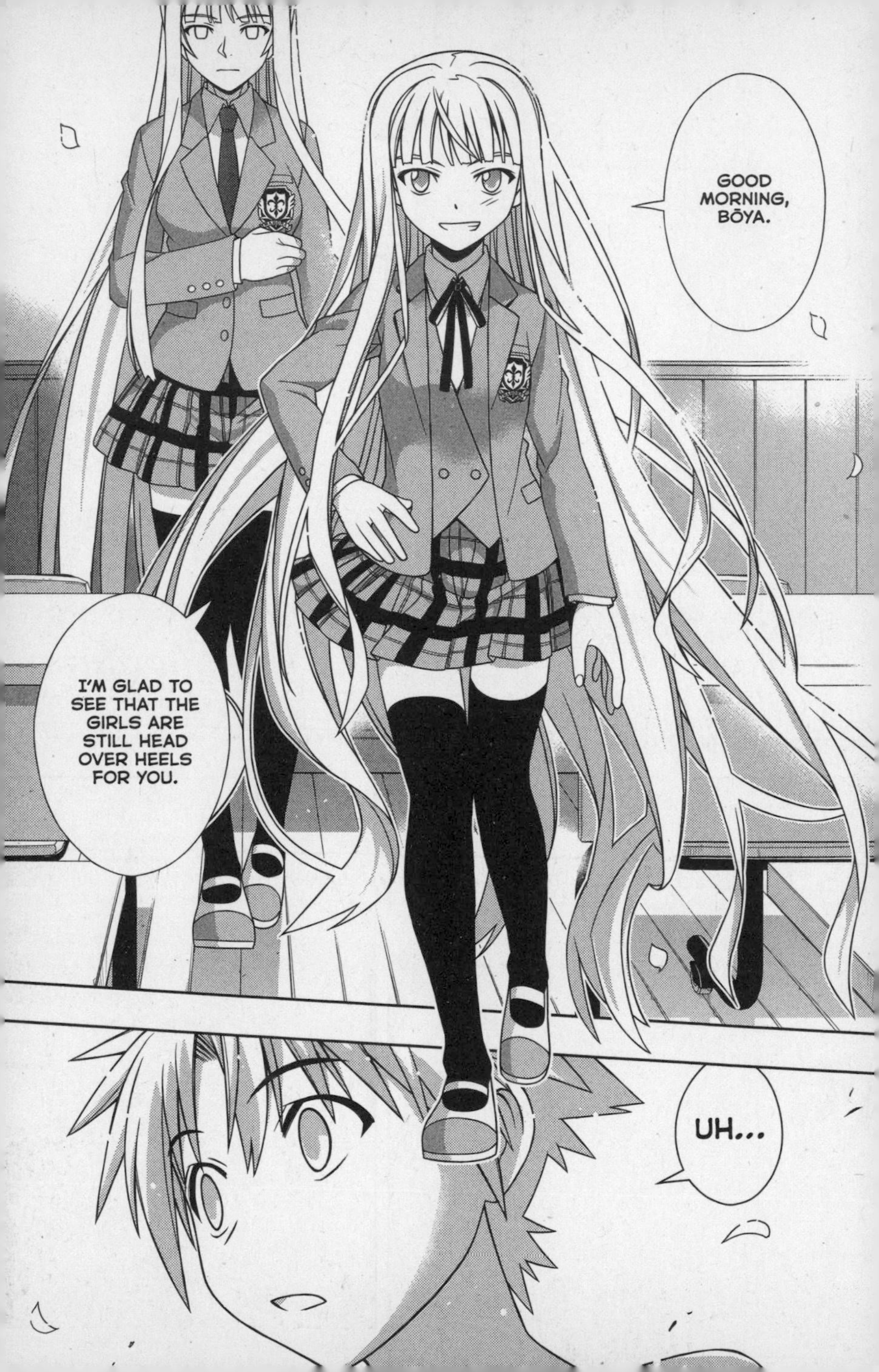
GOOD MORNING, BŌYA.
I'M GLAD TO SEE THAT THE GIRLS ARE STILL HEAD OVER HEELS FOR YOU.
UH...

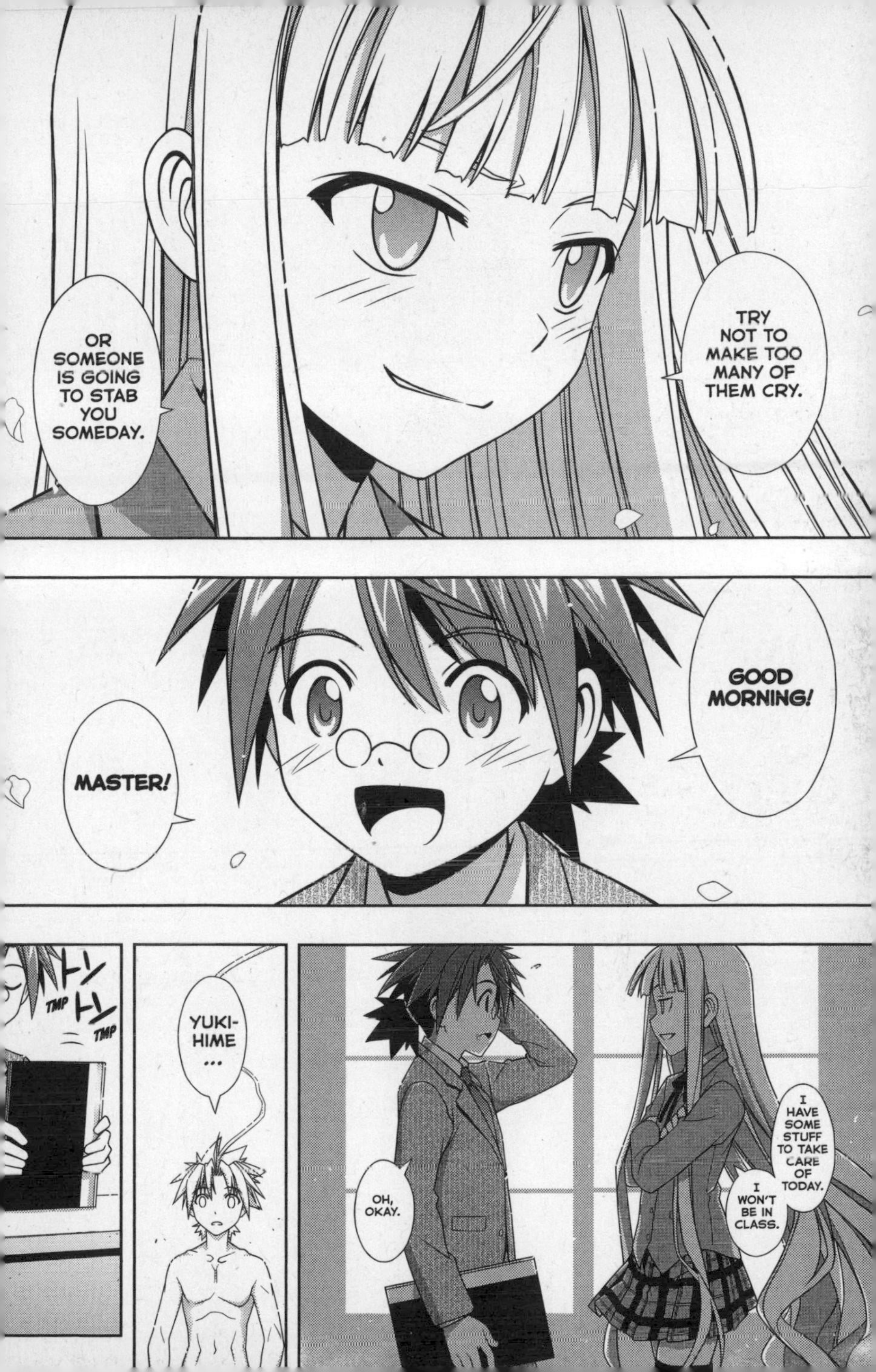
TRY NOT TO MAKE TOO MANY OF THEM CRY.
OR SOMEONE IS GOING TO STAB YOU SOMEDAY.
GOOD MORNING!
MASTER!
I HAVE SOME STUFF TO TAKE CARE OF TODAY.
I WON'T BE IN CLASS.
OH, OKAY.
YUKI-HIME...
TMP
TMP

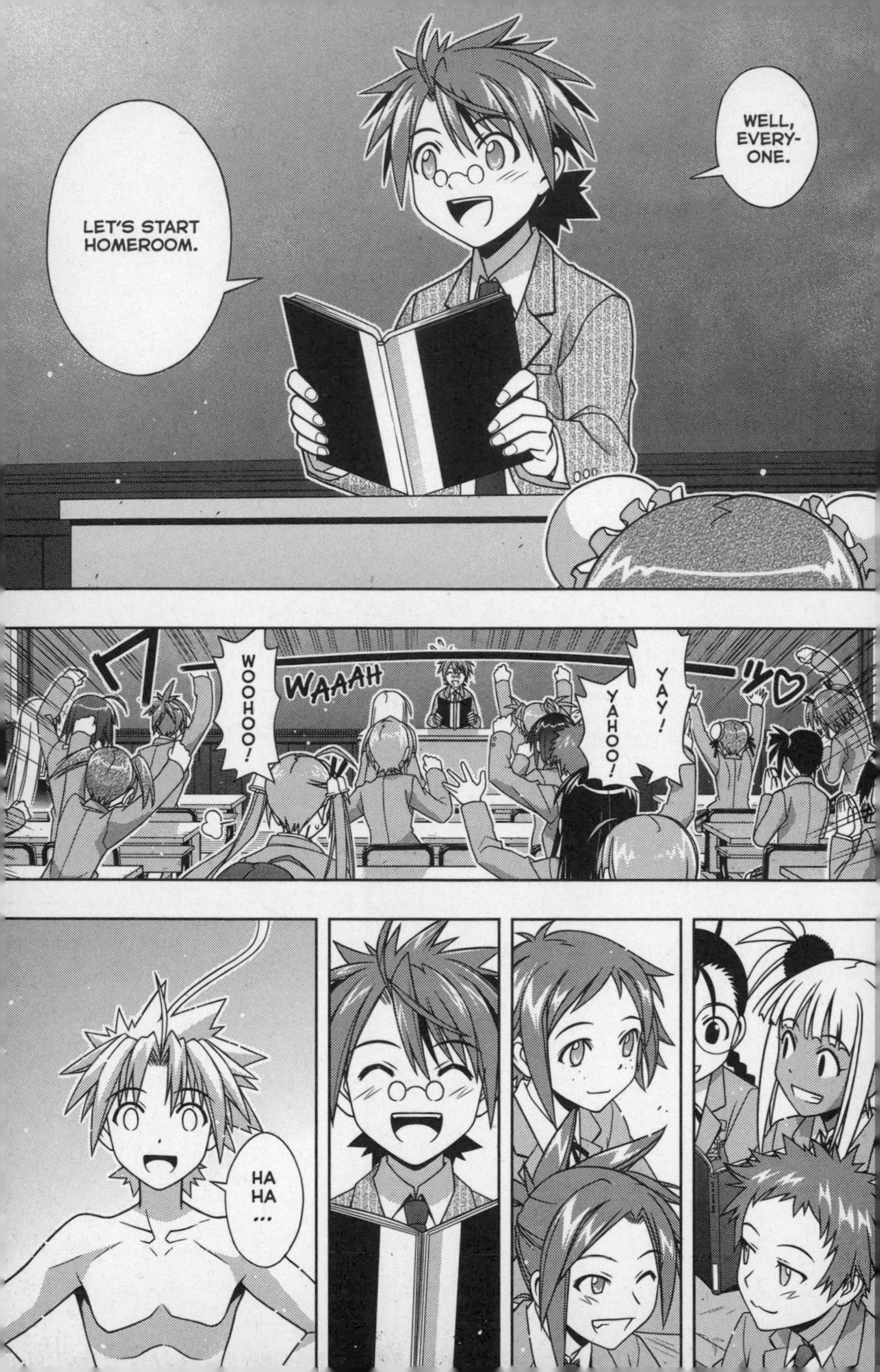
WELL, EVERY-ONE.
LET'S START HOMEROOM.
YAY!
YAHOO!
WAAAH
WOOHOO!
HA HA ...

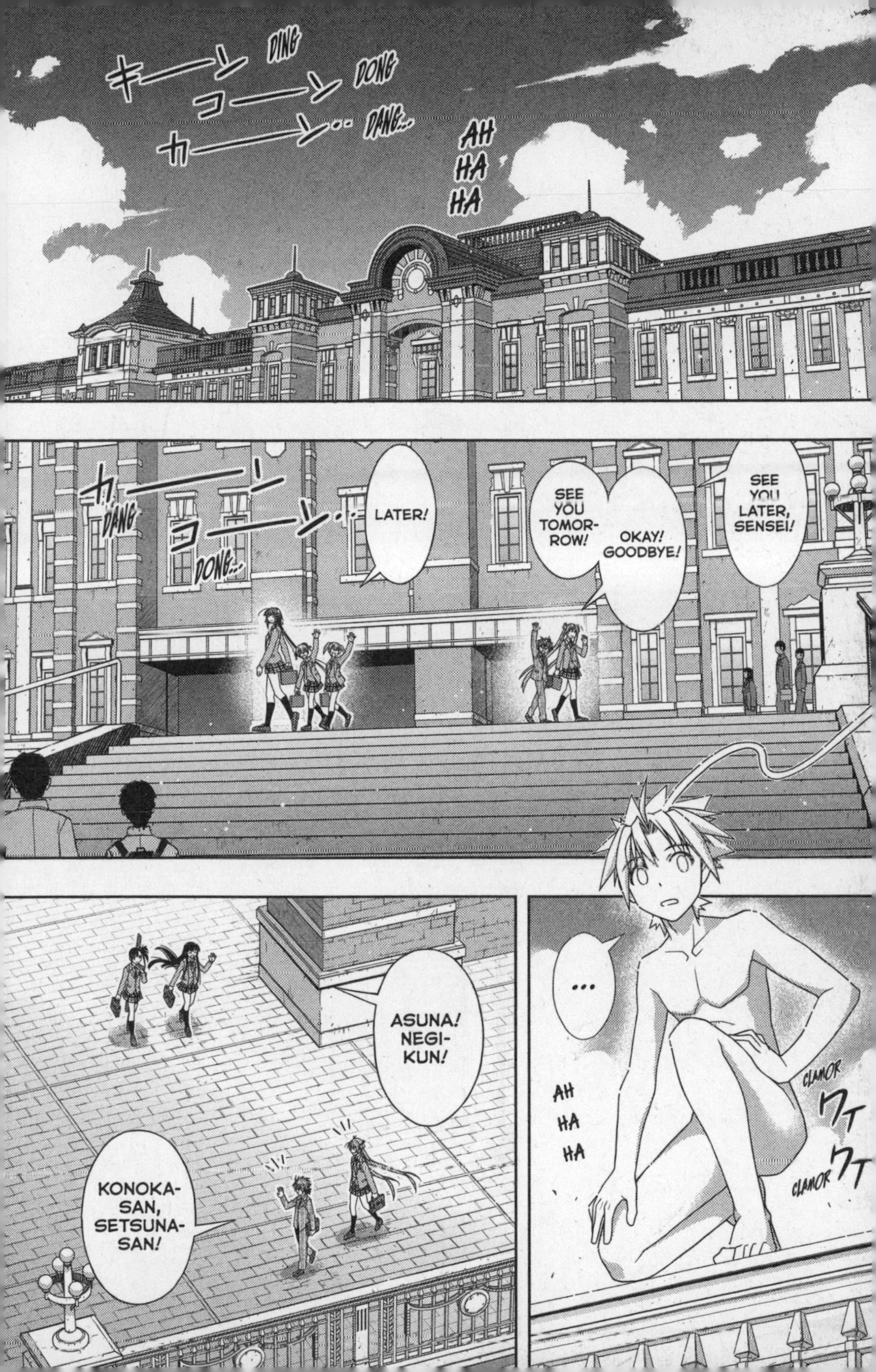
DING
DONG
DANG...
AH HA HA
SEE YOU LATER, SENSEI!
OKAY! GOODBYE!
SEE YOU TOMORROW!
LATER!
DANG
DONG...
...
CLAMOR
CLAMOR
AH HA HA
ASUNA! NEGI-KUN!
KONOKA-SAN, SETSUNA-SAN!

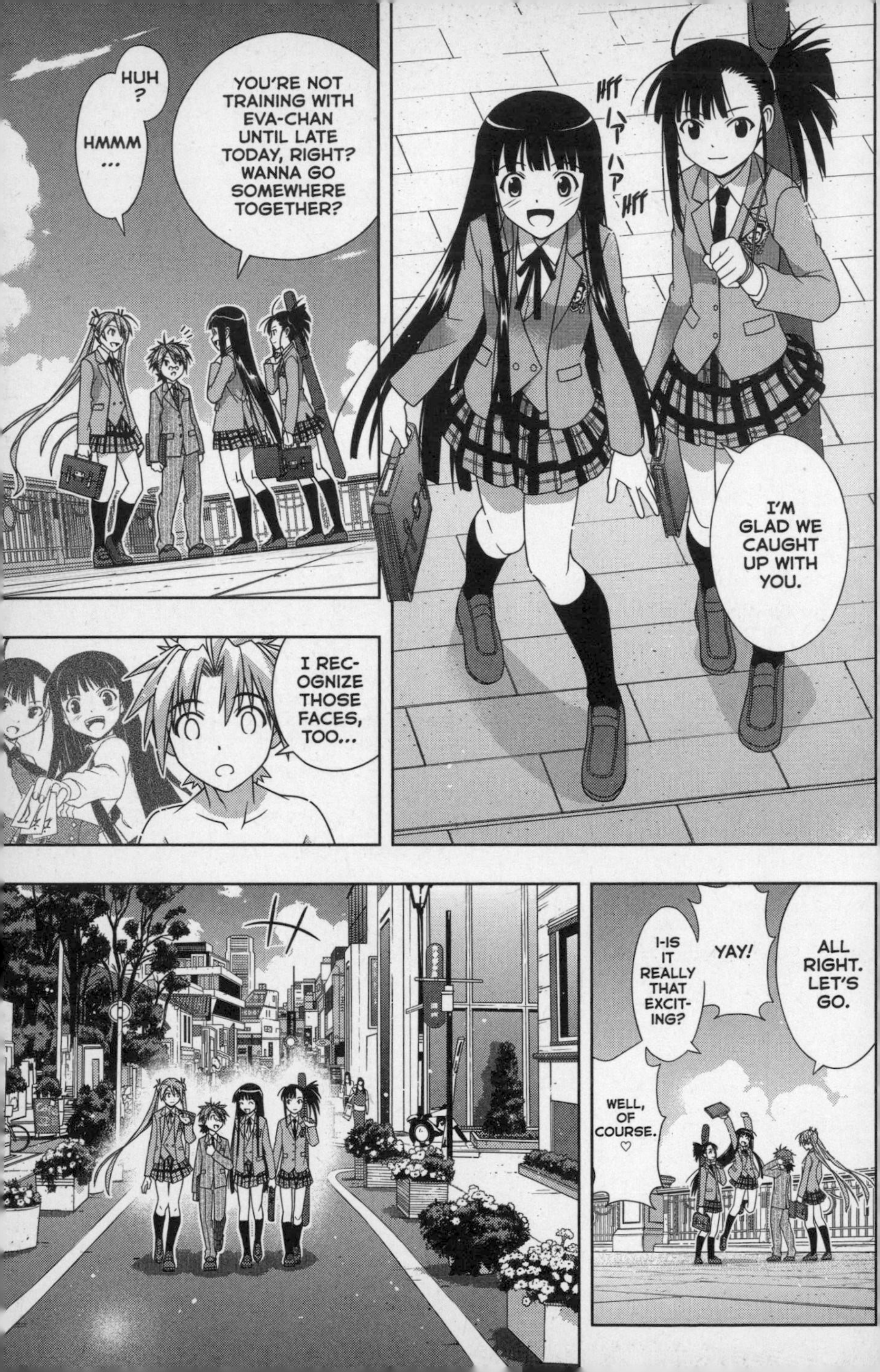
HFF
ハア ハア
HFF
I'M GLAD WE CAUGHT UP WITH YOU.
YOU'RE NOT TRAINING WITH EVA-CHAN UNTIL LATE TODAY, RIGHT? WANNA GO SOMEWHERE TOGETHER?
HUH?
HMMM...
I REC-OGNIZE THOSE FACES, TOO...
ALL RIGHT. LET'S GO.
YAY!
I-IS IT REALLY THAT EXCIT-ING?
WELL, OF COURSE. ♡

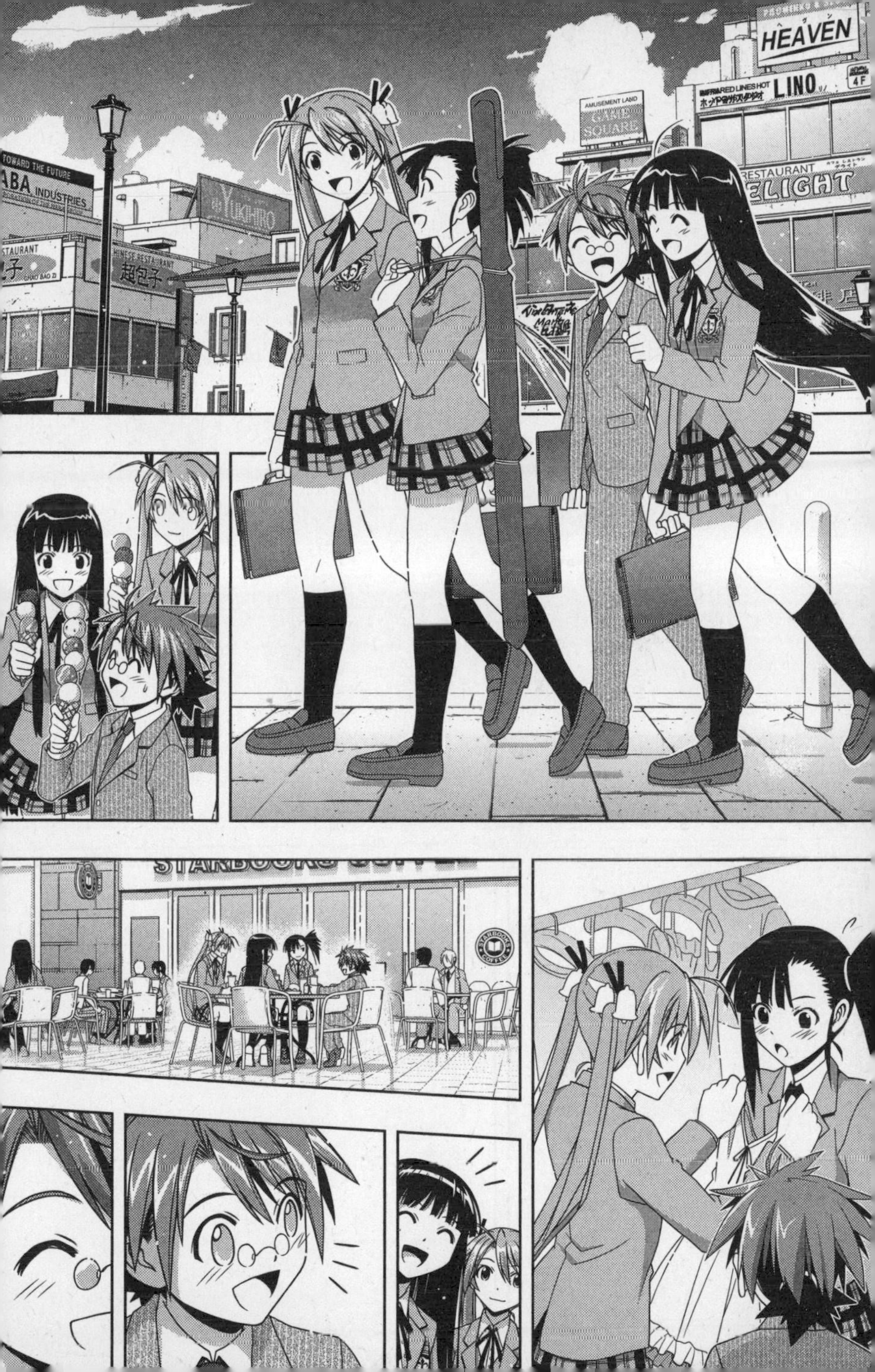
HEAVEN
LINO
4F
INFRARED LINES HOT
AMUSEMENT LAND
GAME SQUARE
RESTAURANT
YUKIHIRO
TOWARD THE FUTURE
INDUSTRIES
超包子
CHAO BAO ZI
STARBOOKS COFFEE

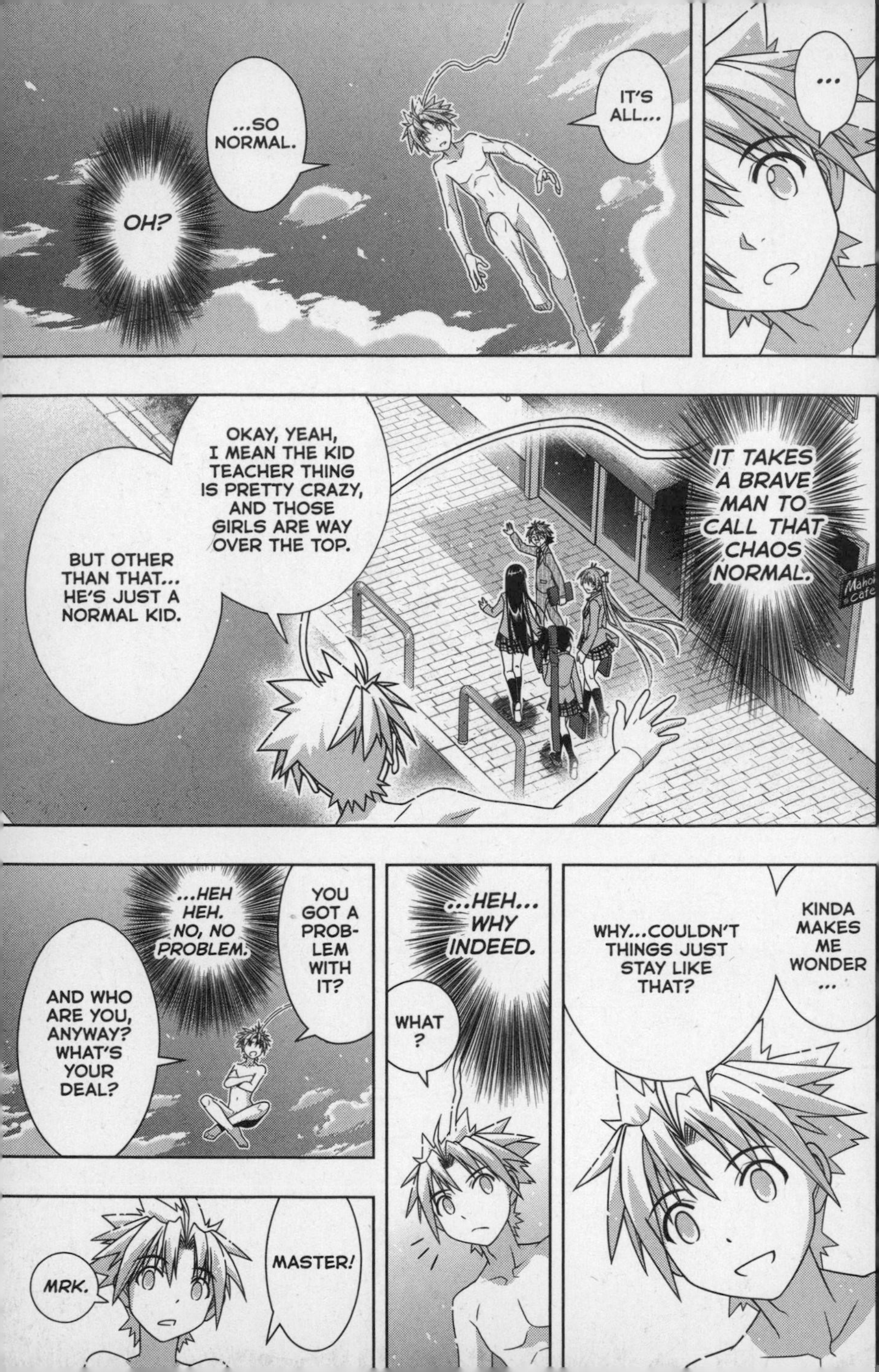
...
IT'S ALL...
...SO NORMAL.
OH?
IT TAKES A BRAVE MAN TO CALL THAT CHAOS NORMAL.
OKAY, YEAH, I MEAN THE KID TEACHER THING IS PRETTY CRAZY, AND THOSE GIRLS ARE WAY OVER THE TOP.
BUT OTHER THAN THAT... HE'S JUST A NORMAL KID.
KINDA MAKES ME WONDER...
WHY...COULDN'T THINGS JUST STAY LIKE THAT?
...HEH... WHY INDEED.
WHAT?
YOU GOT A PROB-LEM WITH IT?
...HEH HEH. NO, NO PROBLEM.
AND WHO ARE YOU, ANYWAY? WHAT'S YOUR DEAL?
MASTER!
MRK.

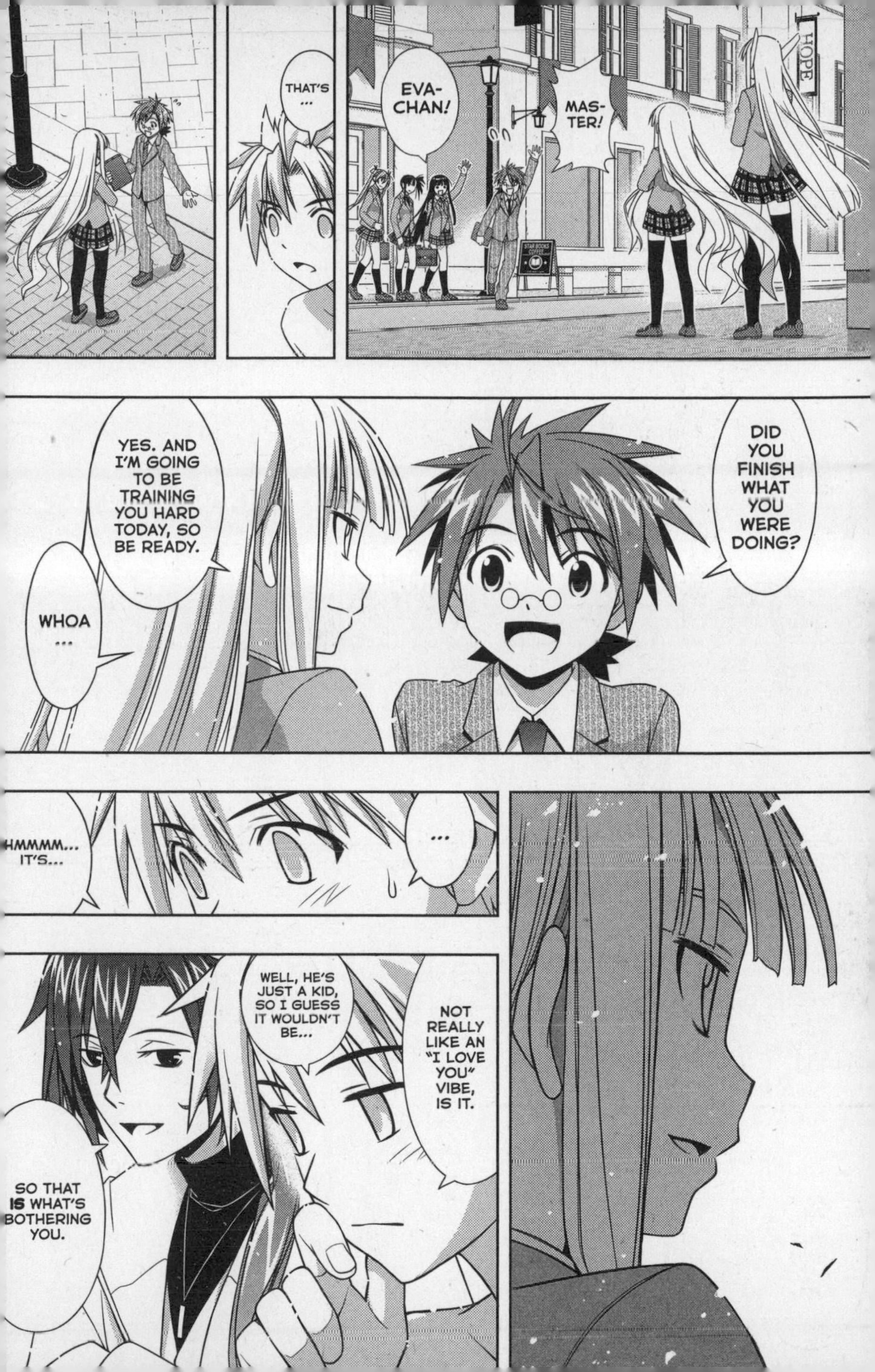
MAS-TER!
EVA-CHAN!
THAT'S ...
DID YOU FINISH WHAT YOU WERE DOING?
YES. AND I'M GOING TO BE TRAINING YOU HARD TODAY, SO BE READY.
WHOA ...
...
HMMMM... IT'S...
NOT REALLY LIKE AN "I LOVE YOU" VIBE, IS IT.
WELL, HE'S JUST A KID, SO I GUESS IT WOULDN'T BE...
SO THAT **IS** WHAT'S BOTHERING YOU.
HOPE

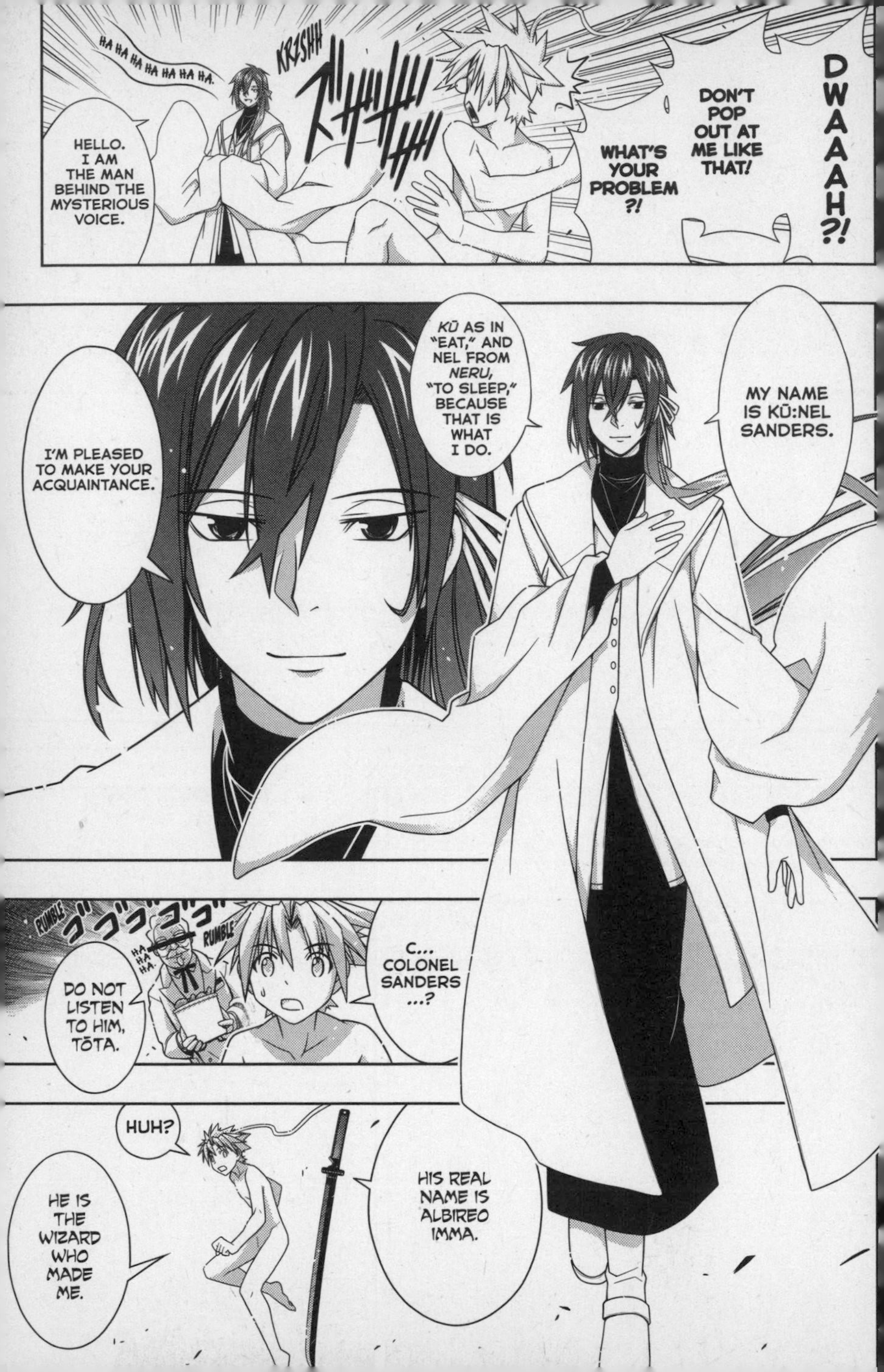
DWAAAAH?!
DON'T POP OUT AT ME LIKE THAT!
WHAT'S YOUR PROBLEM?!
KRISHH
HA HA HA HA HA HA HA HA.
HELLO. I AM THE MAN BEHIND THE MYSTERIOUS VOICE.
MY NAME IS KŪ:NEL SANDERS.
KŪ AS IN "EAT," AND NEL FROM *NERU*, "TO SLEEP," BECAUSE THAT IS WHAT I DO.
I'M PLEASED TO MAKE YOUR ACQUAINTANCE.
C... COLONEL SANDERS ...?
RUMBLE
RUMBLE
HA HA HA.
DO NOT LISTEN TO HIM, TŌTA.
HIS REAL NAME IS ALBIREO IMMA.
HUH?
HE IS THE WIZARD WHO MADE ME.

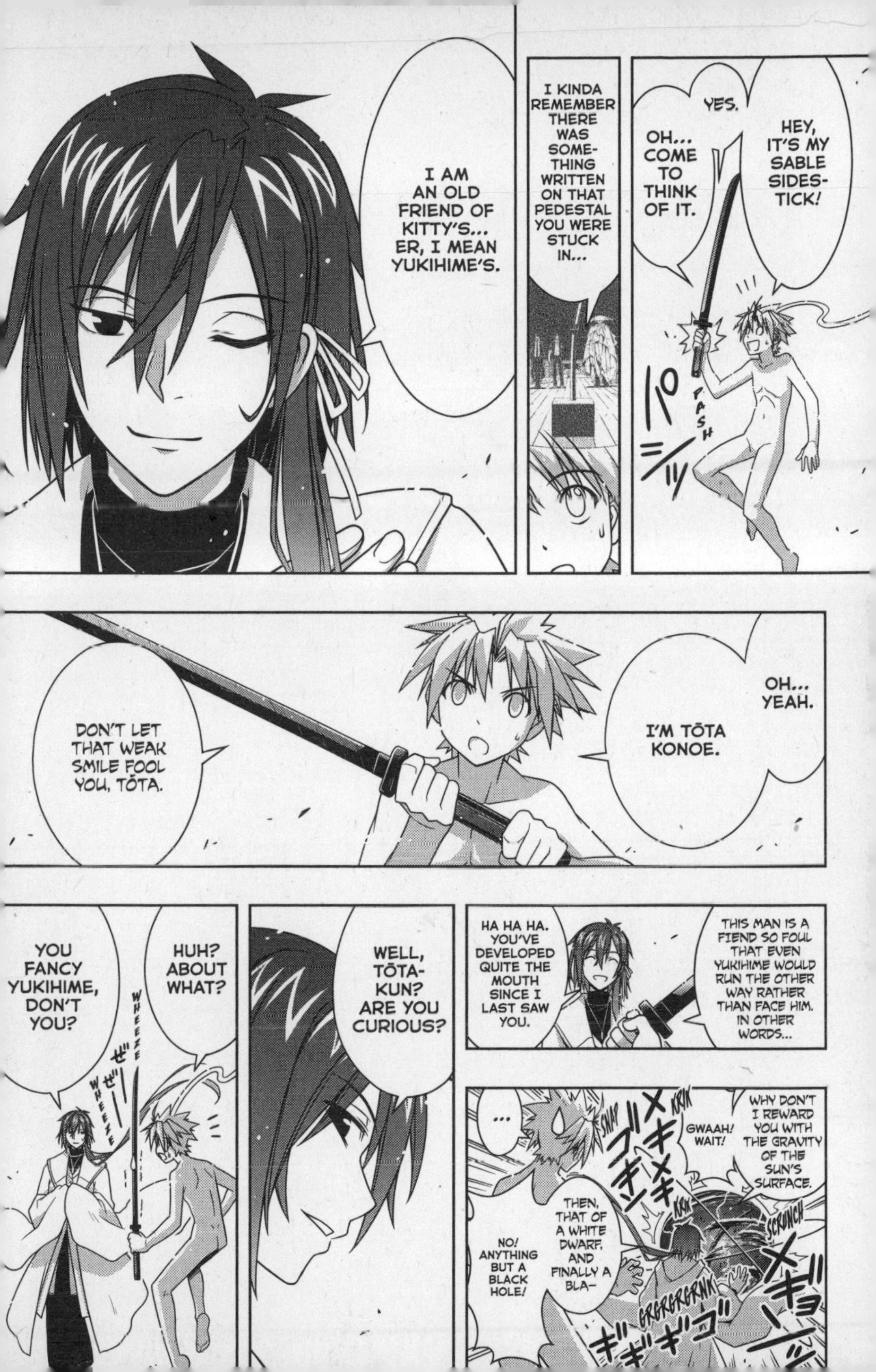
HEY, IT'S MY SABLE SIDES-TICK!
YES.
OH... COME TO THINK OF IT.
パ
PASH
I KINDA REMEMBER THERE WAS SOME-THING WRITTEN ON THAT PEDESTAL YOU WERE STUCK IN...
I AM AN OLD FRIEND OF KITTY'S... ER, I MEAN YUKIHIME'S.
OH... YEAH.
I'M TŌTA KONOE.
DON'T LET THAT WEAK SMILE FOOL YOU, TŌTA.
THIS MAN IS A FIEND SO FOUL THAT EVEN YUKIHIME WOULD RUN THE OTHER WAY RATHER THAN FACE HIM. IN OTHER WORDS...
HA HA HA. YOU'VE DEVELOPED QUITE THE MOUTH SINCE I LAST SAW YOU.
WHY DON'T I REWARD YOU WITH THE GRAVITY OF THE SUN'S SURFACE.
GWAAH! WAIT!
...
KRIK
SNAP
THEN, THAT OF A WHITE DWARF, AND FINALLY A BLA—
NO! ANYTHING BUT A BLACK HOLE!
KRIK
SCRUNCH
GRGRGRGRNK
WELL, TŌTA-KUN? ARE YOU CURIOUS?
HUH? ABOUT WHAT?
YOU FANCY YUKIHIME, DON'T YOU?
WHEEZE
WHEEZE

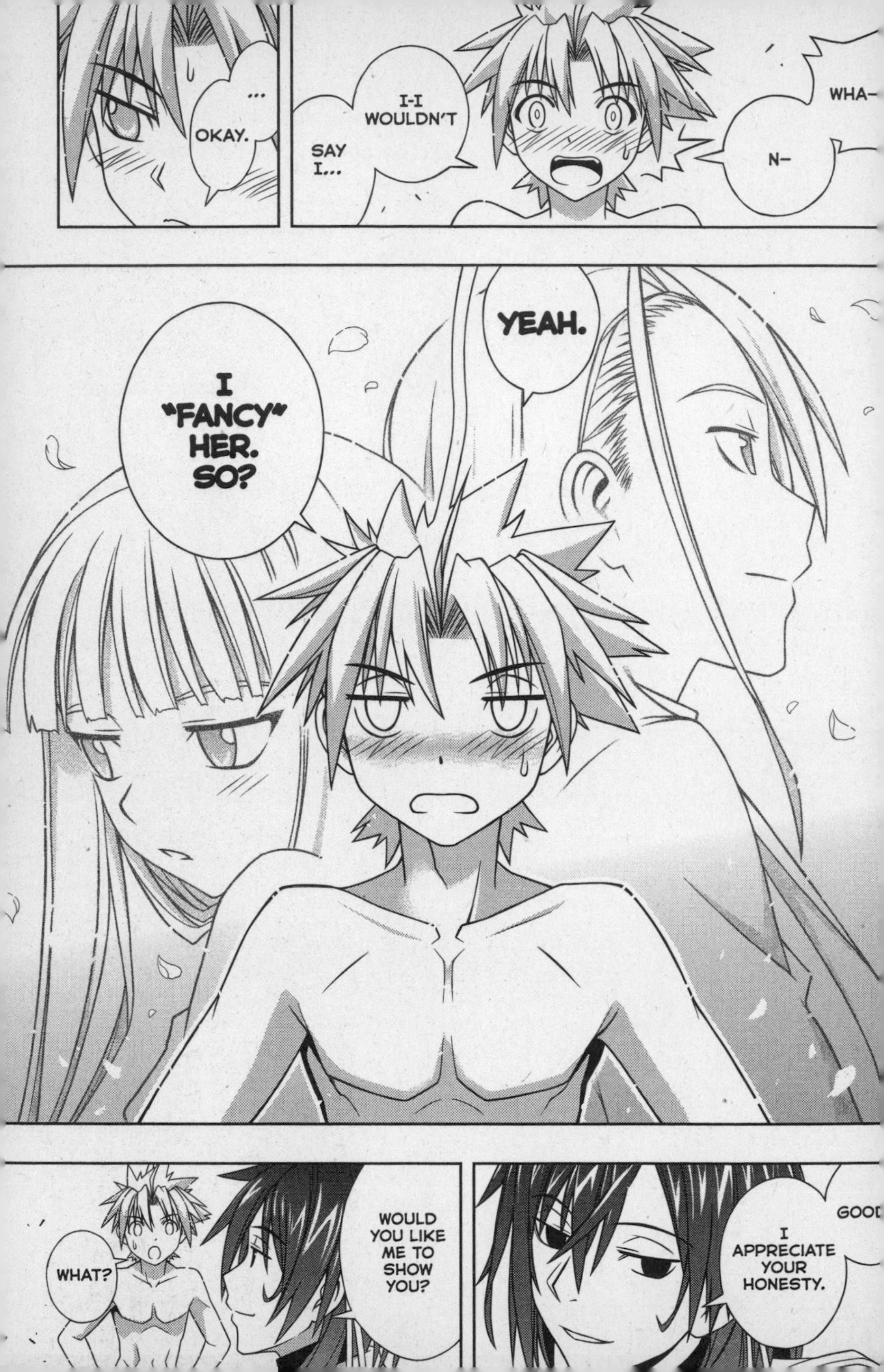
WHA— N—
I-I WOULDN'T SAY I...
... OKAY.
YEAH.
I "FANCY" HER. SO?
GOOD
I APPRECIATE YOUR HONESTY.
WOULD YOU LIKE ME TO SHOW YOU?
WHAT?

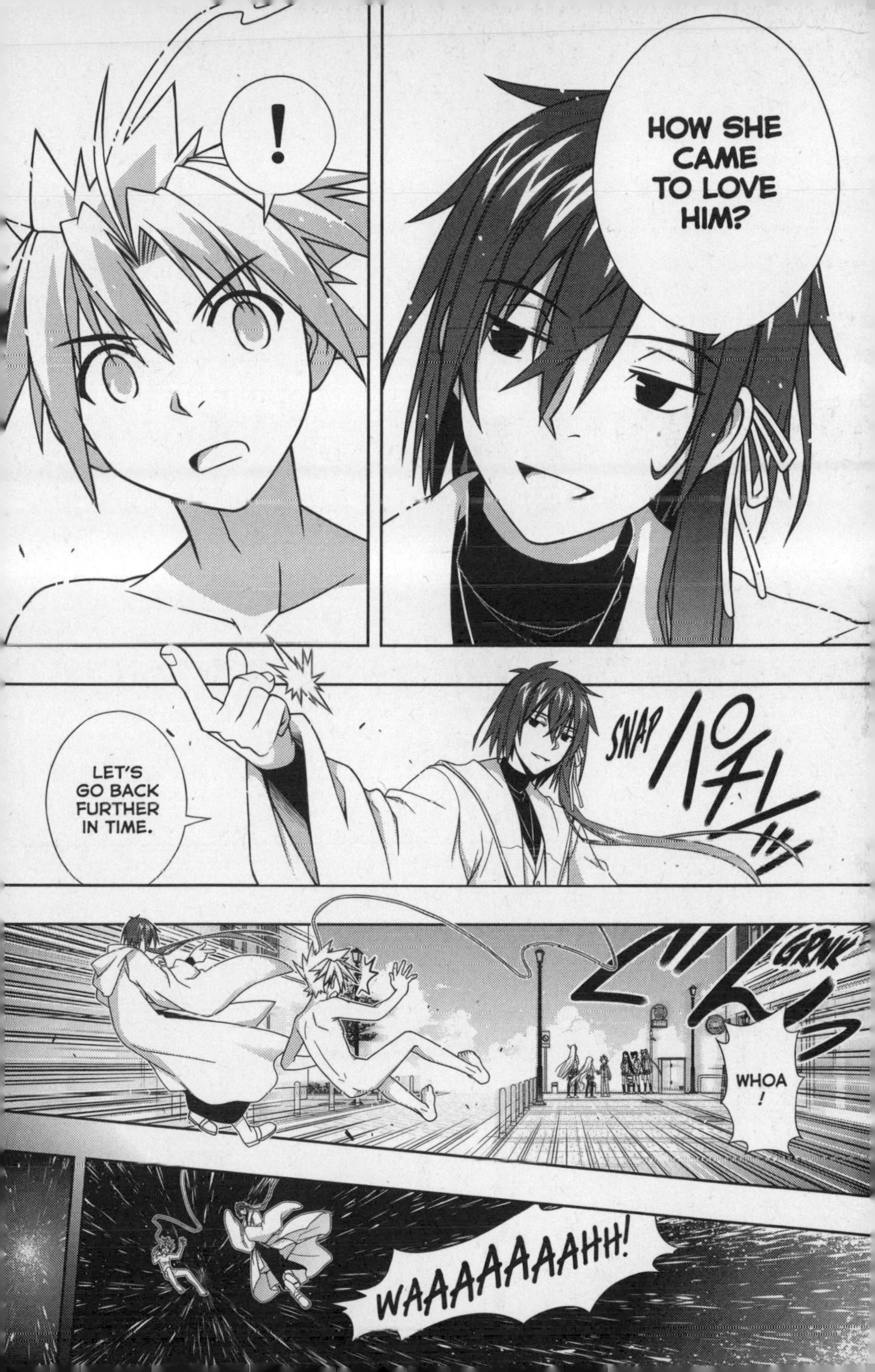
HOW SHE CAME TO LOVE HIM?
!
SNAP
LET'S GO BACK FURTHER IN TIME.
GRNK
WHOA!
WAAAAAAAHH!

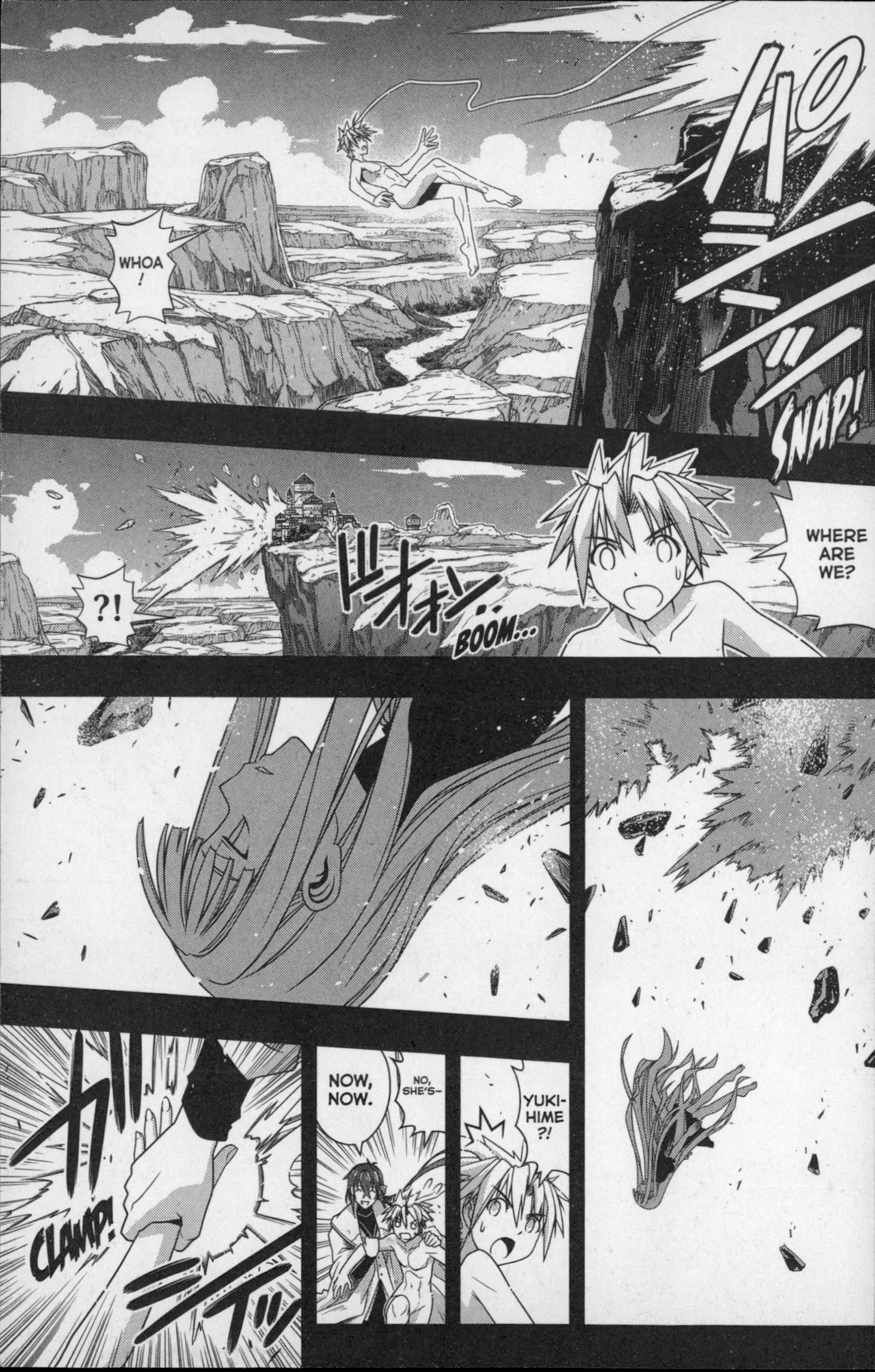
SNAP!
WHOA!
WHERE ARE WE?
ドオン…
BOOM...
?!
YUKI-HIME?!
NO, SHE'S–
NOW, NOW.
CLAMP!

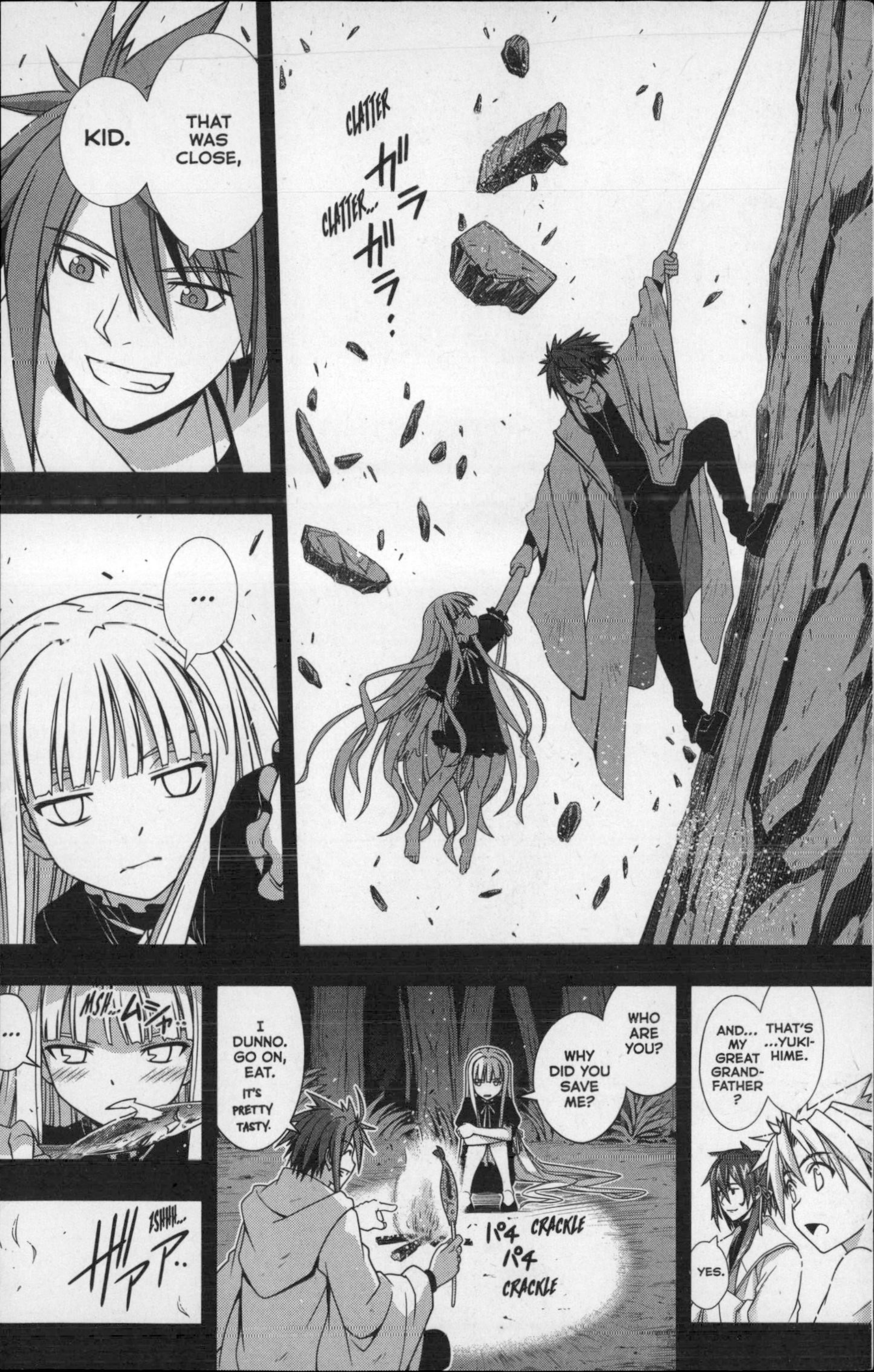
CLATTER
ガラ
CLATTER...
ガラ
THAT WAS CLOSE,
KID.
...
THAT'S ...YUKI-HIME.
AND... MY GREAT GRAND-FATHER?
YES.
WHO ARE YOU?
WHY DID YOU SAVE ME?
I DUNNO. GO ON, EAT.
IT'S PRETTY TASTY.
パチ CRACKLE
パチ CRACKLE
...
MSH... ムシャ
ISHHH...
ガアア..

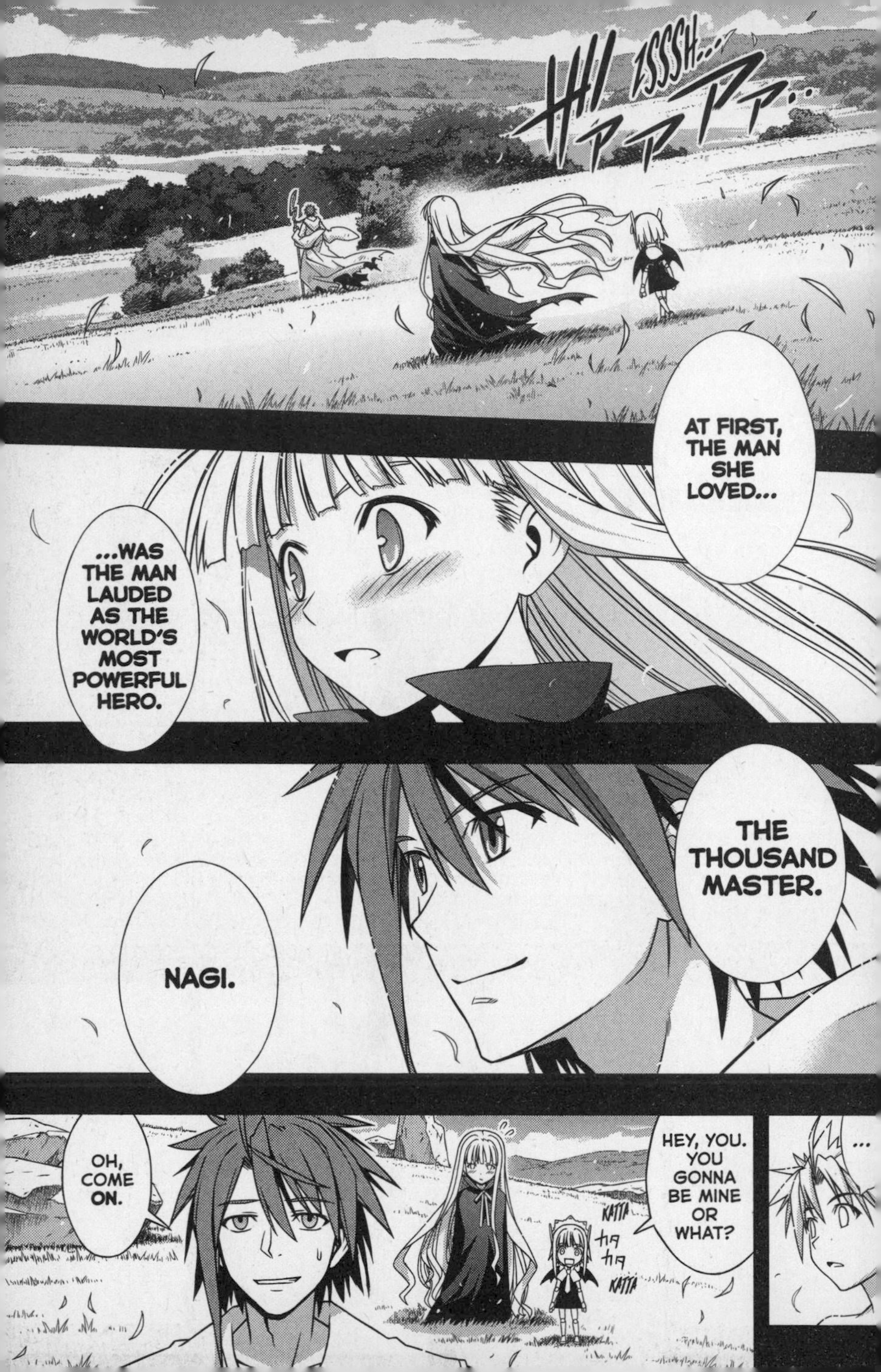
ZSSSH...
AT FIRST, THE MAN SHE LOVED...
...WAS THE MAN LAUDED AS THE WORLD'S MOST POWERFUL HERO.
THE THOUSAND MASTER.
NAGI.
...
HEY, YOU. YOU GONNA BE MINE OR WHAT?
KATTA
カタ カタ
KATTA
OH, COME ON.

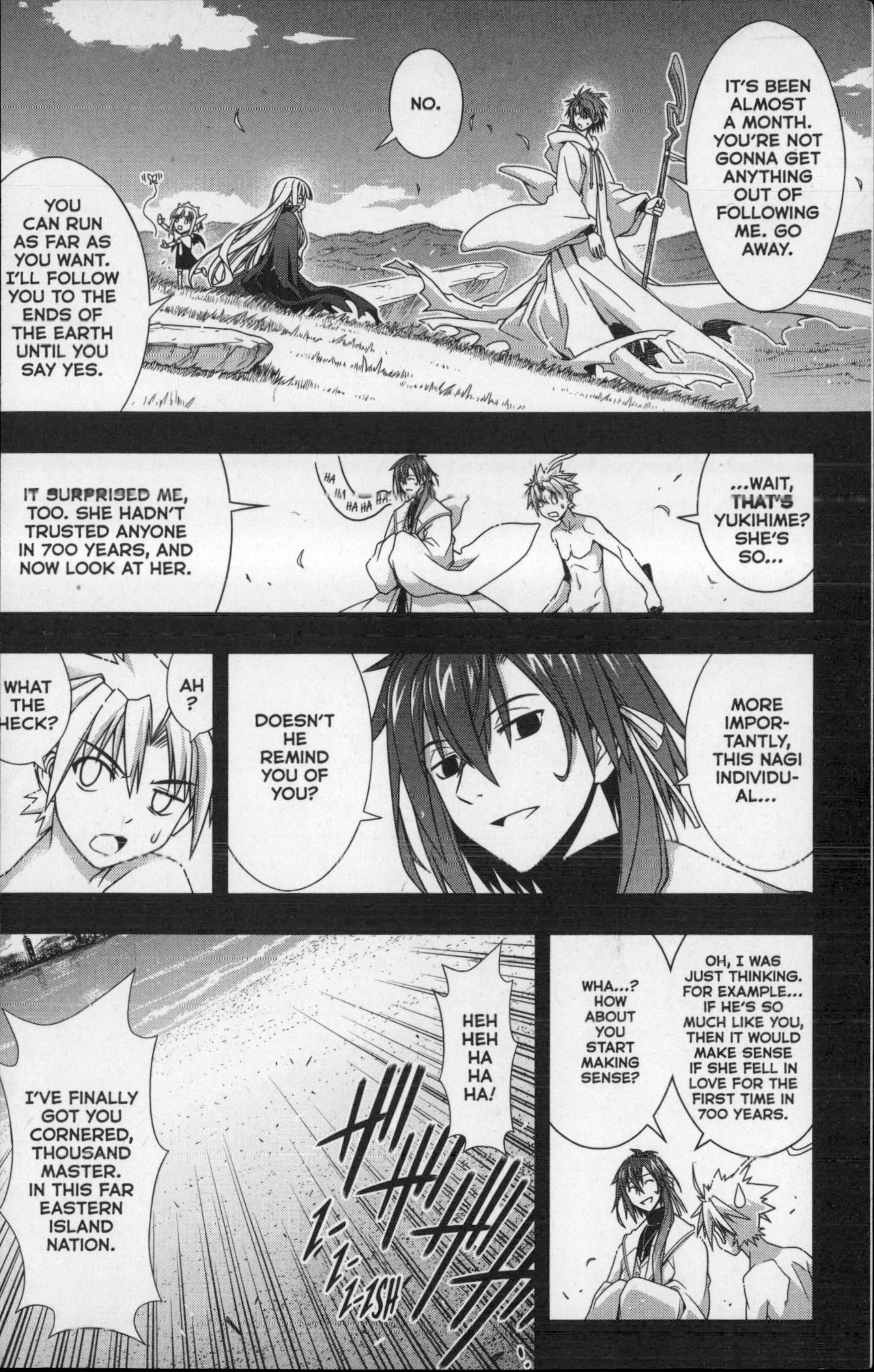
IT'S BEEN ALMOST A MONTH. YOU'RE NOT GONNA GET ANYTHING OUT OF FOLLOWING ME. GO AWAY.
NO.
YOU CAN RUN AS FAR AS YOU WANT. I'LL FOLLOW YOU TO THE ENDS OF THE EARTH UNTIL YOU SAY YES.
...WAIT, THAT'S YUKIHIME? SHE'S SO...
IT SURPRISED ME, TOO. SHE HADN'T TRUSTED ANYONE IN 700 YEARS, AND NOW LOOK AT HER.
MORE IMPOR-TANTLY, THIS NAGI INDIVIDU-AL...
DOESN'T HE REMIND YOU OF YOU?
AH?
WHAT THE HECK?
OH, I WAS JUST THINKING. FOR EXAMPLE... IF HE'S SO MUCH LIKE YOU, THEN IT WOULD MAKE SENSE IF SHE FELL IN LOVE FOR THE FIRST TIME IN 700 YEARS.
WHA...? HOW ABOUT YOU START MAKING SENSE?
HEH HEH HA HA HA!
I'VE FINALLY GOT YOU CORNERED, THOUSAND MASTER. IN THIS FAR EASTERN ISLAND NATION.
Z-Z-Z-ZSH

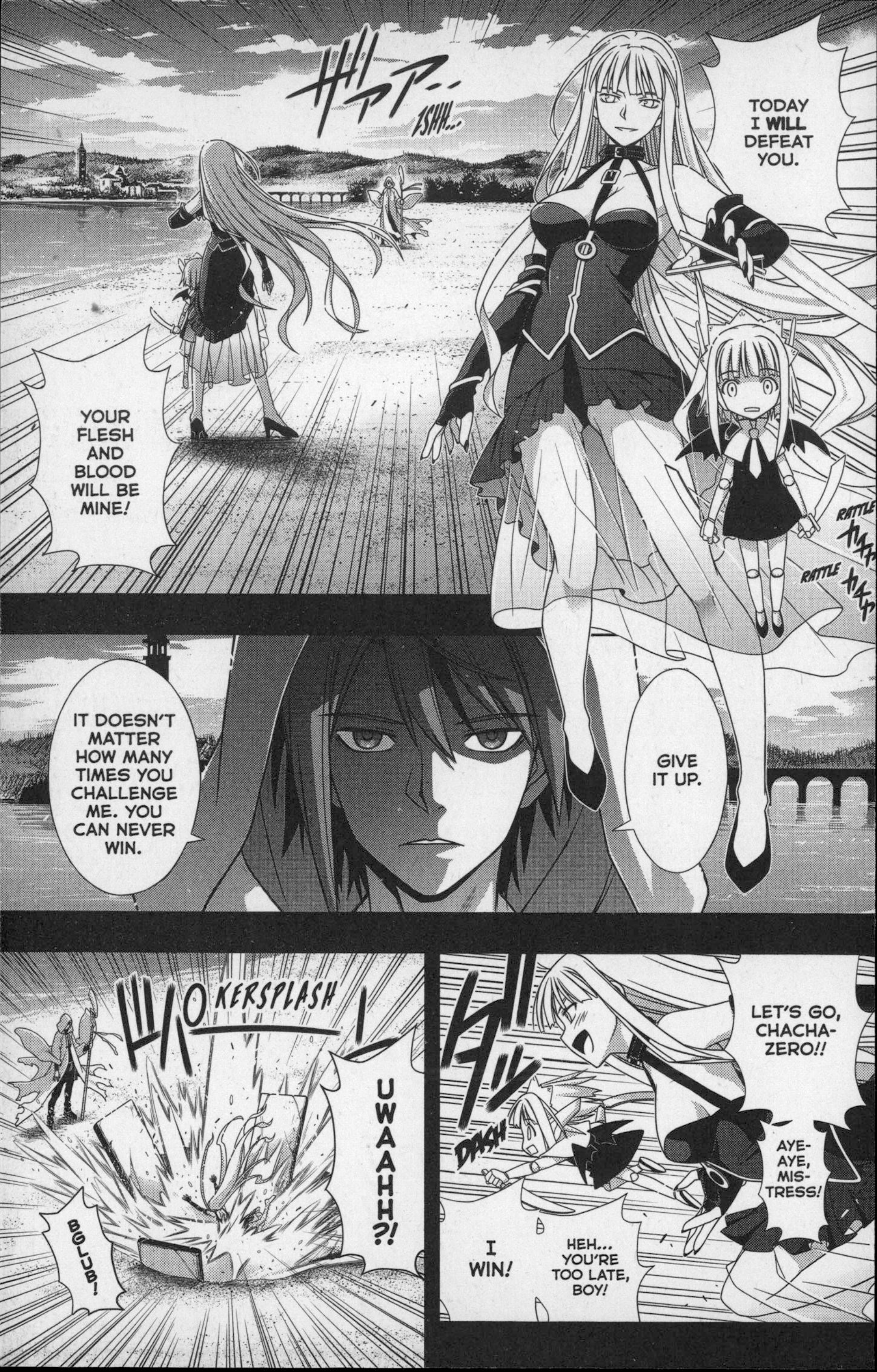

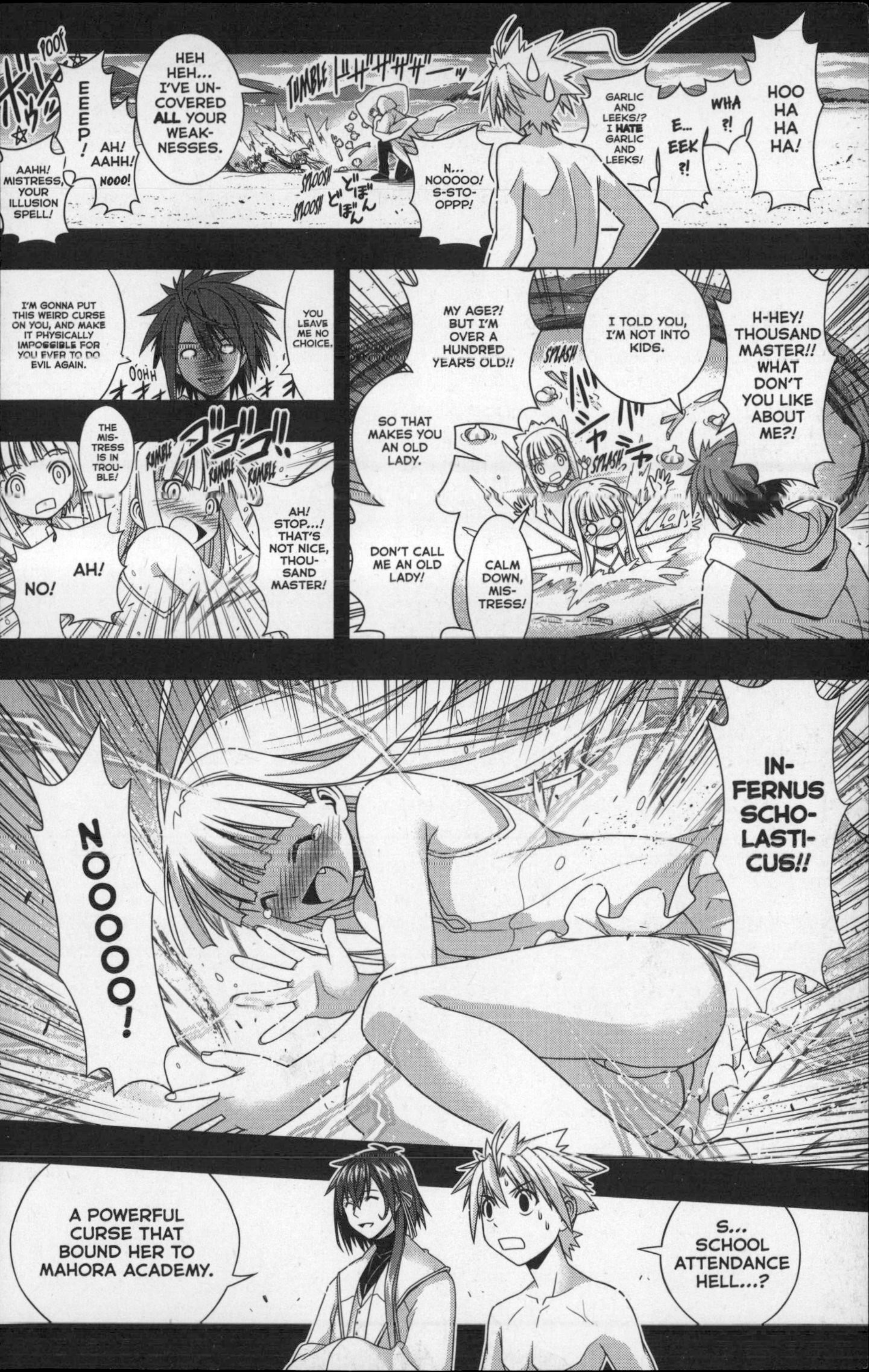
HOO HA HA HA!
WHA ?!
E... EEK ?!
GARLIC AND LEEKS!? I HATE GARLIC AND LEEKS!
N... NOOOOO! S-STO-OPPP!
SPLOOSH SPLOOSH
TUMBLE
HEH HEH... I'VE UN-COVERED ALL YOUR WEAK-NESSES.
AH! AAHH! NOOO!
EEEP!
AAHH! MISTRESS, YOUR ILLUSION SPELL!
POOF
H-HEY! THOUSAND MASTER!! WHAT DON'T YOU LIKE ABOUT ME?!
I TOLD YOU, I'M NOT INTO KIDS.
MY AGE?! BUT I'M OVER A HUNDRED YEARS OLD!!
SPLASH
SO THAT MAKES YOU AN OLD LADY.
SPLASH
CALM DOWN, MIS-TRESS!
DON'T CALL ME AN OLD LADY!
YOU LEAVE ME NO CHOICE.
I'M GONNA PUT THIS WEIRD CURSE ON YOU, AND MAKE IT PHYSICALLY IMPOSSIBLE FOR YOU EVER TO DO EVIL AGAIN.
O'OHH
THE MIS-TRESS IS IN TROU-BLE!
RUMBLE RUMBLE RUMBLE
AH! STOP...! THAT'S NOT NICE, THOU-SAND MASTER!
AH!
NO!
IN-FERNUS SCHO-LASTI-CUS!!
NOOOOO!
S... SCHOOL ATTENDANCE HELL...?
A POWERFUL CURSE THAT BOUND HER TO MAHORA ACADEMY.

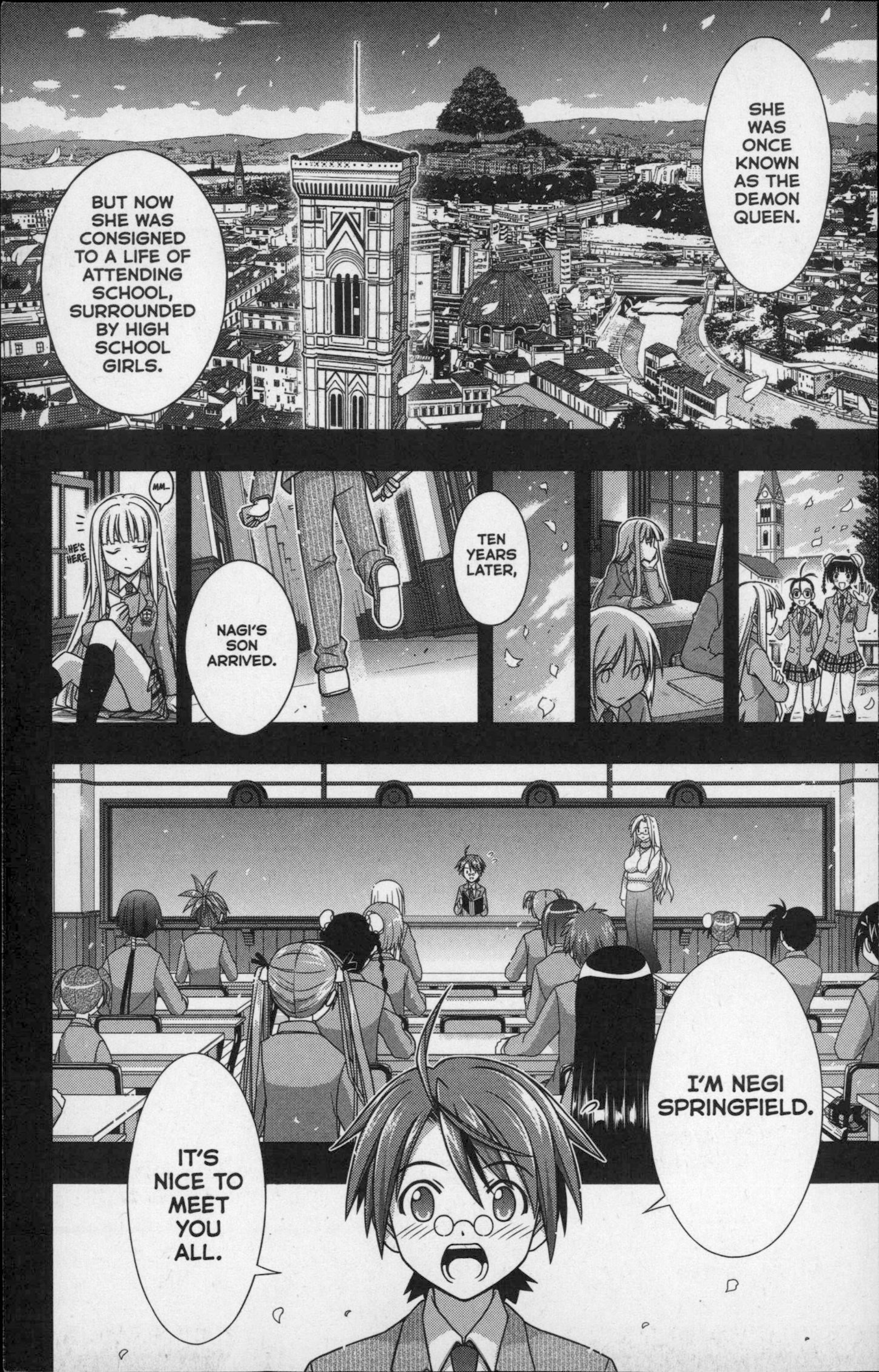
SHE WAS ONCE KNOWN AS THE DEMON QUEEN.
BUT NOW SHE WAS CONSIGNED TO A LIFE OF ATTENDING SCHOOL, SURROUNDED BY HIGH SCHOOL GIRLS.
TEN YEARS LATER,
NAGI'S SON ARRIVED.
MM...
HE'S HERE
I'M NEGI SPRINGFIELD.
IT'S NICE TO MEET YOU ALL.

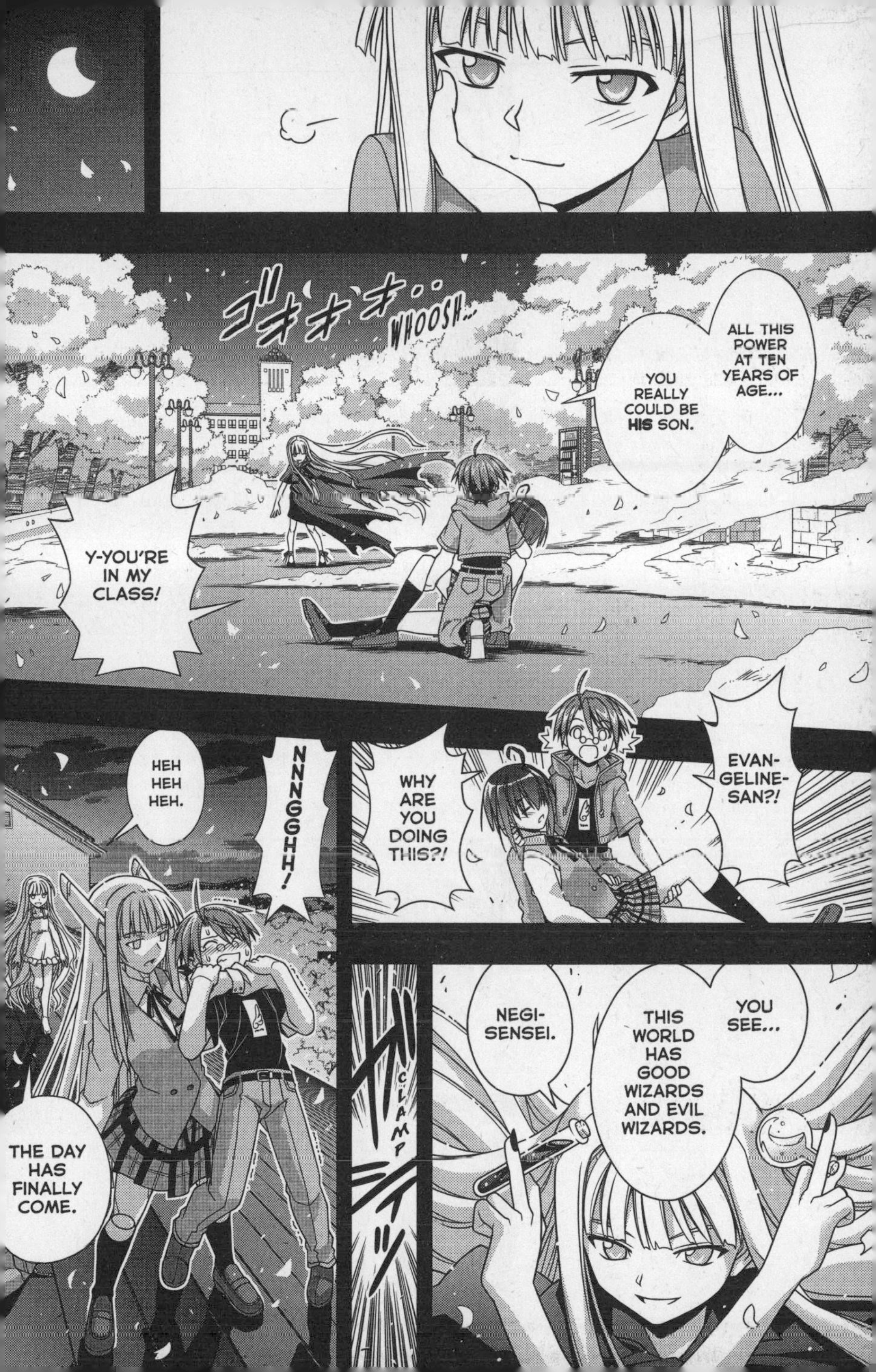
ゴオオオ..
WHOOSH...
ALL THIS POWER AT TEN YEARS OF AGE...
YOU REALLY COULD BE **HIS** SON.
Y-YOU'RE IN MY CLASS!
EVAN-GELINE-SAN?!
WHY ARE YOU DOING THIS?!
YOU SEE...
NEGI-SENSEI.
THIS WORLD HAS GOOD WIZARDS AND EVIL WIZARDS.
CLAMP
NNNGGHH!
HEH HEH HEH.
THE DAY HAS FINALLY COME.

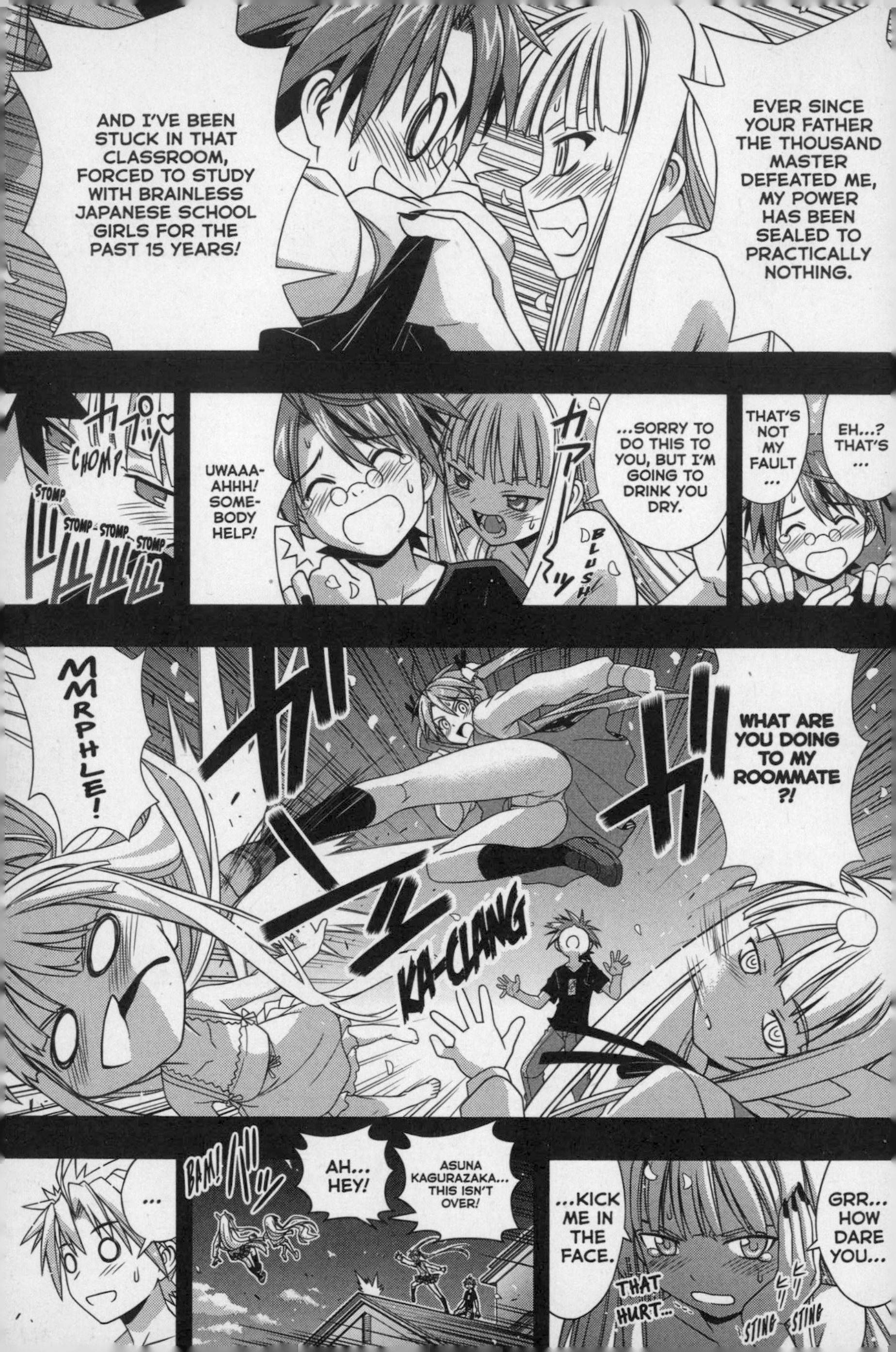
EVER SINCE YOUR FATHER THE THOUSAND MASTER DEFEATED ME, MY POWER HAS BEEN SEALED TO PRACTICALLY NOTHING.
AND I'VE BEEN STUCK IN THAT CLASSROOM, FORCED TO STUDY WITH BRAINLESS JAPANESE SCHOOL GIRLS FOR THE PAST 15 YEARS!
EH...? THAT'S ...
THAT'S NOT MY FAULT ...
...SORRY TO DO THIS TO YOU, BUT I'M GOING TO DRINK YOU DRY.
BLUSH
UWAAA-AHHH! SOME-BODY HELP!
CHOMP
STOMP
STOMP STOMP STOMP
WHAT ARE YOU DOING TO MY ROOMMATE ?!
KA-CLANG
MMRPHLE!
GRR... HOW DARE YOU...
...KICK ME IN THE FACE.
THAT HURT...
STING STING
ASUNA KAGURAZAKA... THIS ISN'T OVER!
AH... HEY!
BAM!
...

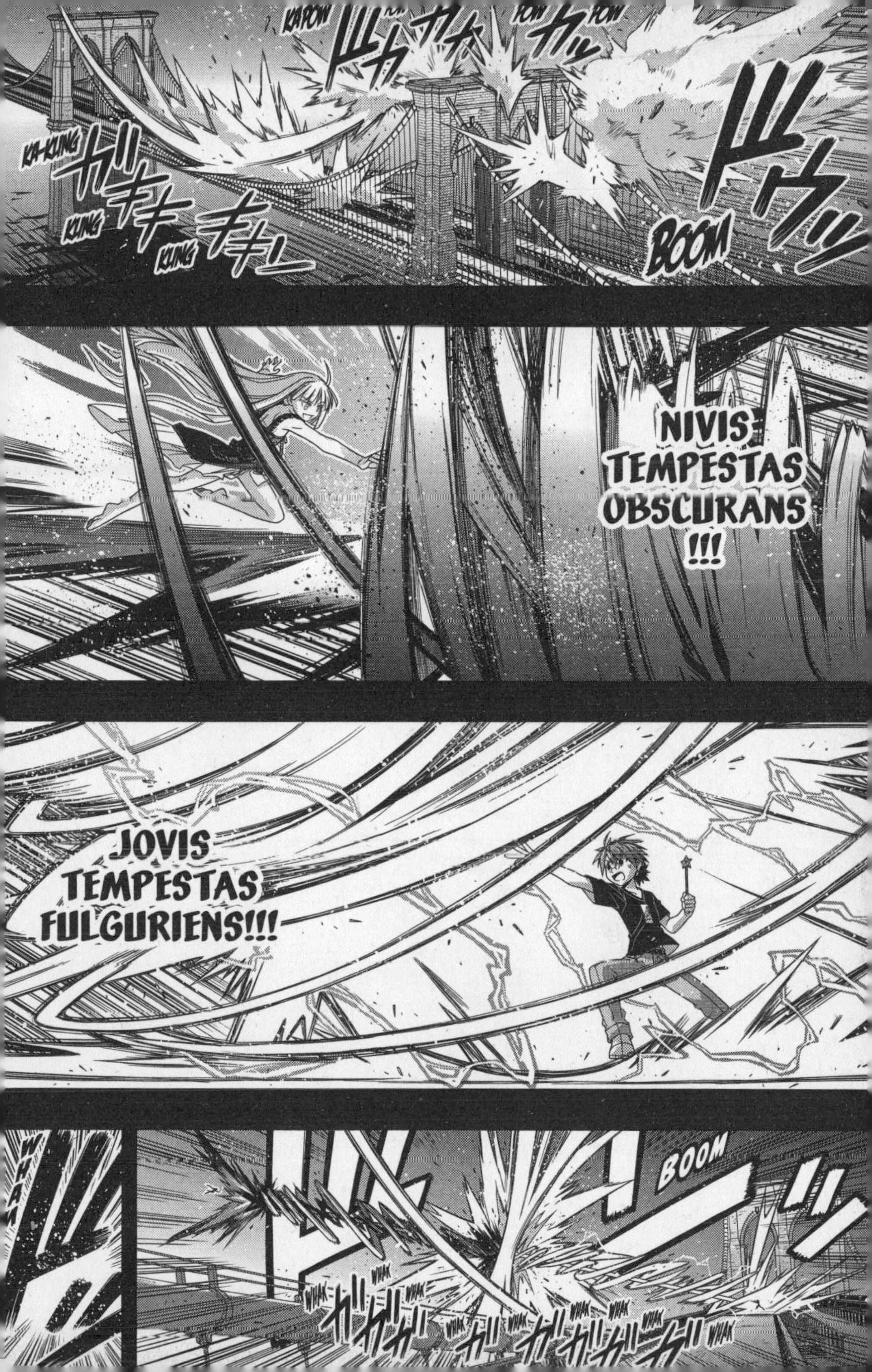
BOOM
POW
POW
KAPOW
KA-KUNG
KUNG
KUNG
NIVIS TEMPESTAS OBSCURANS !!!
JOVIS TEMPESTAS FULGURIENS!!!
BOOM
WHAK
WHAK
WHAK
WHAK
WHAK
WHAK
WHAM

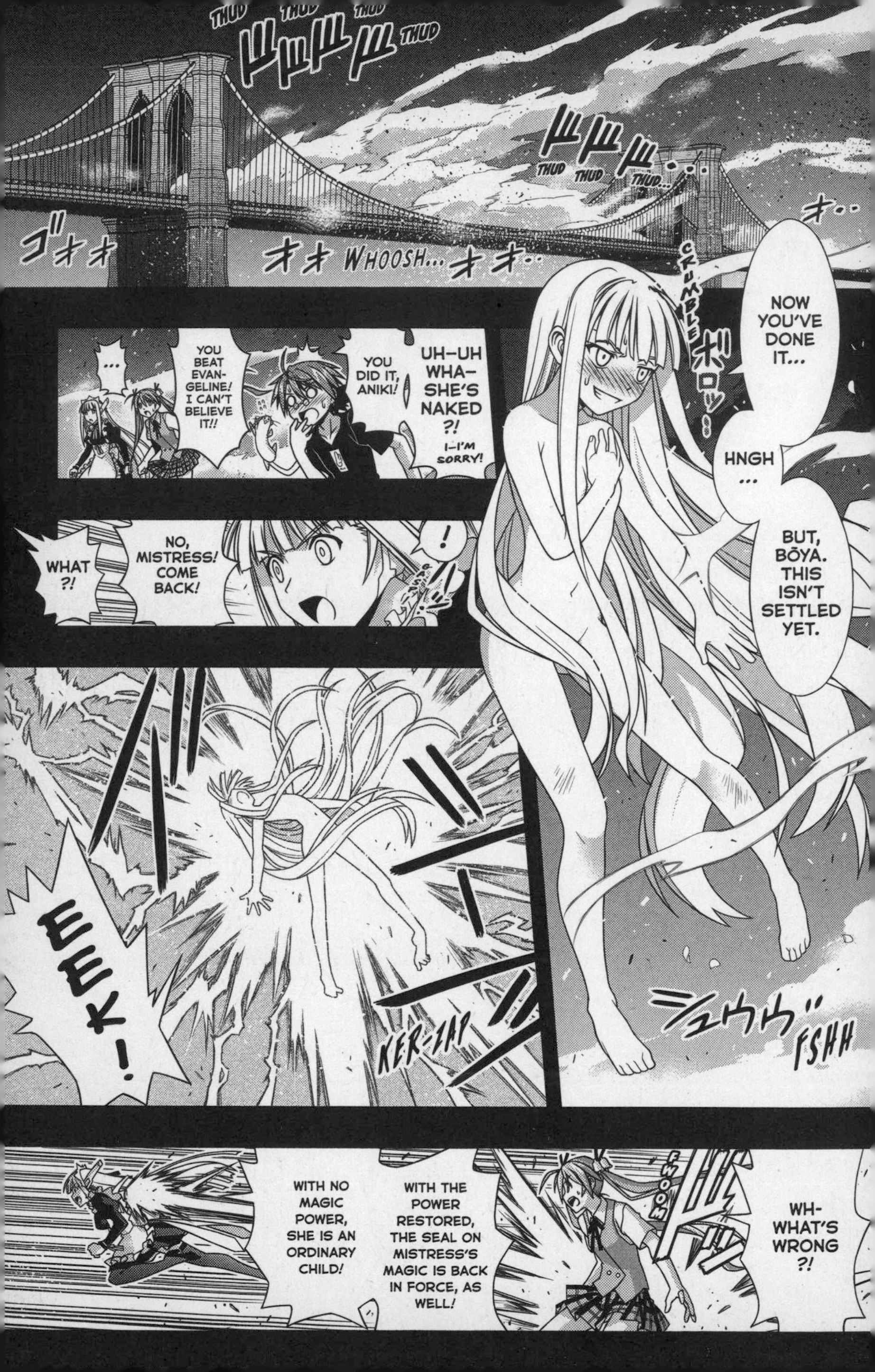
THUD THUD THUD THUD
THUD THUD THUD...
WHOOSH...
CRUMBLE
NOW YOU'VE DONE IT...
HNGH...
BUT, BŌYA. THIS ISN'T SETTLED YET.
FSHH
UH-UH WHA- SHE'S NAKED?!
I-I'M SORRY!
YOU DID IT, ANIKI!
YOU BEAT EVAN-GELINE! I CAN'T BELIEVE IT!!
...
!
NO, MISTRESS! COME BACK!
WHAT?!
KER-ZAP
EEK!
WH-WHAT'S WRONG?!
FWOOM
WITH THE POWER RESTORED, THE SEAL ON MISTRESS'S MAGIC IS BACK IN FORCE, AS WELL!
WITH NO MAGIC POWER, SHE IS AN ORDINARY CHILD!

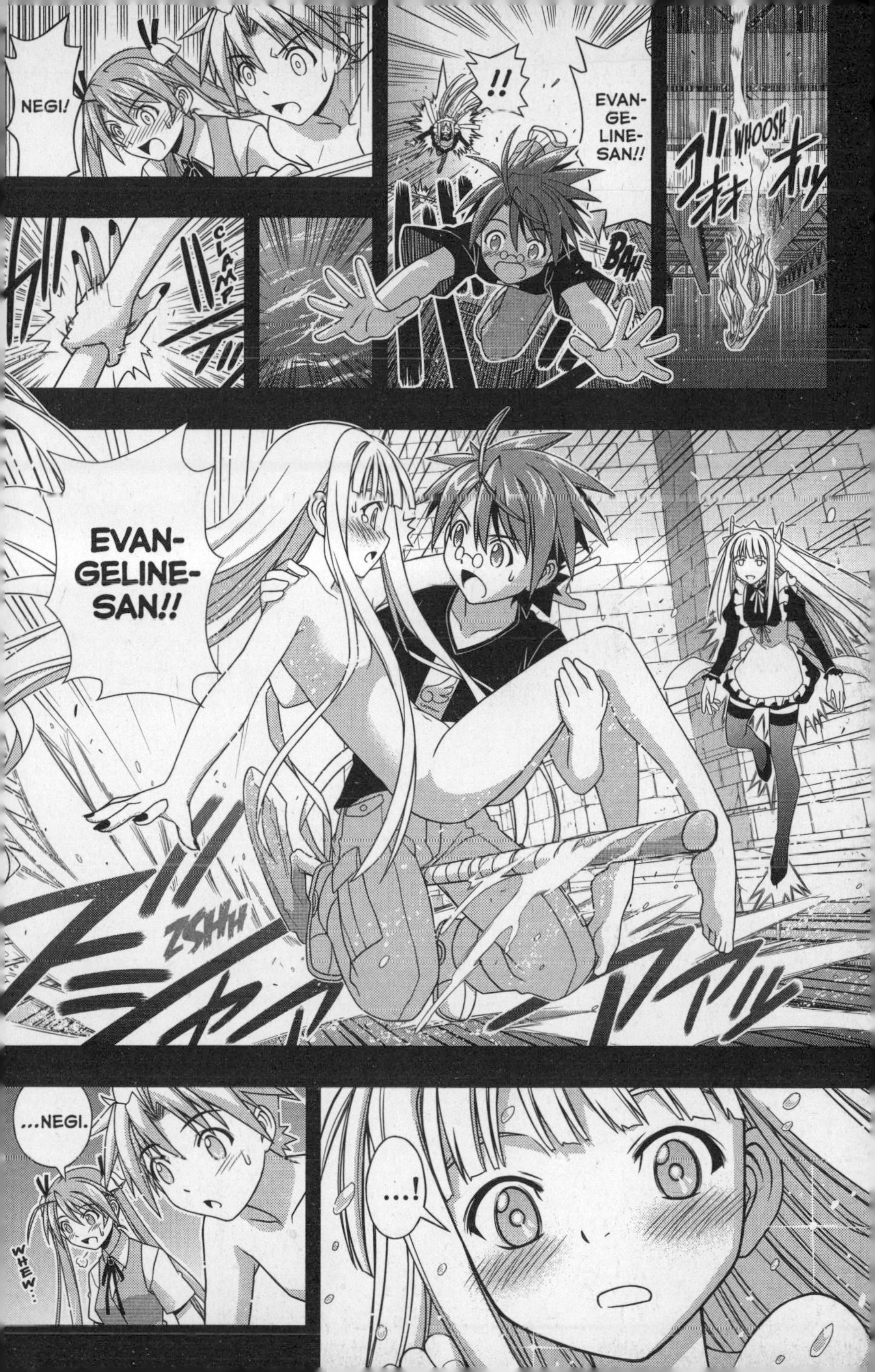
WHOOSH
!!
EVAN-GE-LINE-SAN!!
BAH
NEGI!
CLAMP
EVAN-GELINE-SAN!!
ZSHHH
...!
...NEGI.
WHEW...

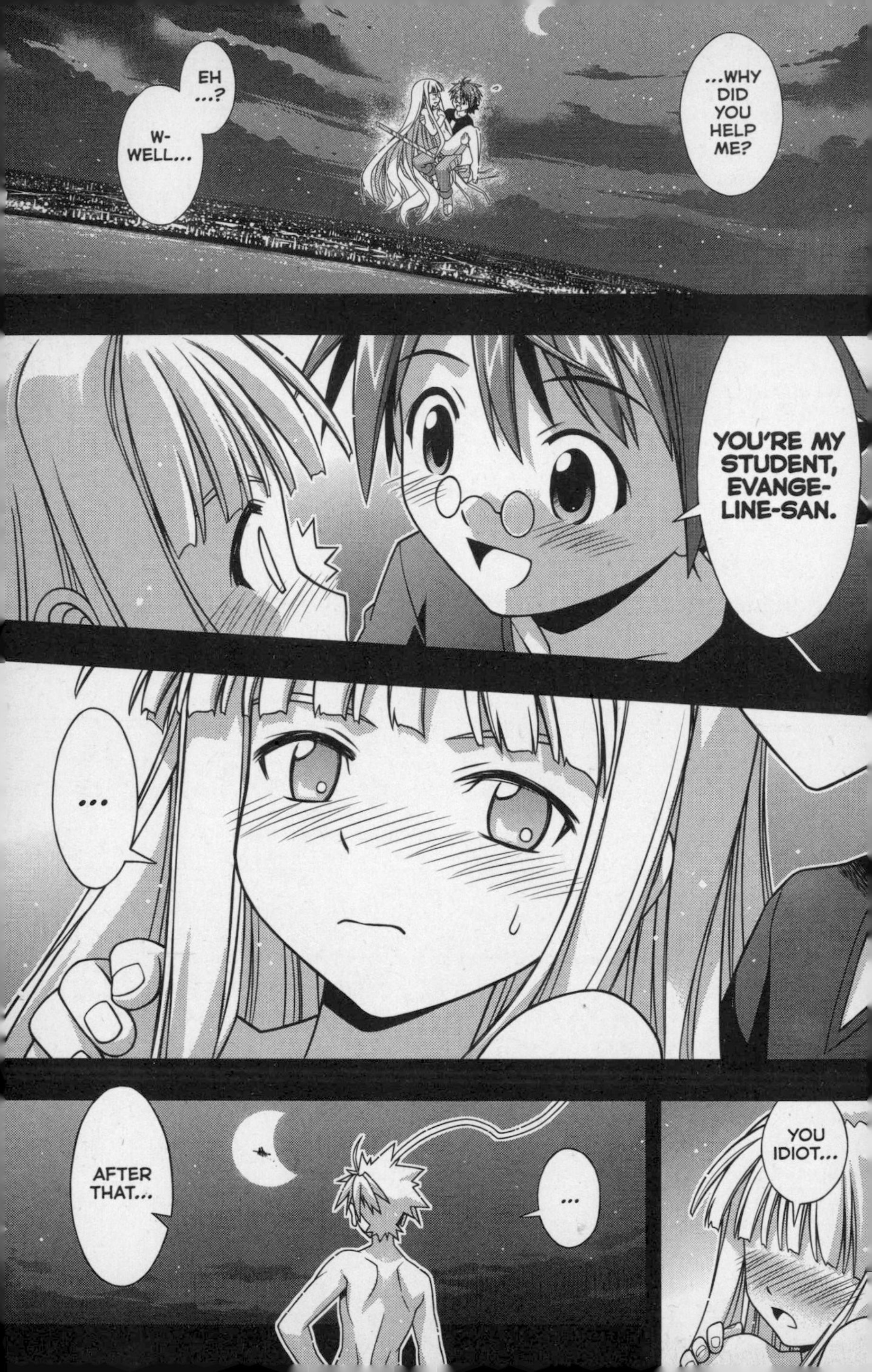
...WHY DID YOU HELP ME?
EH ...?
W-WELL...
YOU'RE MY STUDENT, EVANGE-LINE-SAN.
...
YOU IDIOT...
...
AFTER THAT...

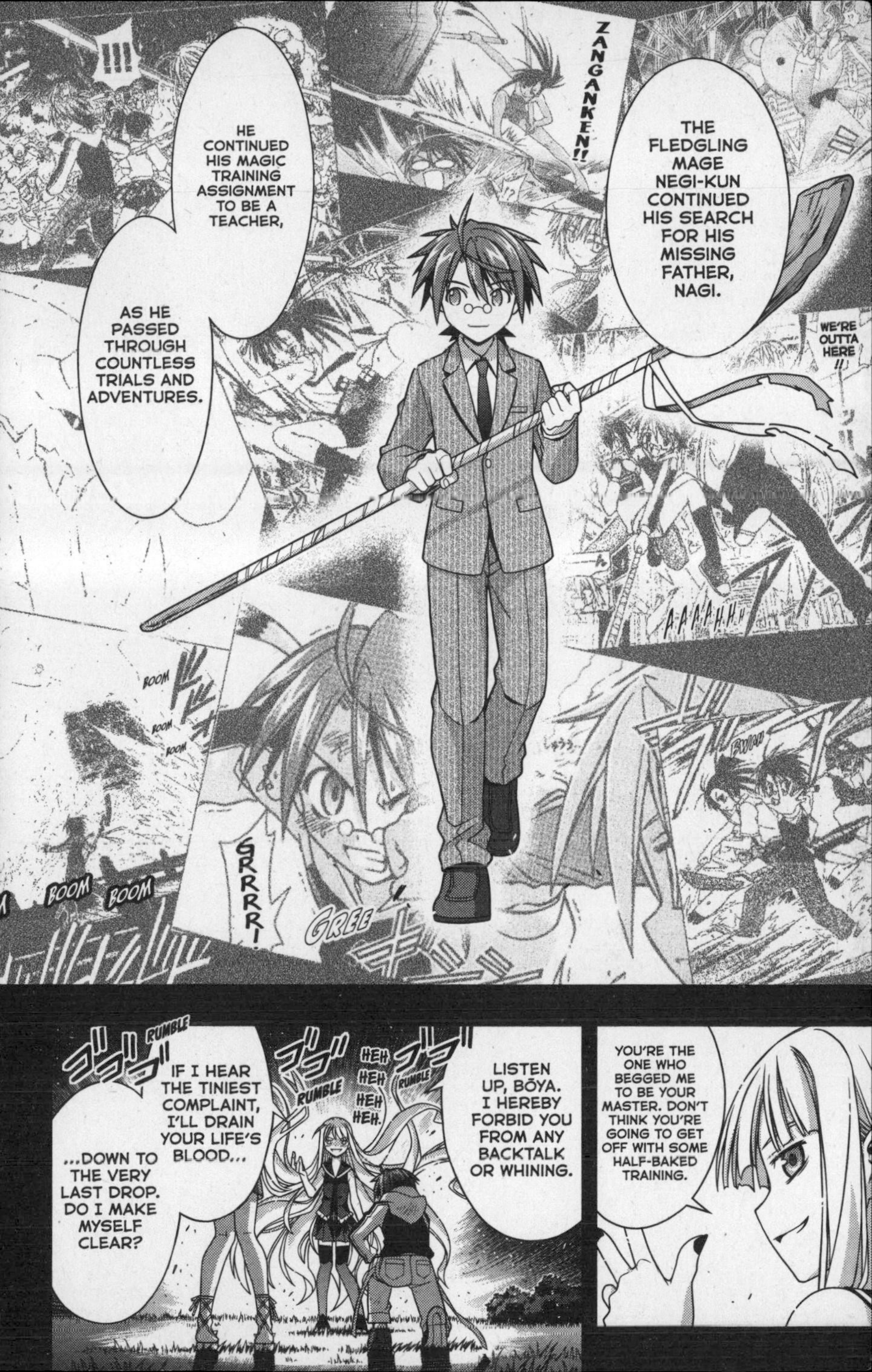

ZANGANKEN!!
THE FLEDGLING MAGE NEGI-KUN CONTINUED HIS SEARCH FOR HIS MISSING FATHER, NAGI.
!!!
HE CONTINUED HIS MAGIC TRAINING ASSIGNMENT TO BE A TEACHER,
AS HE PASSED THROUGH COUNTLESS TRIALS AND ADVENTURES.
WE'RE OUTTA HERE!!
AAAAHH
BOOM BOOM BOOM
GRRRR!
GREE
BOOM BOOM
YOU'RE THE ONE WHO BEGGED ME TO BE YOUR MASTER. DON'T THINK YOU'RE GOING TO GET OFF WITH SOME HALF-BAKED TRAINING.
LISTEN UP, BŌYA. I HEREBY FORBID YOU FROM ANY BACKTALK OR WHINING.
RUMBLE
HEH HEH HEH HEH.
RUMBLE
IF I HEAR THE TINIEST COMPLAINT, I'LL DRAIN YOUR LIFE'S BLOOD...
RUMBLE
...DOWN TO THE VERY LAST DROP. DO I MAKE MYSELF CLEAR?

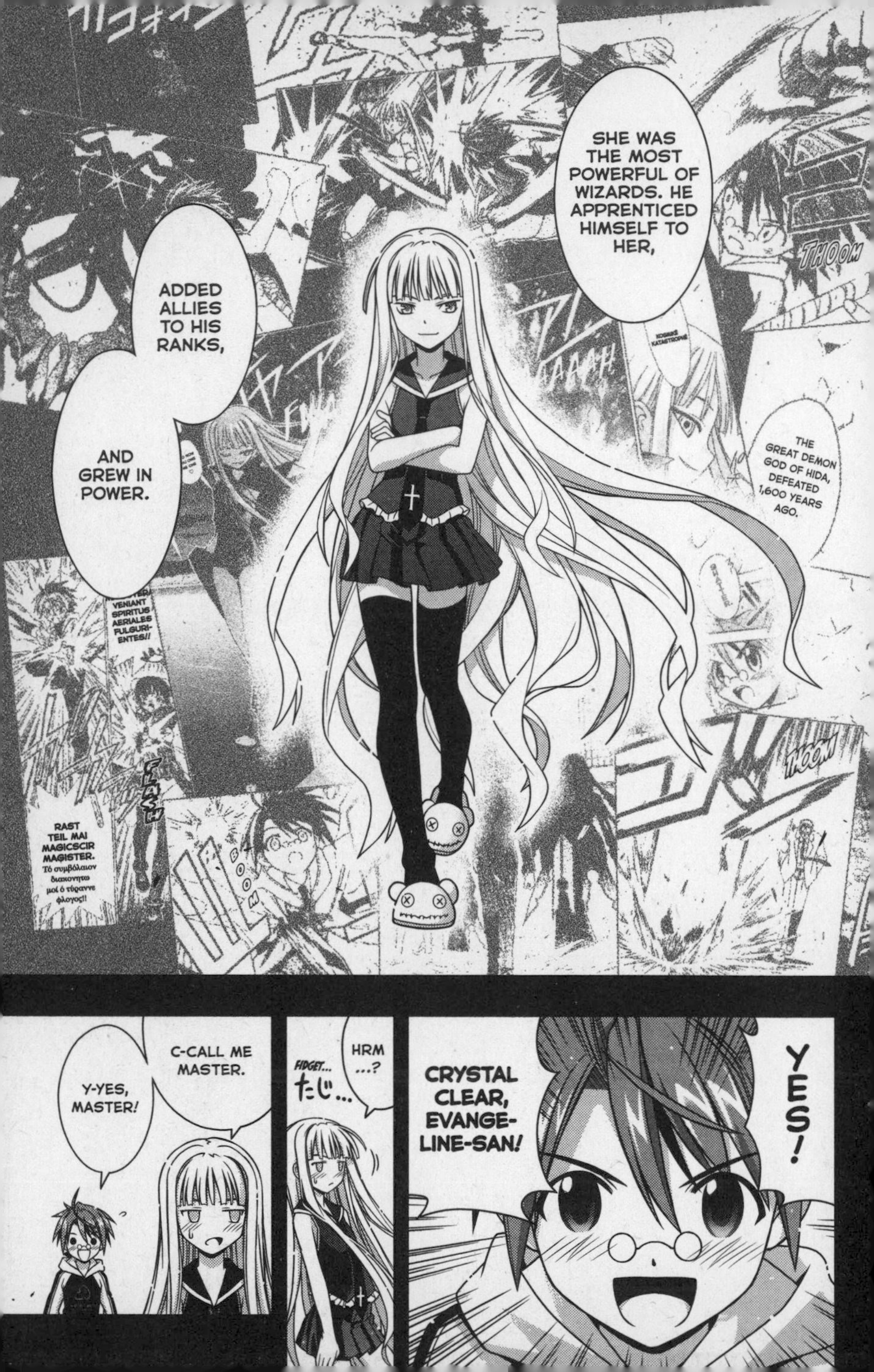
SHE WAS THE MOST POWERFUL OF WIZARDS. HE APPRENTICED HIMSELF TO HER,
THOOM
ADDED ALLIES TO HIS RANKS,
AND GREW IN POWER.
THE GREAT DEMON GOD OF HIDA, DEFEATED 1,600 YEARS AGO.
VENIANT SPIRITUS AERIALES FULGURIENTES!!
THOOM
FLASH
RAST TEIL MAI MAGICSCIR MAGISTER. Τὸ συμβόλαιον διακονητω μοί ὁ τύραννε φλογος!!
BOOM
YES!
CRYSTAL CLEAR, EVANGE-LINE-SAN!
HRM ...?
FIDGET... たじ...
C-CALL ME MASTER.
Y-YES, MASTER!

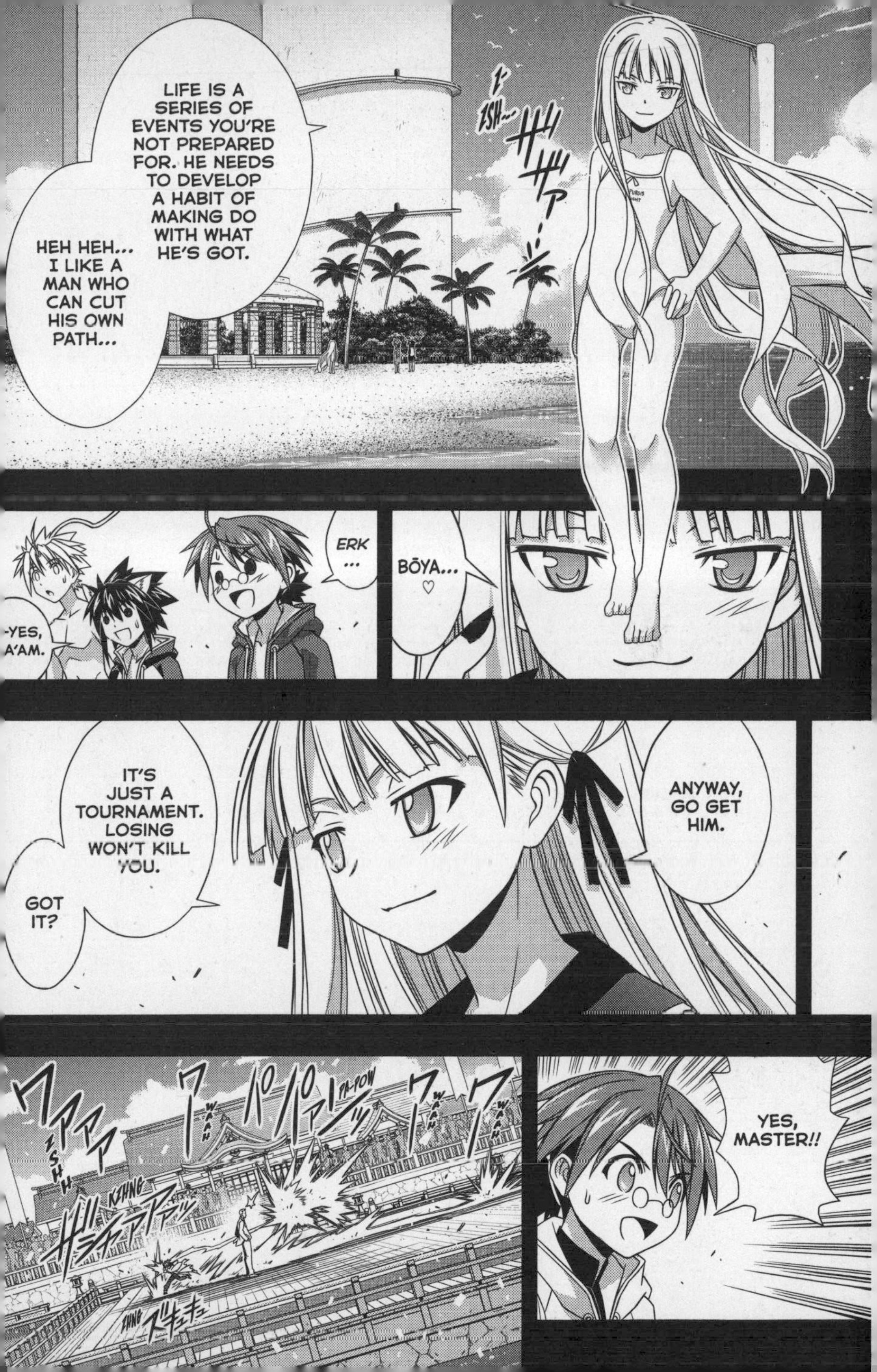
ZSH...
LIFE IS A SERIES OF EVENTS YOU'RE NOT PREPARED FOR. HE NEEDS TO DEVELOP A HABIT OF MAKING DO WITH WHAT HE'S GOT.
HEH HEH... I LIKE A MAN WHO CAN CUT HIS OWN PATH...
BŌYA... ♡
ERK...
-YES, A'AM.
ANYWAY, GO GET HIM.
IT'S JUST A TOURNAMENT. LOSING WON'T KILL YOU.
GOT IT?
YES, MASTER!!
WAAAH
PA-POW
ZSHH
KZHNG
ZHNG

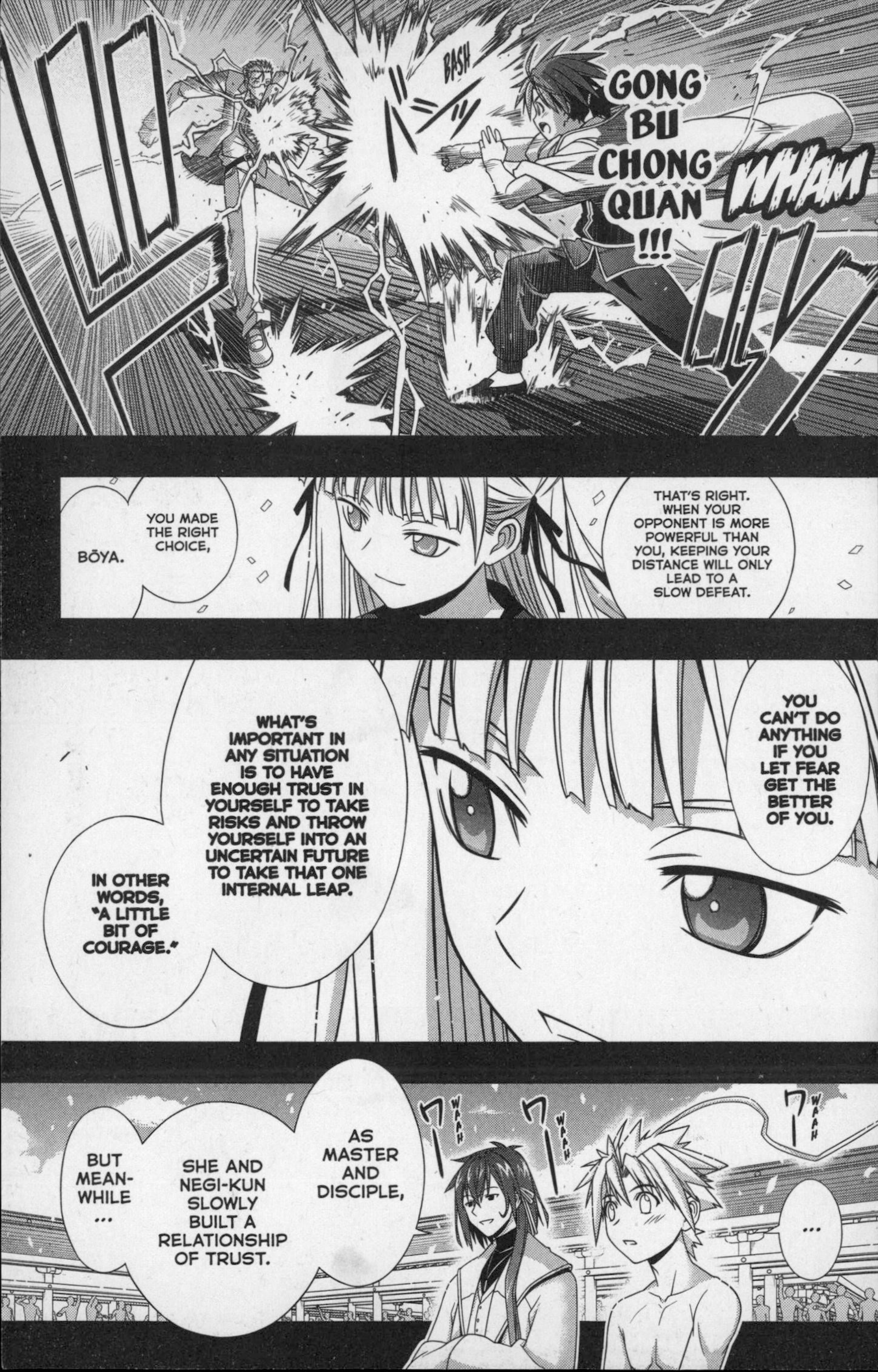
BASH
GONG BU CHONG QUAN !!!
WHAM
THAT'S RIGHT. WHEN YOUR OPPONENT IS MORE POWERFUL THAN YOU, KEEPING YOUR DISTANCE WILL ONLY LEAD TO A SLOW DEFEAT.
YOU MADE THE RIGHT CHOICE,
BŌYA.
YOU CAN'T DO ANYTHING IF YOU LET FEAR GET THE BETTER OF YOU.
WHAT'S IMPORTANT IN ANY SITUATION IS TO HAVE ENOUGH TRUST IN YOURSELF TO TAKE RISKS AND THROW YOURSELF INTO AN UNCERTAIN FUTURE TO TAKE THAT ONE INTERNAL LEAP.
IN OTHER WORDS, "A LITTLE BIT OF COURAGE."
WAAH
...
WAAH
WAAH
AS MASTER AND DISCIPLE,
SHE AND NEGI-KUN SLOWLY BUILT A RELATIONSHIP OF TRUST.
BUT MEAN-WHILE ...

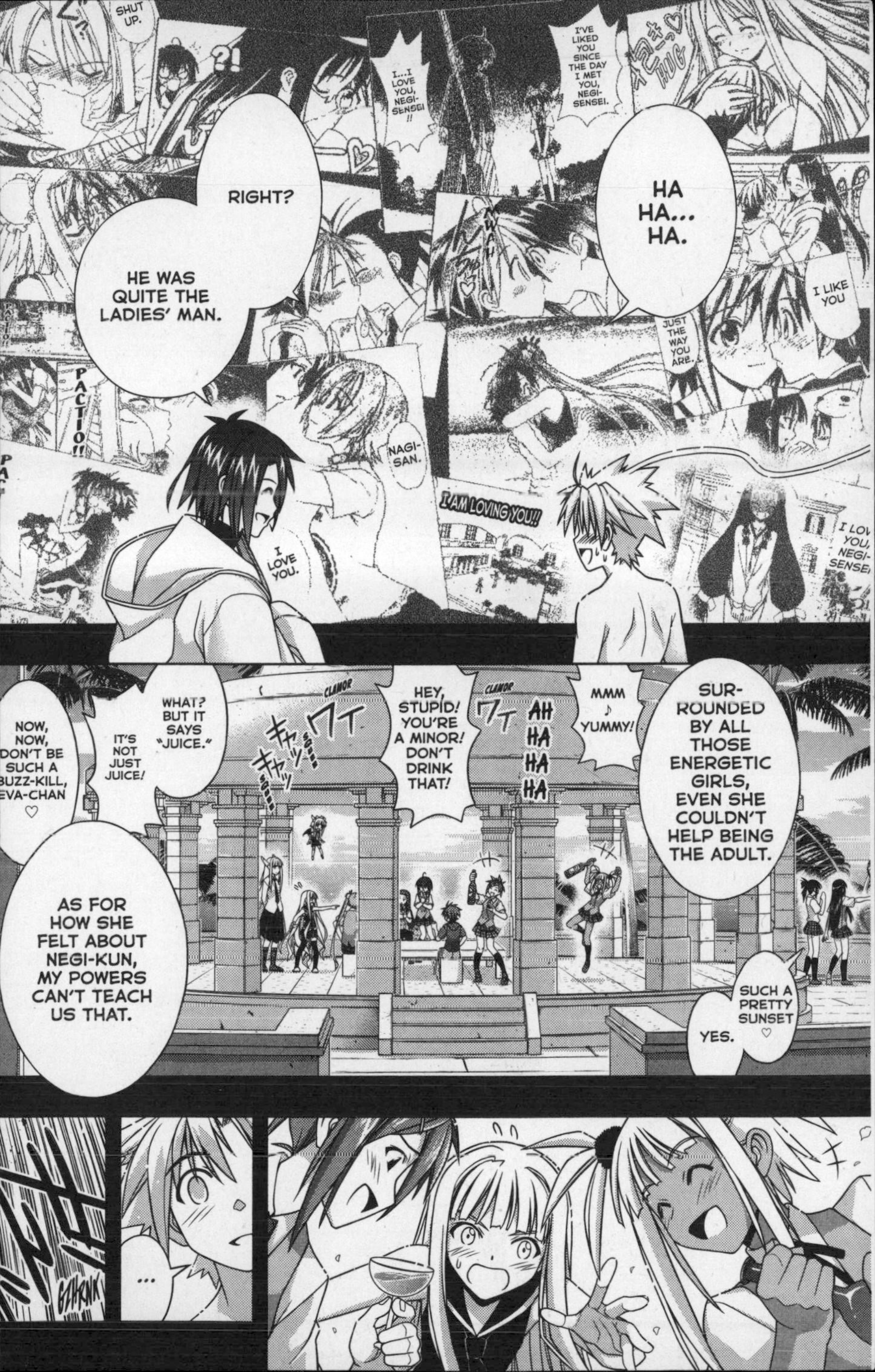
I'VE LIKED YOU SINCE THE DAY I MET YOU, NEGI-SENSEI.
HUG
I...I LOVE YOU, NEGI-SENSEI!!
SHUT UP.
?!
HA HA... HA.
RIGHT?
HE WAS QUITE THE LADIES' MAN.
I LIKE YOU
JUST THE WAY YOU ARE.
PACTIO!!
NAGI-SAN.
I LOVE YOU, NEGI-SENSEI
I AM LOVING YOU!!
I LOVE YOU.
SUR-ROUNDED BY ALL THOSE ENERGETIC GIRLS, EVEN SHE COULDN'T HELP BEING THE ADULT.
MMM ♪ YUMMY!
AH HA HA HA HA
CLAMOR
HEY, STUPID! YOU'RE A MINOR! DON'T DRINK THAT!
CLAMOR
WHAT? BUT IT SAYS "JUICE."
IT'S NOT JUST JUICE!
NOW, NOW, DON'T BE SUCH A BUZZ-KILL, EVA-CHAN ♡
SUCH A PRETTY SUNSET ♡
YES.
AS FOR HOW SHE FELT ABOUT NEGI-KUN, MY POWERS CAN'T TEACH US THAT.
...
GLHRNK

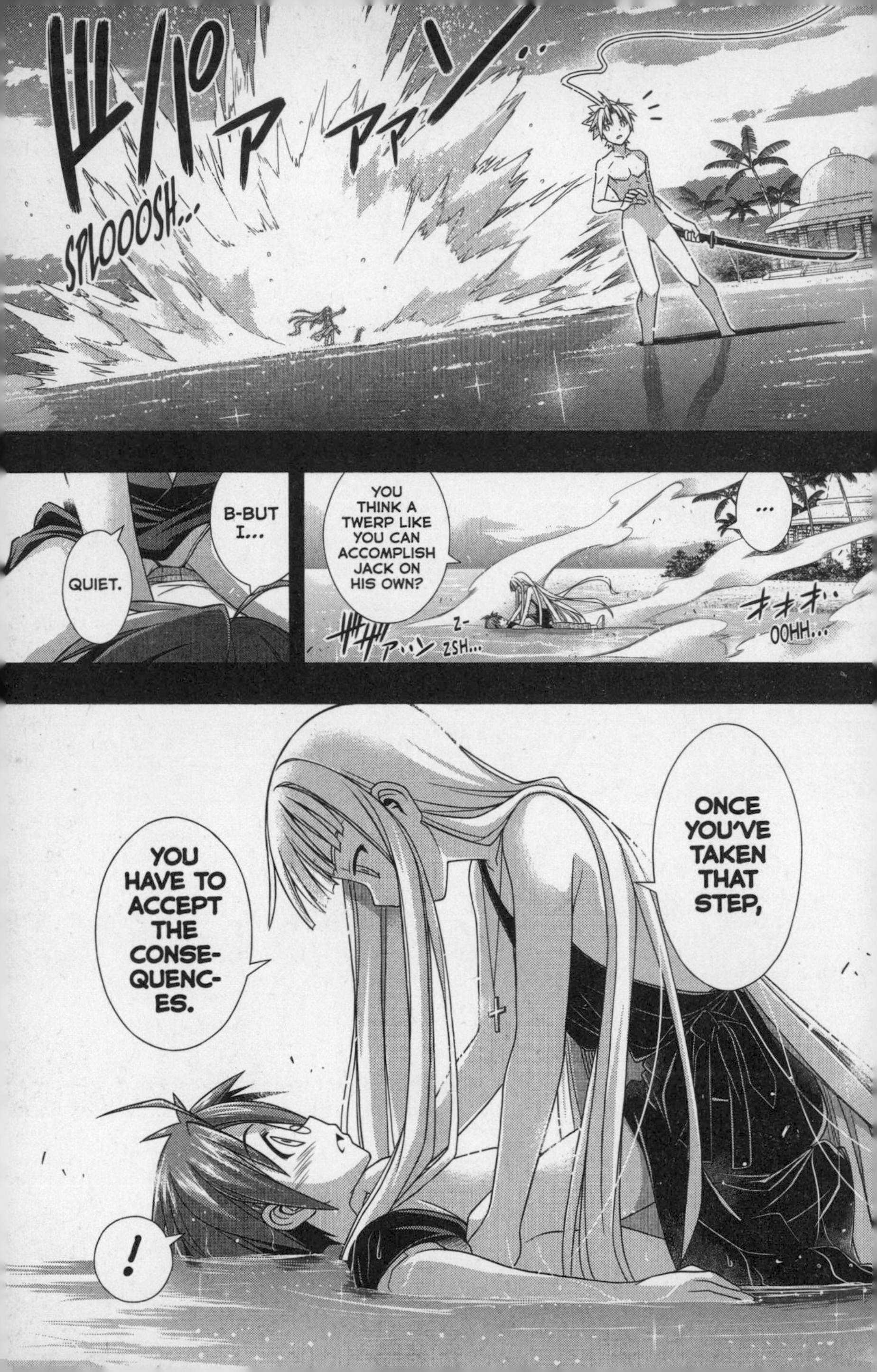
SPLOOOSH...
...
YOU THINK A TWERP LIKE YOU CAN ACCOMPLISH JACK ON HIS OWN?
Z-ZSH...
OOHH...
B-BUT I...
QUIET.
ONCE YOU'VE TAKEN THAT STEP,
YOU HAVE TO ACCEPT THE CONSE-QUENC-ES.
!

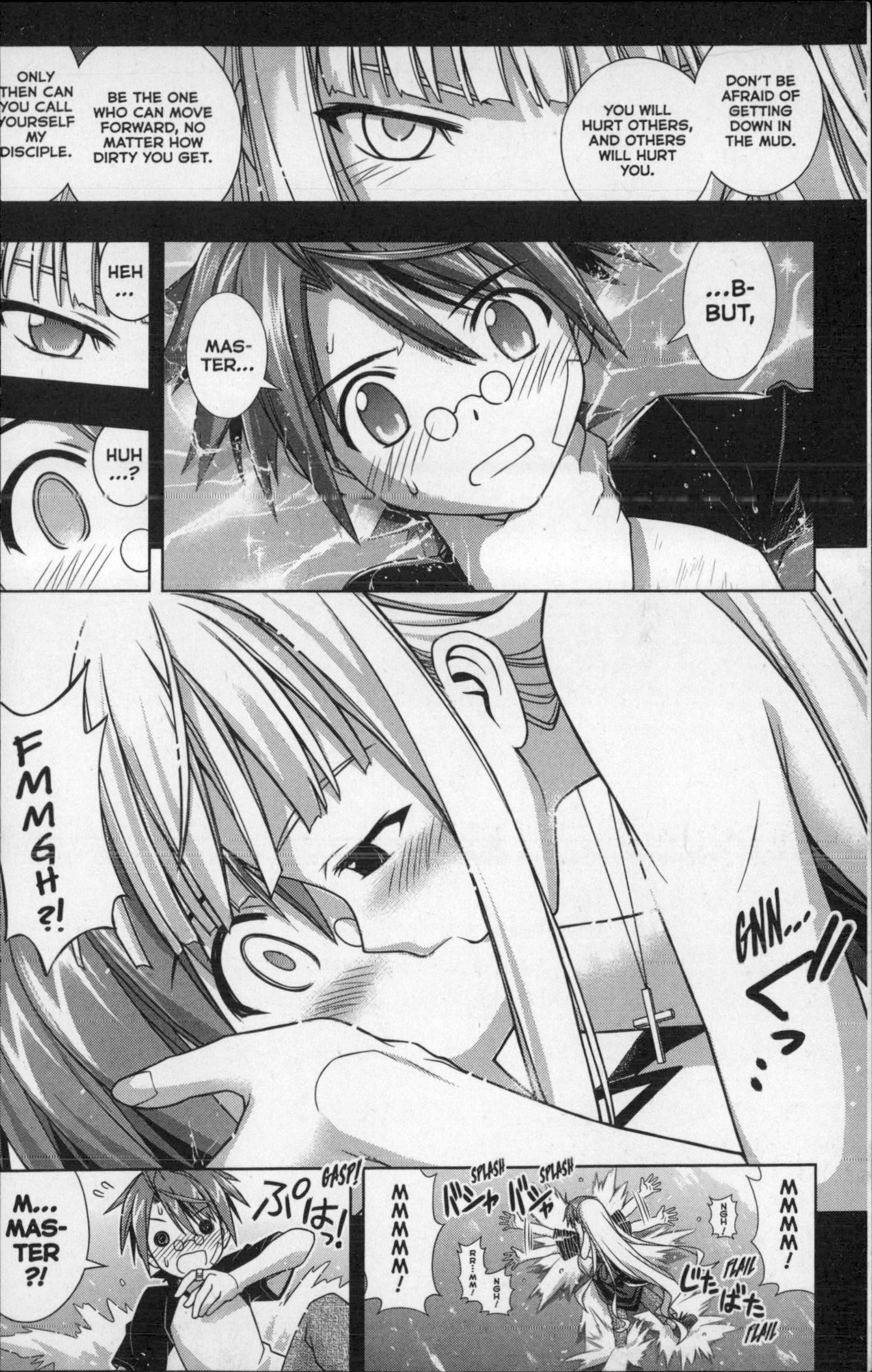
DON'T BE AFRAID OF GETTING DOWN IN THE MUD.
YOU WILL HURT OTHERS, AND OTHERS WILL HURT YOU.
BE THE ONE WHO CAN MOVE FORWARD, NO MATTER HOW DIRTY YOU GET.
ONLY THEN CAN YOU CALL YOURSELF MY DISCIPLE.
...B-BUT,
MAS-TER...
HEH ...
HUH ...?
GNN...
FMMGH ?!
MMMM!
NGH!
SPLASH
SPLASH
RR...MM!
NGH!
FLAIL
FLAIL
MMMMM!
GASP!
M... MAS-TER ?!

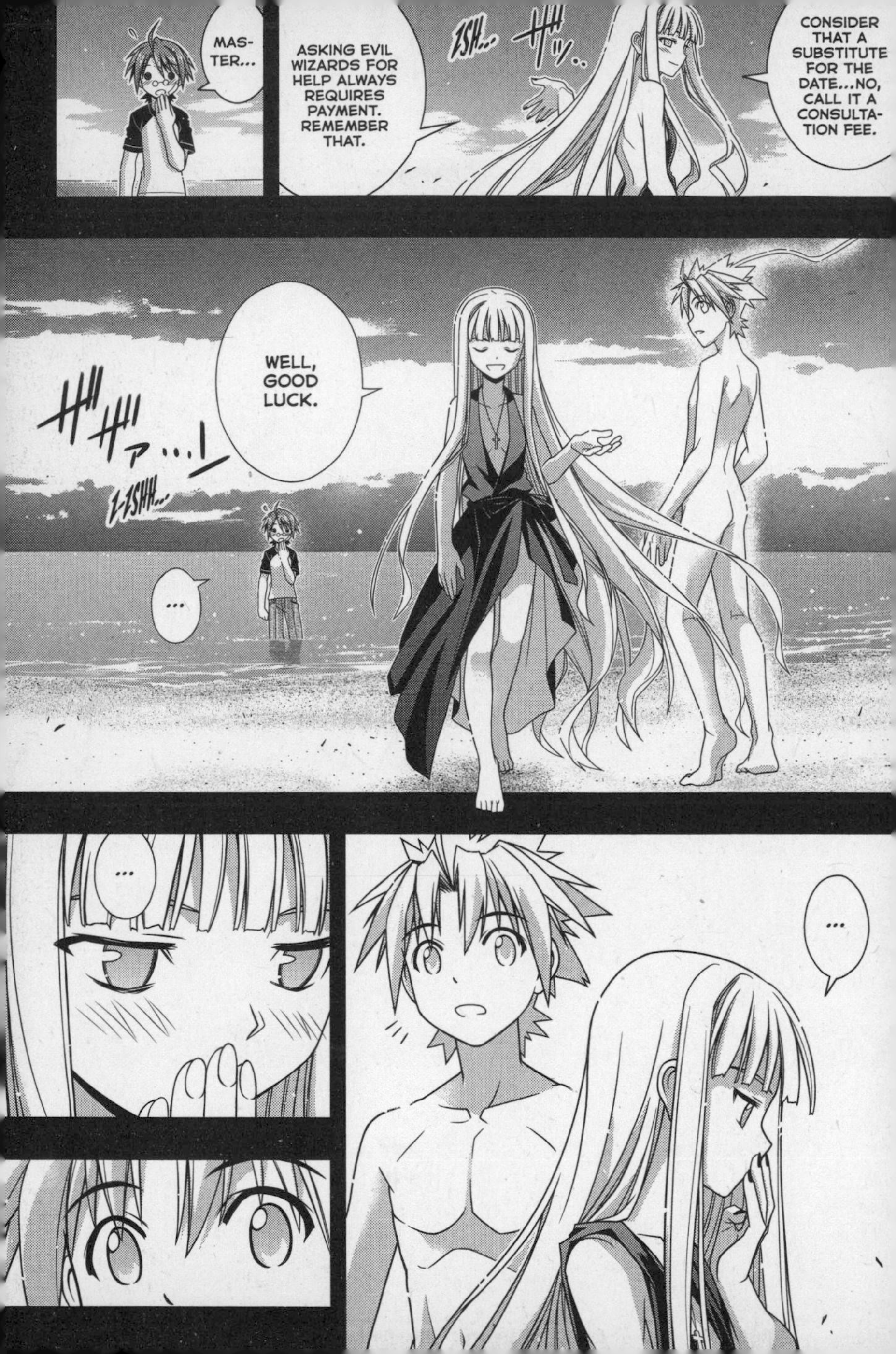

CONSIDER THAT A SUBSTITUTE FOR THE DATE...NO, CALL IT A CONSULTATION FEE.
ZSH... ザッ..
ASKING EVIL WIZARDS FOR HELP ALWAYS REQUIRES PAYMENT. REMEMBER THAT.
MASTER...
WELL, GOOD LUCK.
ザザァ...!
Z-ZSHH...
...
...
...

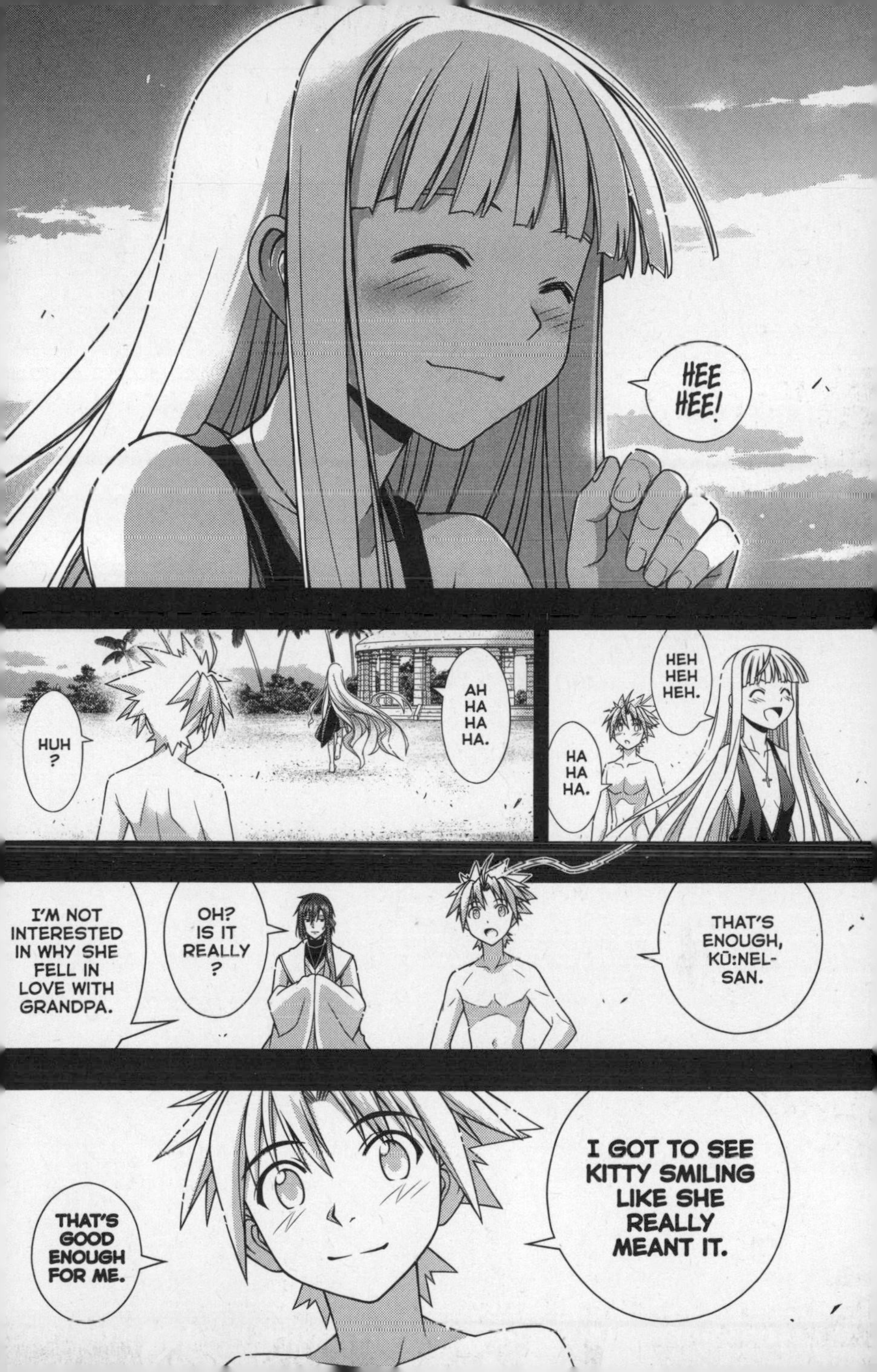
HEE HEE!
HEH HEH HEH.
HA HA HA.
AH HA HA HA.
HUH?
THAT'S ENOUGH, KŪ:NEL-SAN.
OH? IS IT REALLY?
I'M NOT INTERESTED IN WHY SHE FELL IN LOVE WITH GRANDPA.
I GOT TO SEE KITTY SMILING LIKE SHE REALLY MEANT IT.
THAT'S GOOD ENOUGH FOR ME.

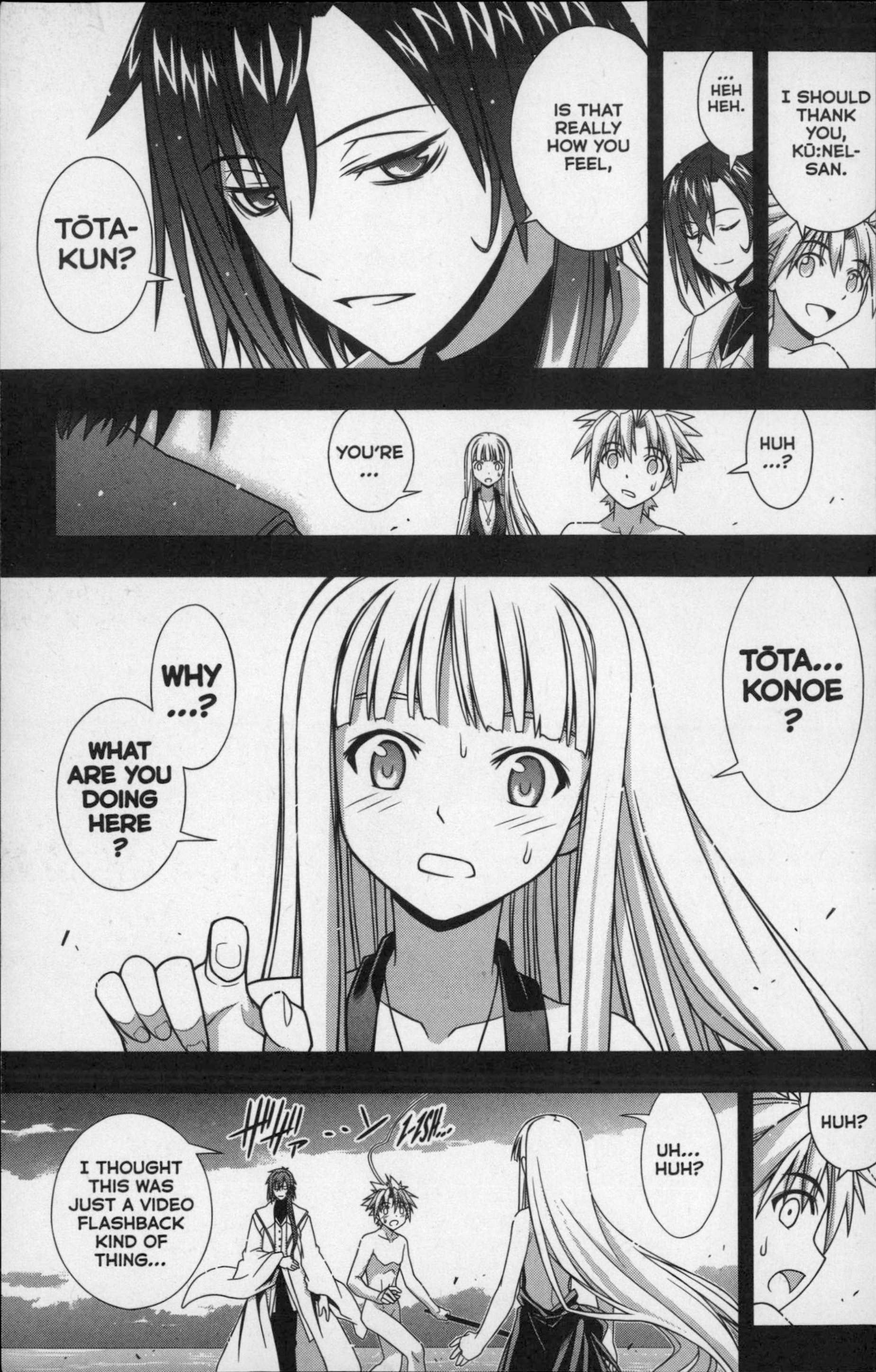
I SHOULD THANK YOU, KŪ:NEL-SAN.
...HEH HEH.
IS THAT REALLY HOW YOU FEEL,
TŌTA-KUN?
HUH ...?
YOU'RE ...
TŌTA... KONOE ?
WHY ...? WHAT ARE YOU DOING HERE ?
HUH?
UH... HUH?
I THOUGHT THIS WAS JUST A VIDEO FLASHBACK KIND OF THING...

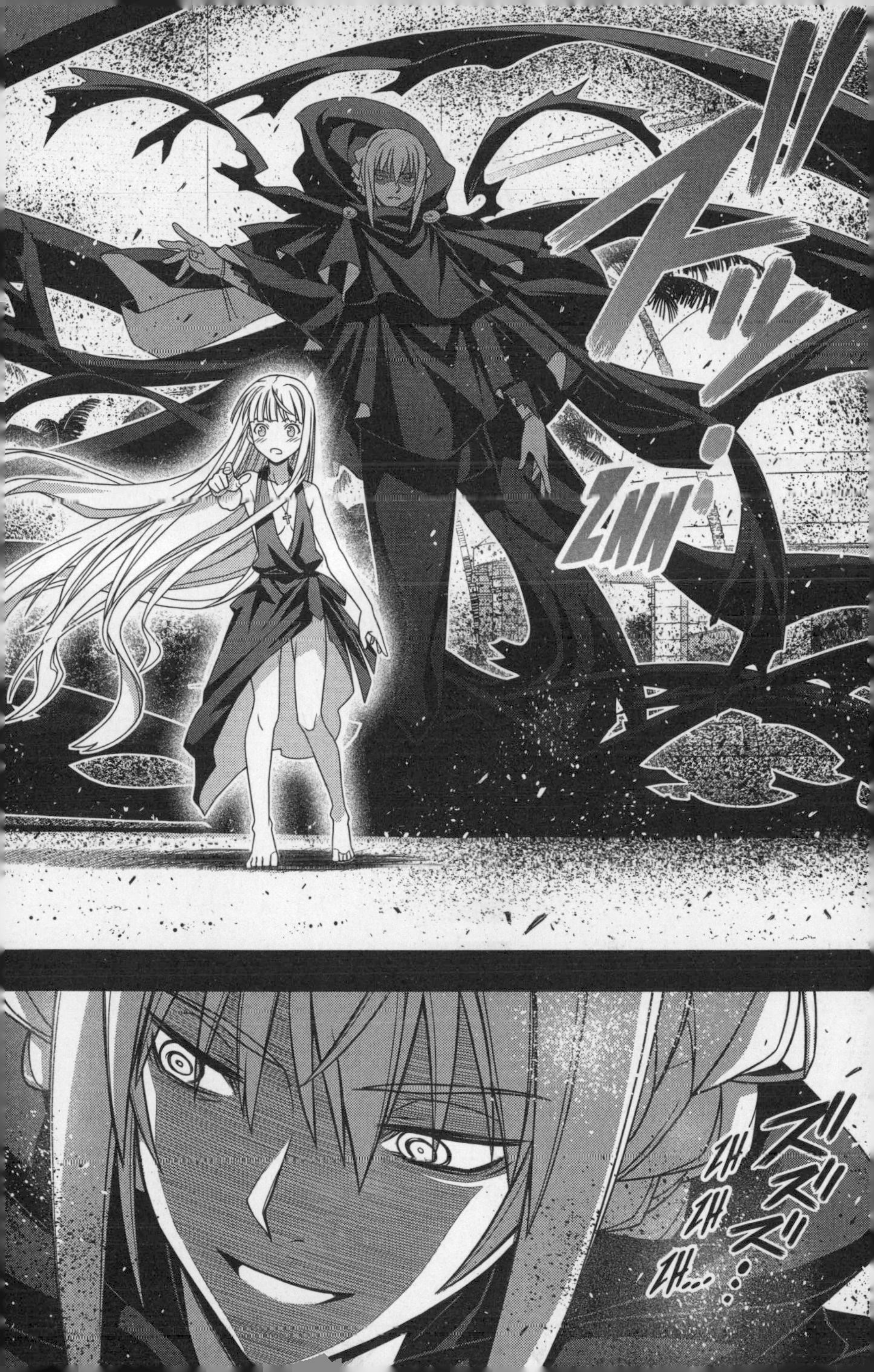
ズッ
ZNN
ズズズ…

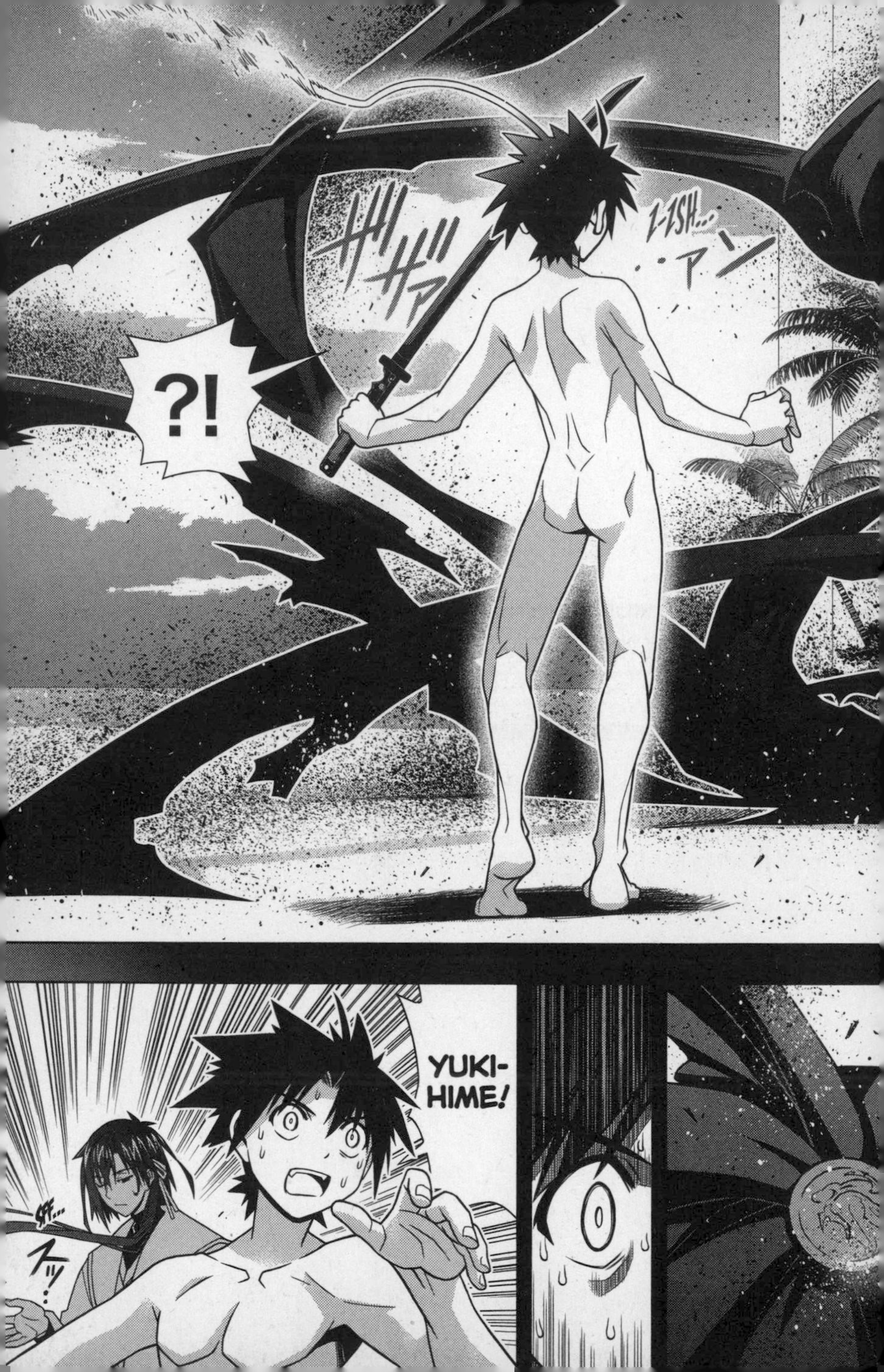
Z-ZSH...
?!
YUKI-HIME!
SFF...
スッ...

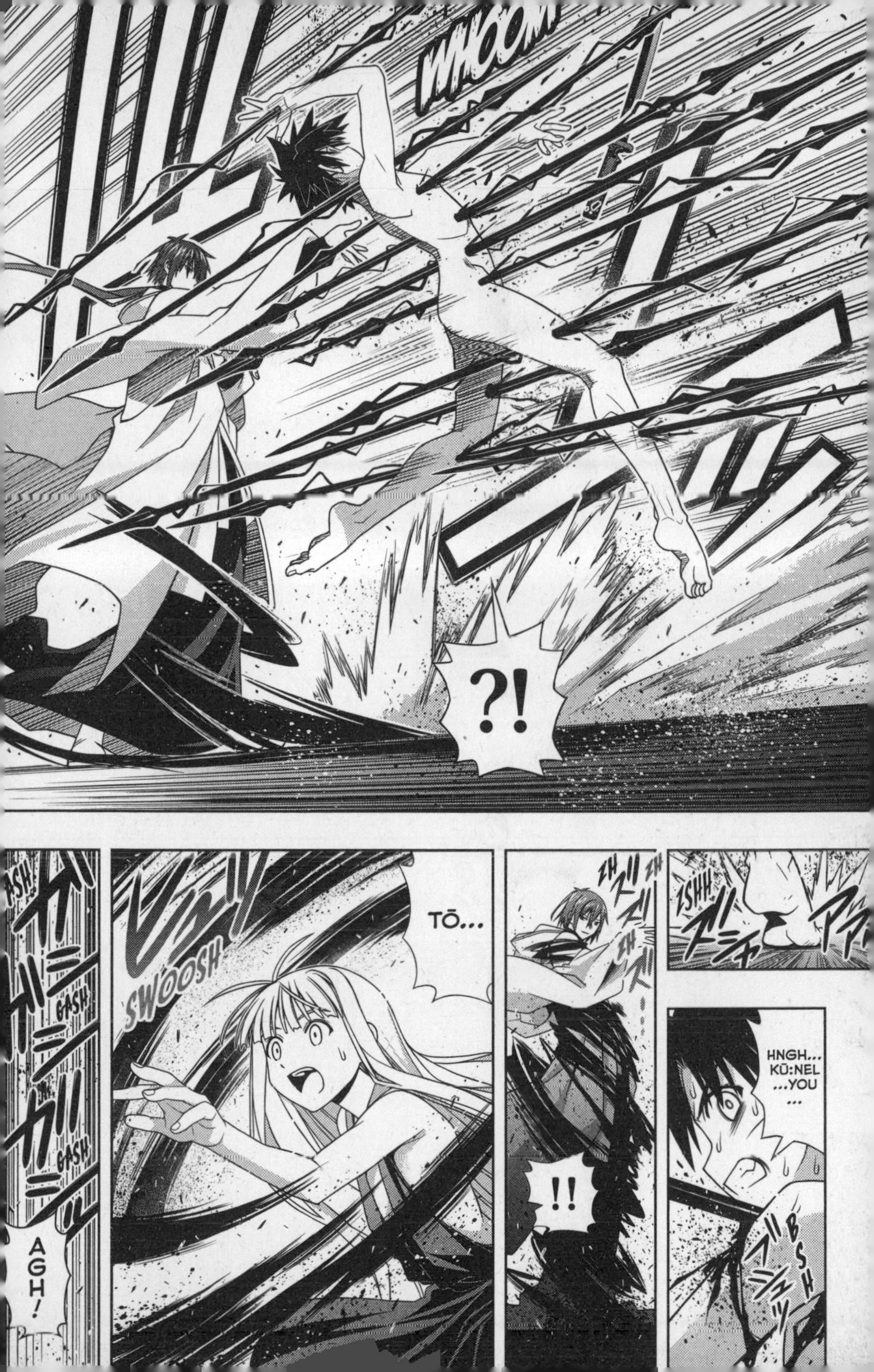
WHOOM
?!
ZSHH
HNGH... KŪ:NEL ...YOU ...
BSH
ZH
ZH
ZH
!!
TŌ...
SWOOSH
GASH
GASH
GASH
AGH!

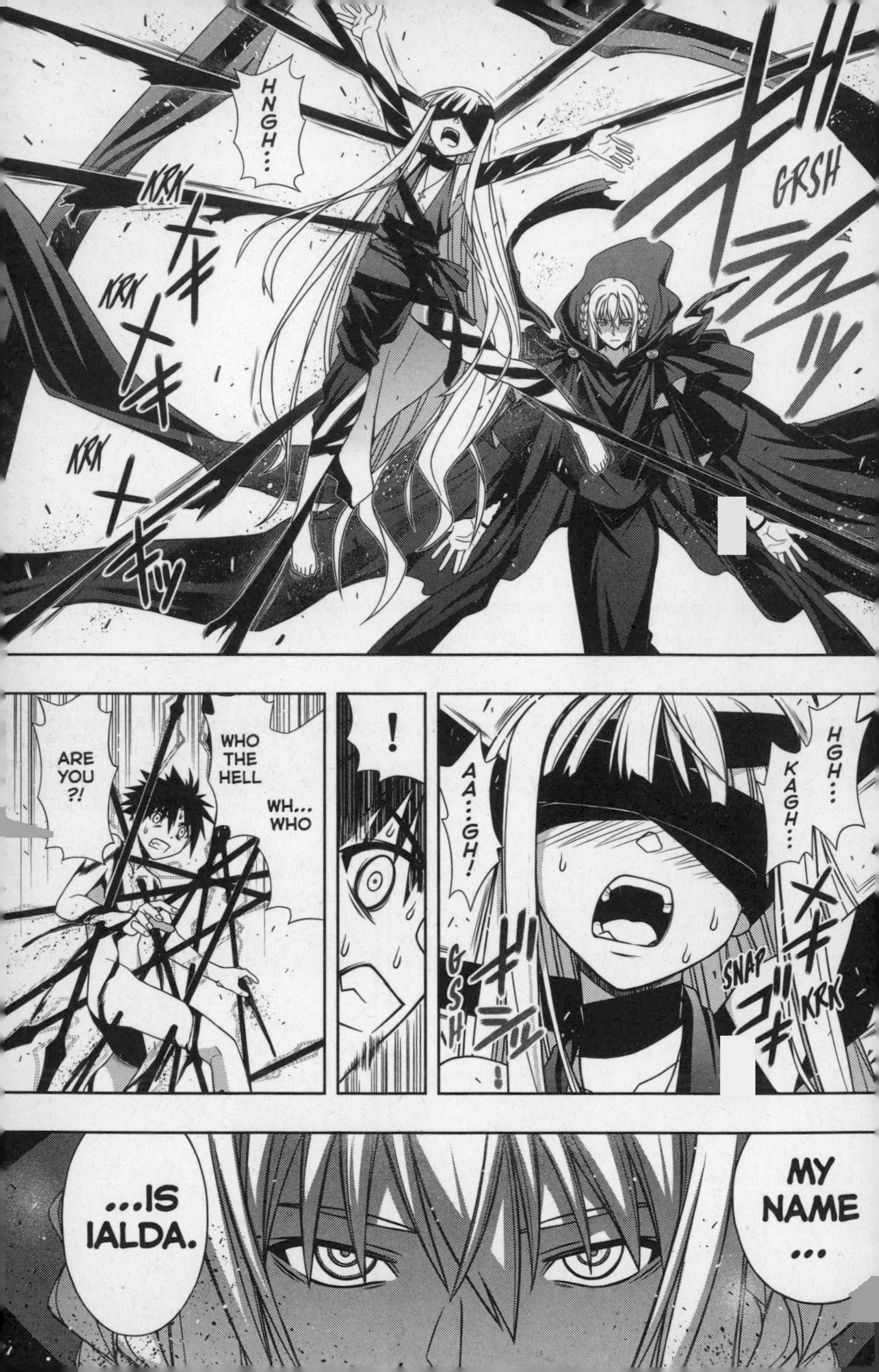
GRSH
HNGH...
KRK
KRK
KRK
HGH... KAGH...
SNAP
KRK
AA...GH!
GSH
!
WH... WHO
WHO THE HELL
ARE YOU ?!
MY NAME ...
...IS IALDA.

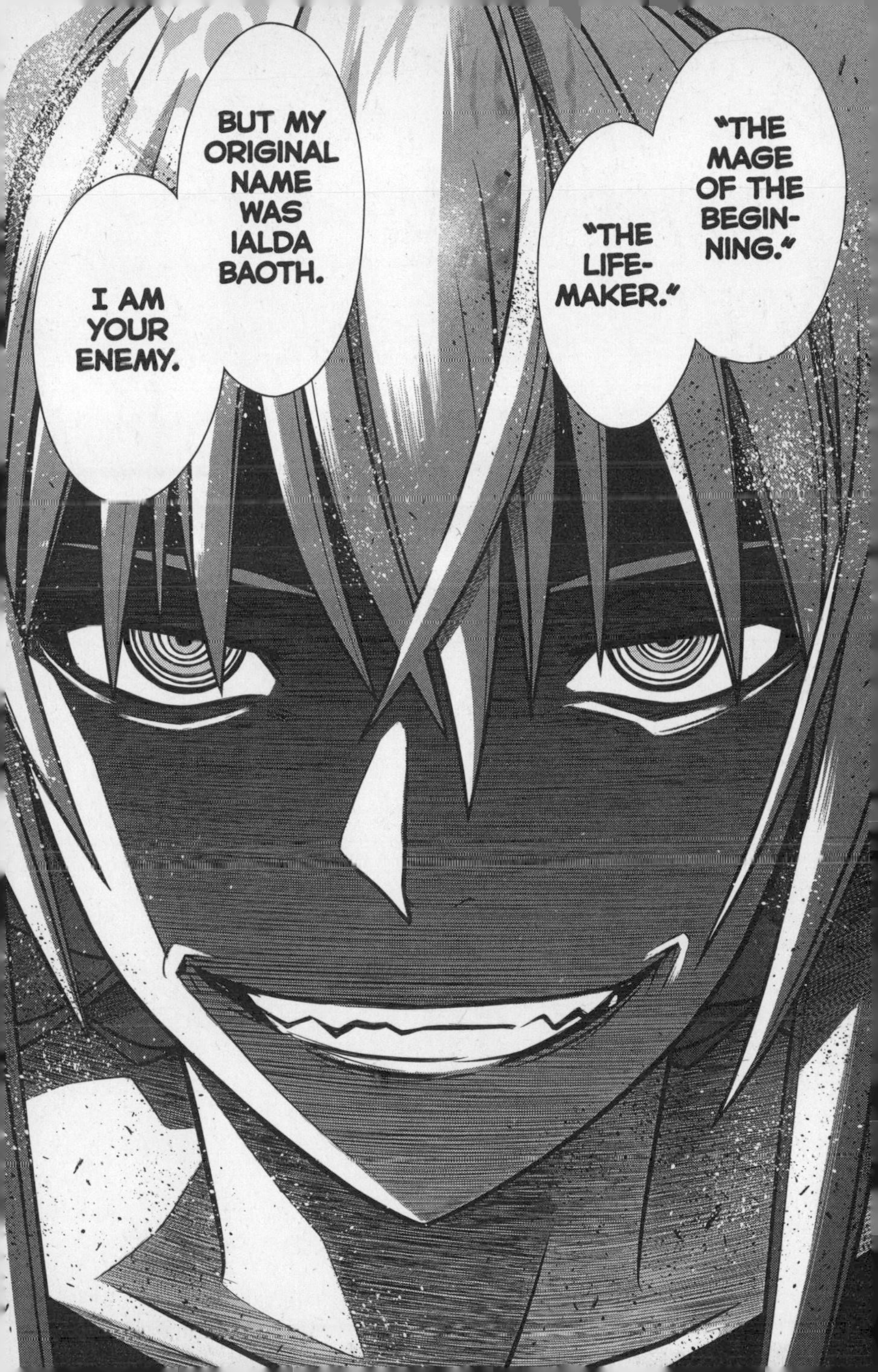
"THE MAGE OF THE BEGIN-NING."
"THE LIFE-MAKER."
BUT MY ORIGINAL NAME WAS IALDA BAOTH.
I AM YOUR ENEMY.

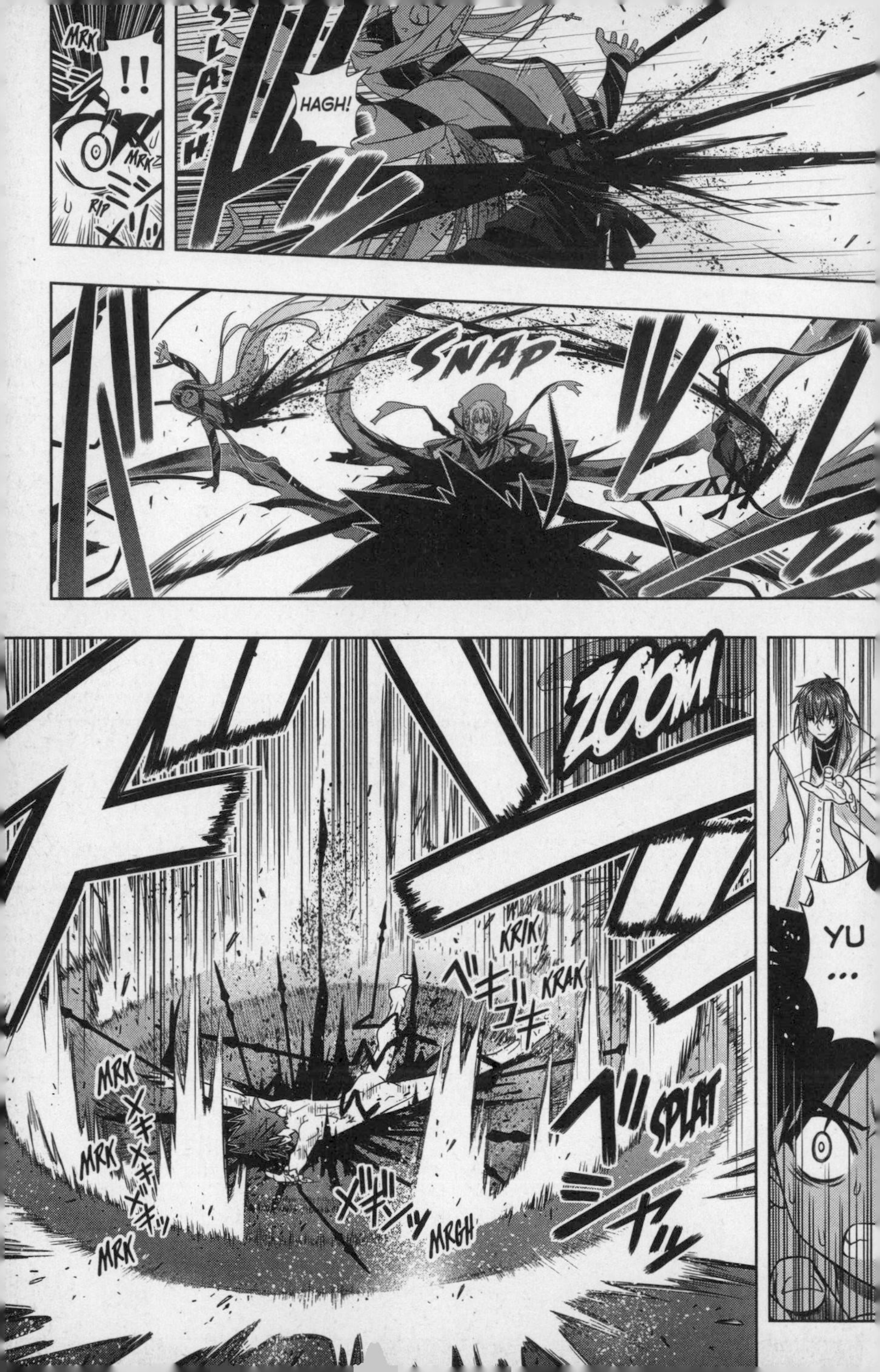
SLASH
HAGH!
MRK
!!
MRK
RIP
SNAP
YU ...
ZOOM
KRIK
KRAK
SPLAT
MRK
MRK
MRK
MRGH

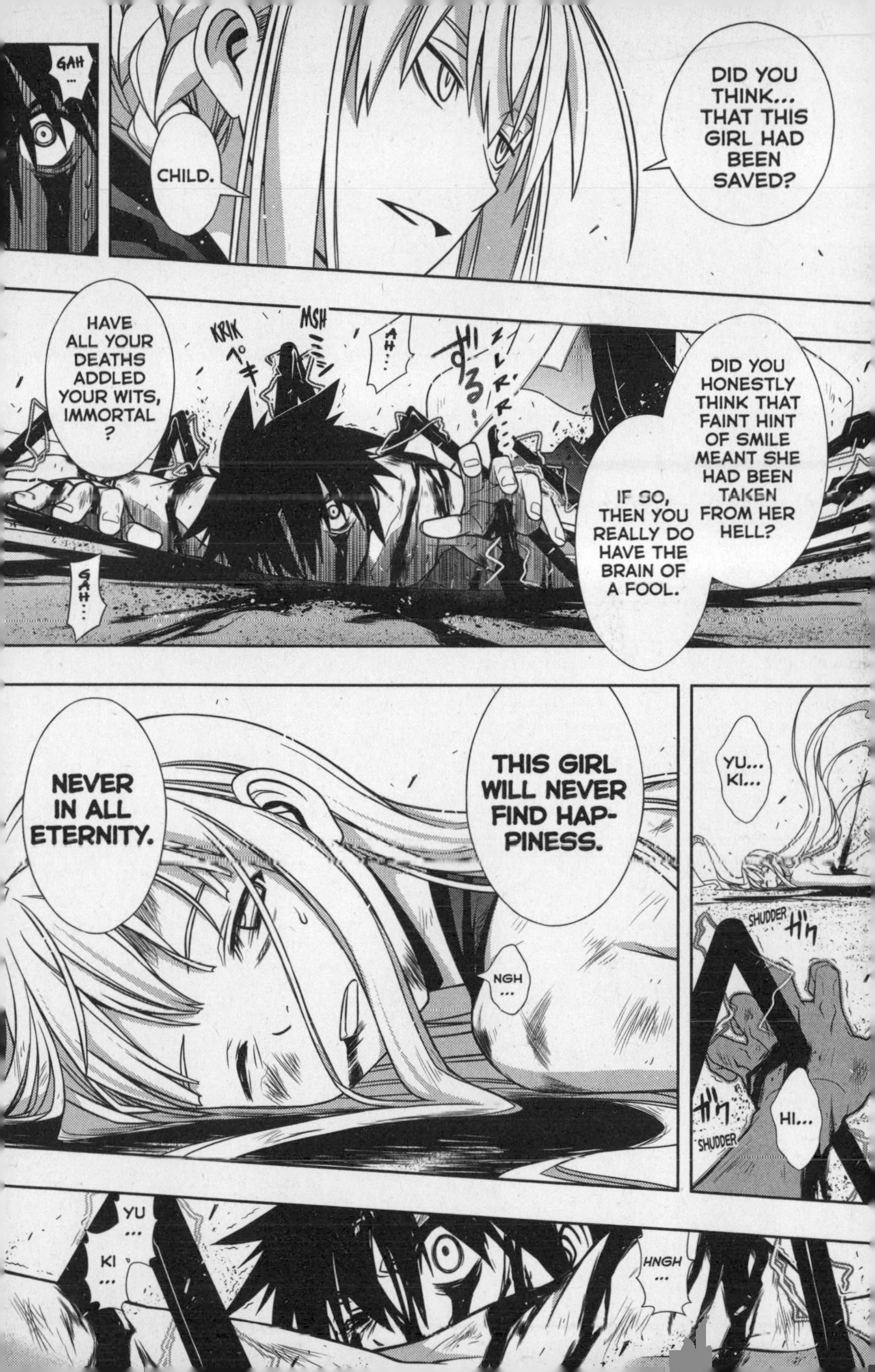
DID YOU THINK... THAT THIS GIRL HAD BEEN SAVED?
CHILD.
GAH ...
DID YOU HONESTLY THINK THAT FAINT HINT OF SMILE MEANT SHE HAD BEEN TAKEN FROM HER HELL?
IF SO, THEN YOU REALLY DO HAVE THE BRAIN OF A FOOL.
ZLRK ずる...
AH...
MSH ミシ
KRIK ペキ
HAVE ALL YOUR DEATHS ADDLED YOUR WITS, IMMORTAL?
GAH...
YU... KI...
SHUDDER ガク
HI...
SHUDDER ガク
THIS GIRL WILL NEVER FIND HAP-PINESS.
NEVER IN ALL ETERNITY.
NGH ...
HNGH ...
YU ...
KI ...

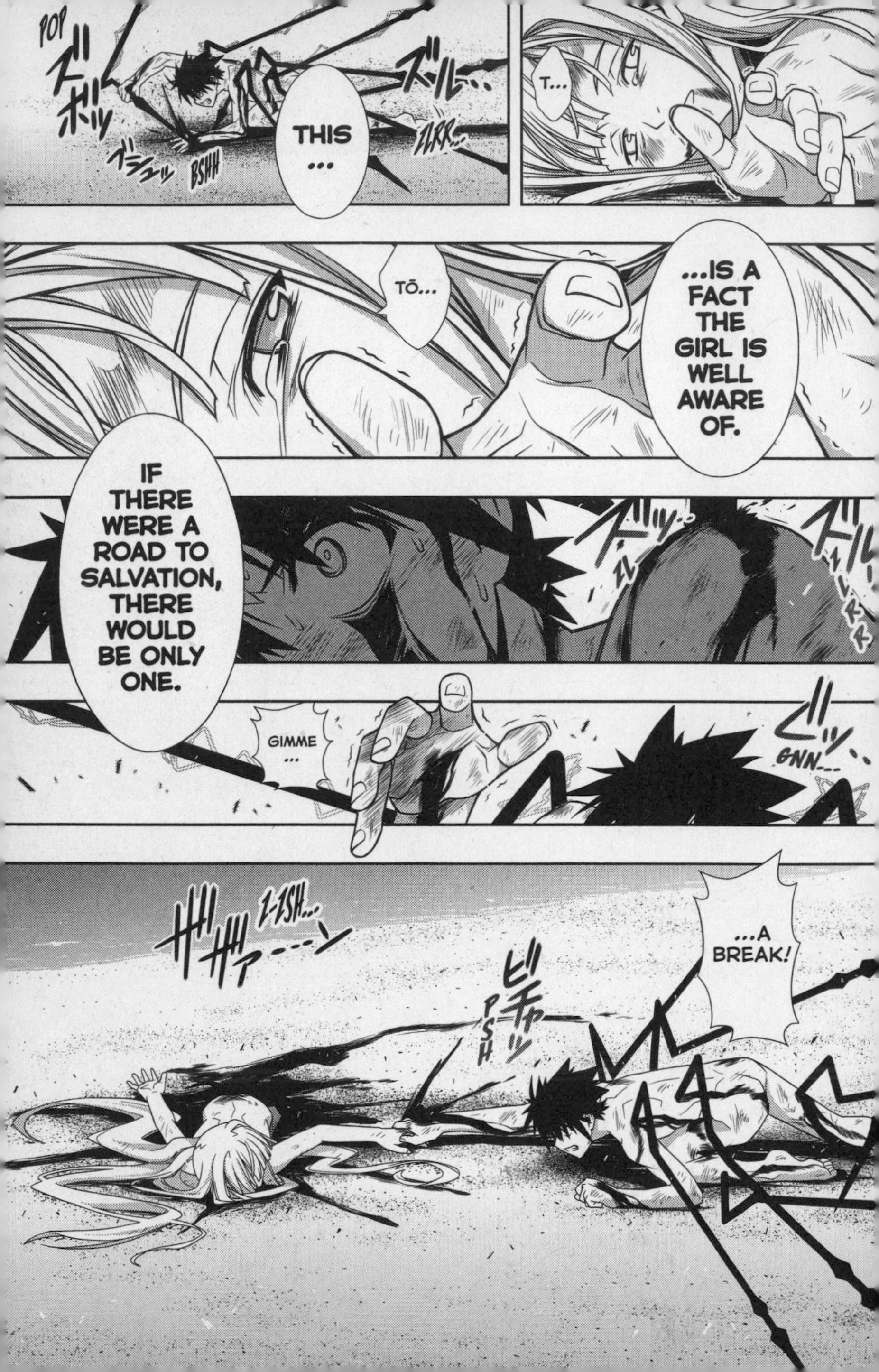
T...
ズル...
ZLRR...
THIS ...
POP
ズボッ
ズシュッ
BSHH
...IS A FACT THE GIRL IS WELL AWARE OF.
TŌ...
ZLRR
ZL
IF THERE WERE A ROAD TO SALVATION, THERE WOULD BE ONLY ONE.
GNN...
GIMME ...
...A BREAK!
ビチャッ
PSH
Z-ZSH...

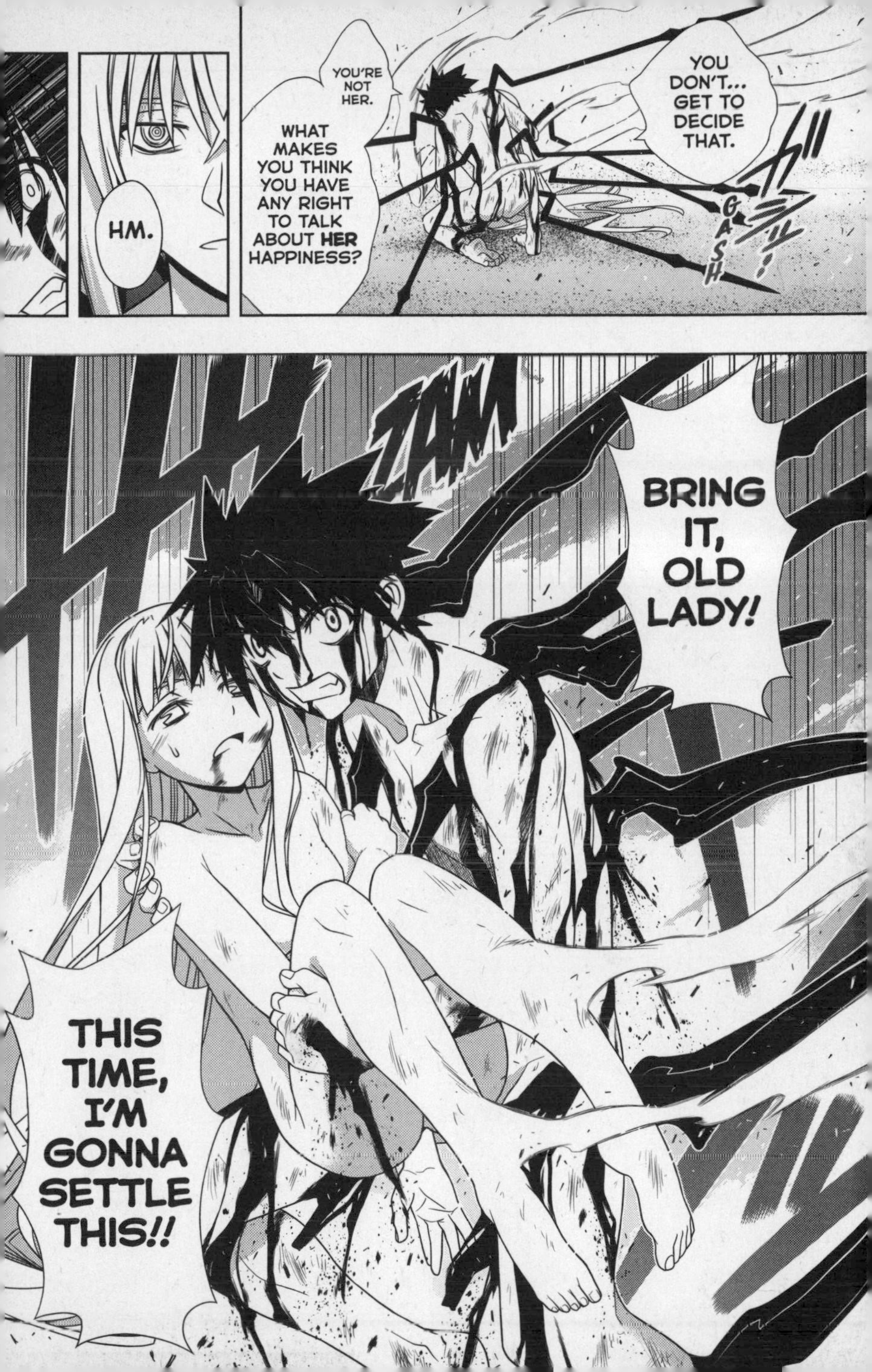
YOU DON'T... GET TO DECIDE THAT.
GASH
YOU'RE NOT HER.
WHAT MAKES YOU THINK YOU HAVE ANY RIGHT TO TALK ABOUT **HER** HAPPINESS?
HM.
ZAM
BRING IT, OLD LADY!
THIS TIME, I'M GONNA SETTLE THIS!!

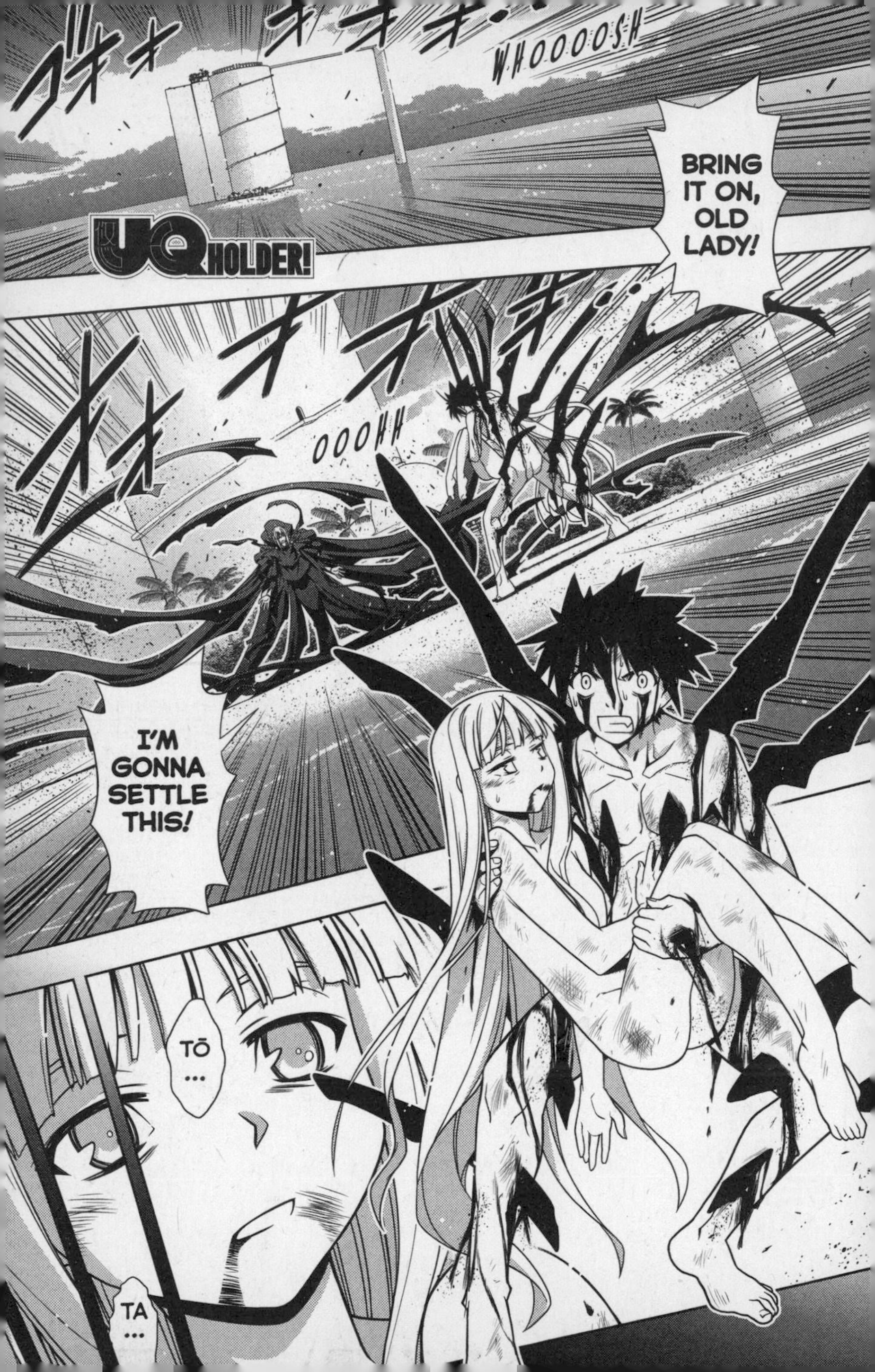
BRING IT ON, OLD LADY!
WHOOOOSH
UQ HOLDER!
OOOOHH
I'M GONNA SETTLE THIS!
TŌ...
TA...

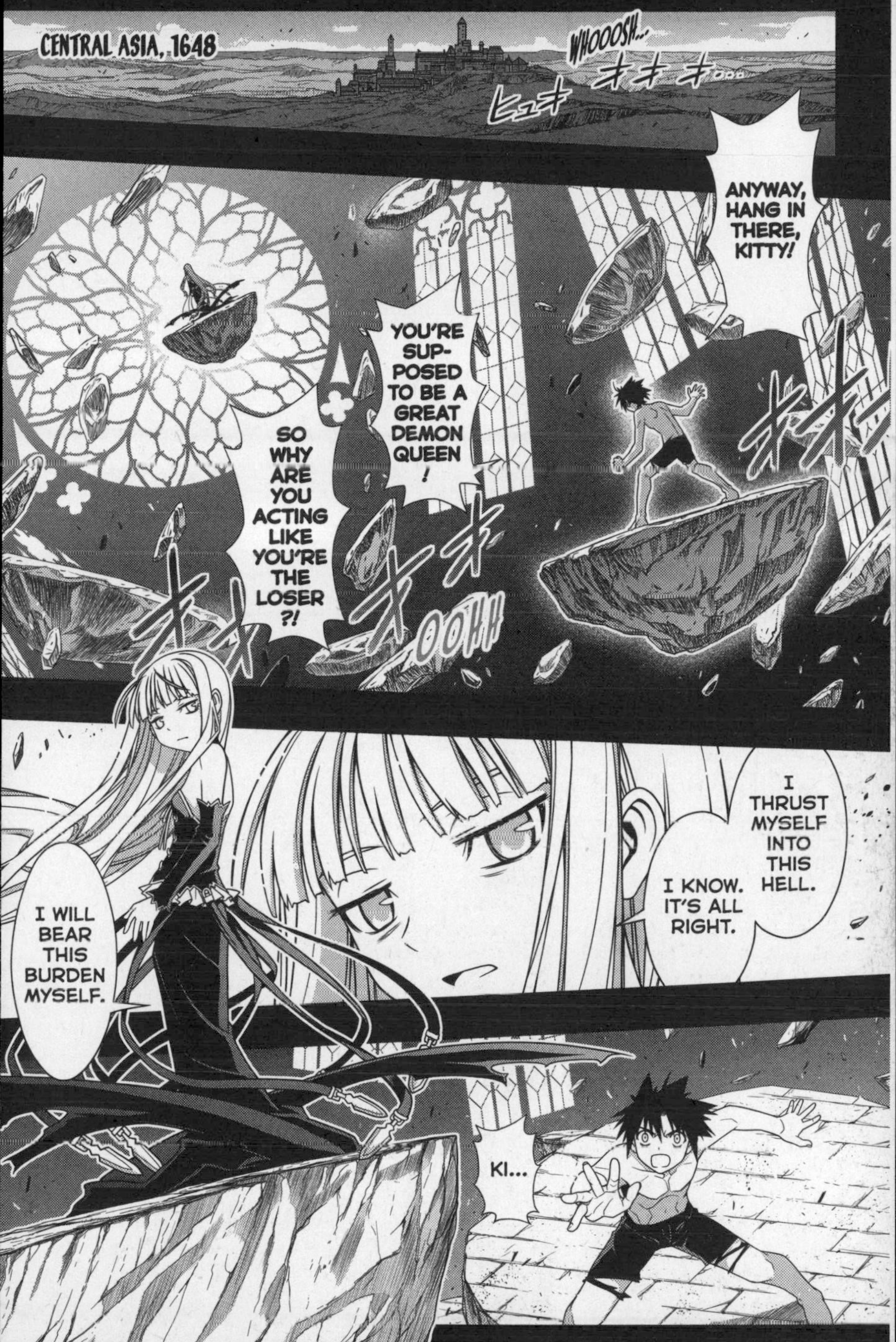
CENTRAL ASIA, 1648
WHOOOSH...
ヒュオ オオオ...
ANYWAY, HANG IN THERE, KITTY!
YOU'RE SUPPOSED TO BE A GREAT DEMON QUEEN!
SO WHY ARE YOU ACTING LIKE YOU'RE THE LOSER?!
OOHH
I THRUST MYSELF INTO THIS HELL.
I KNOW. IT'S ALL RIGHT.
I WILL BEAR THIS BURDEN MYSELF.
KI...

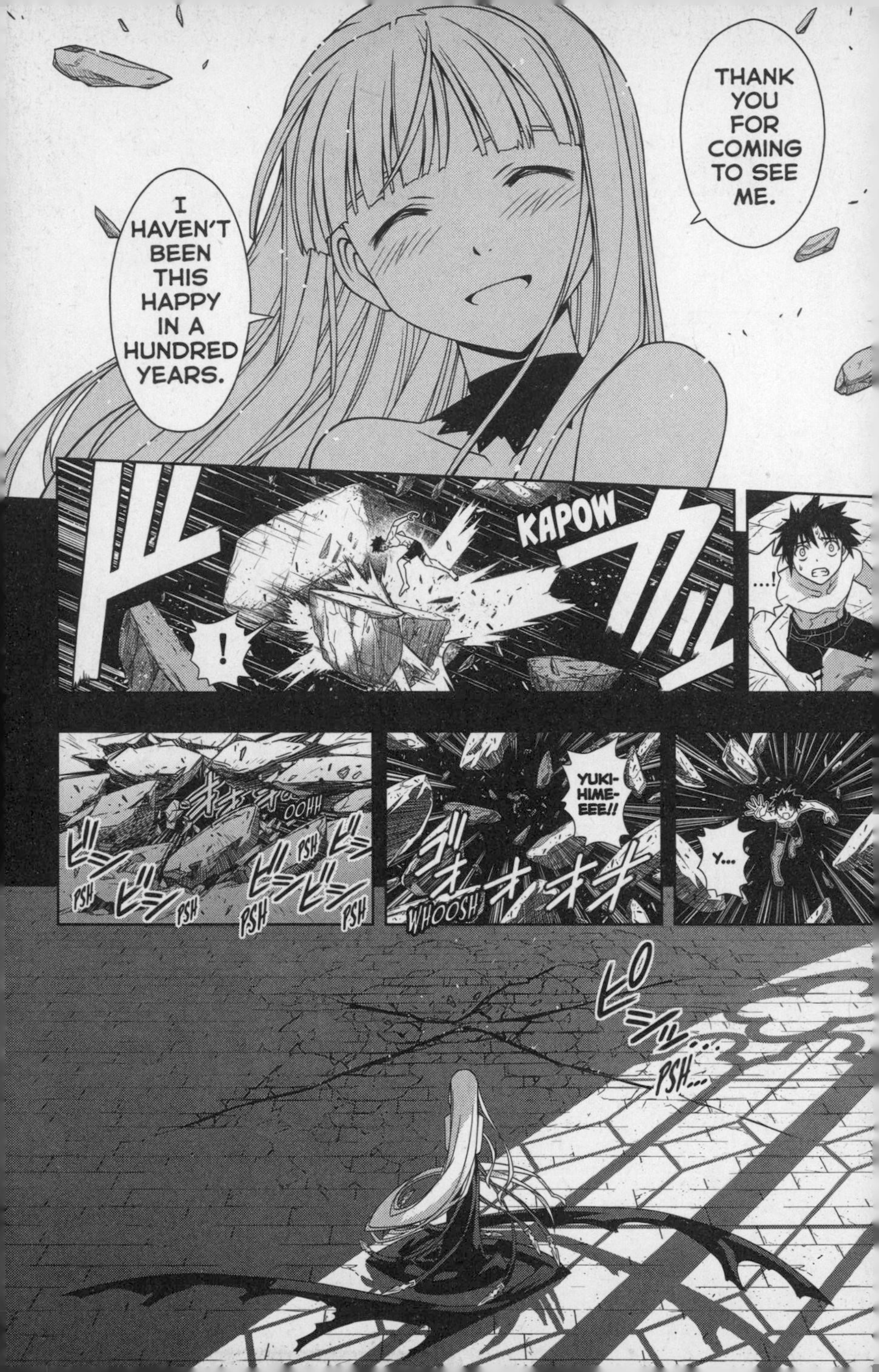
THANK YOU FOR COMING TO SEE ME.
I HAVEN'T BEEN THIS HAPPY IN A HUNDRED YEARS.
...!
KAPOW
!
Y...
YUKI-HIME-EEE!!
WHOOSH
OOHH
PSH
PSH
PSH
PSH
PSH...

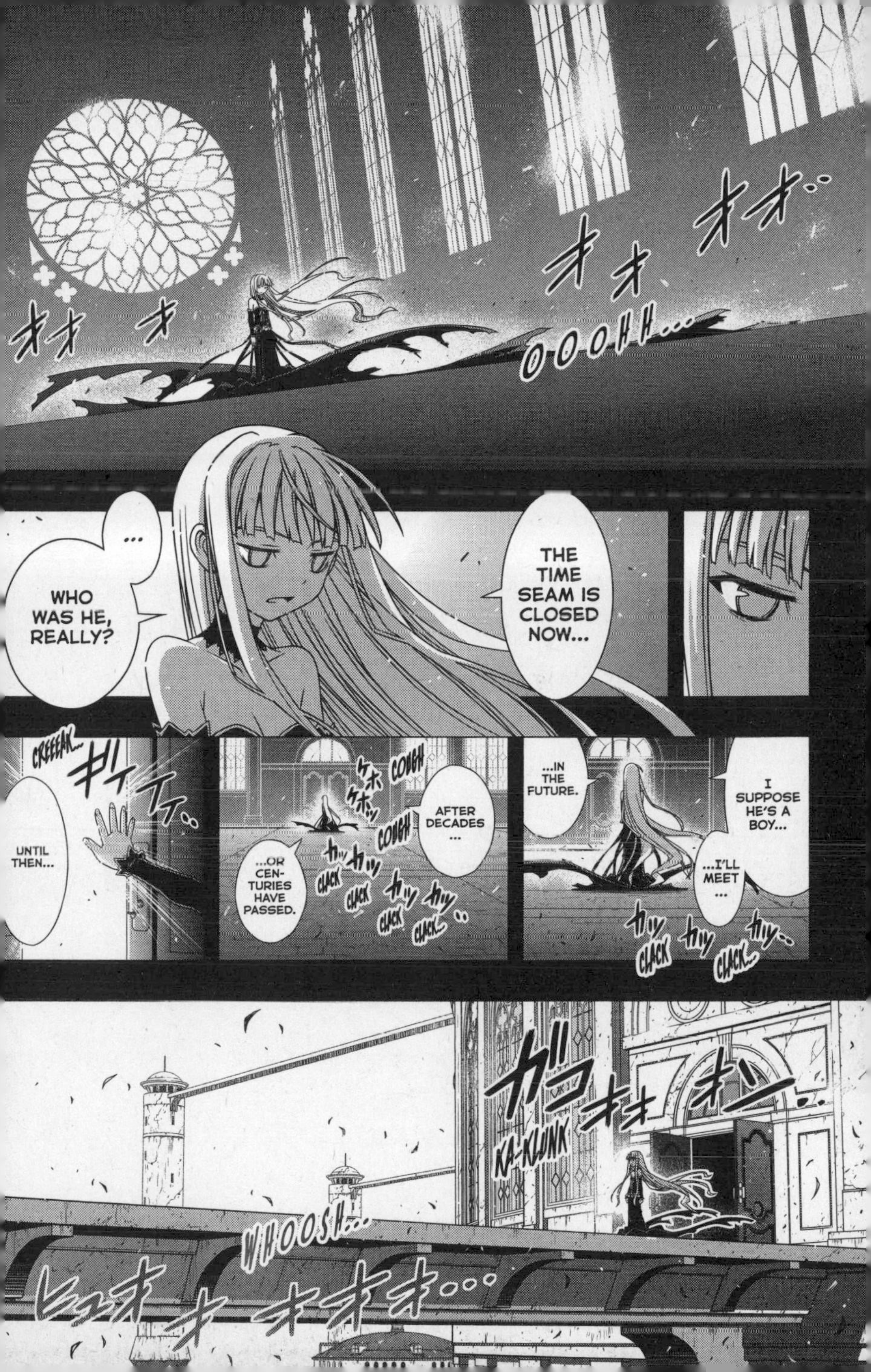
OOOHH...
THE TIME SEAM IS CLOSED NOW...
...
WHO WAS HE, REALLY?
I SUPPOSE HE'S A BOY...
...I'LL MEET ...
...IN THE FUTURE.
CLACK
CLACK...
COUGH
COUGH
AFTER DECADES ...
...OR CENTURIES HAVE PASSED.
CLACK
CLACK
CLACK
CLACK...
CREEEAK...
UNTIL THEN...
KA-KLUNK
WHOOSH...

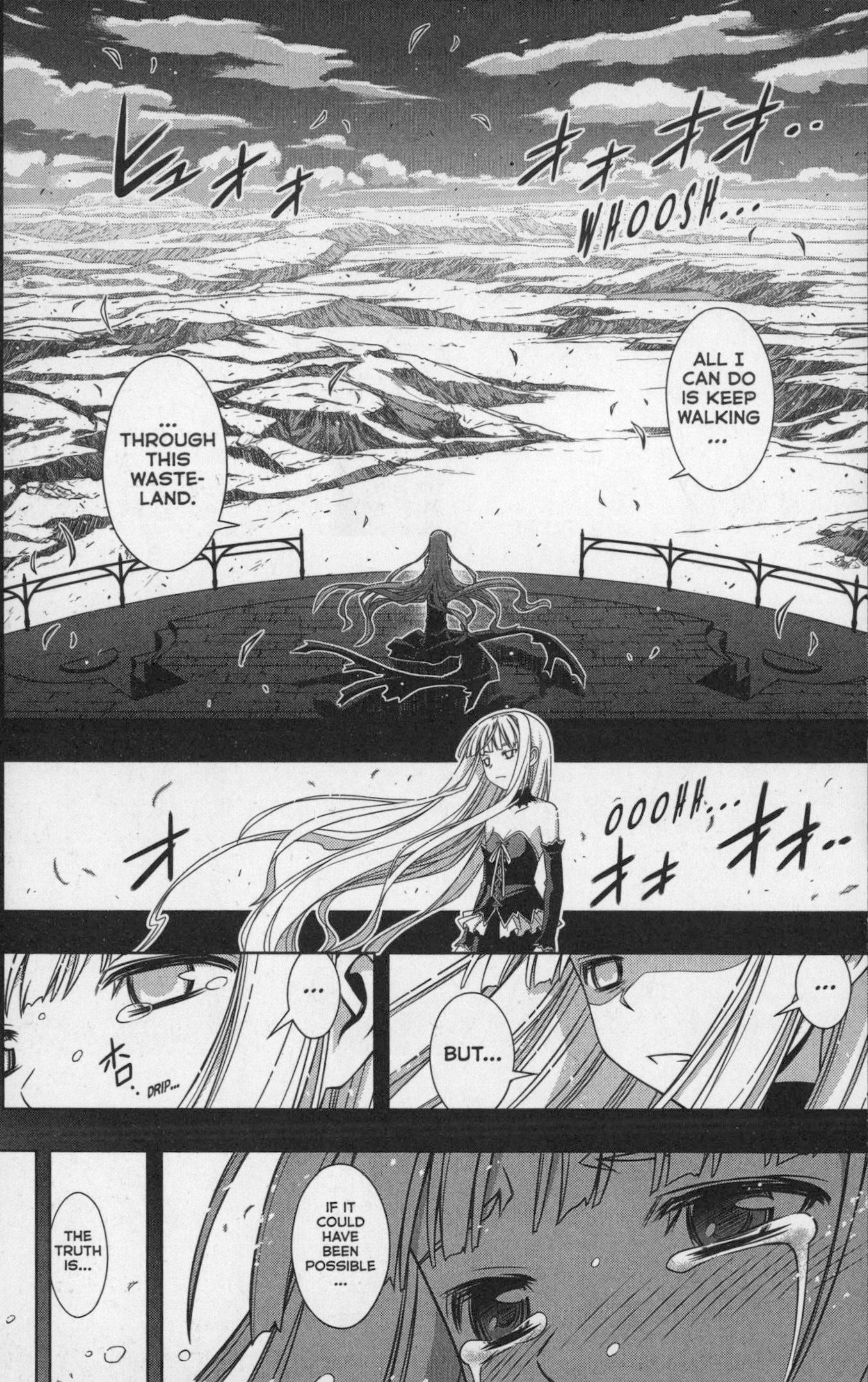
ヒュオオ
オォオオオ..
WHOOSH...
ALL I CAN DO IS KEEP WALKING ...
... THROUGH THIS WASTE-LAND.
オォオ オオ..
OOOHH...
...
BUT...
...
DRIP...
IF IT COULD HAVE BEEN POSSIBLE ...
THE TRUTH IS...

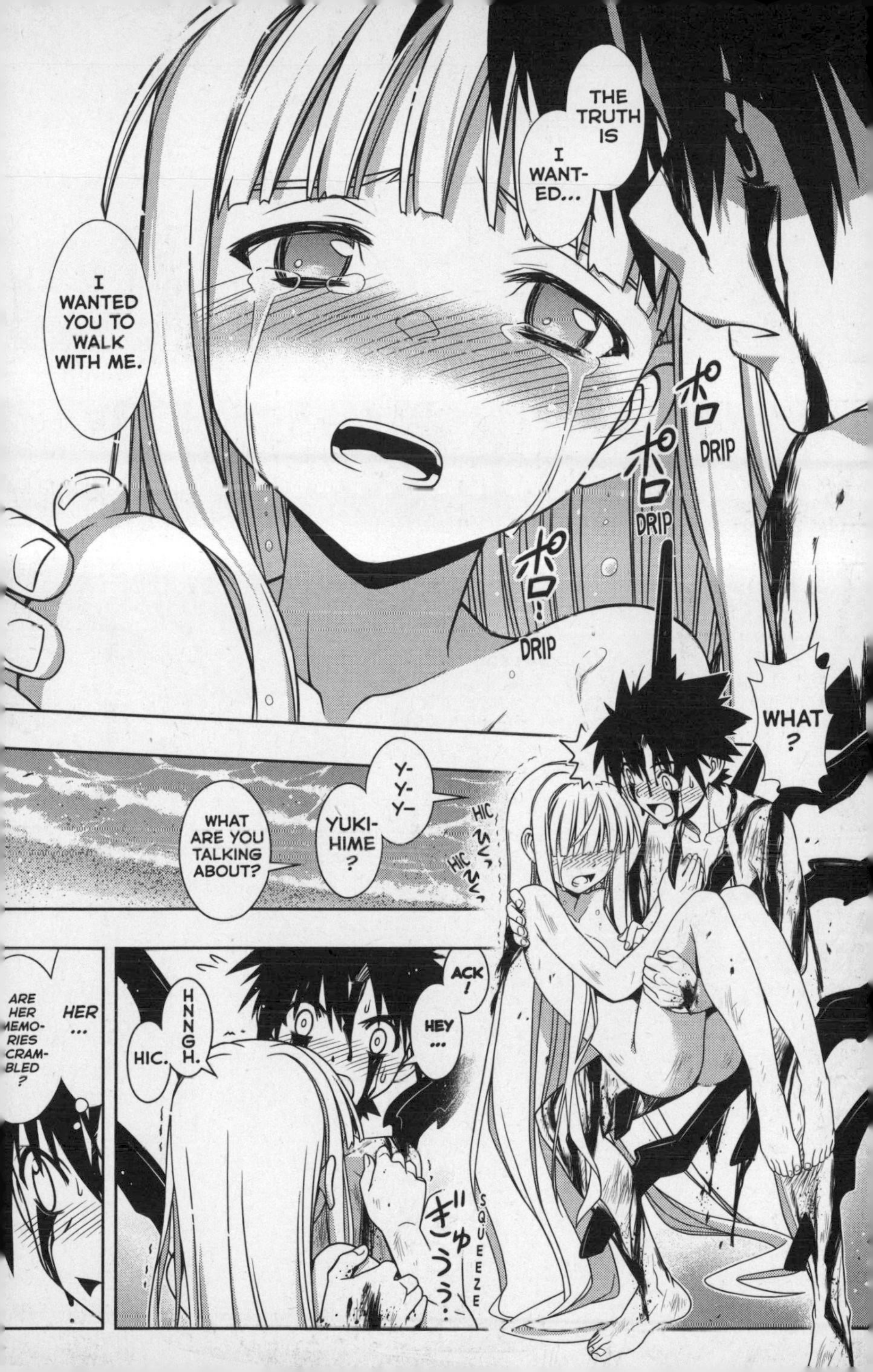
THE TRUTH IS
I WANTED...
I WANTED YOU TO WALK WITH ME.
ポロ DRIP
ポロ DRIP
ポロ DRIP
WHAT?
Y-Y-Y- YUKI-HIME?
WHAT ARE YOU TALKING ABOUT?
HIC
HIC
ACK!
HEY...
HNNGH.
HIC.
ぎゅうう SQUEEZE
HER...
ARE HER MEMORIES SCRAMBLED?

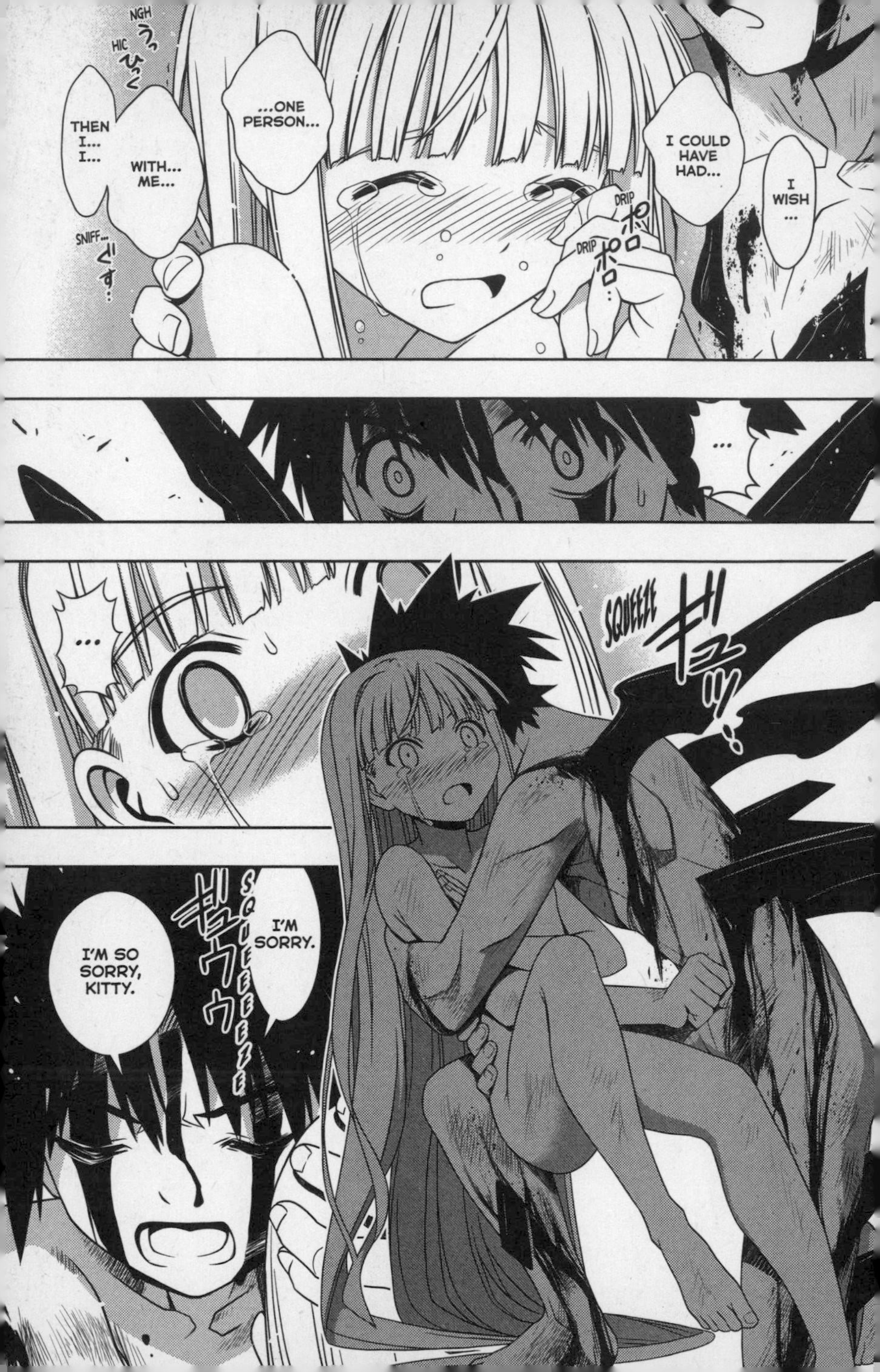
I WISH ...
I COULD HAVE HAD...
DRIP ポロ
DRIP ポロ...
...ONE PERSON...
WITH... ME...
NGH うっ
HIC ひっく
THEN I... I...
SNIFF... ぐす...
...
SQUEEEE ギュッ
...
I'M SORRY.
SQUEEEEZE ギュウウ
I'M SO SORRY, KITTY.

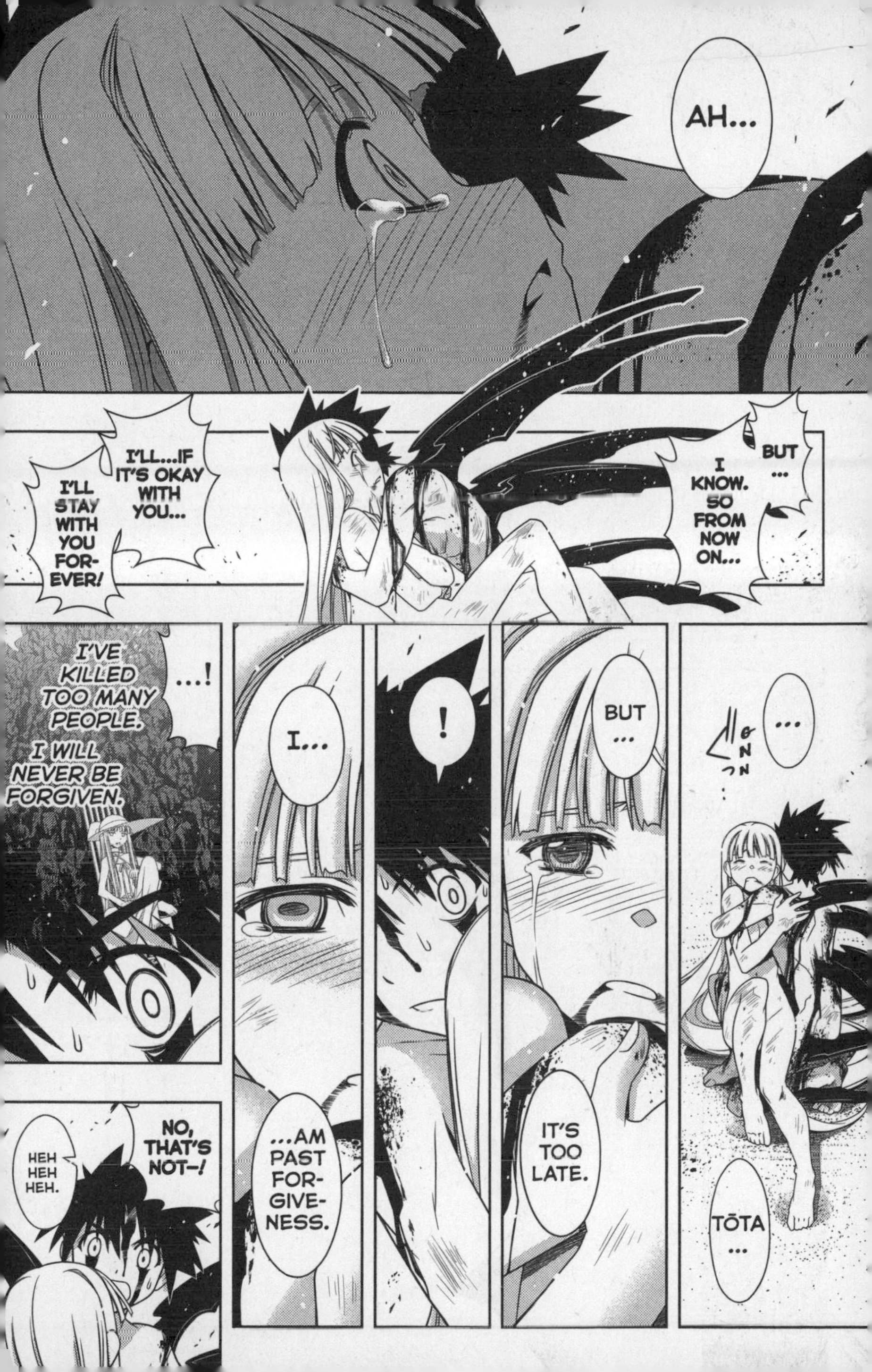
AH...
BUT ...
I KNOW. SO FROM NOW ON...
I'LL...IF IT'S OKAY WITH YOU...
I'LL STAY WITH YOU FOREVER!
...
TŌTA ...
BUT ...
IT'S TOO LATE.
!
I...
...AM PAST FORGIVENESS.
...!
I'VE KILLED TOO MANY PEOPLE.
I WILL NEVER BE FORGIVEN.
NO, THAT'S NOT–!
HEH HEH HEH.

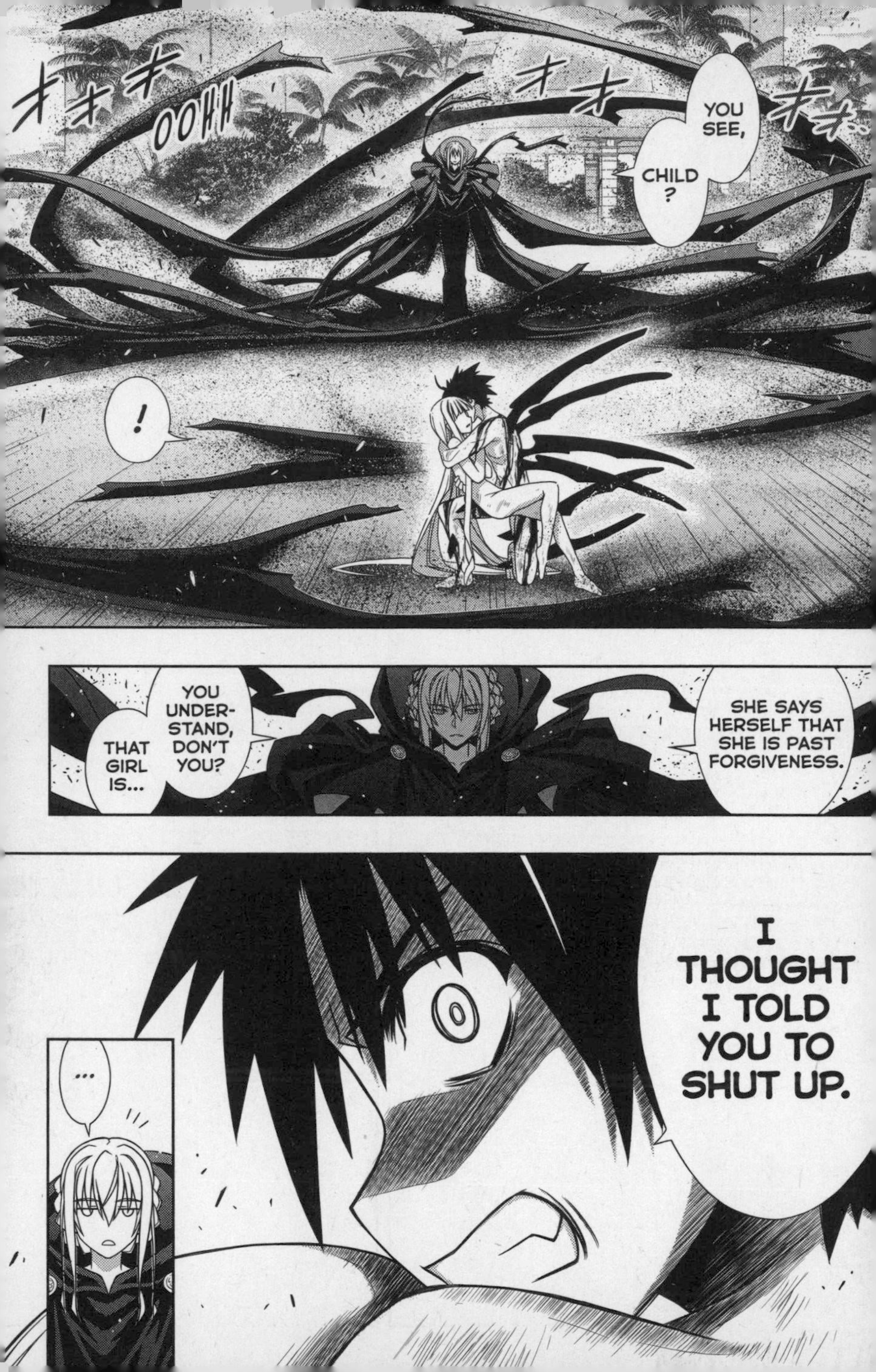
YOU SEE, CHILD?
OOHH
!
SHE SAYS HERSELF THAT SHE IS PAST FORGIVENESS.
YOU UNDERSTAND, DON'T YOU?
THAT GIRL IS...
I THOUGHT I TOLD YOU TO SHUT UP.
...

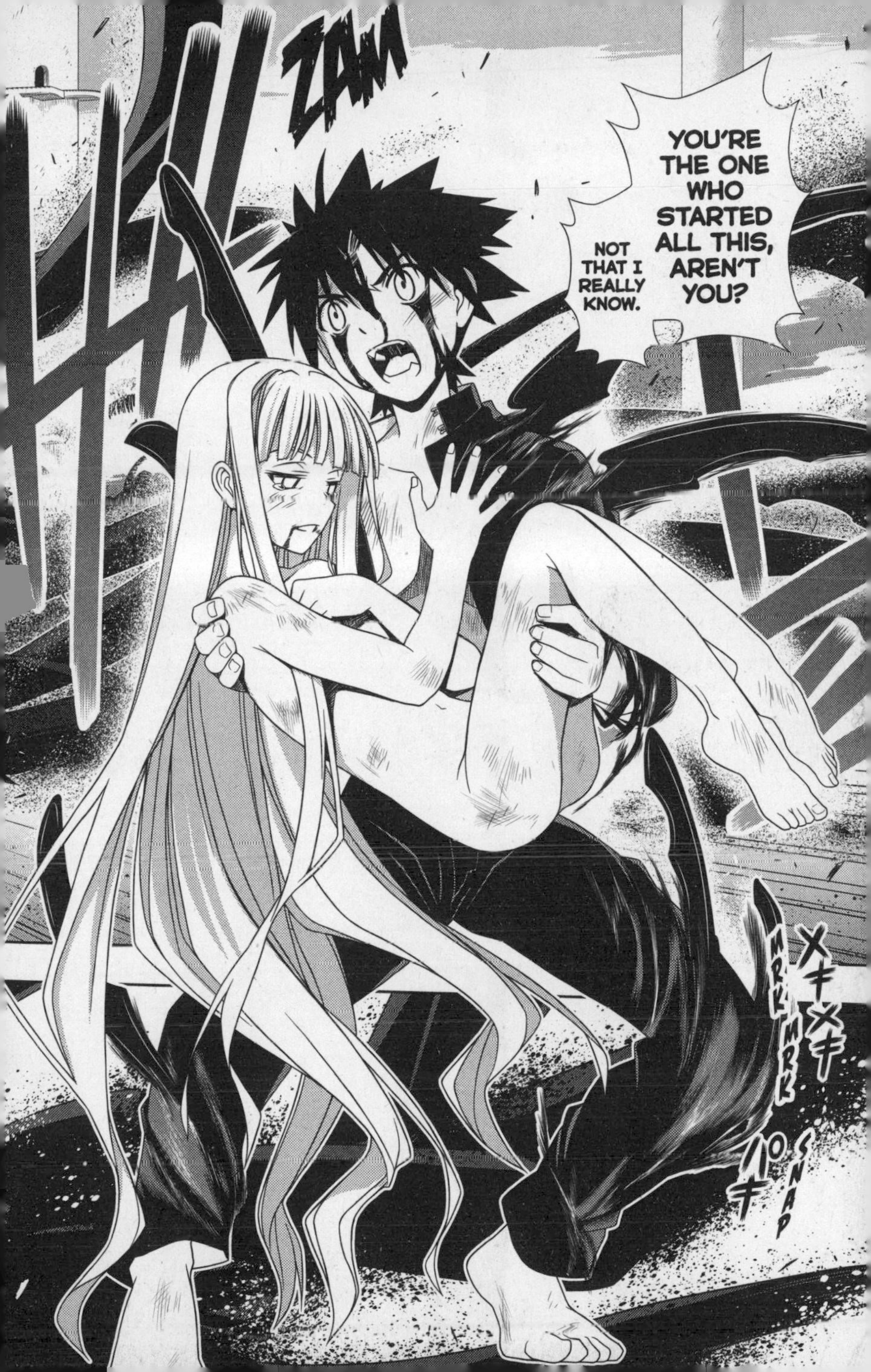
ZAM
YOU'RE THE ONE WHO STARTED ALL THIS, AREN'T YOU?
NOT THAT I REALLY KNOW.
MRK MRK
SNAP

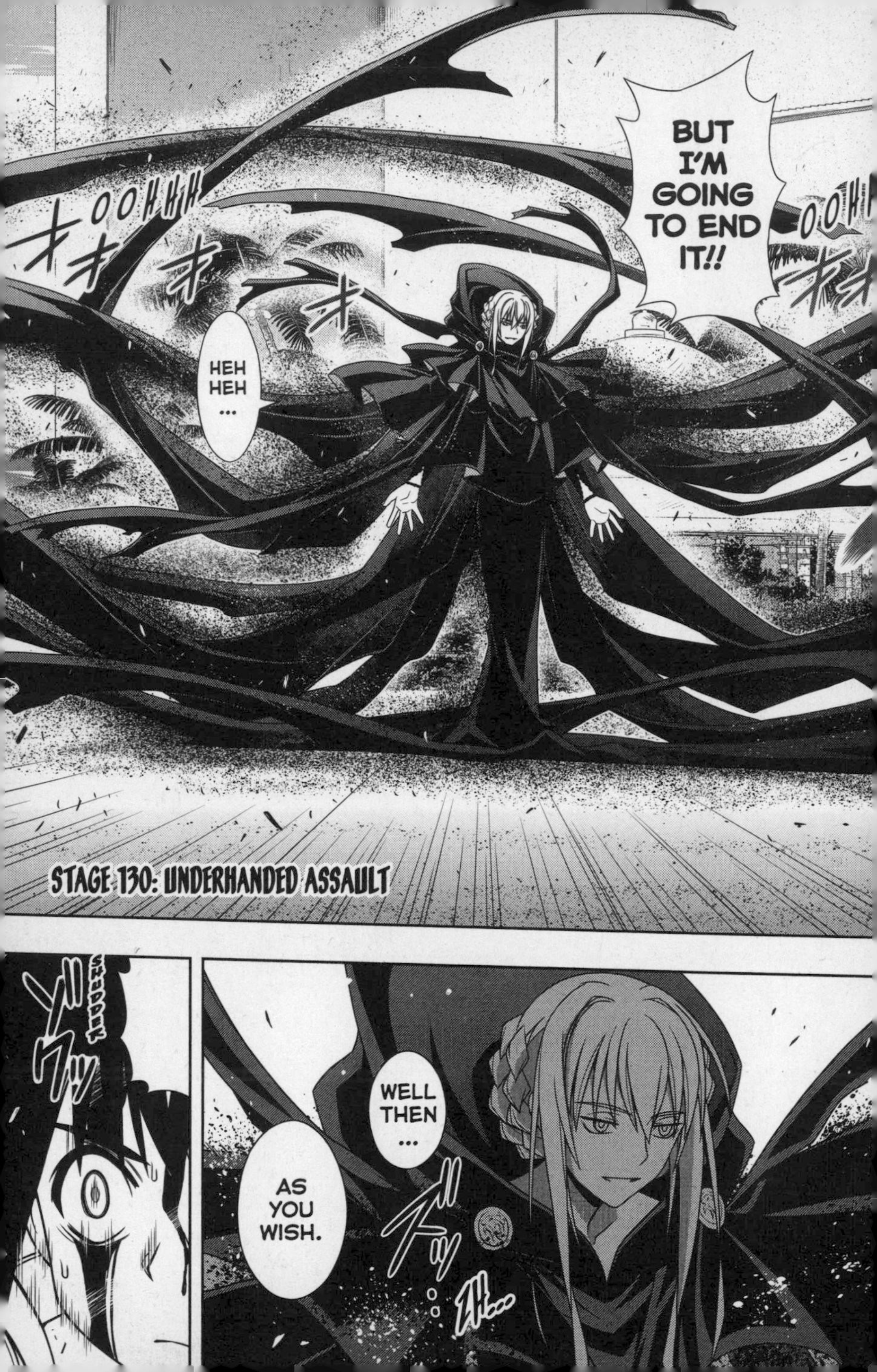
BUT I'M GOING TO END IT!!
HEH HEH ...
STAGE 130: UNDERHANDED ASSAULT
WELL THEN ...
AS YOU WISH.
SHUDDER

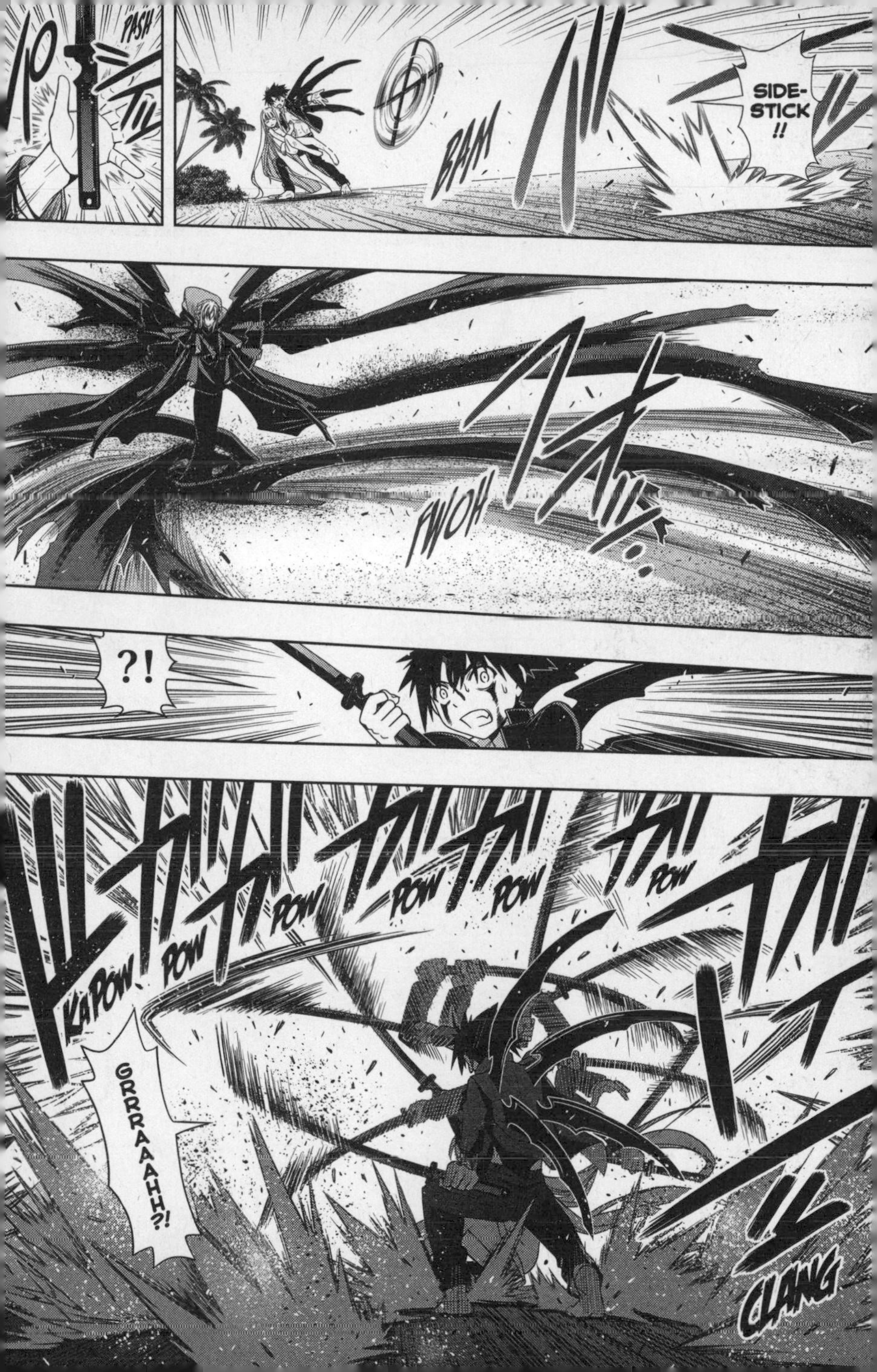
SIDE-STICK!!
BAM
PASH
FWOH
?!
POW
POW
POW
POW
POW
KAPOW
GRRRAAAHH?!
CLANG

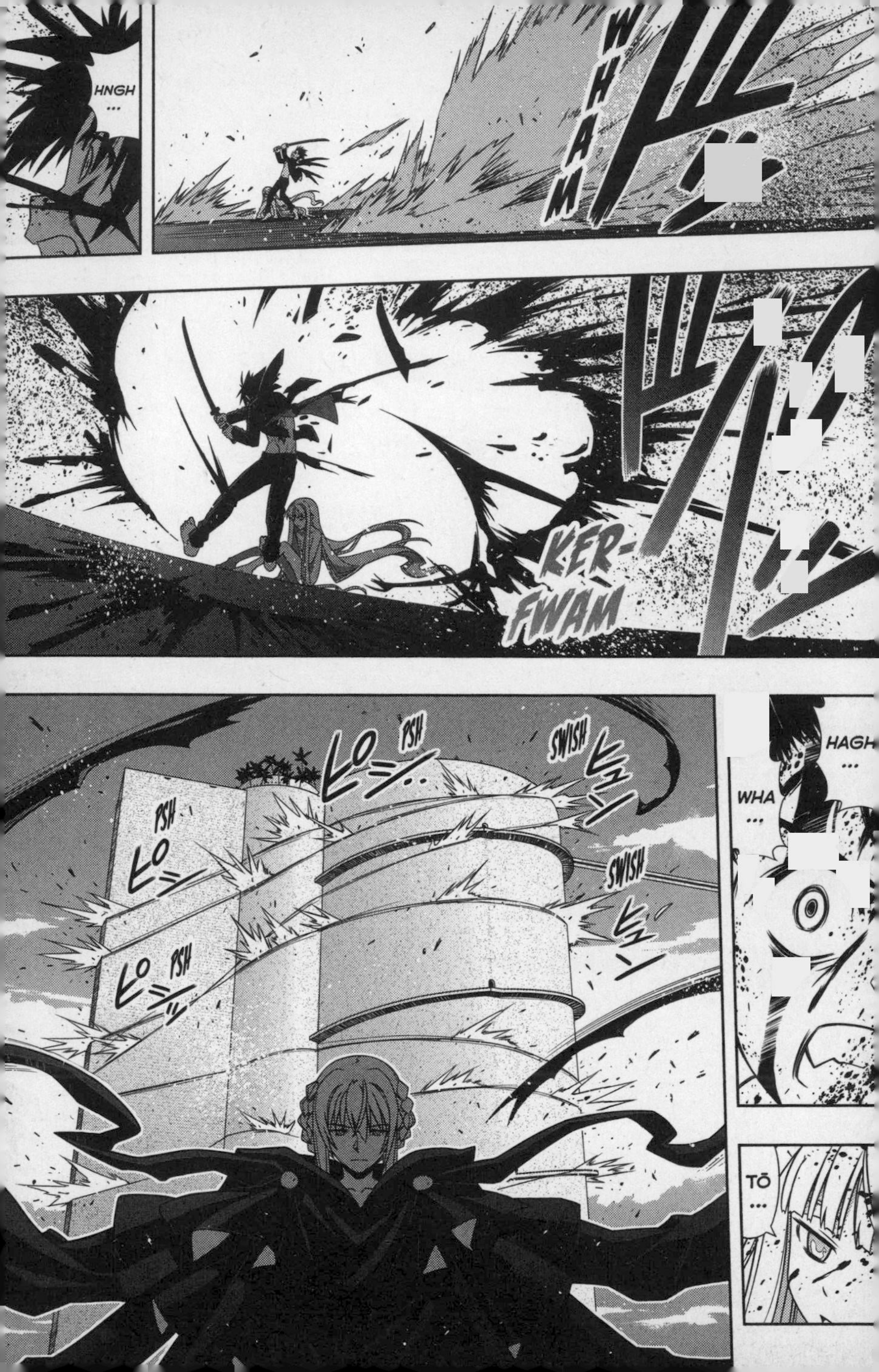
WHAM
HNGH ...
KER-FWAM
HAGH ...
WHA ...
TŌ ...
SWISH
PSH
SWISH
PSH
PSH

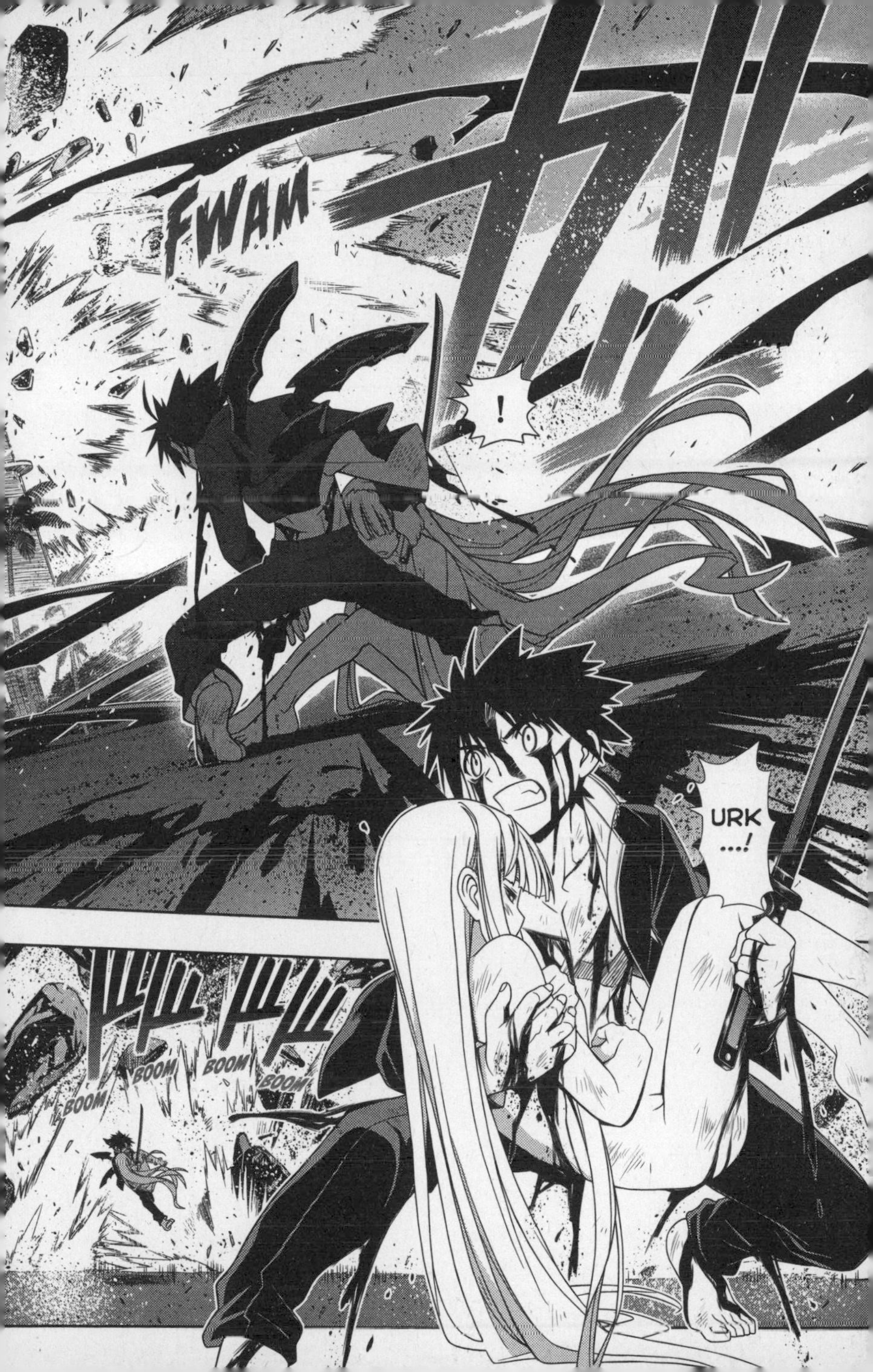
FWAM
!
URK ....!
BOOM
BOOM
BOOM
BOOM

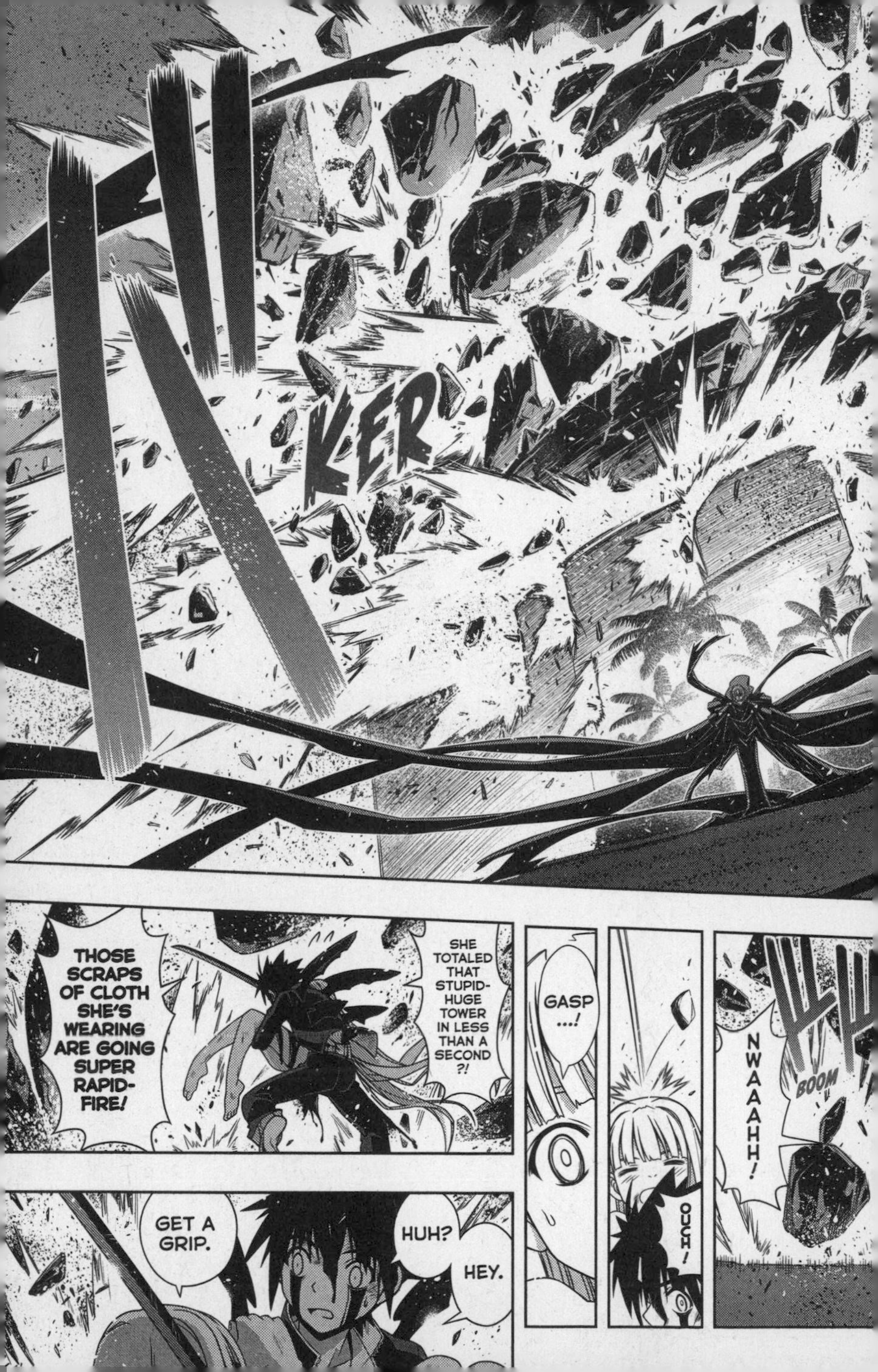

KER-
NWAAAHH!
BOOM
OUCH!
GASP...!
SHE TOTALED THAT STUPID-HUGE TOWER IN LESS THAN A SECOND?!
THOSE SCRAPS OF CLOTH SHE'S WEARING ARE GOING SUPER RAPID-FIRE!
HUH?
HEY.
GET A GRIP.

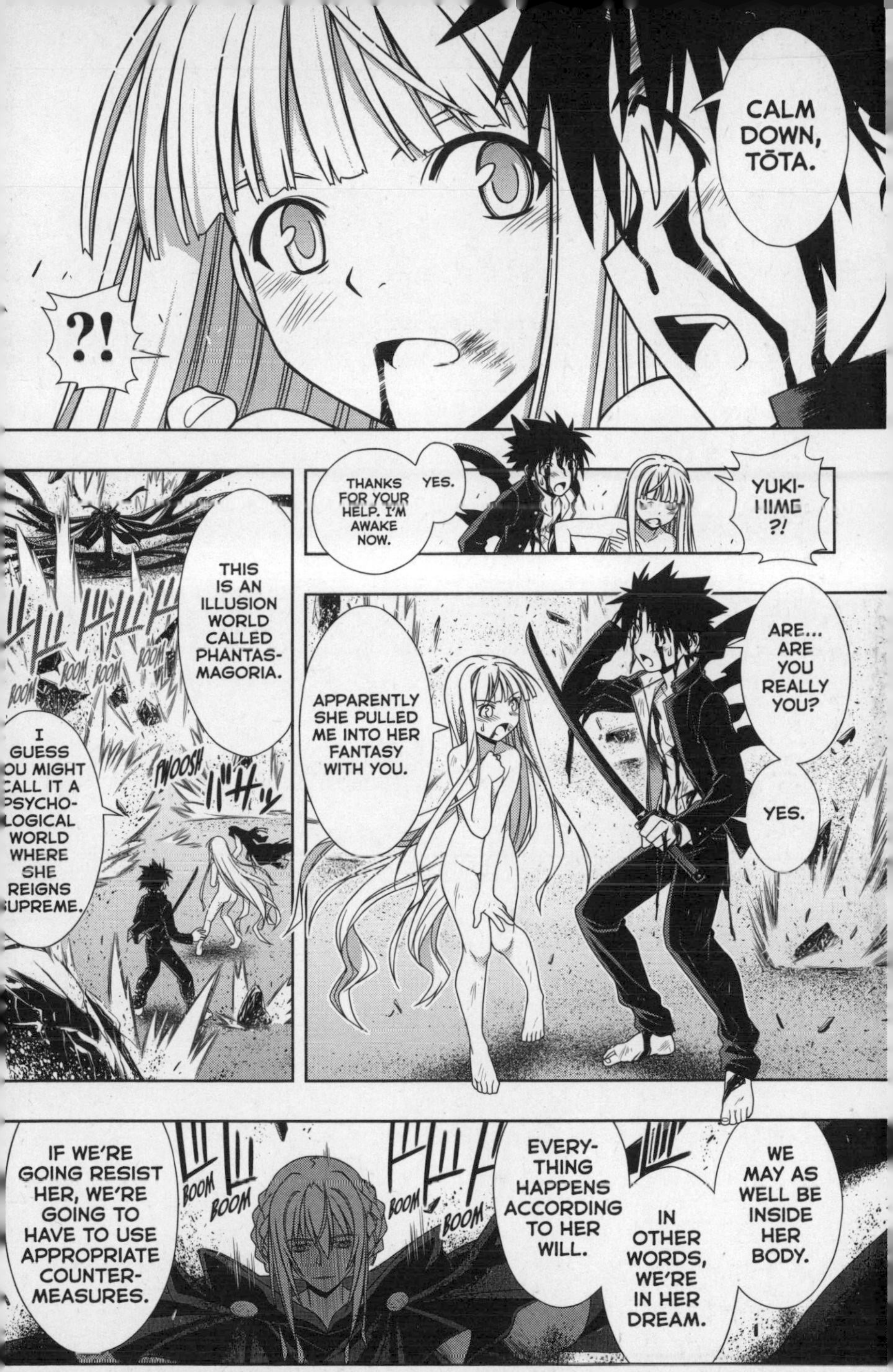
CALM DOWN, TŌTA.
?!
YUKI-HIME?!
YES.
THANKS FOR YOUR HELP. I'M AWAKE NOW.
ARE... ARE YOU REALLY YOU?
YES.
APPARENTLY SHE PULLED ME INTO HER FANTASY WITH YOU.
THIS IS AN ILLUSION WORLD CALLED PHANTAS-MAGORIA.
BOOM BOOM BOOM BOOM
WOOSH
I GUESS YOU MIGHT CALL IT A PSYCHO-LOGICAL WORLD WHERE SHE REIGNS SUPREME.
WE MAY AS WELL BE INSIDE HER BODY.
IN OTHER WORDS, WE'RE IN HER DREAM.
EVERY-THING HAPPENS ACCORDING TO HER WILL.
BOOM BOOM BOOM BOOM
IF WE'RE GOING RESIST HER, WE'RE GOING TO HAVE TO USE APPROPRIATE COUNTER-MEASURES.

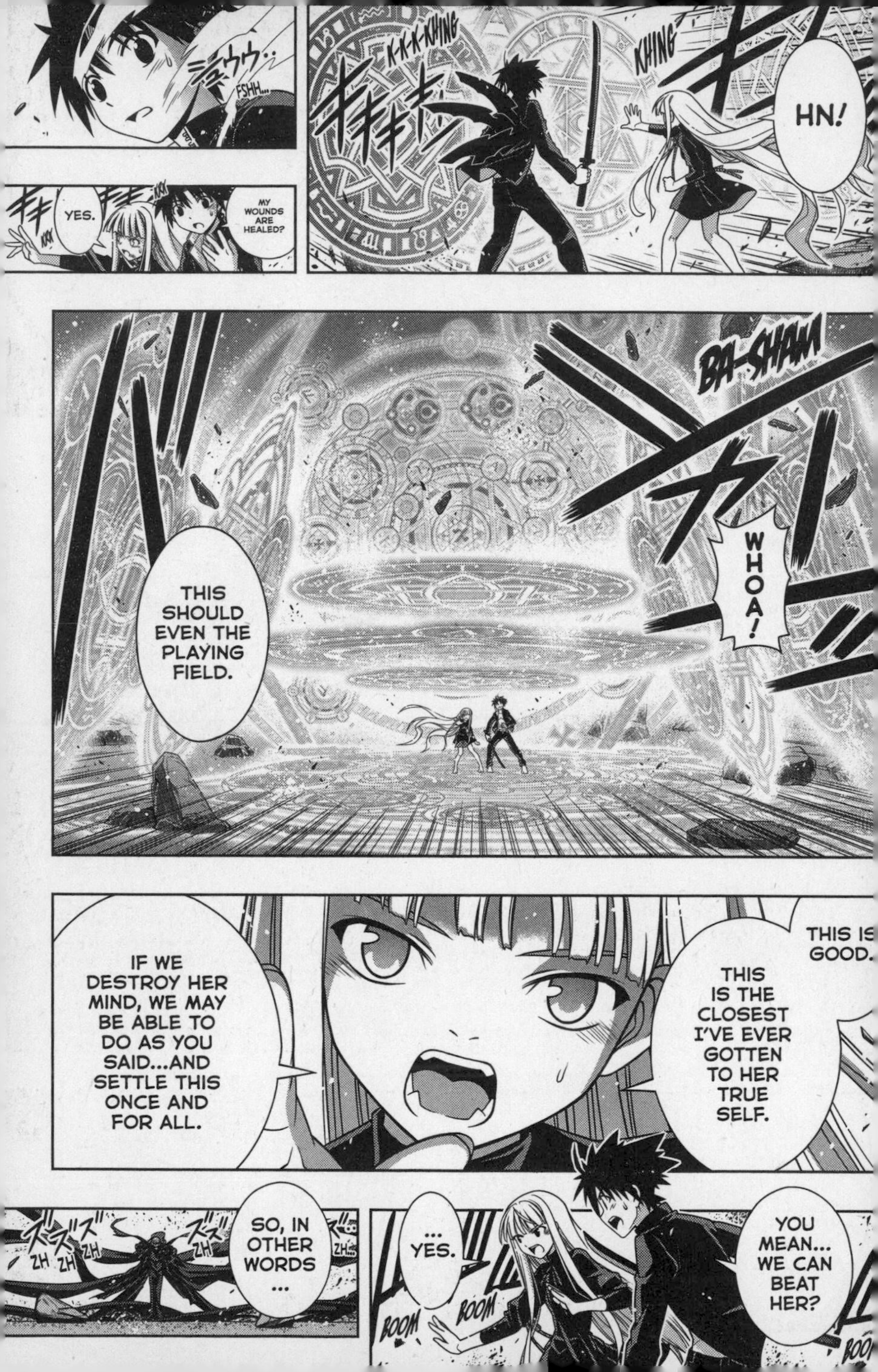
HN!
KHING
K-K-K-KHING
FSHH...
MY WOUNDS ARE HEALED?
YES.
BA-SHAM
WHOA!
THIS SHOULD EVEN THE PLAYING FIELD.
THIS IS GOOD.
THIS IS THE CLOSEST I'VE EVER GOTTEN TO HER TRUE SELF.
IF WE DESTROY HER MIND, WE MAY BE ABLE TO DO AS YOU SAID...AND SETTLE THIS ONCE AND FOR ALL.
YOU MEAN... WE CAN BEAT HER?
...YES.
BOOM
BOOM
BOOM
SO, IN OTHER WORDS...
ZH
ZH
ZH
ZH...

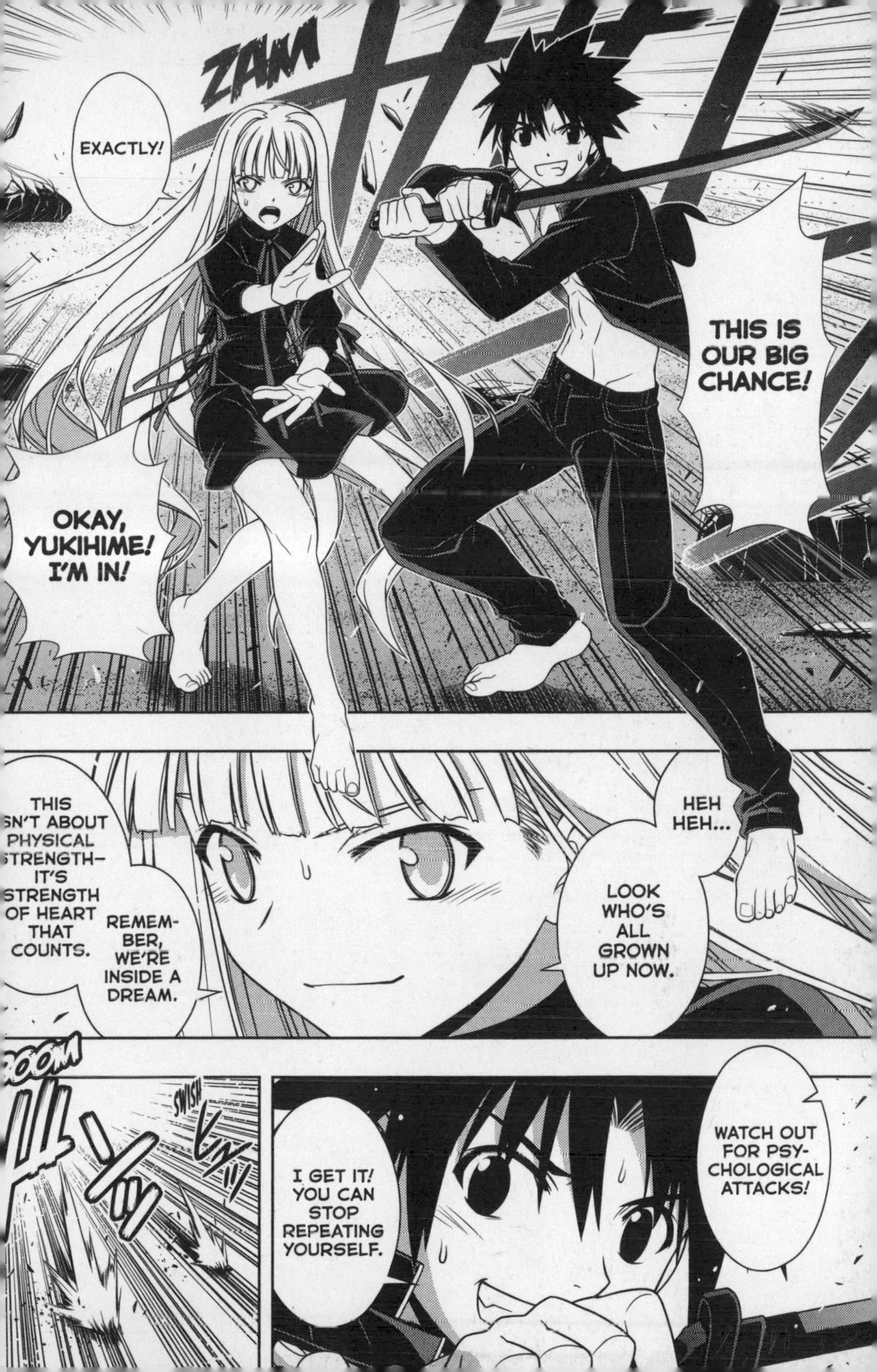
ZAM
THIS IS OUR BIG CHANCE!
EXACTLY!
OKAY, YUKIHIME! I'M IN!
HEH HEH...
LOOK WHO'S ALL GROWN UP NOW.
REMEMBER, WE'RE INSIDE A DREAM.
THIS SN'T ABOUT PHYSICAL TRENGTH— IT'S STRENGTH OF HEART THAT COUNTS.
WATCH OUT FOR PSYCHOLOGICAL ATTACKS!
I GET IT! YOU CAN STOP REPEATING YOURSELF.
SWISH

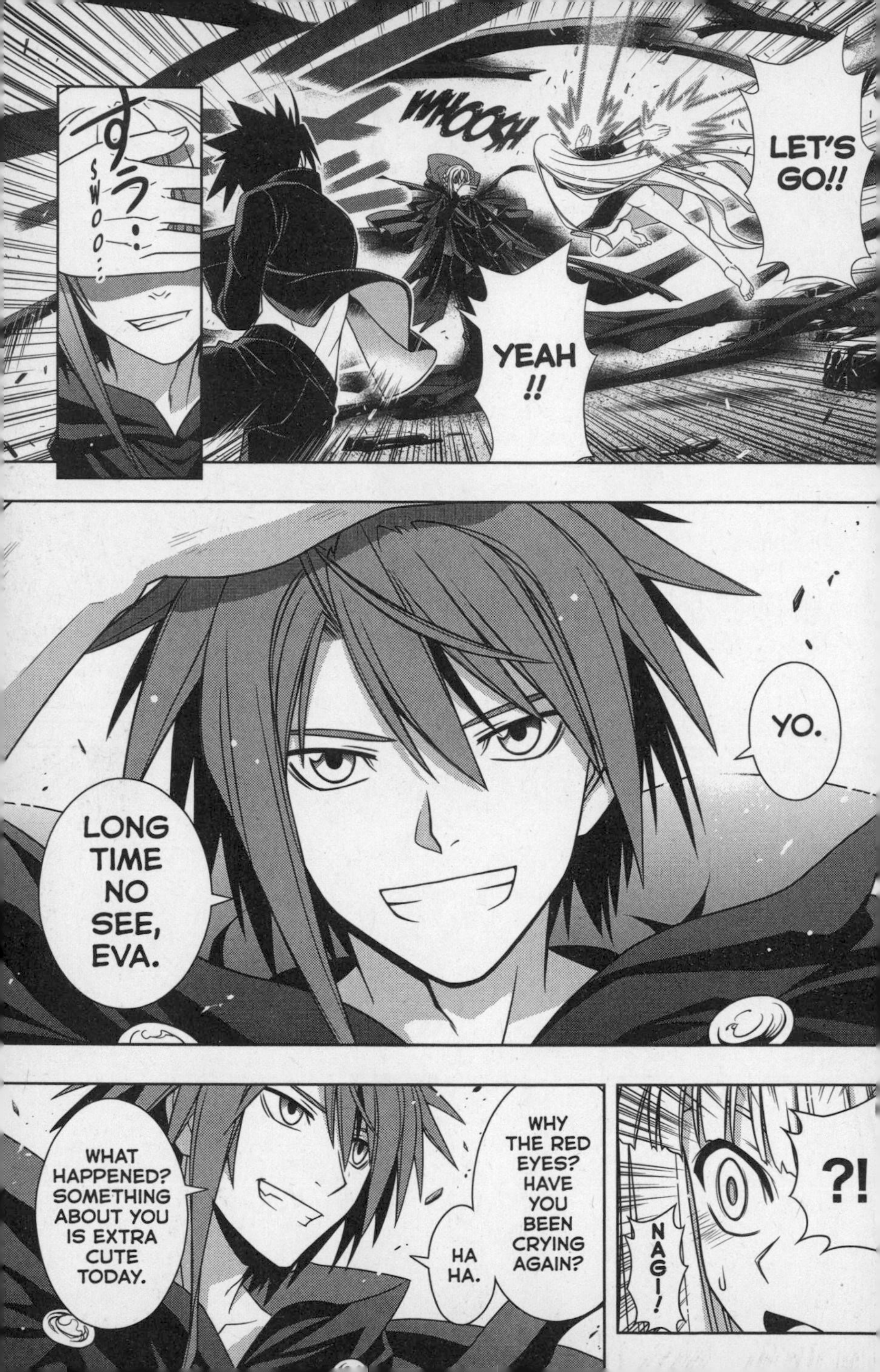
LET'S GO!!
WHOOSH
YEAH!!
すう…
SWOO…
YO.
LONG TIME NO SEE, EVA.
?!
NAGI!
WHY THE RED EYES? HAVE YOU BEEN CRYING AGAIN?
HA HA.
WHAT HAPPENED? SOMETHING ABOUT YOU IS EXTRA CUTE TODAY.

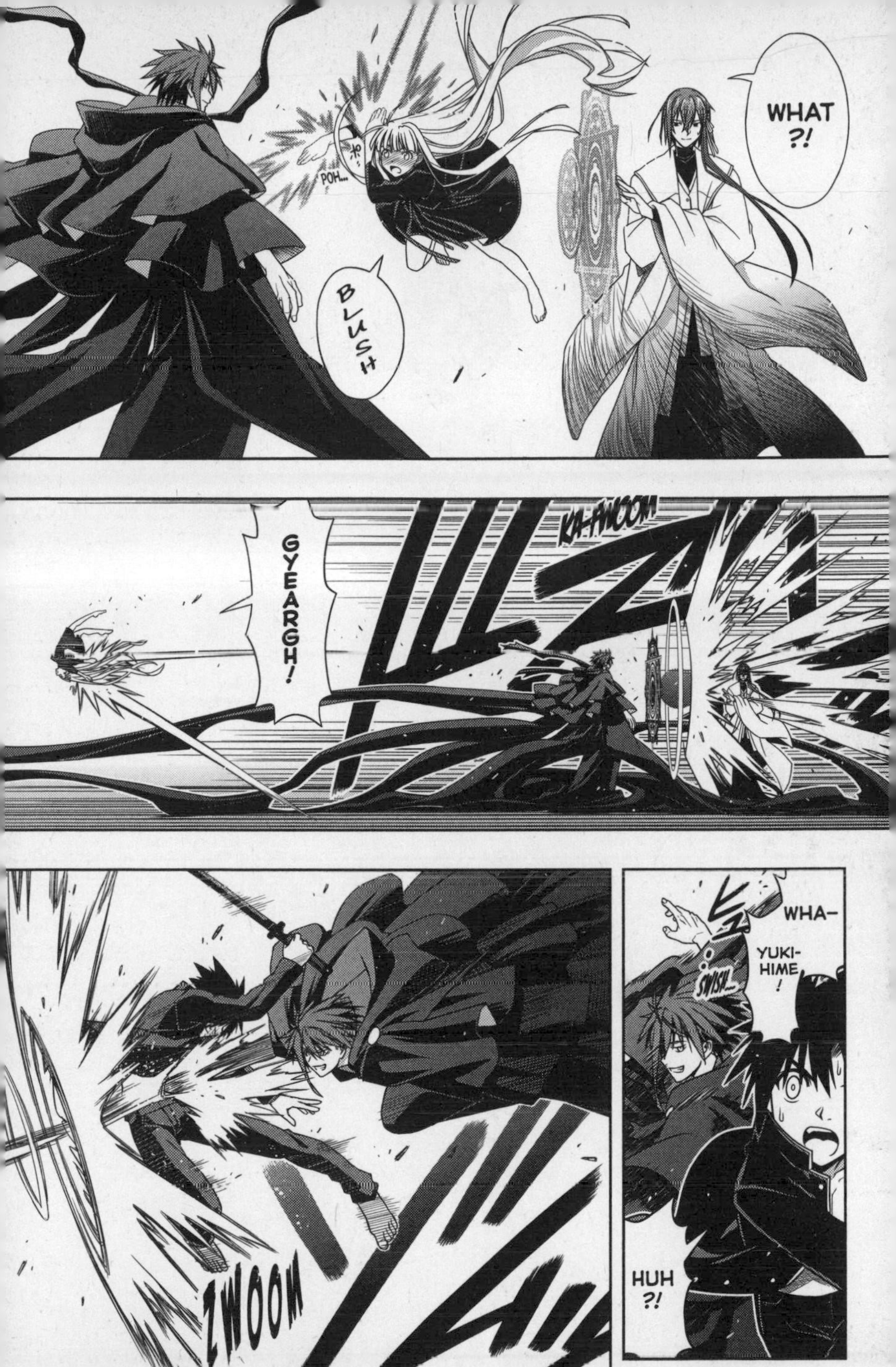
WHAT ?!
POH...
BLUSH
KA-FWOOM
GYEARGH!
WHA-
YUKI-HIME!
SWISH...
HUH ?!
ZWOOM

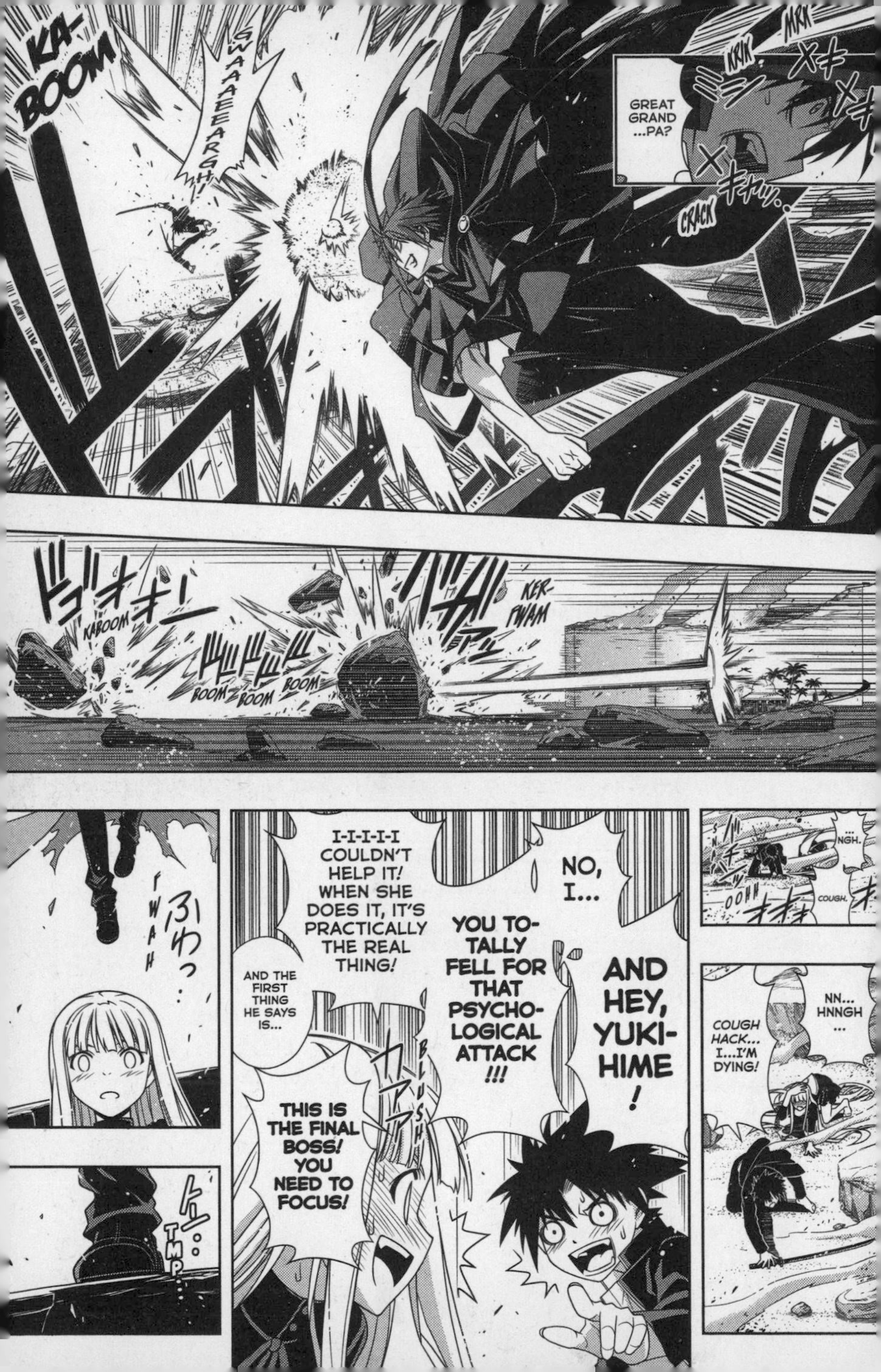
MRK
KRIK
GREAT GRAND ...PA?
CRACK
KA-BOOM
GWAAAAEEEARGH!
KER-FWAM
BOOM BOOM BOOM
KABOOM
...NGH.
OOHH
COUGH.
NN... HNNGH ...
COUGH HACK... I...I'M DYING!
AND HEY, YUKI-HIME!
NO, I...
YOU TO-TALLY FELL FOR THAT PSYCHO-LOGICAL ATTACK!!!
I-I-I-I-I COULDN'T HELP IT! WHEN SHE DOES IT, IT'S PRACTICALLY THE REAL THING!
AND THE FIRST THING HE SAYS IS...
BLUSH
THIS IS THE FINAL BOSS! YOU NEED TO FOCUS!
FWAH
TMP...

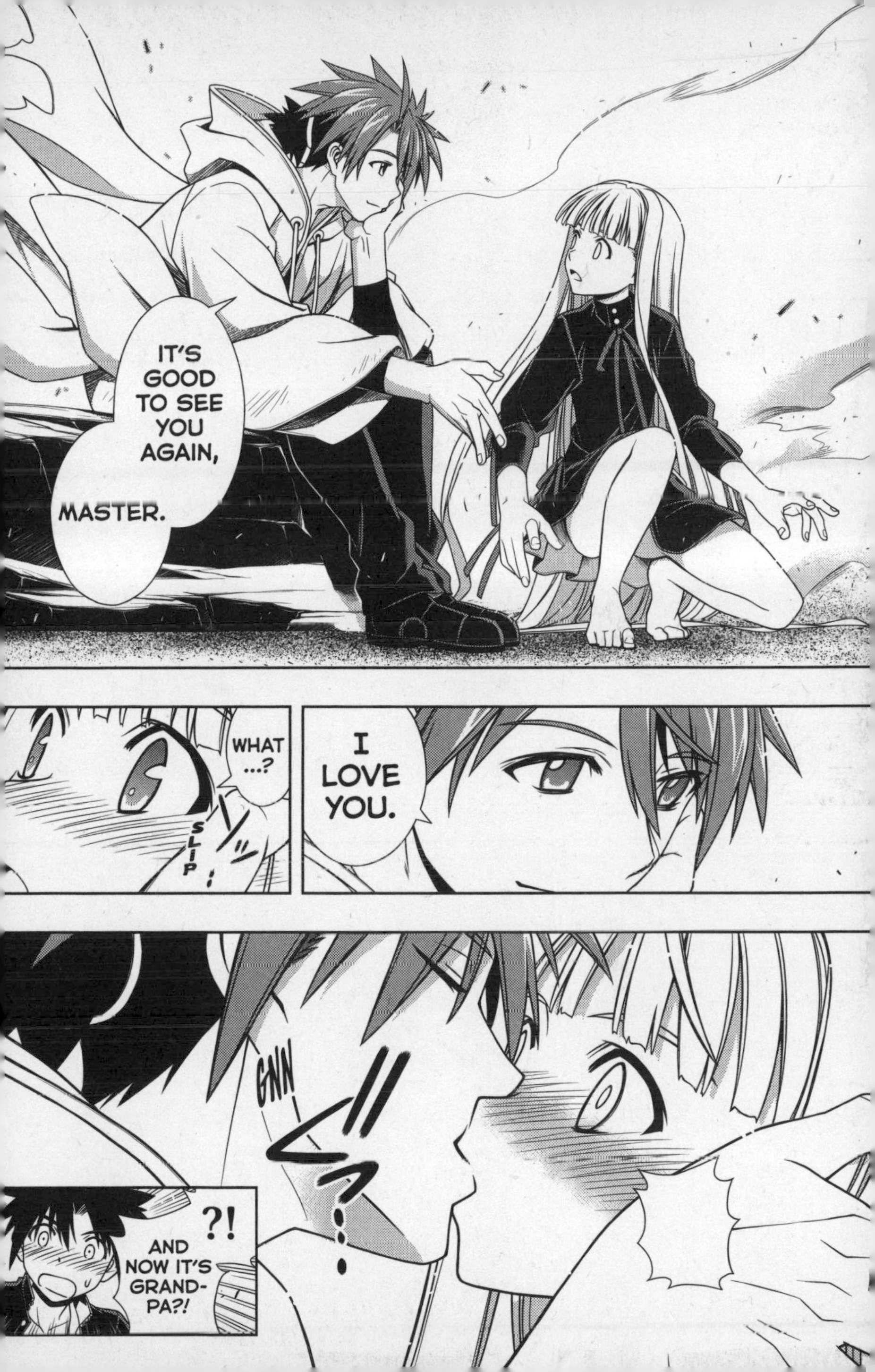
IT'S GOOD TO SEE YOU AGAIN,
MASTER.
I LOVE YOU.
WHAT ...?
SLIP
GNN
?!
AND NOW IT'S GRAND-PA?!

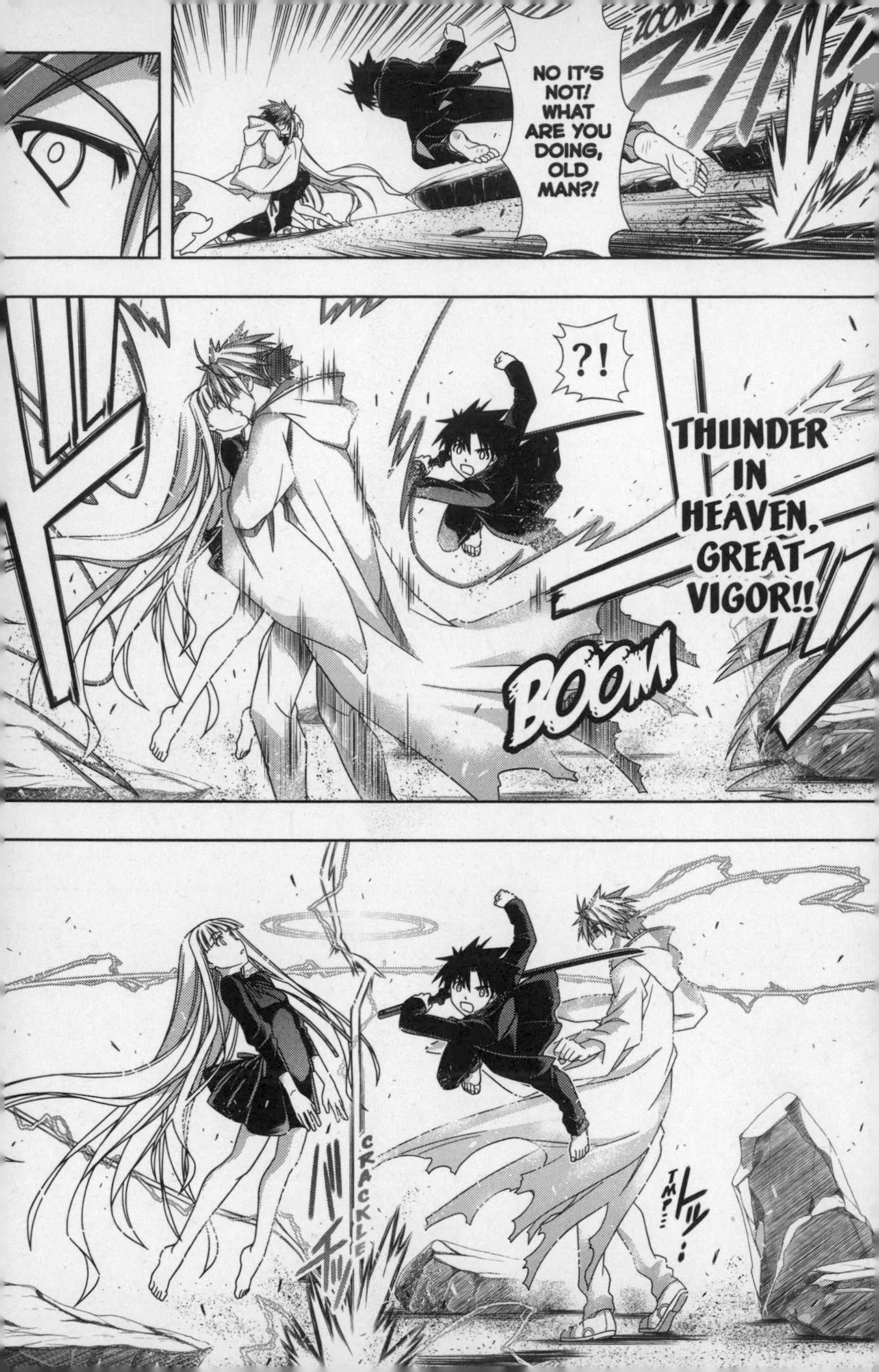
ZOOM
NO IT'S NOT! WHAT ARE YOU DOING, OLD MAN?!
THUNDER IN HEAVEN, GREAT VIGOR!!
?!
BOOM
TMP...
CRACKLE

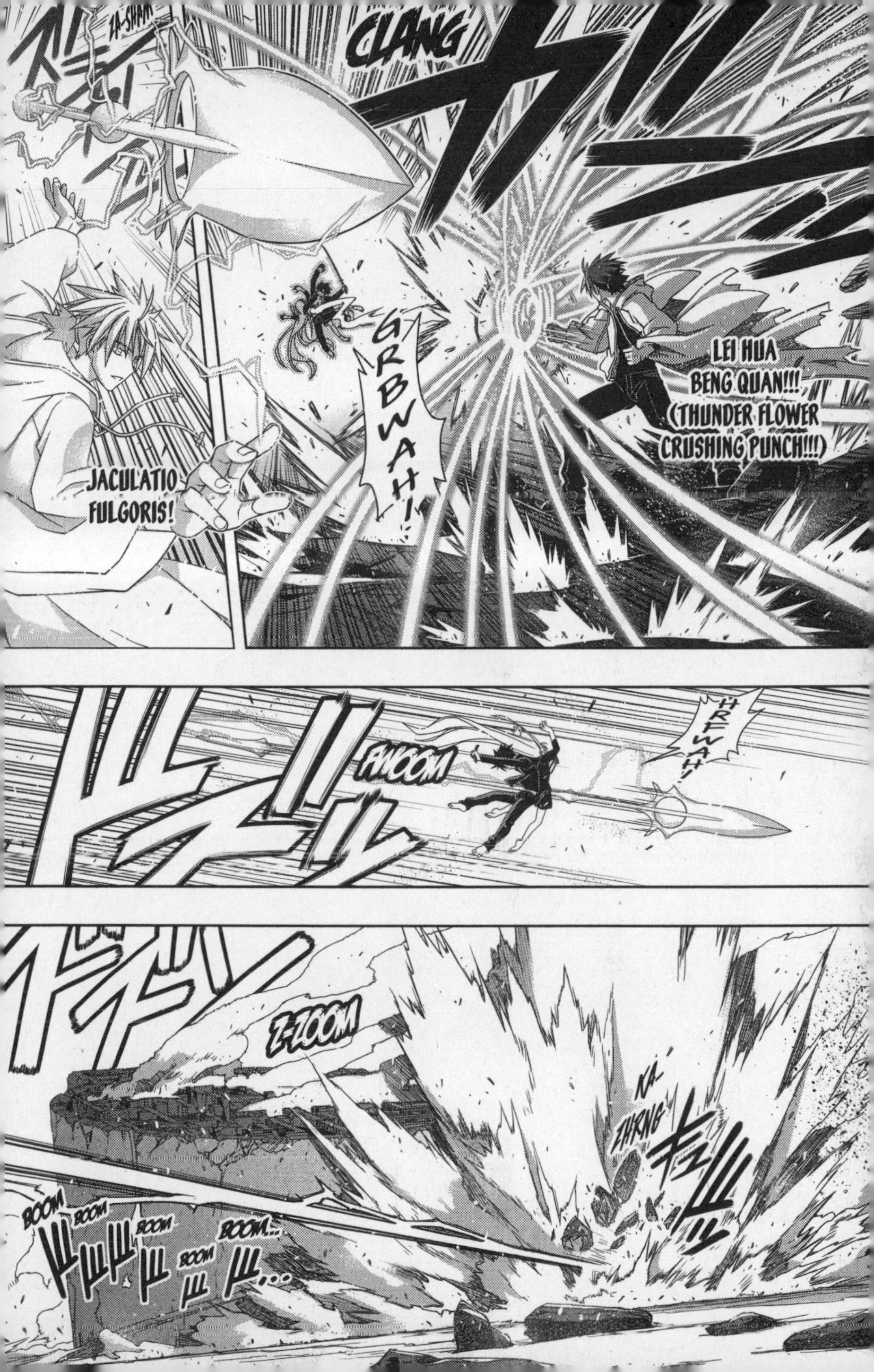
CLANG
ZA-SHAM
LEI HUA BENG QUAN!!! (THUNDER FLOWER CRUSHING PUNCH!!!)
GRBWAH!
JACULATIO FULGORIS!
HRFWAH!
FWOOM
KA-ZHRNG
Z-ZOOM
BOOM BOOM BOOM BOOM BOOM...

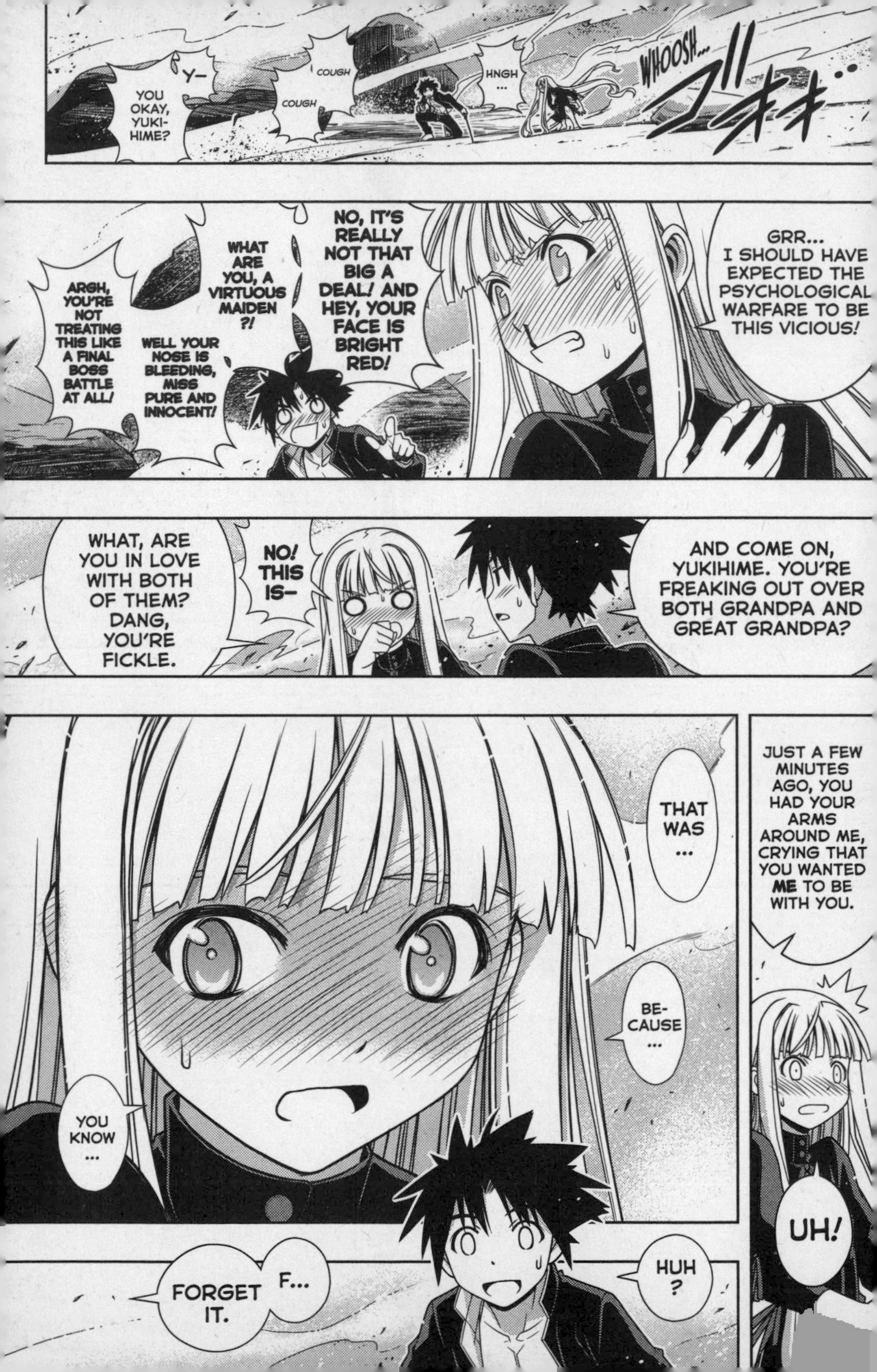
WHOOSH...
ゴオオ
HNGH...
COUGH
COUGH
Y–
YOU OKAY, YUKI-HIME?
GRR... I SHOULD HAVE EXPECTED THE PSYCHOLOGICAL WARFARE TO BE THIS VICIOUS!
NO, IT'S REALLY NOT THAT BIG A DEAL! AND HEY, YOUR FACE IS BRIGHT RED!
WHAT ARE YOU, A VIRTUOUS MAIDEN?!
ARGH, YOU'RE NOT TREATING THIS LIKE A FINAL BOSS BATTLE AT ALL!
WELL YOUR NOSE IS BLEEDING, MISS PURE AND INNOCENT!
AND COME ON, YUKIHIME. YOU'RE FREAKING OUT OVER BOTH GRANDPA AND GREAT GRANDPA?
NO! THIS IS–
WHAT, ARE YOU IN LOVE WITH BOTH OF THEM? DANG, YOU'RE FICKLE.
JUST A FEW MINUTES AGO, YOU HAD YOUR ARMS AROUND ME, CRYING THAT YOU WANTED **ME** TO BE WITH YOU.
UH!
THAT WAS...
BE-CAUSE...
YOU KNOW...
HUH?
F...
FORGET IT.

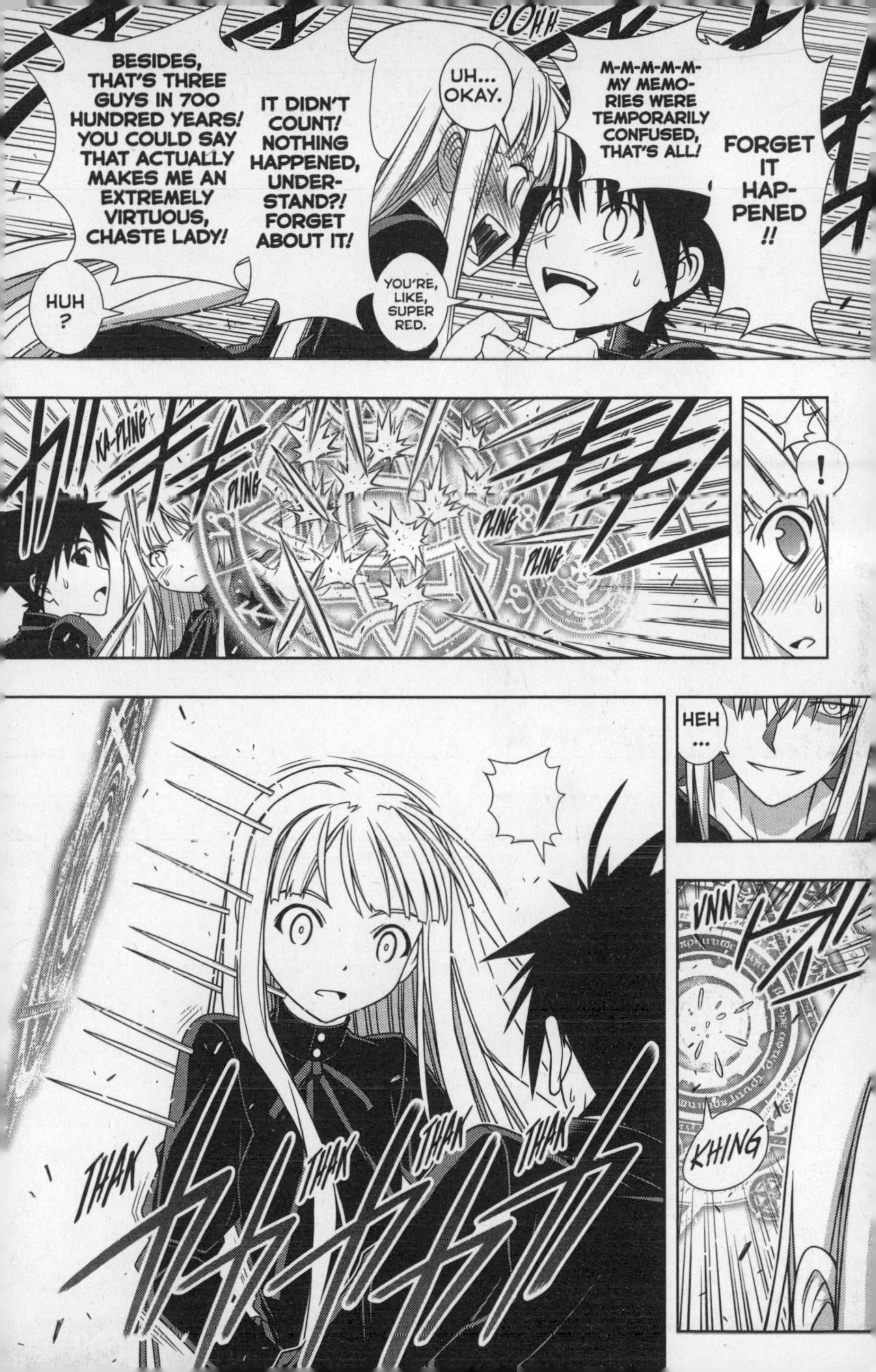

FORGET IT HAP-PENED!!
M-M-M-M-M-MY MEMO-RIES WERE TEMPORARILY CONFUSED, THAT'S ALL!
OOHH
UH... OKAY.
YOU'RE, LIKE, SUPER RED.
IT DIDN'T COUNT! NOTHING HAPPENED, UNDER-STAND?! FORGET ABOUT IT!
BESIDES, THAT'S THREE GUYS IN 700 HUNDRED YEARS! YOU COULD SAY THAT ACTUALLY MAKES ME AN EXTREMELY VIRTUOUS, CHASTE LADY!
HUH?
!
PLING
PLING
PLING
KA-PLING
HEH ...
VNN
KHING
THAK
THAK
THAK
THAK

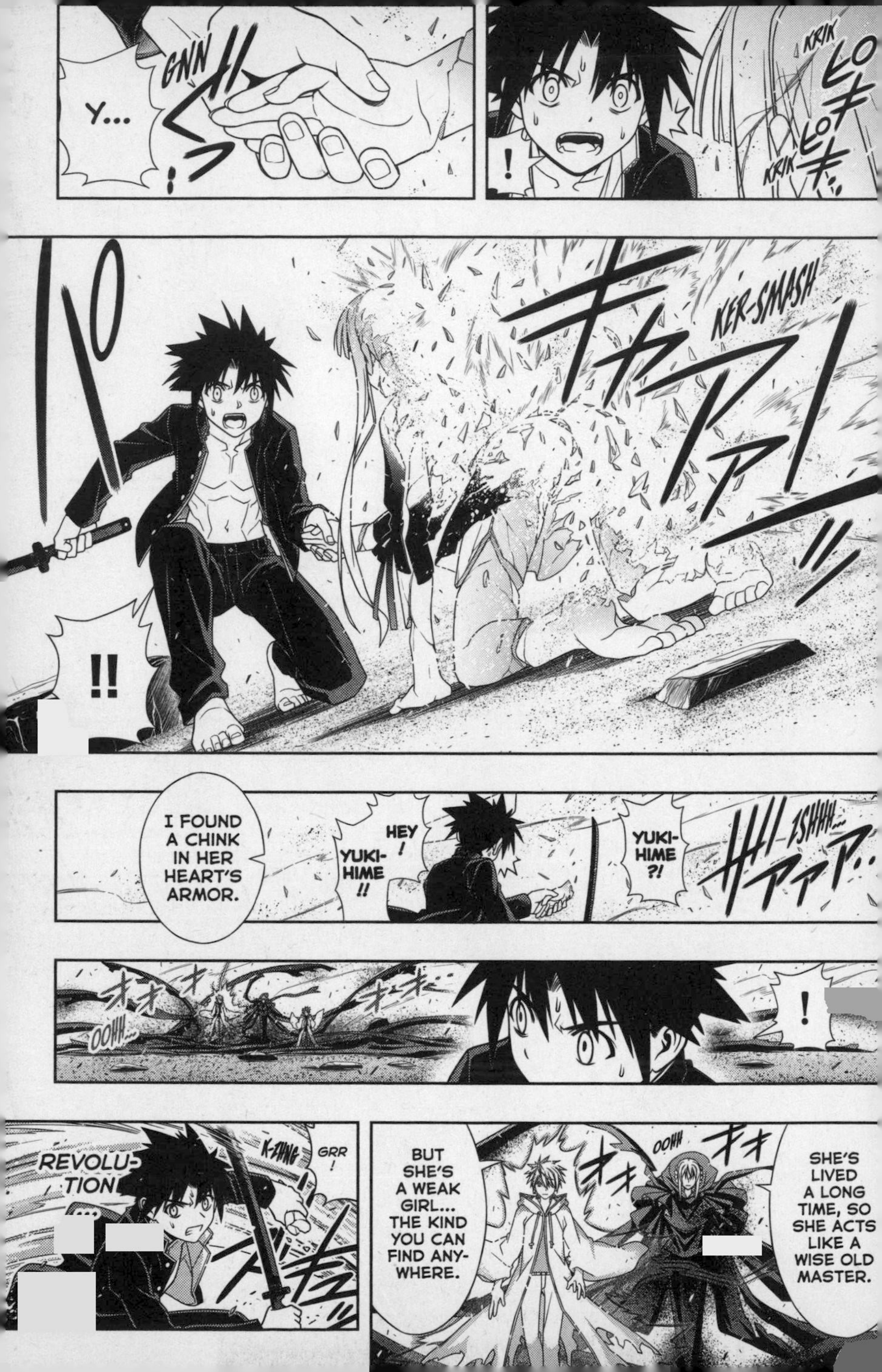
KRIK
KRIK
!
GNN
Y...
KER-SMASH
!!
TSHHH...
YUKI-HIME ?!
HEY! YUKI-HIME !!
I FOUND A CHINK IN HER HEART'S ARMOR.
!
OOHH...
SHE'S LIVED A LONG TIME, SO SHE ACTS LIKE A WISE OLD MASTER.
OOHH
BUT SHE'S A WEAK GIRL... THE KIND YOU CAN FIND ANY-WHERE.
GRR!
K-ZING
REVOLU-TION...

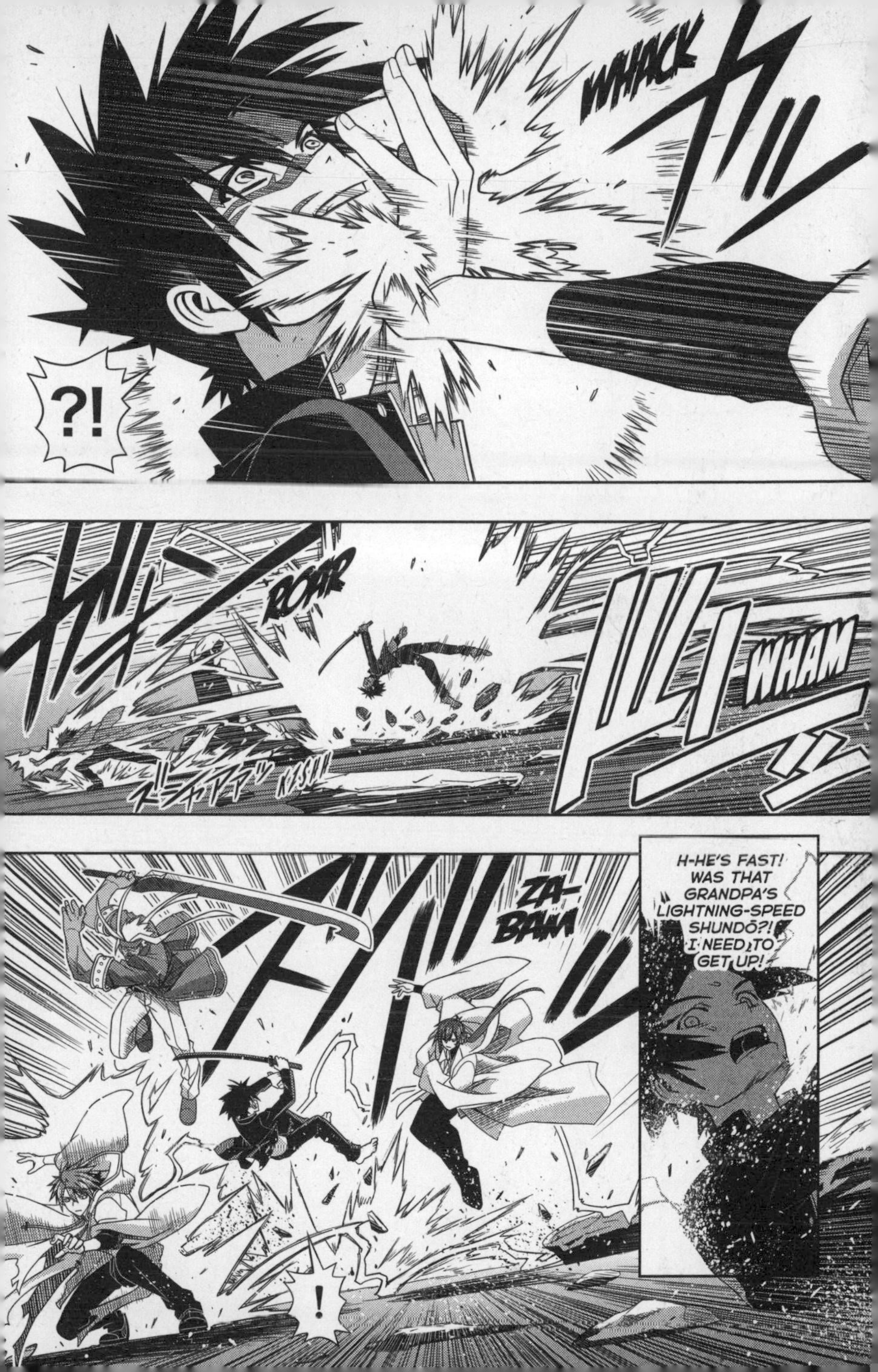

WHACK
?!
WHAM
ROAR
H-HE'S FAST! WAS THAT GRANDPA'S LIGHTNING-SPEED SHUNDŌ?! I NEED TO GET UP!
ZA-BAM
!

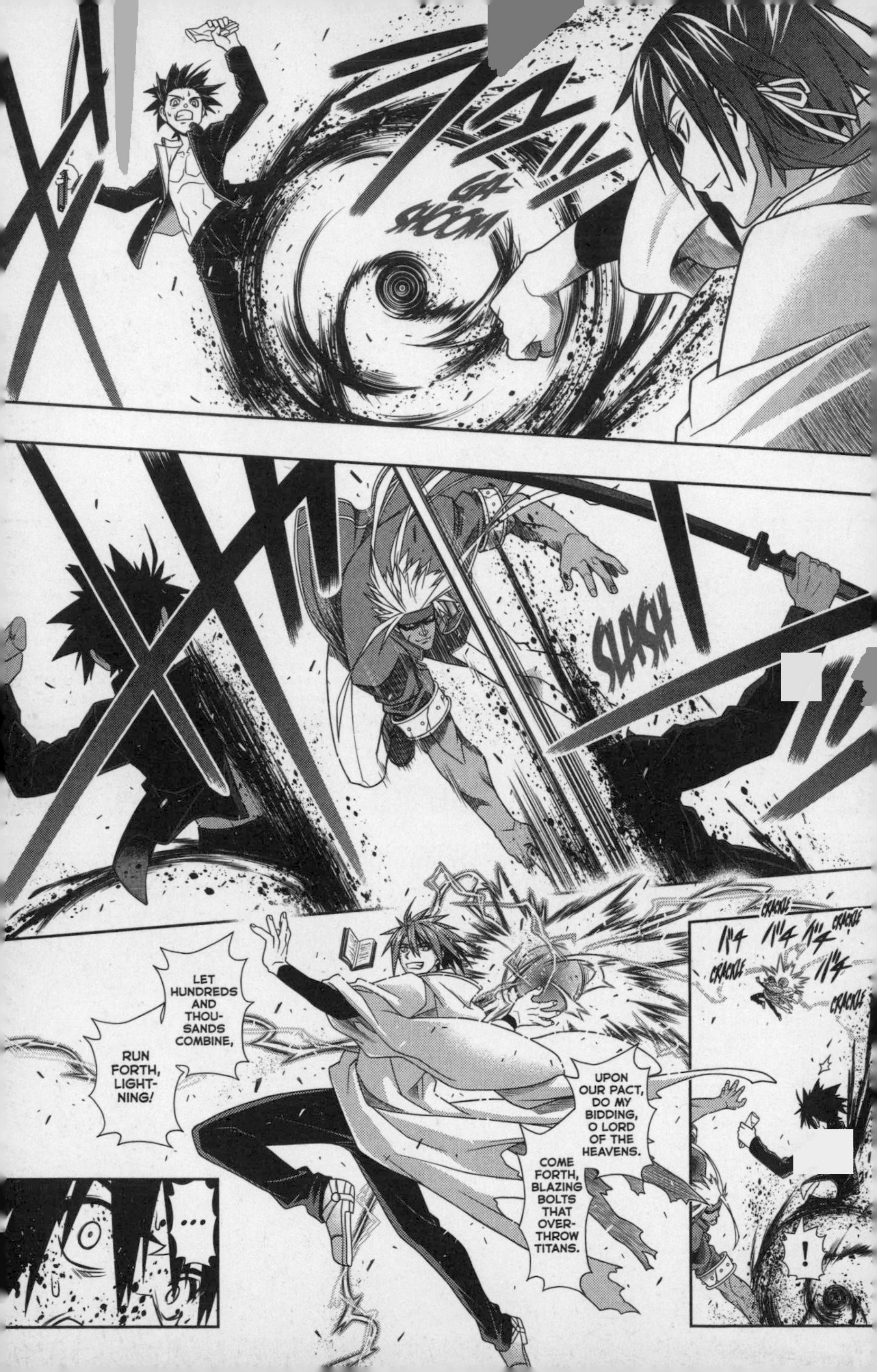
GA-SHOOM
SLASH
CRACKLE
バチ バチ バチ
CRACKLE
バチ
CRACKLE
CRACKLE
!
UPON OUR PACT, DO MY BIDDING, O LORD OF THE HEAVENS.
COME FORTH, BLAZING BOLTS THAT OVER-THROW TITANS.
LET HUNDREDS AND THOU-SANDS COMBINE,
RUN FORTH, LIGHT-NING!
...

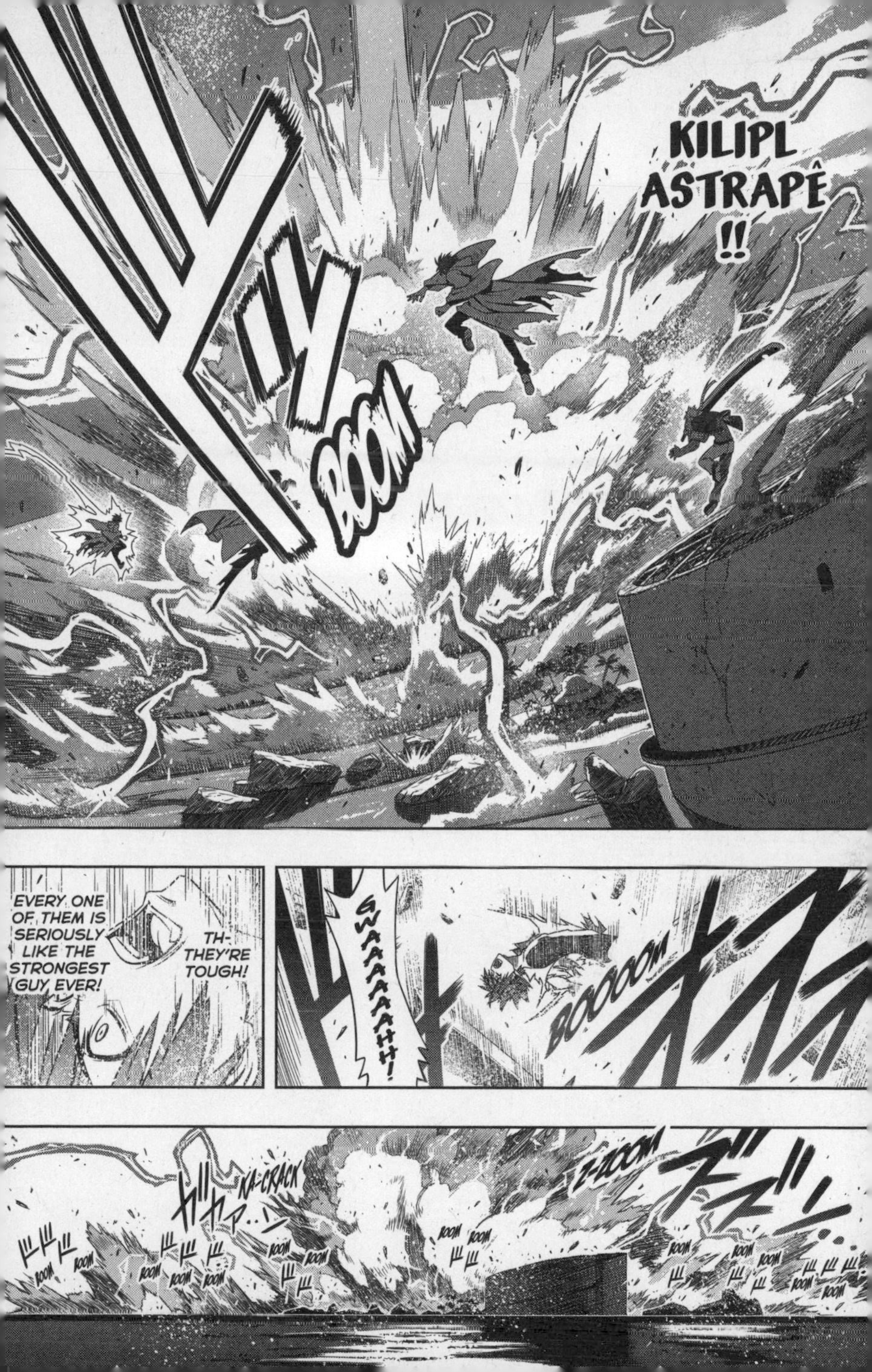
KILIPL ASTRAPÊ !!
BOOM
GWAAAAAAAAHH!
BOOOOM
TH- THEY'RE TOUGH!
EVERY ONE OF THEM IS SERIOUSLY LIKE THE STRONGEST GUY EVER!
Z-ZOOM
KA-CRACK
BOOM
BOOM
BOOM
BOOM
BOOM
BOOM
BOOM
BOOM
BOOM
BOOM
BOOM

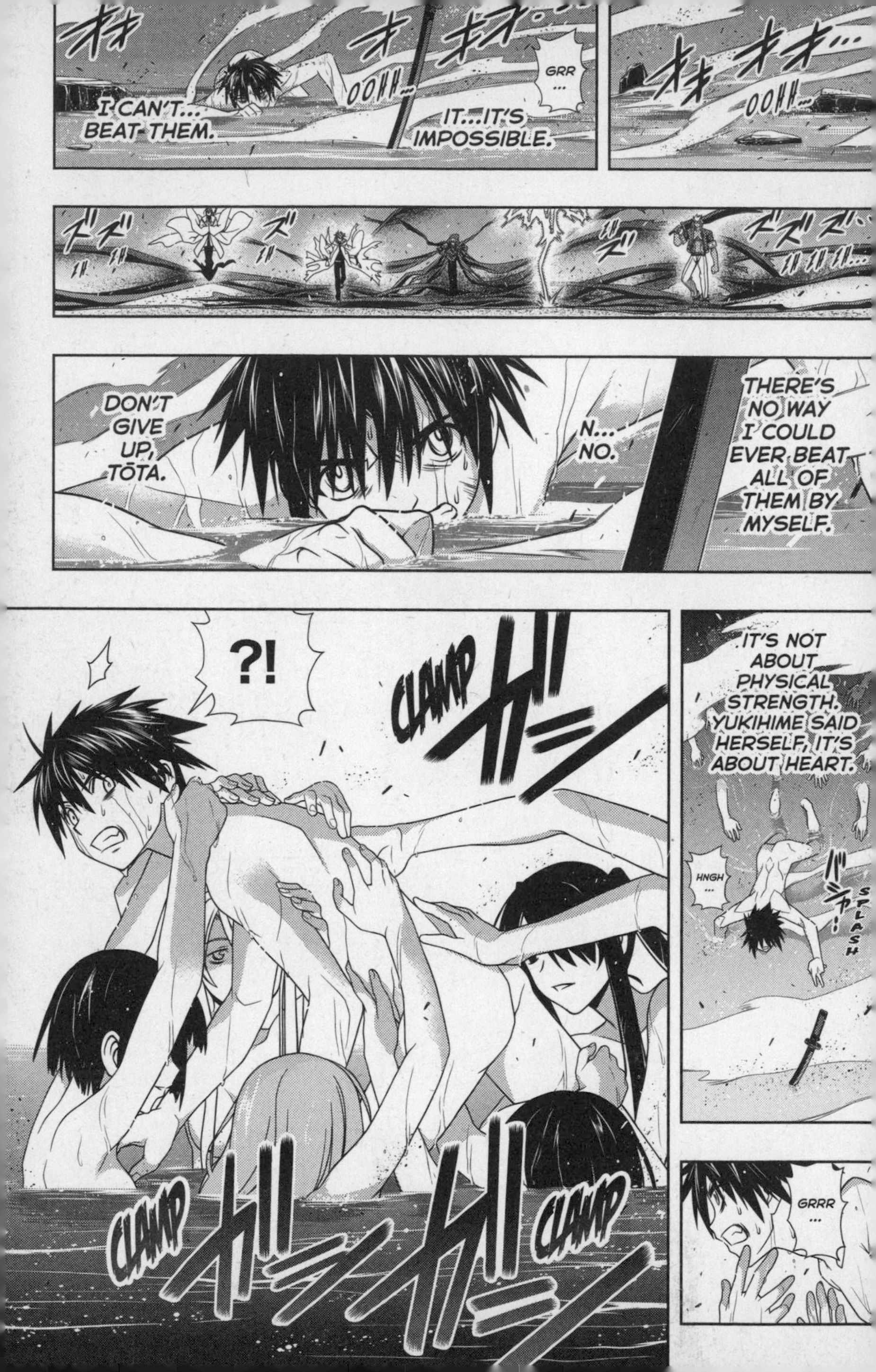
OOHH...
GRR ...
IT...IT'S IMPOSSIBLE.
OOHH...
I CAN'T... BEAT THEM.
THERE'S NO WAY I COULD EVER BEAT ALL OF THEM BY MYSELF.
N... NO.
DON'T GIVE UP, TŌTA.
IT'S NOT ABOUT PHYSICAL STRENGTH. YUKIHIME SAID HERSELF, IT'S ABOUT HEART.
SPLASH
HNGH ...
GRRR ...
?!
CLAMP
CLAMP
CLAMP

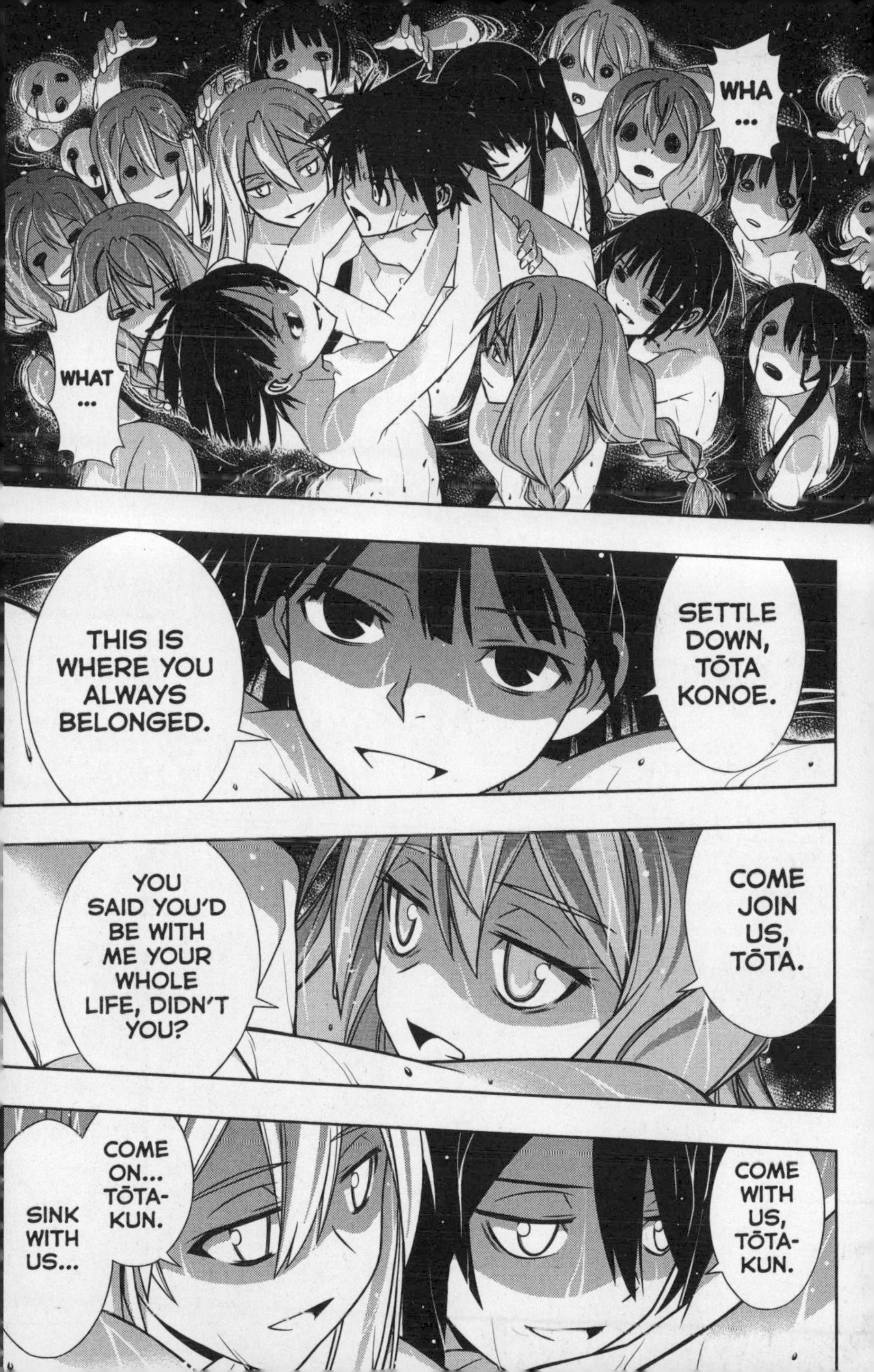
WHA ...
WHAT ...
SETTLE DOWN, TŌTA KONOE.
THIS IS WHERE YOU ALWAYS BELONGED.
COME JOIN US, TŌTA.
YOU SAID YOU'D BE WITH ME YOUR WHOLE LIFE, DIDN'T YOU?
COME WITH US, TŌTA-KUN.
COME ON... TŌTA-KUN.
SINK WITH US...

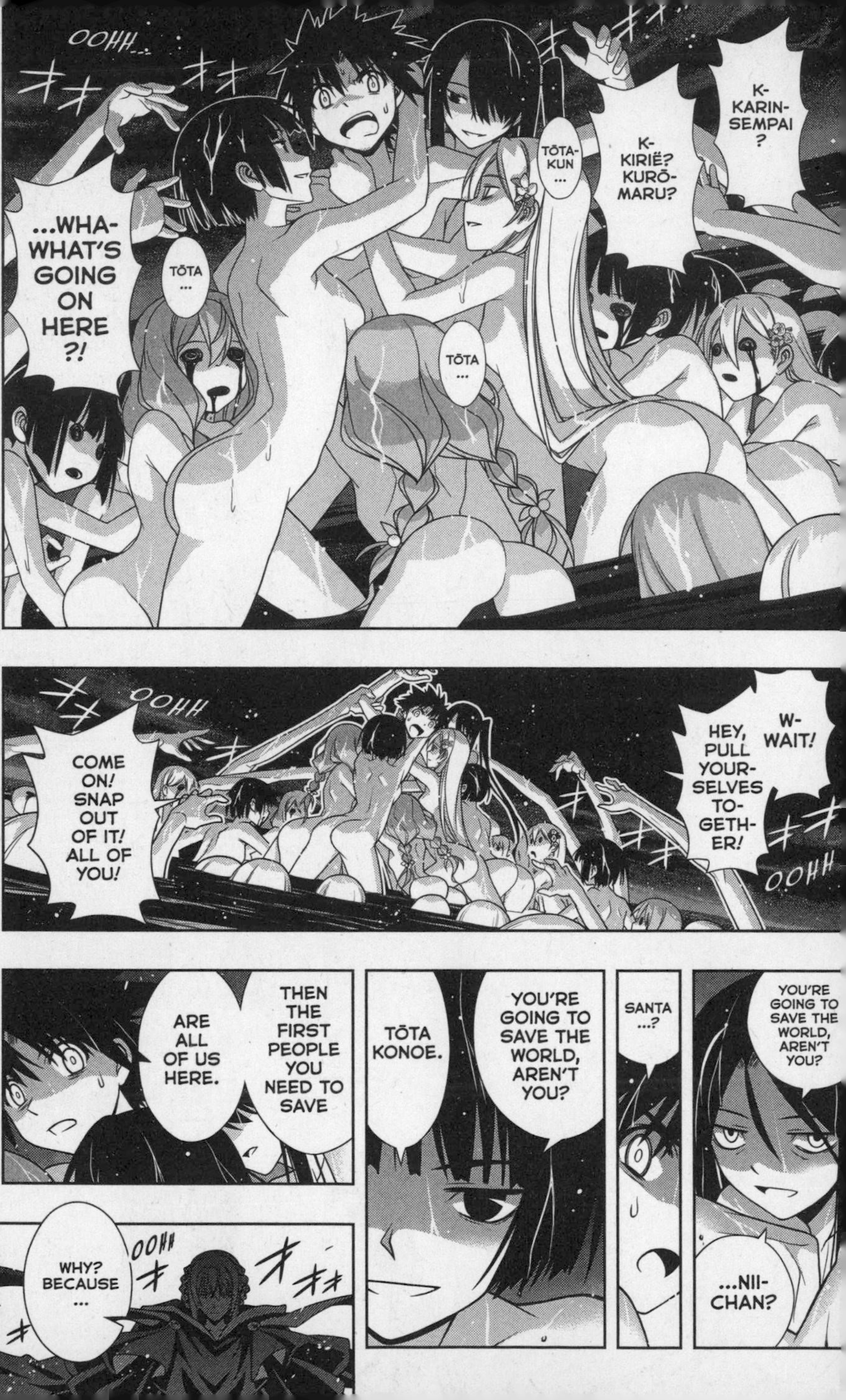
OOHH...
K-KARIN-SEMPAI?
K-KIRIË? KURŌ-MARU?
TŌTA-KUN...
TŌTA...
TŌTA...
...WHA-WHAT'S GOING ON HERE?!
W-WAIT!
HEY, PULL YOURSELVES TOGETHER!
OOHH
OOHH
COME ON! SNAP OUT OF IT! ALL OF YOU!
YOU'RE GOING TO SAVE THE WORLD, AREN'T YOU?
...NII-CHAN?
SANTA...?
YOU'RE GOING TO SAVE THE WORLD, AREN'T YOU?
TŌTA KONOE.
THEN THE FIRST PEOPLE YOU NEED TO SAVE
ARE ALL OF US HERE.
OOHH
WHY? BECAUSE...

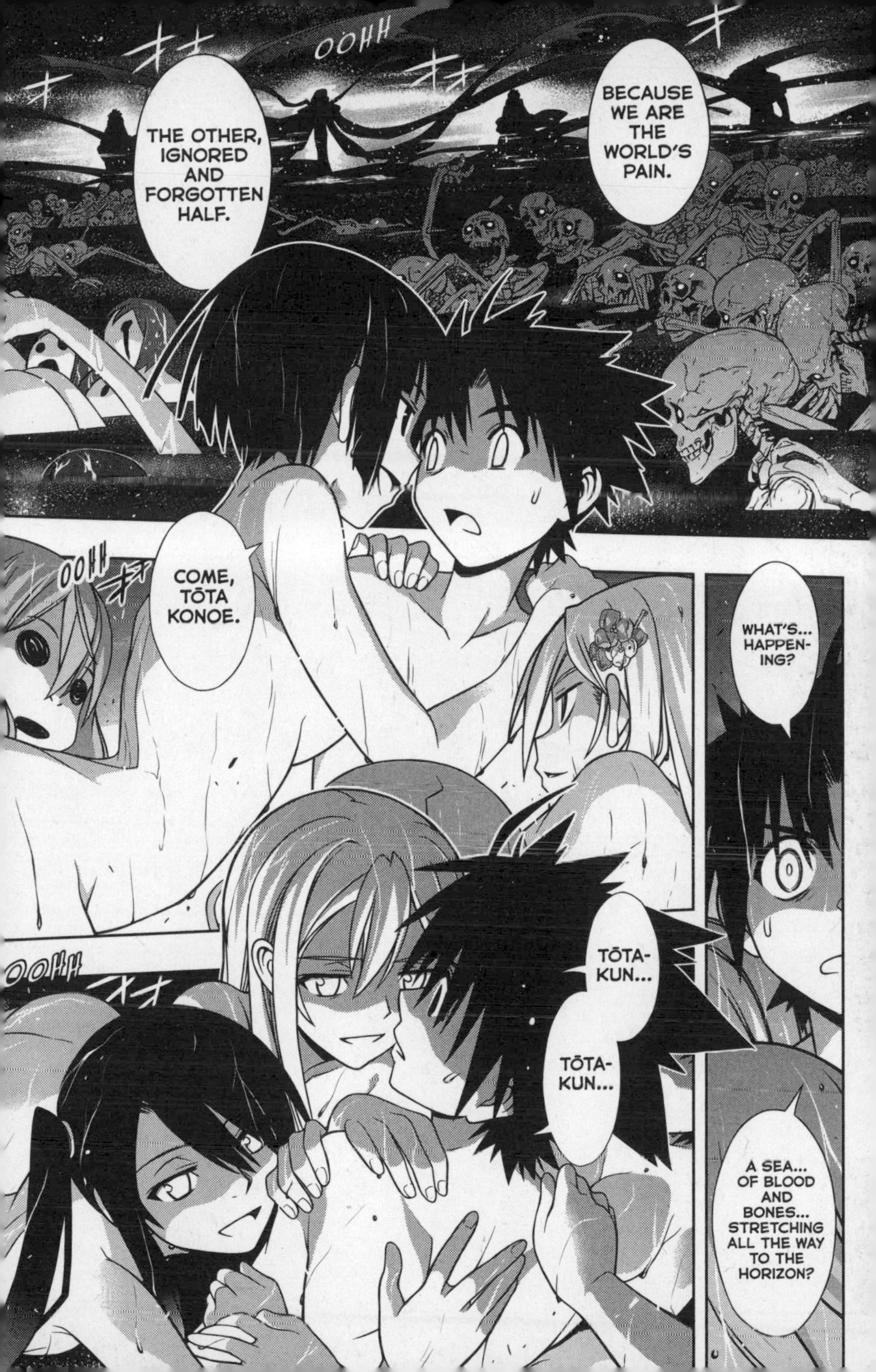
OOHH
BECAUSE WE ARE THE WORLD'S PAIN.
THE OTHER, IGNORED AND FORGOTTEN HALF.
WHAT'S... HAPPEN-ING?
A SEA... OF BLOOD AND BONES... STRETCHING ALL THE WAY TO THE HORIZON?
OOHH
COME, TŌTA KONOE.
OOHH
TŌTA-KUN...
TŌTA-KUN...

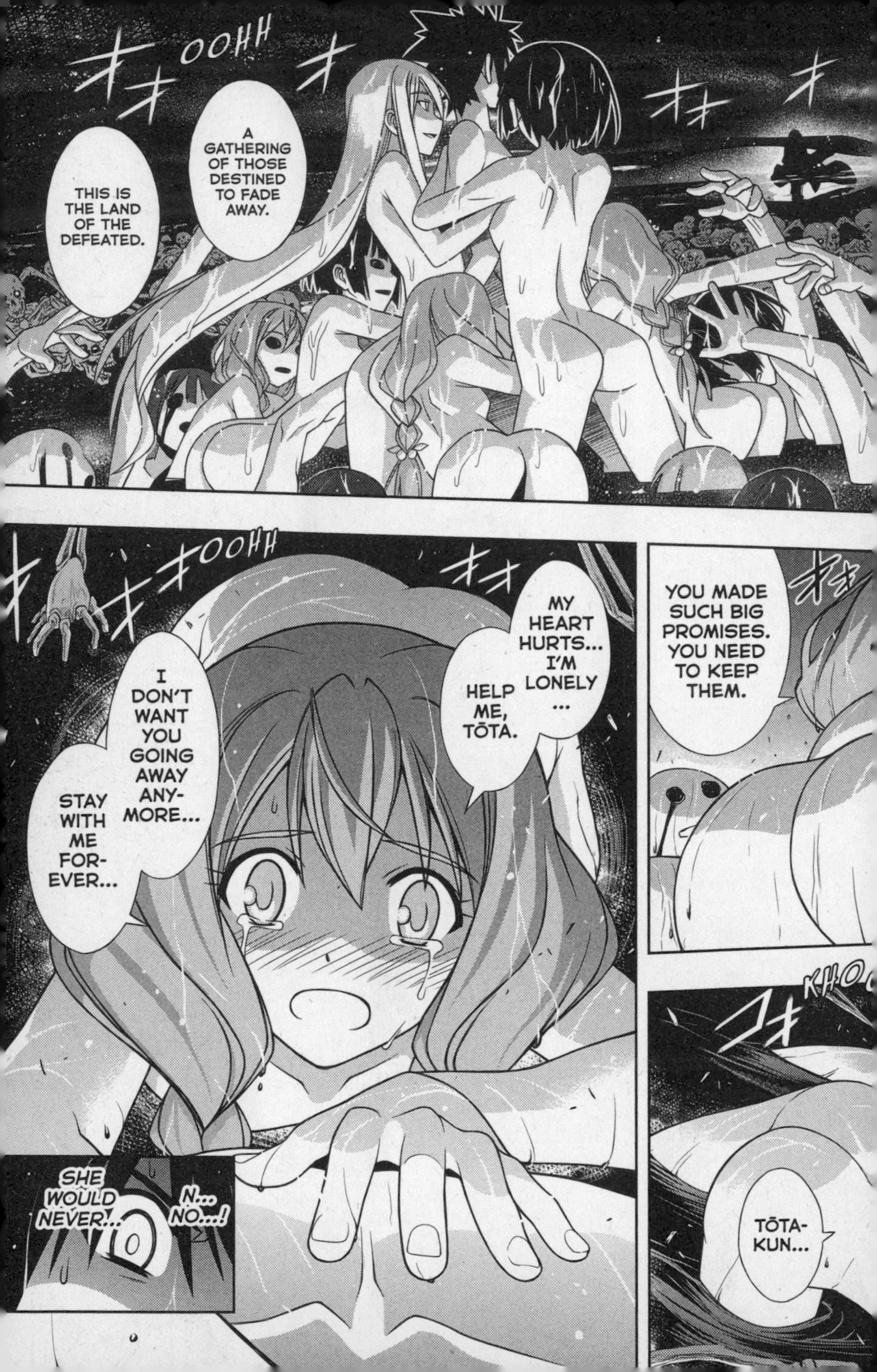
OOHH
A GATHERING OF THOSE DESTINED TO FADE AWAY.
THIS IS THE LAND OF THE DEFEATED.
YOU MADE SUCH BIG PROMISES. YOU NEED TO KEEP THEM.
KHO
TŌTA-KUN...
OOHH
MY HEART HURTS... I'M LONELY...
HELP ME, TŌTA.
I DON'T WANT YOU GOING AWAY ANYMORE...
STAY WITH ME FOREVER...
N... NO...!
SHE WOULD NEVER...

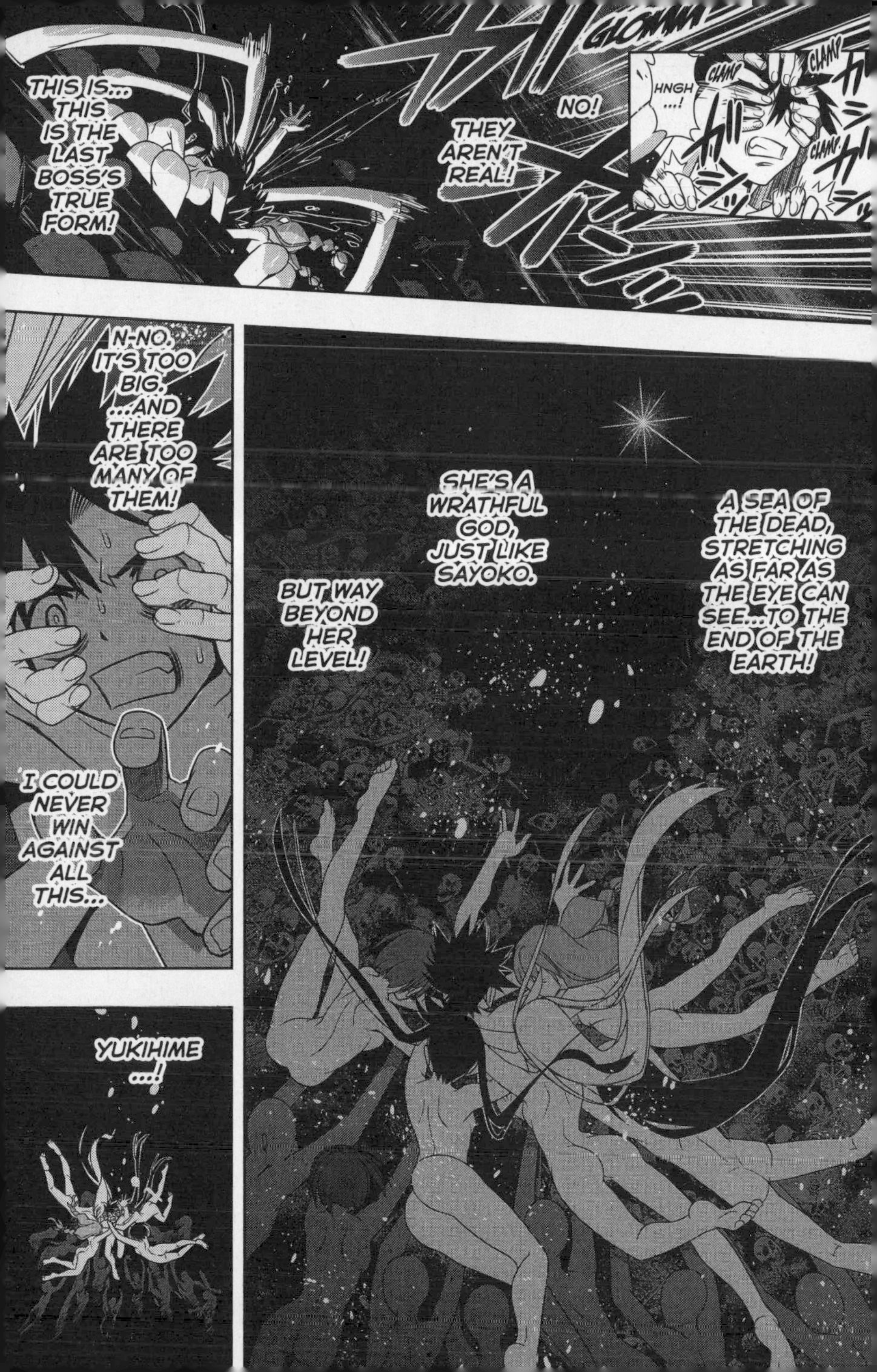
CLAMP
CLAMP
CLAMP
HNGH ...!
GLOMMM
NO!
THEY AREN'T REAL!
THIS IS... THIS IS THE LAST BOSS'S TRUE FORM!
A SEA OF THE DEAD, STRETCHING AS FAR AS THE EYE CAN SEE...TO THE END OF THE EARTH!
SHE'S A WRATHFUL GOD, JUST LIKE SAYOKO.
BUT WAY BEYOND HER LEVEL!
N-NO. IT'S TOO BIG. ...AND THERE ARE TOO MANY OF THEM!
I COULD NEVER WIN AGAINST ALL THIS...
YUKIHIME ...!

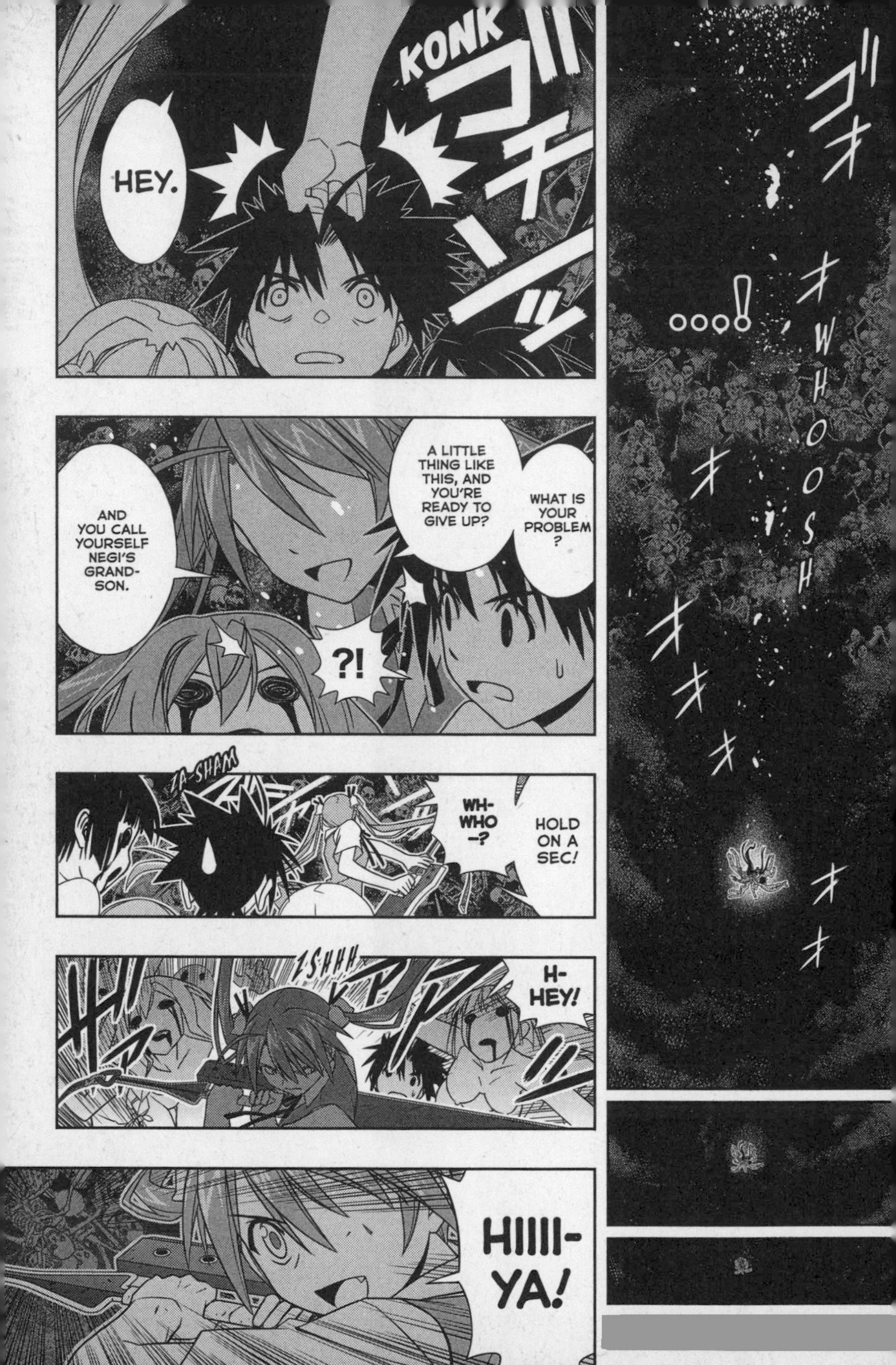
WHOOSH
...!
KONK
HEY.
WHAT IS YOUR PROBLEM?
A LITTLE THING LIKE THIS, AND YOU'RE READY TO GIVE UP?
AND YOU CALL YOURSELF NEGI'S GRAND-SON.
?!
HOLD ON A SEC!
WH-WHO-?
ZA-SHAM
H-HEY!
ZSHHH
HIIII-YA!

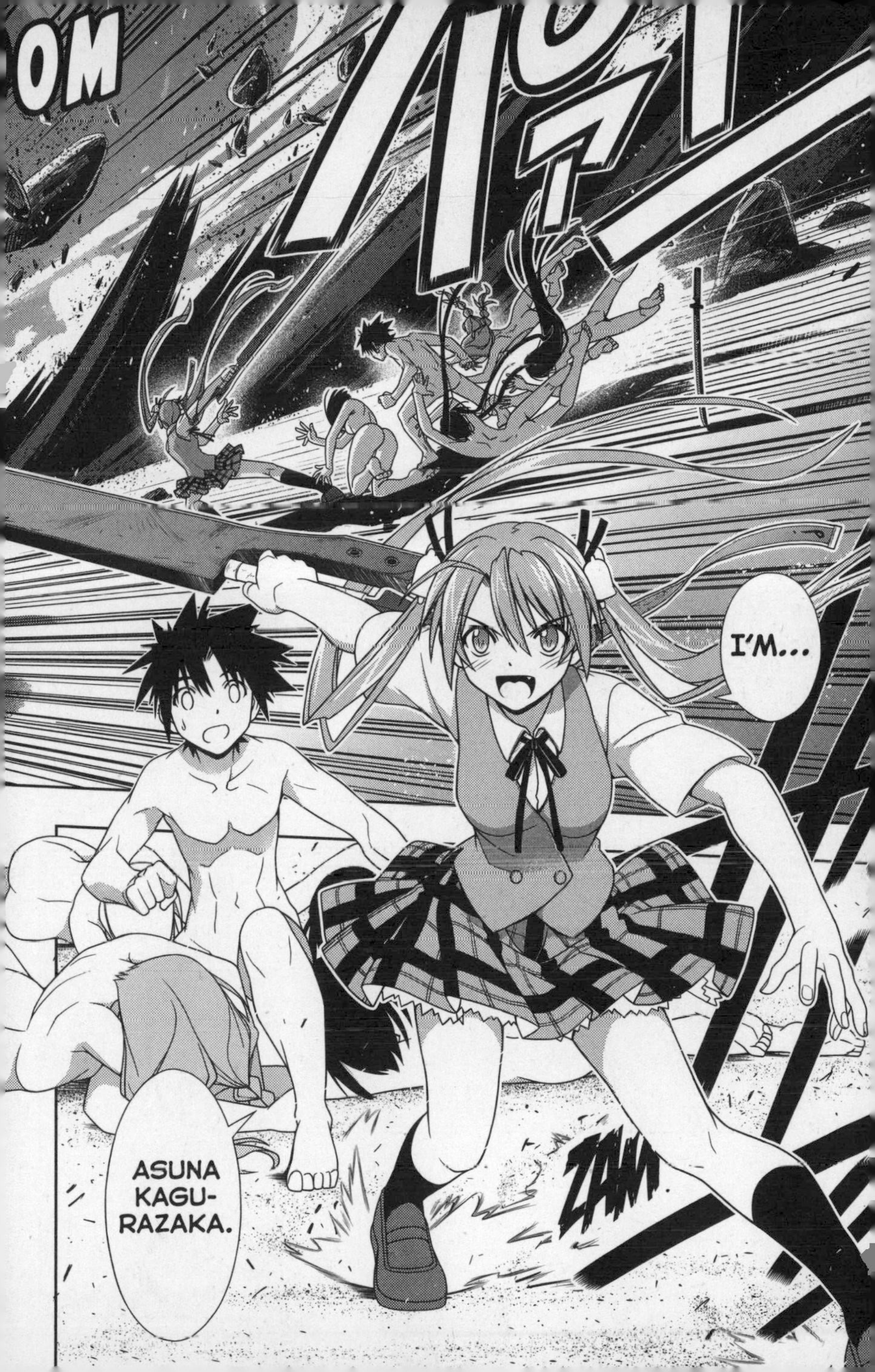
OM
I'M...
ZAM
ASUNA KAGU-RAZAKA.

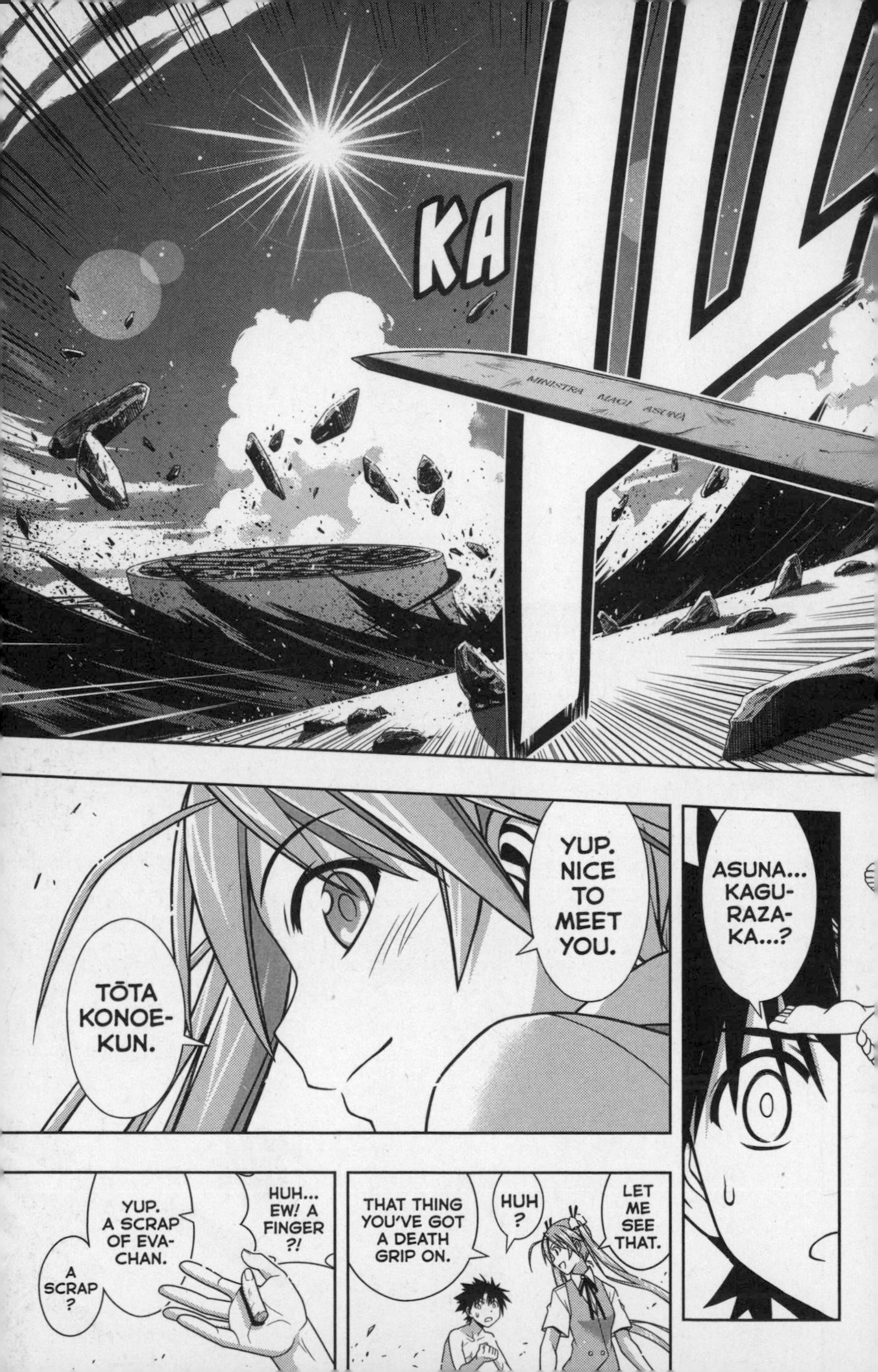
KA
MINISTRA MAGI ASUNA
ASUNA... KAGURAZAKA...?
YUP. NICE TO MEET YOU.
TŌTA KONOE-KUN.
LET ME SEE THAT.
HUH?
THAT THING YOU'VE GOT A DEATH GRIP ON.
HUH... EW! A FINGER?!
YUP. A SCRAP OF EVA-CHAN.
A SCRAP?

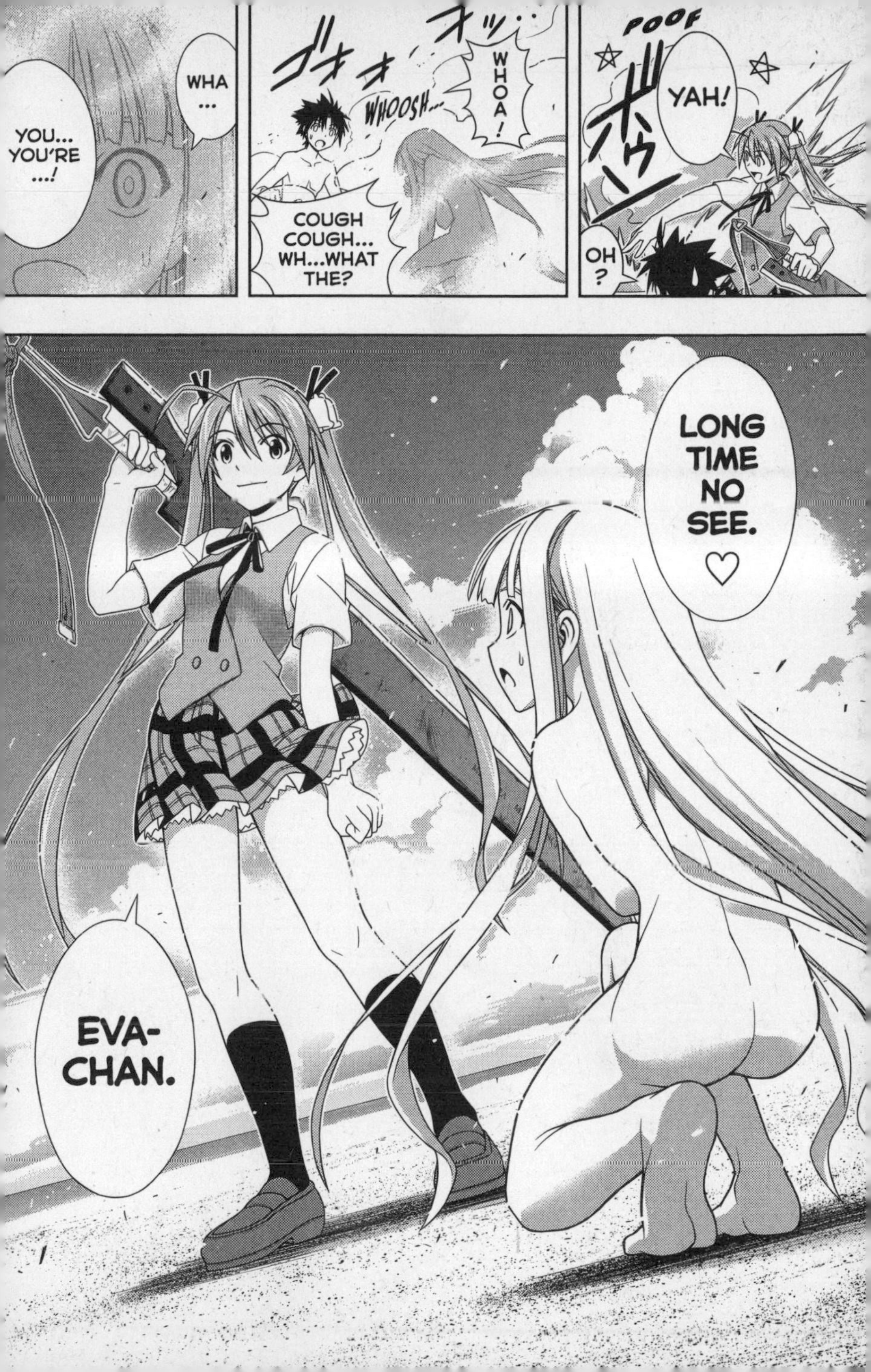
POOF
YAH!
OH?
WHOA!
WHOOSH...
COUGH COUGH... WH...WHAT THE?
WHA ...
YOU... YOU'RE ...!
LONG TIME NO SEE. ♡
EVA-CHAN.

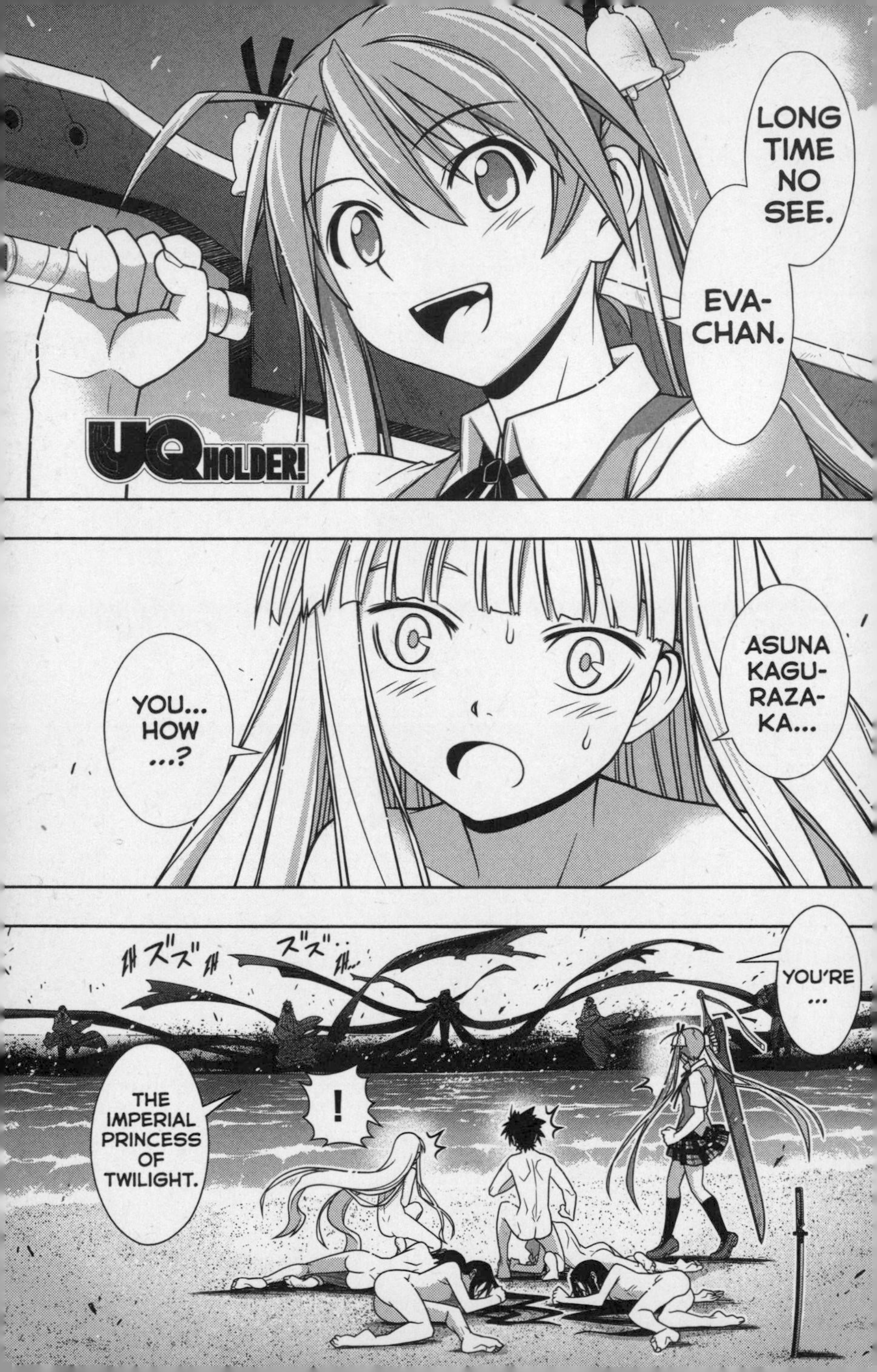
LONG TIME NO SEE.
EVA-CHAN.
UQ HOLDER!
ASUNA KAGU-RAZA-KA...
YOU... HOW ...?
ズズ.. ZH...
ズズ ZH
YOU'RE ...
!
THE IMPERIAL PRINCESS OF TWILIGHT.

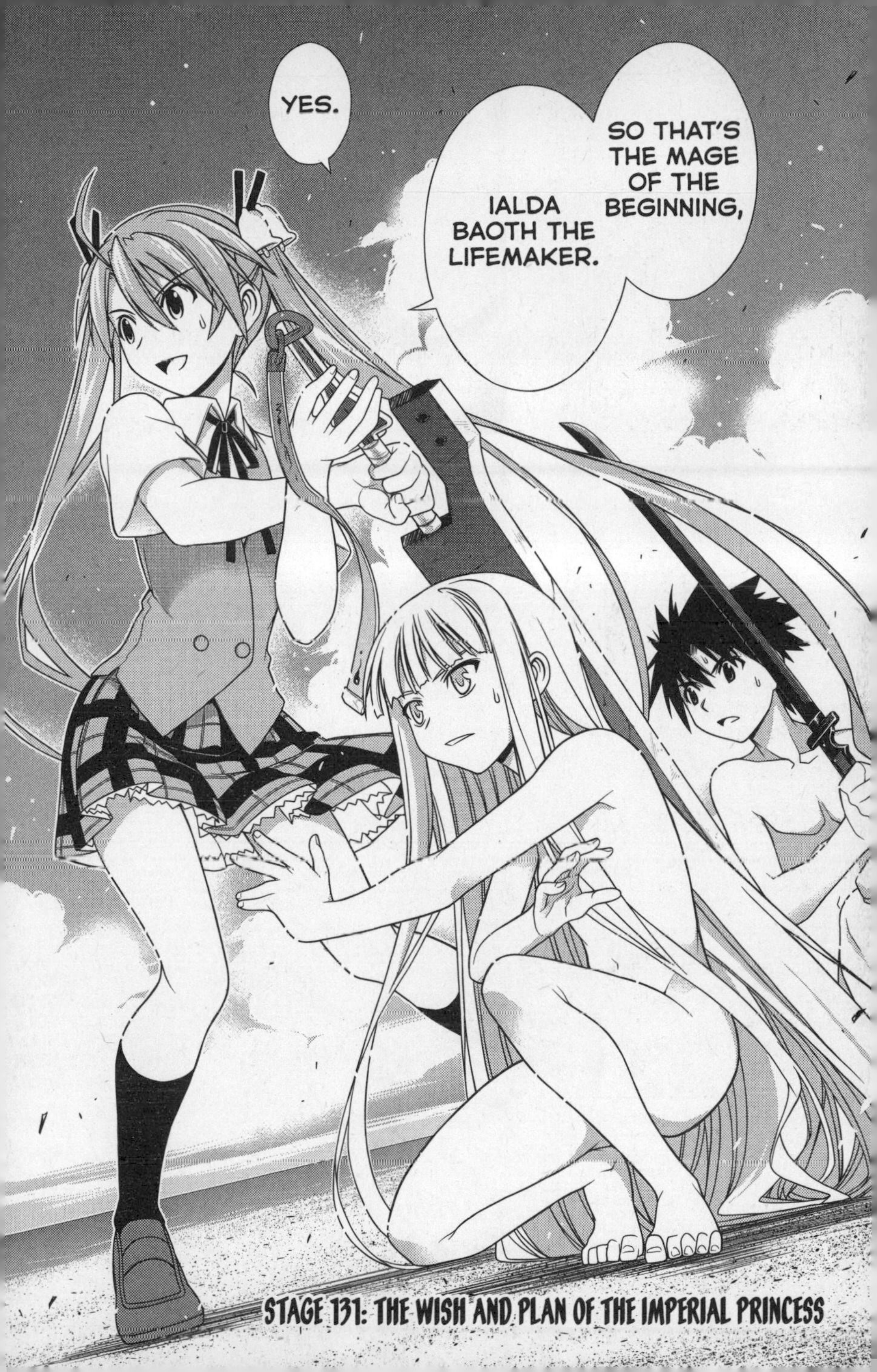
SO THAT'S THE MAGE OF THE BEGINNING, IALDA BAOTH THE LIFEMAKER.
YES.
STAGE 131: THE WISH AND PLAN OF THE IMPERIAL PRINCESS

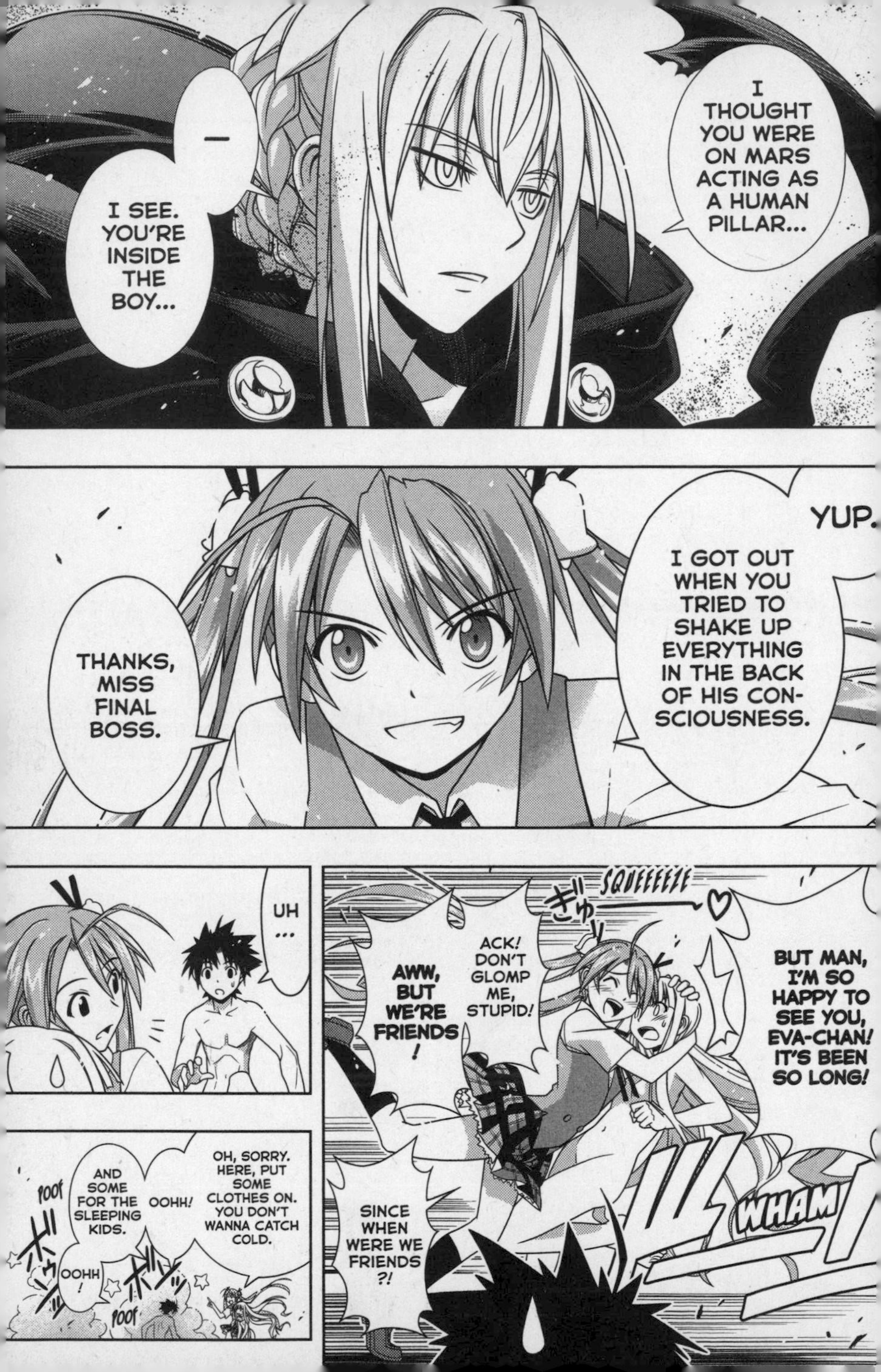
I THOUGHT YOU WERE ON MARS ACTING AS A HUMAN PILLAR...
—
I SEE. YOU'RE INSIDE THE BOY...
YUP.
I GOT OUT WHEN YOU TRIED TO SHAKE UP EVERYTHING IN THE BACK OF HIS CON-SCIOUSNESS.
THANKS, MISS FINAL BOSS.
SQUEEEEZE
BUT MAN, I'M SO HAPPY TO SEE YOU, EVA-CHAN! IT'S BEEN SO LONG!
ACK! DON'T GLOMP ME, STUPID!
AWW, BUT WE'RE FRIENDS!
WHAM
SINCE WHEN WERE WE FRIENDS?!
UH ...
OH, SORRY. HERE, PUT SOME CLOTHES ON. YOU DON'T WANNA CATCH COLD.
OOHH!
AND SOME FOR THE SLEEPING KIDS.
OOHH!
POOF
POOF

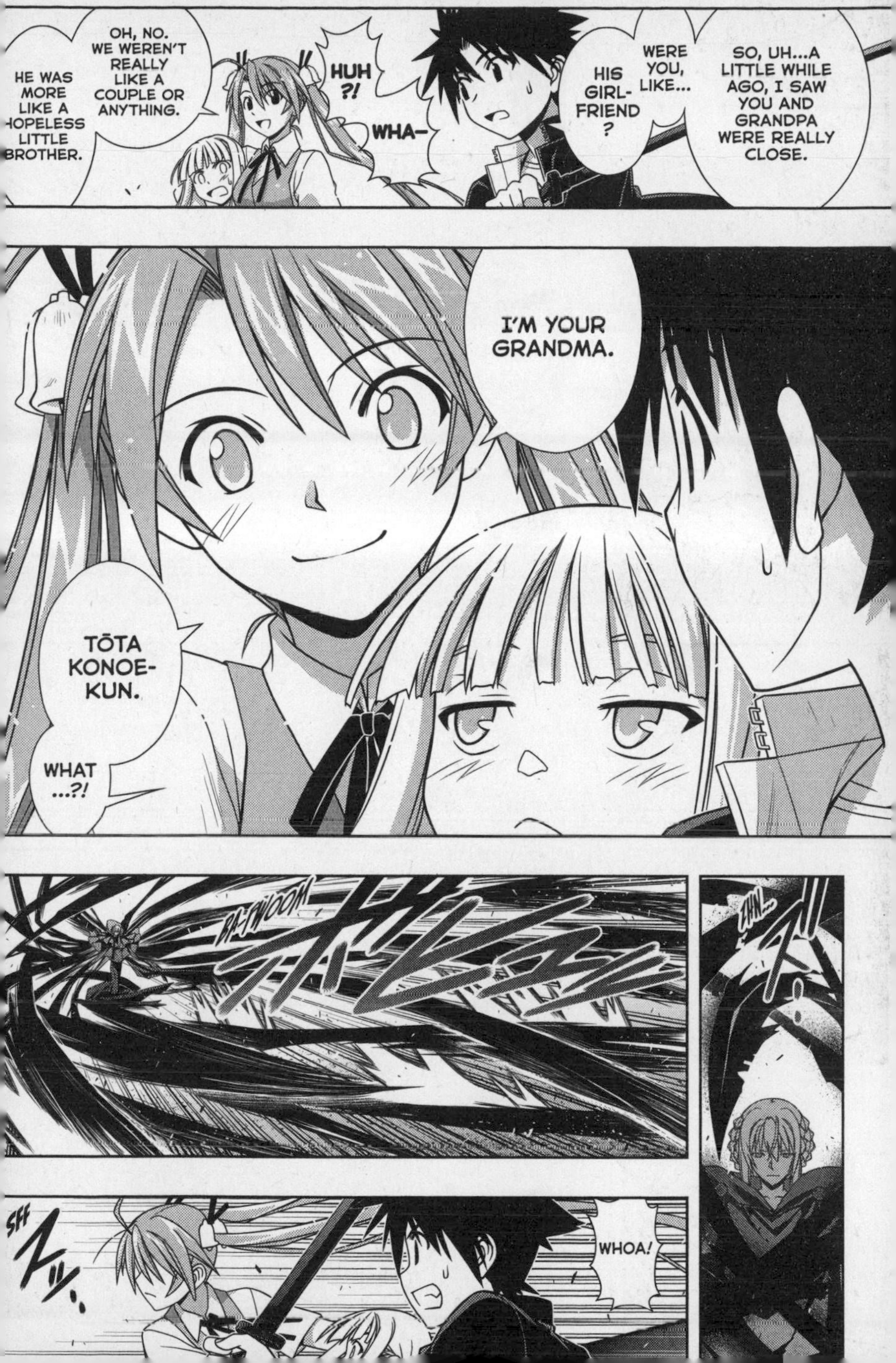
SO, UH...A LITTLE WHILE AGO, I SAW YOU AND GRANDPA WERE REALLY CLOSE.
WERE YOU, LIKE...
HIS GIRL-FRIEND?
WHA-
HUH?!
OH, NO. WE WEREN'T REALLY LIKE A COUPLE OR ANYTHING.
HE WAS MORE LIKE A HOPELESS LITTLE BROTHER.
I'M YOUR GRANDMA.
TŌTA KONOE-KUN.
WHAT...?!
ZHN...
BA-DWOOM
WHOA!
SFF

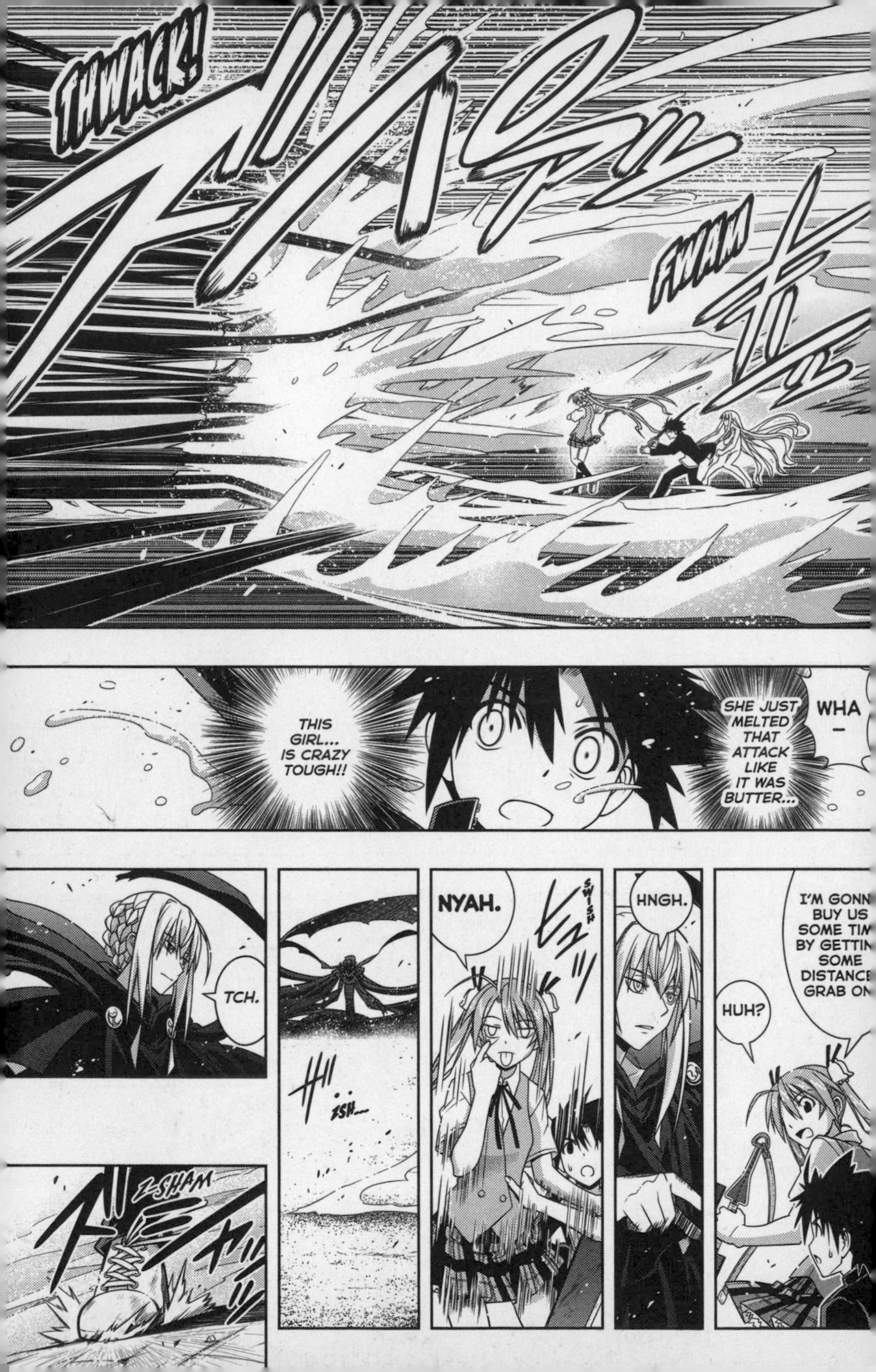
THWACK!
FWAM
WHA –
SHE JUST MELTED THAT ATTACK LIKE IT WAS BUTTER...
THIS GIRL... IS CRAZY TOUGH!!
I'M GONN BUY US SOME TIM BY GETTIN SOME DISTANCE GRAB ON
HUH?
HNGH.
NYAH.
SWISH
ZSH...
TCH.
Z-SHAM

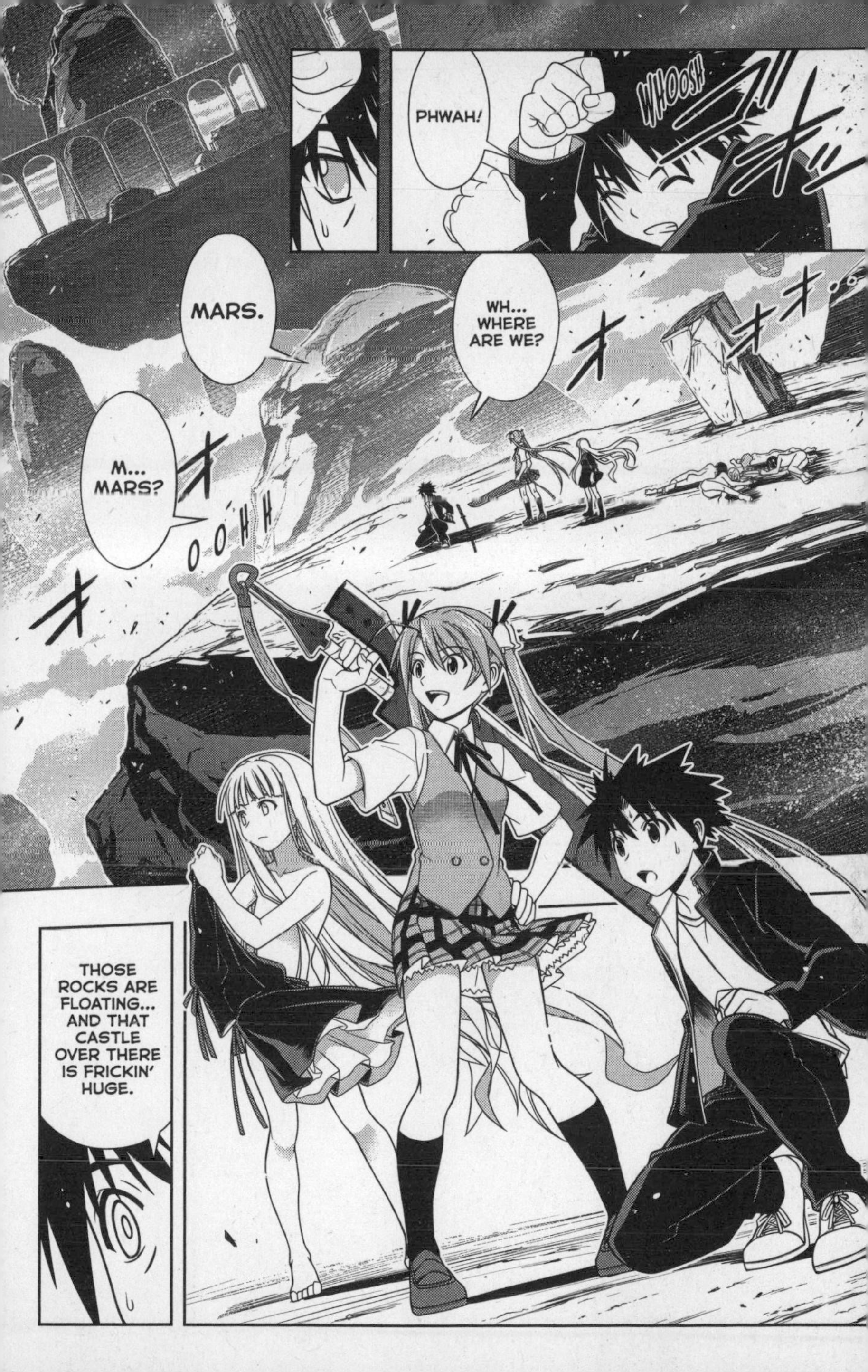
WHOOSH
PHWAH!
WH... WHERE ARE WE?
MARS.
M... MARS?
OOHH
THOSE ROCKS ARE FLOATING... AND THAT CASTLE OVER THERE IS FRICKIN' HUGE.

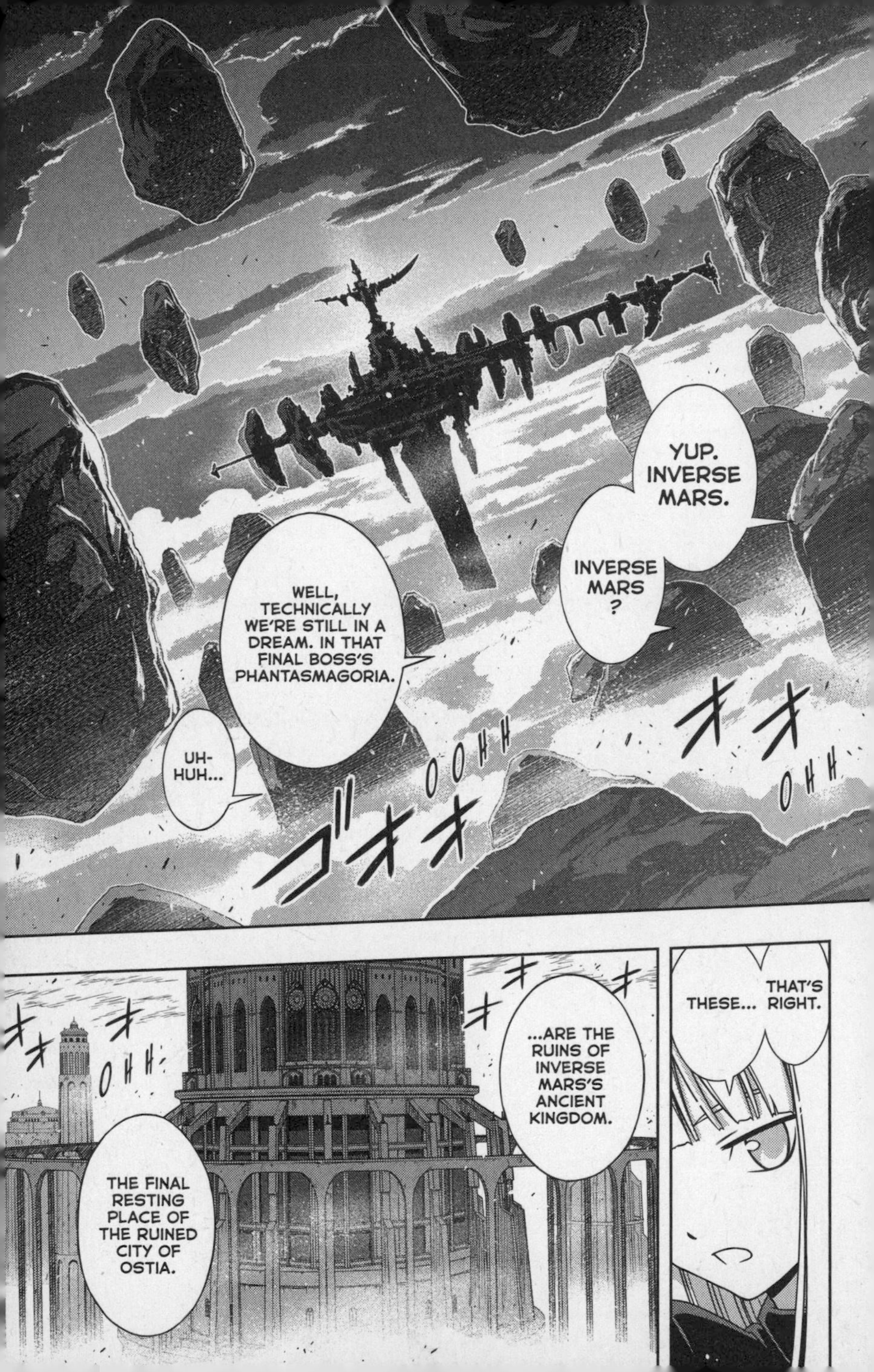
YUP. INVERSE MARS.
INVERSE MARS?
WELL, TECHNICALLY WE'RE STILL IN A DREAM. IN THAT FINAL BOSS'S PHANTASMAGORIA.
UH-HUH...
オオ
OHH
ゴオオ
OOHH
THAT'S RIGHT.
THESE...
...ARE THE RUINS OF INVERSE MARS'S ANCIENT KINGDOM.
オオオ
OHH
THE FINAL RESTING PLACE OF THE RUINED CITY OF OSTIA.

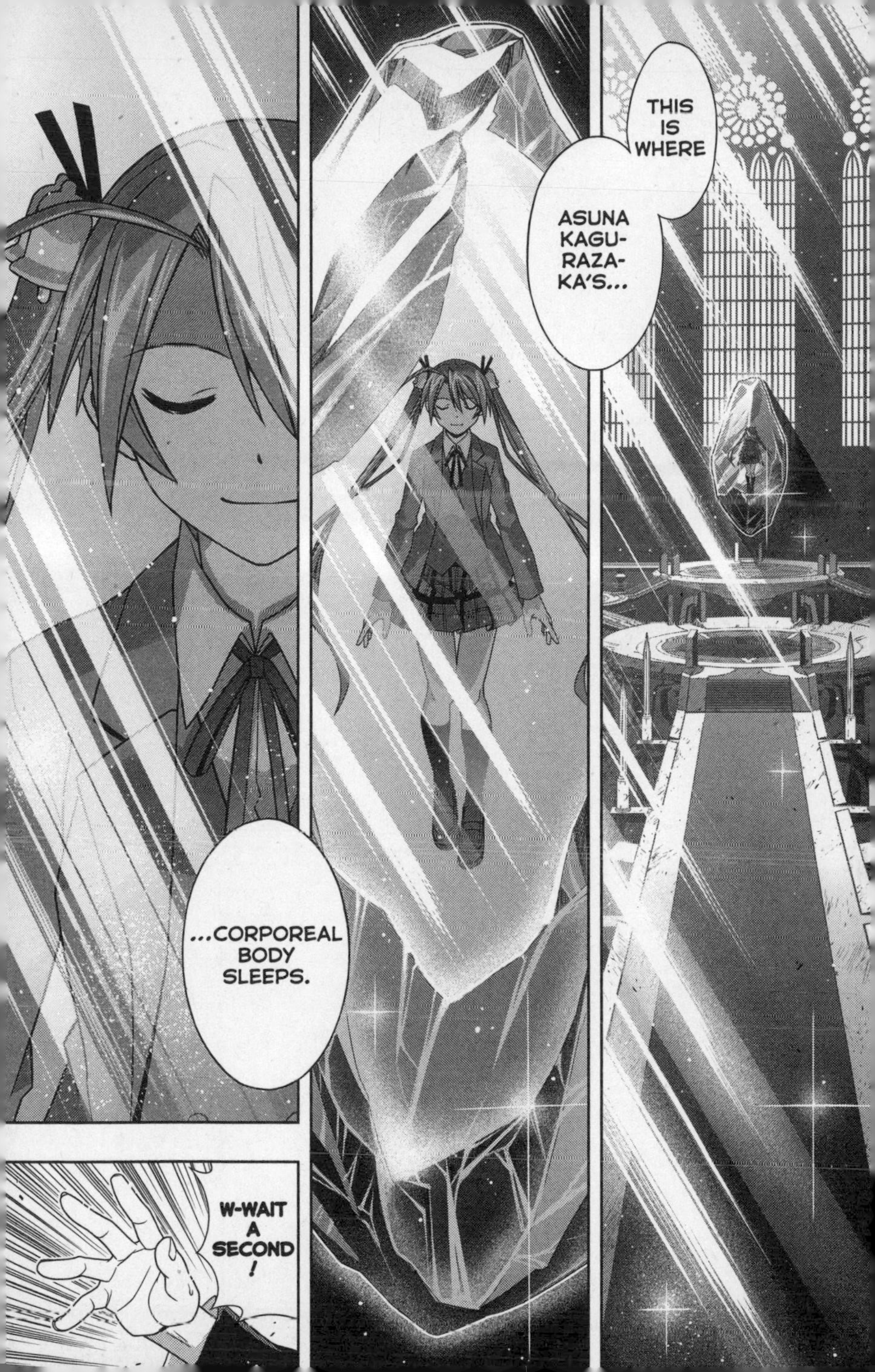
THIS IS WHERE
ASUNA KAGURAZAKA'S...
...CORPOREAL BODY SLEEPS.
W-WAIT A SECOND!

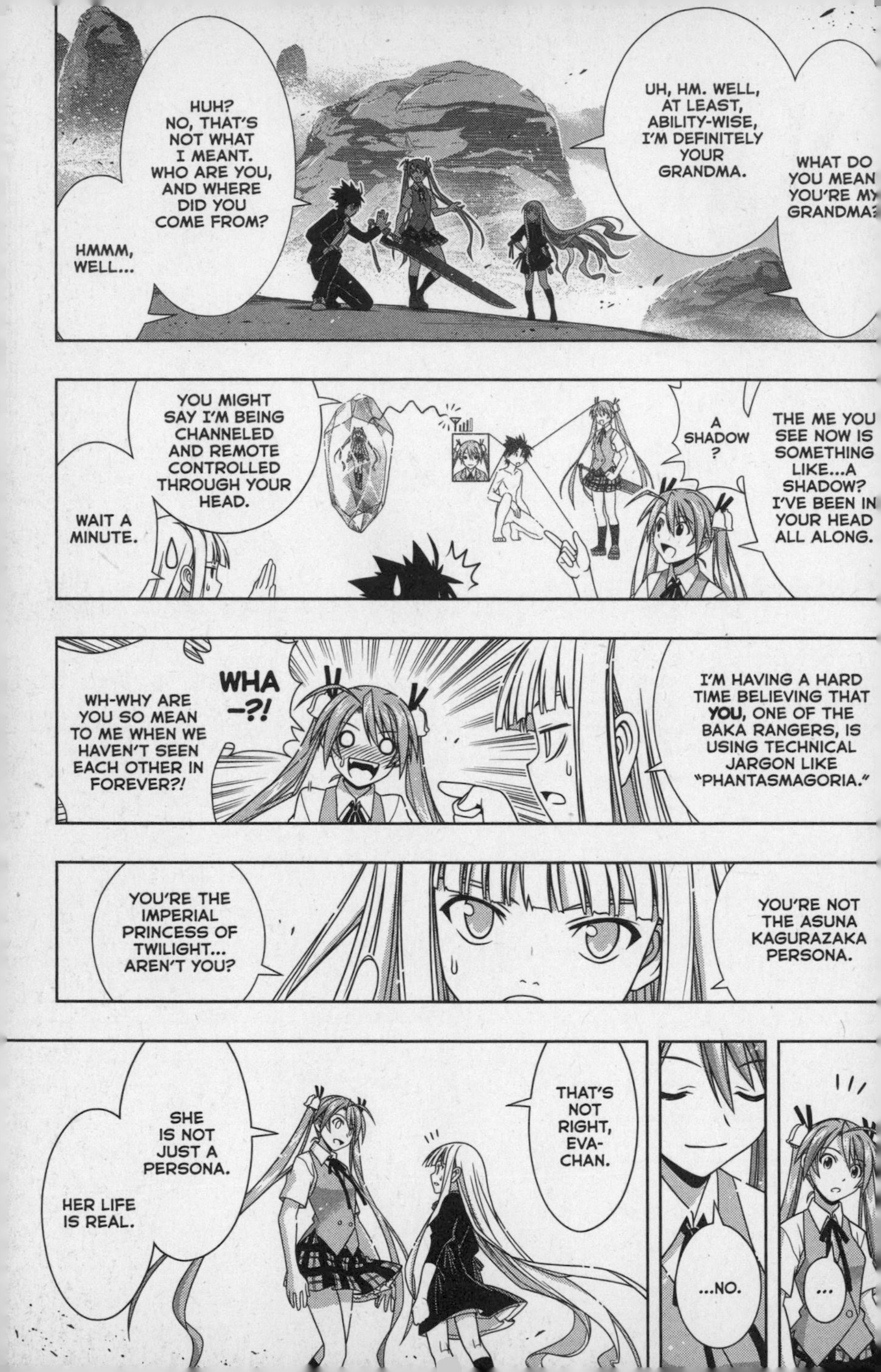
WHAT DO YOU MEAN YOU'RE MY GRANDMA?
UH, HM. WELL, AT LEAST, ABILITY-WISE, I'M DEFINITELY YOUR GRANDMA.
HUH? NO, THAT'S NOT WHAT I MEANT. WHO ARE YOU, AND WHERE DID YOU COME FROM?
HMMM, WELL...
THE ME YOU SEE NOW IS SOMETHING LIKE...A SHADOW? I'VE BEEN IN YOUR HEAD ALL ALONG.
A SHADOW?
YOU MIGHT SAY I'M BEING CHANNELED AND REMOTE CONTROLLED THROUGH YOUR HEAD.
WAIT A MINUTE.
I'M HAVING A HARD TIME BELIEVING THAT **YOU**, ONE OF THE BAKA RANGERS, IS USING TECHNICAL JARGON LIKE "PHANTASMAGORIA."
WHA—?!
WH-WHY ARE YOU SO MEAN TO ME WHEN WE HAVEN'T SEEN EACH OTHER IN FOREVER?!
YOU'RE NOT THE ASUNA KAGURAZAKA PERSONA.
YOU'RE THE IMPERIAL PRINCESS OF TWILIGHT... AREN'T YOU?
...
...NO.
THAT'S NOT RIGHT, EVA-CHAN.
SHE IS NOT JUST A PERSONA.
HER LIFE IS REAL.

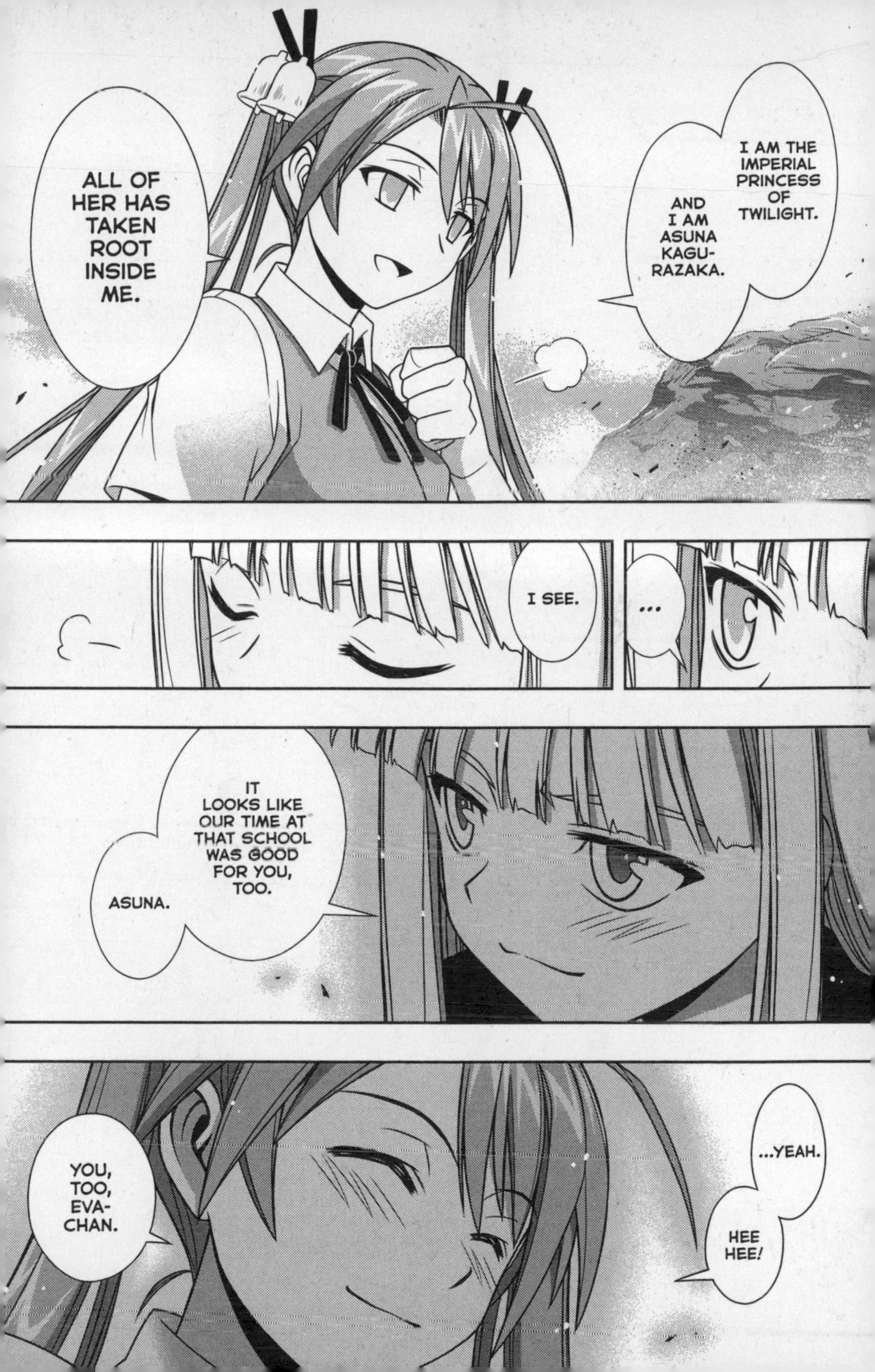
I AM THE IMPERIAL PRINCESS OF TWILIGHT.
AND I AM ASUNA KAGURAZAKA.
ALL OF HER HAS TAKEN ROOT INSIDE ME.
...
I SEE.
IT LOOKS LIKE OUR TIME AT THAT SCHOOL WAS GOOD FOR YOU, TOO.
ASUNA.
...YEAH.
HEE HEE!
YOU, TOO, EVA-CHAN.

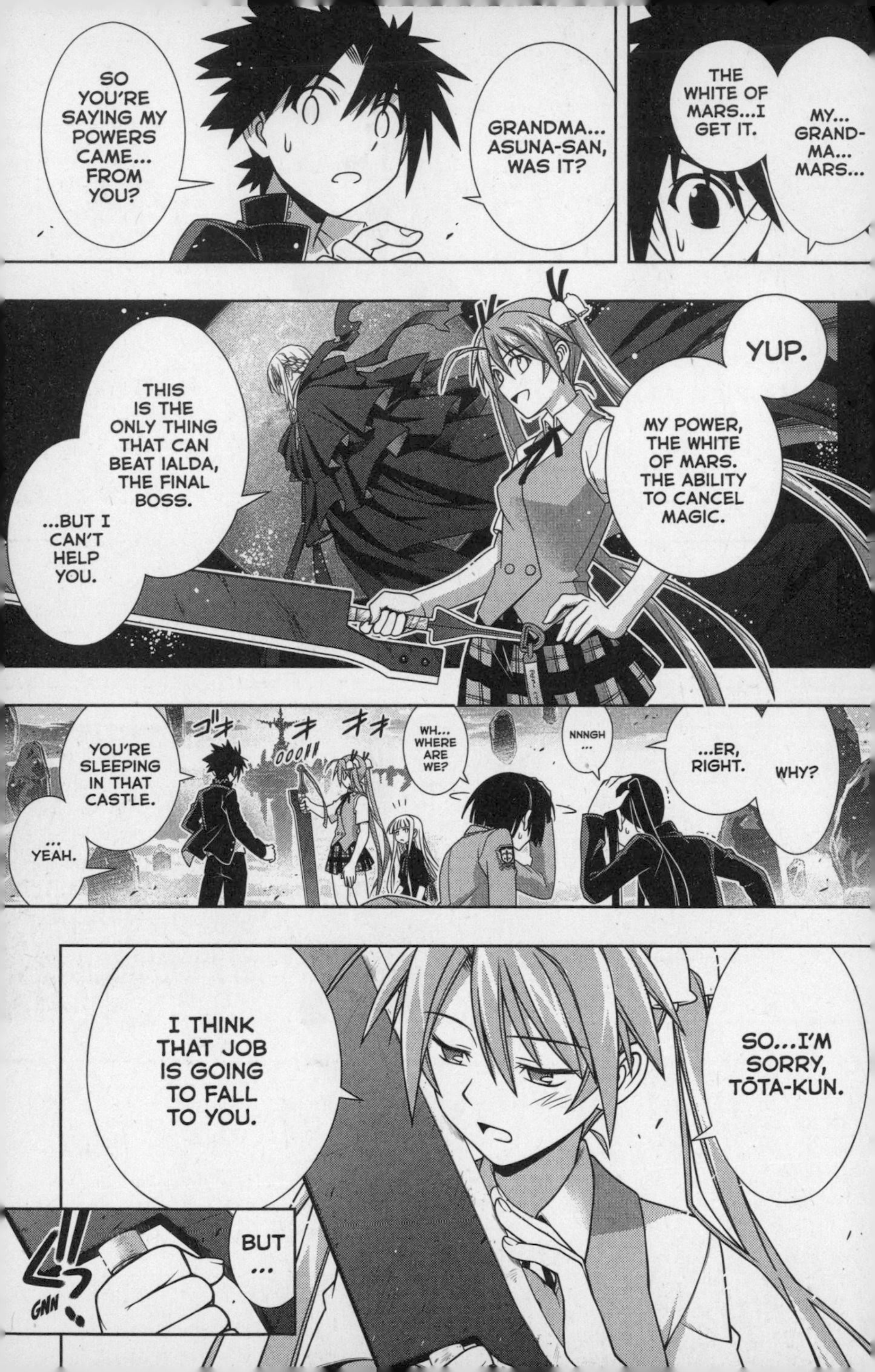

MY... GRAND-MA... MARS...
THE WHITE OF MARS...I GET IT.
GRANDMA... ASUNA-SAN, WAS IT?
SO YOU'RE SAYING MY POWERS CAME... FROM YOU?
YUP.
MY POWER, THE WHITE OF MARS. THE ABILITY TO CANCEL MAGIC.
THIS IS THE ONLY THING THAT CAN BEAT IALDA, THE FINAL BOSS.
...BUT I CAN'T HELP YOU.
WHY?
...ER, RIGHT.
NNNGH...
WH... WHERE ARE WE?
ゴオオオオ
OOO!!!
YOU'RE SLEEPING IN THAT CASTLE.
... YEAH.
SO...I'M SORRY, TŌTA-KUN.
I THINK THAT JOB IS GOING TO FALL TO YOU.
BUT...
ぐっ
GNN

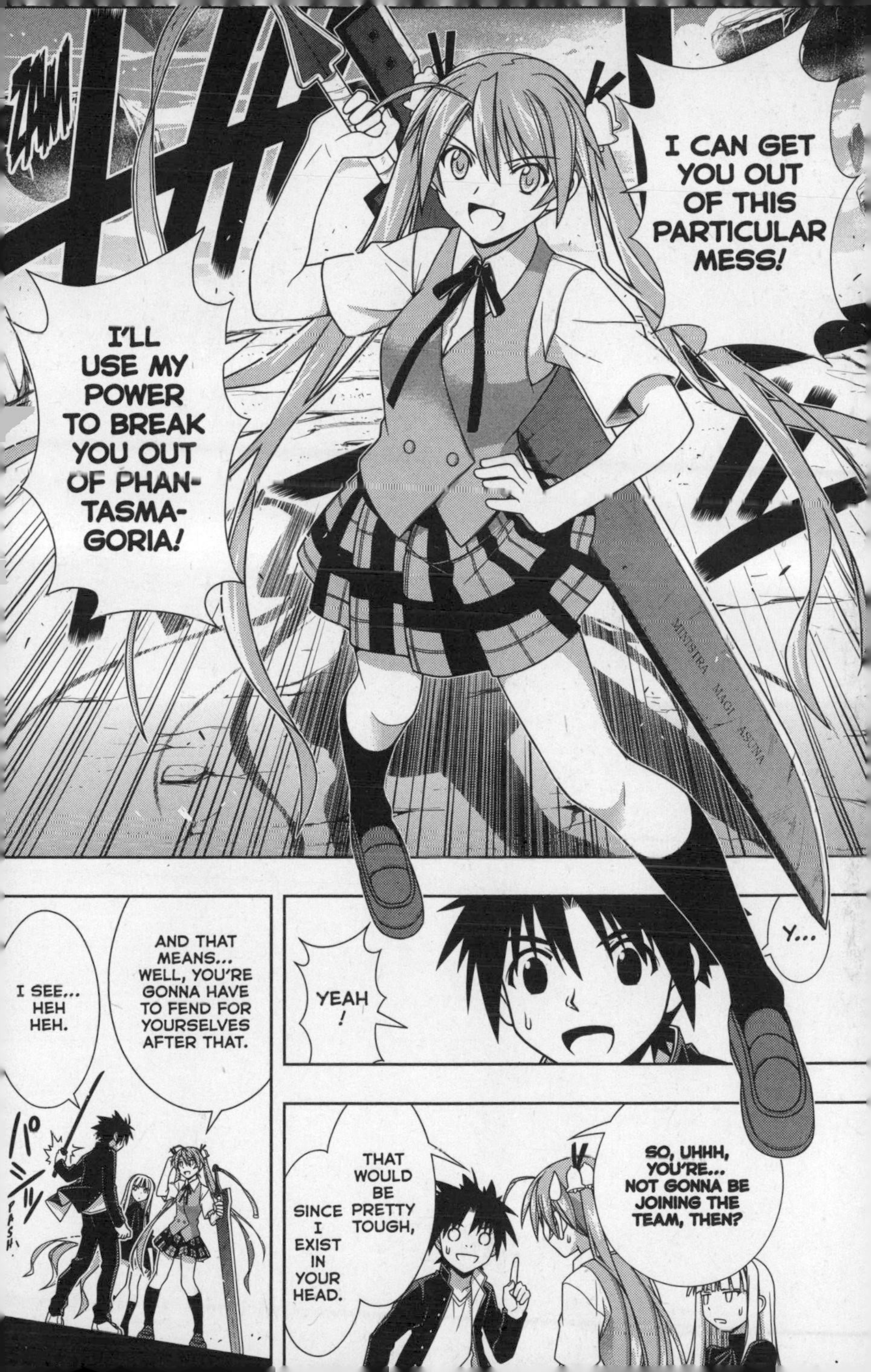
I CAN GET YOU OUT OF THIS PARTICULAR MESS!
I'LL USE MY POWER TO BREAK YOU OUT OF PHANTASMAGORIA!
Y...
YEAH!
SO, UHHH, YOU'RE... NOT GONNA BE JOINING THE TEAM, THEN?
THAT WOULD BE PRETTY TOUGH, SINCE I EXIST IN YOUR HEAD.
AND THAT MEANS... WELL, YOU'RE GONNA HAVE TO FEND FOR YOURSELVES AFTER THAT.
I SEE... HEH HEH.
PASH

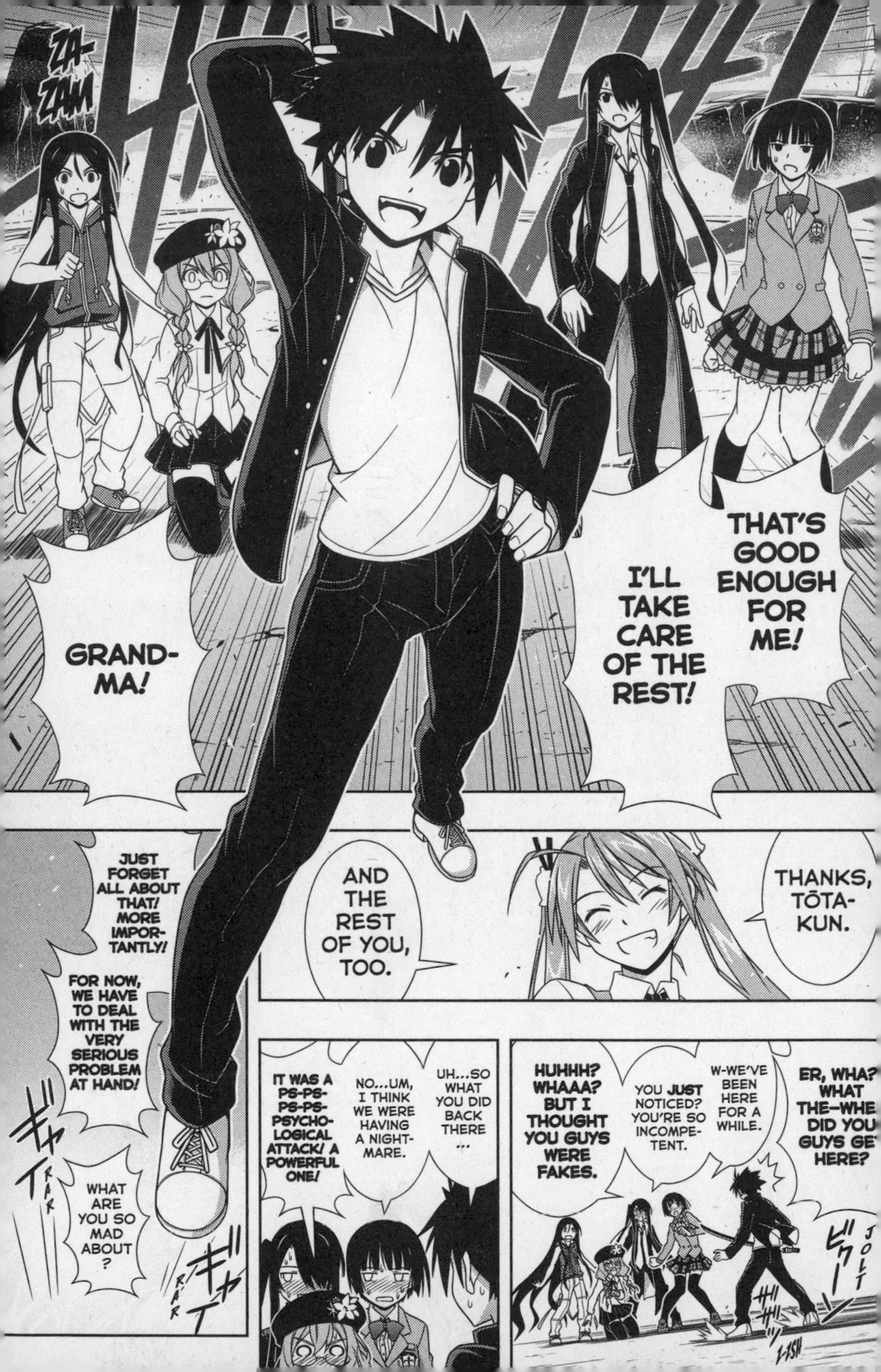
THAT'S GOOD ENOUGH FOR ME!
I'LL TAKE CARE OF THE REST!
ZA-ZAM
GRAND-MA!
THANKS, TŌTA-KUN.
AND THE REST OF YOU, TOO.
ER, WHA? WHAT THE—WHE DID YOU GUYS GE HERE?
JOLT
W-WE'VE BEEN HERE FOR A WHILE.
YOU JUST NOTICED? YOU'RE SO INCOMPETENT.
HUHHH? WHAAA? BUT I THOUGHT YOU GUYS WERE FAKES.
UH...SO WHAT YOU DID BACK THERE ...
NO...UM, I THINK WE WERE HAVING A NIGHTMARE.
IT WAS A PS-PS-PS-PS-PSYCHOLOGICAL ATTACK! A POWERFUL ONE!
JUST FORGET ALL ABOUT THAT! MORE IMPORTANTLY!
FOR NOW, WE HAVE TO DEAL WITH THE VERY SERIOUS PROBLEM AT HAND!
RAR
WHAT ARE YOU SO MAD ABOUT?
RAR

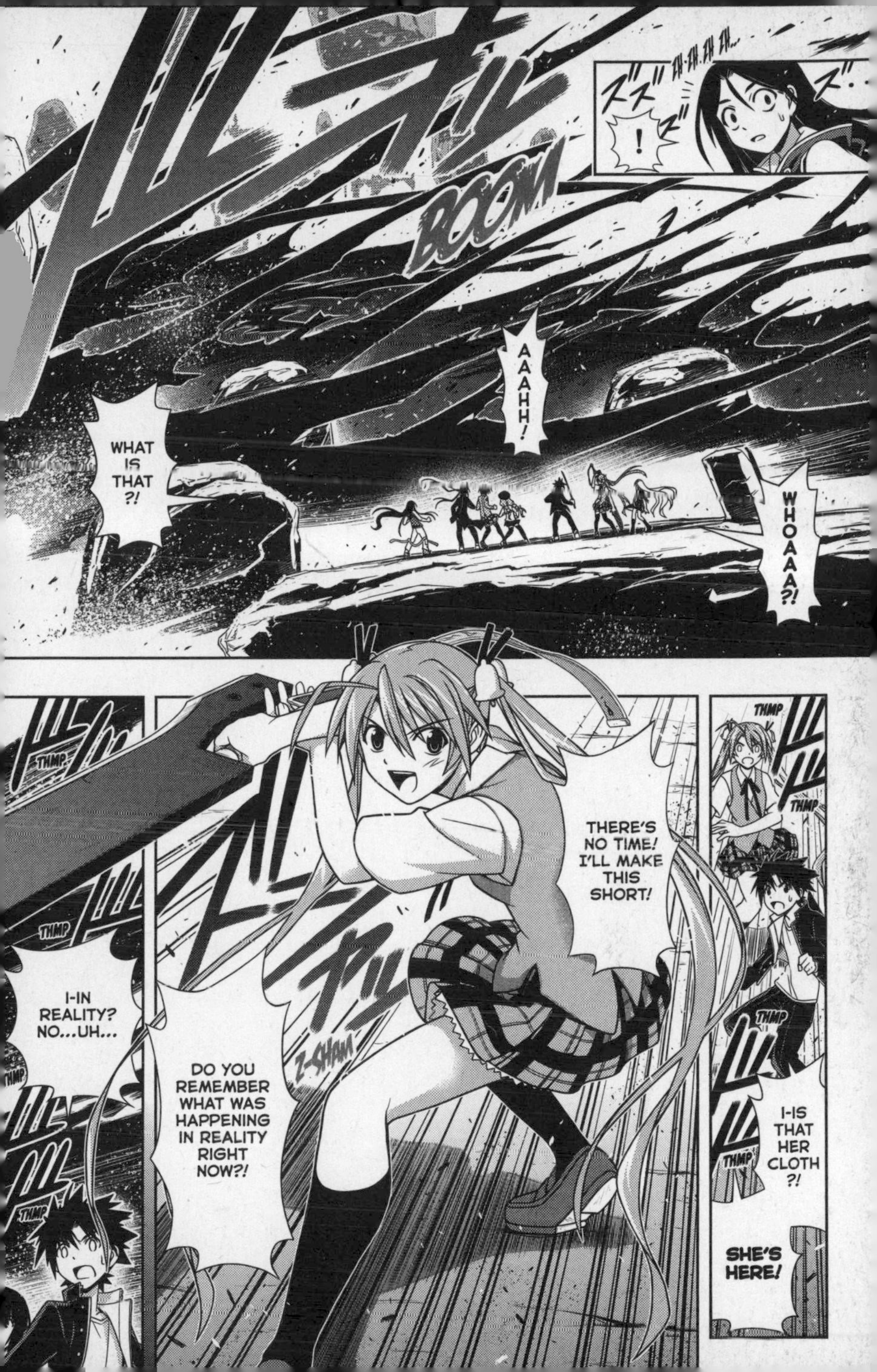
ZH ZH ZH ZH...
!
BOOM
WHOAAAA?!
AAAHH!
WHAT IS THAT?!
THMP
THMP
THMP
I-IS THAT HER CLOTH?!
THMP
SHE'S HERE!
THERE'S NO TIME! I'LL MAKE THIS SHORT!
Z-SHAM
DO YOU REMEMBER WHAT WAS HAPPENING IN REALITY RIGHT NOW?!
THMP
THMP
I-IN REALITY? NO...UH...
THMP
THMP

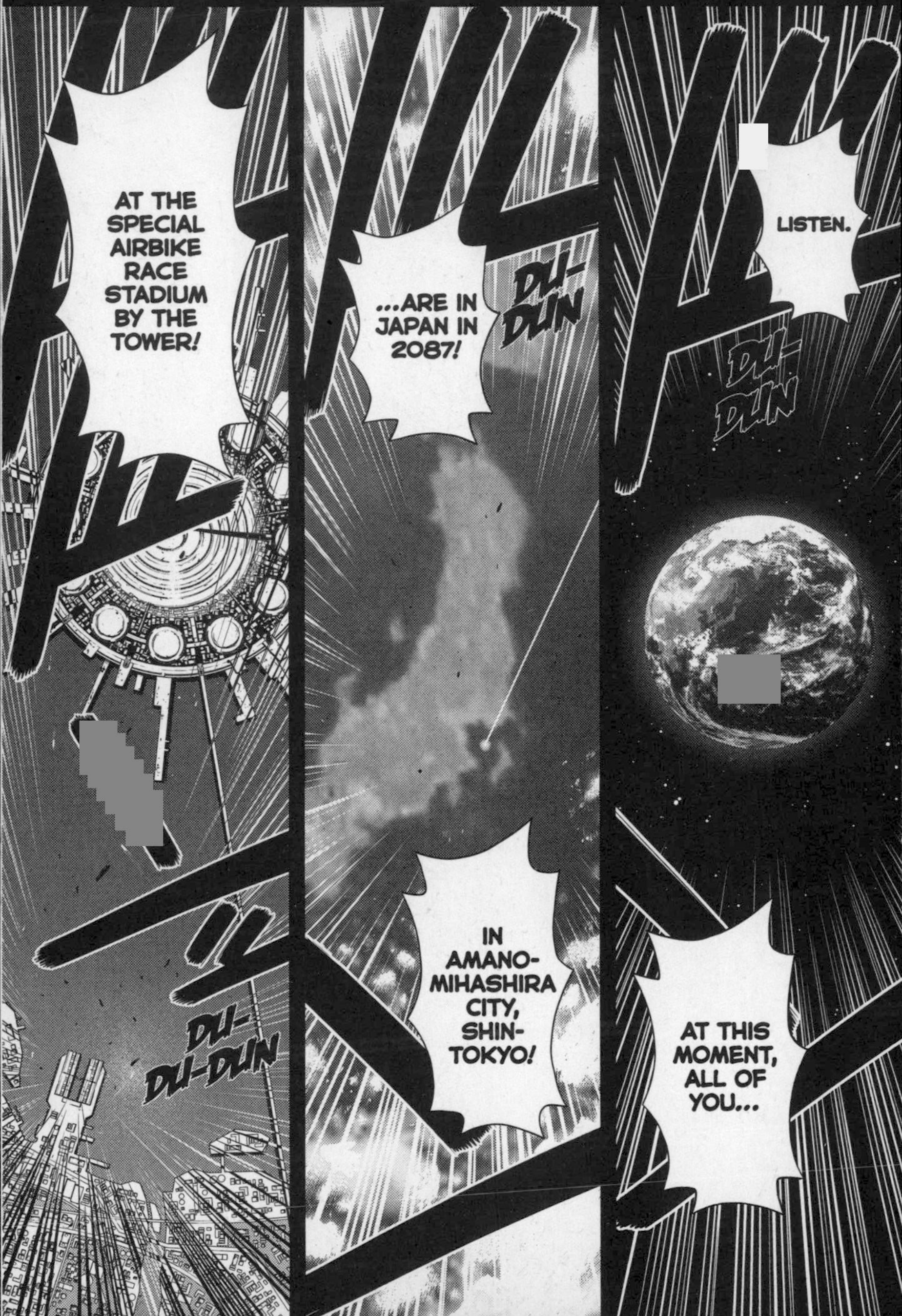
LISTEN.
DU-DUN
AT THIS MOMENT, ALL OF YOU...
...ARE IN JAPAN IN 2087!
DU-DUN
IN AMANO-MIHASHIRA CITY, SHIN-TOKYO!
AT THE SPECIAL AIRBIKE RACE STADIUM BY THE TOWER!
DU-DU-DUN

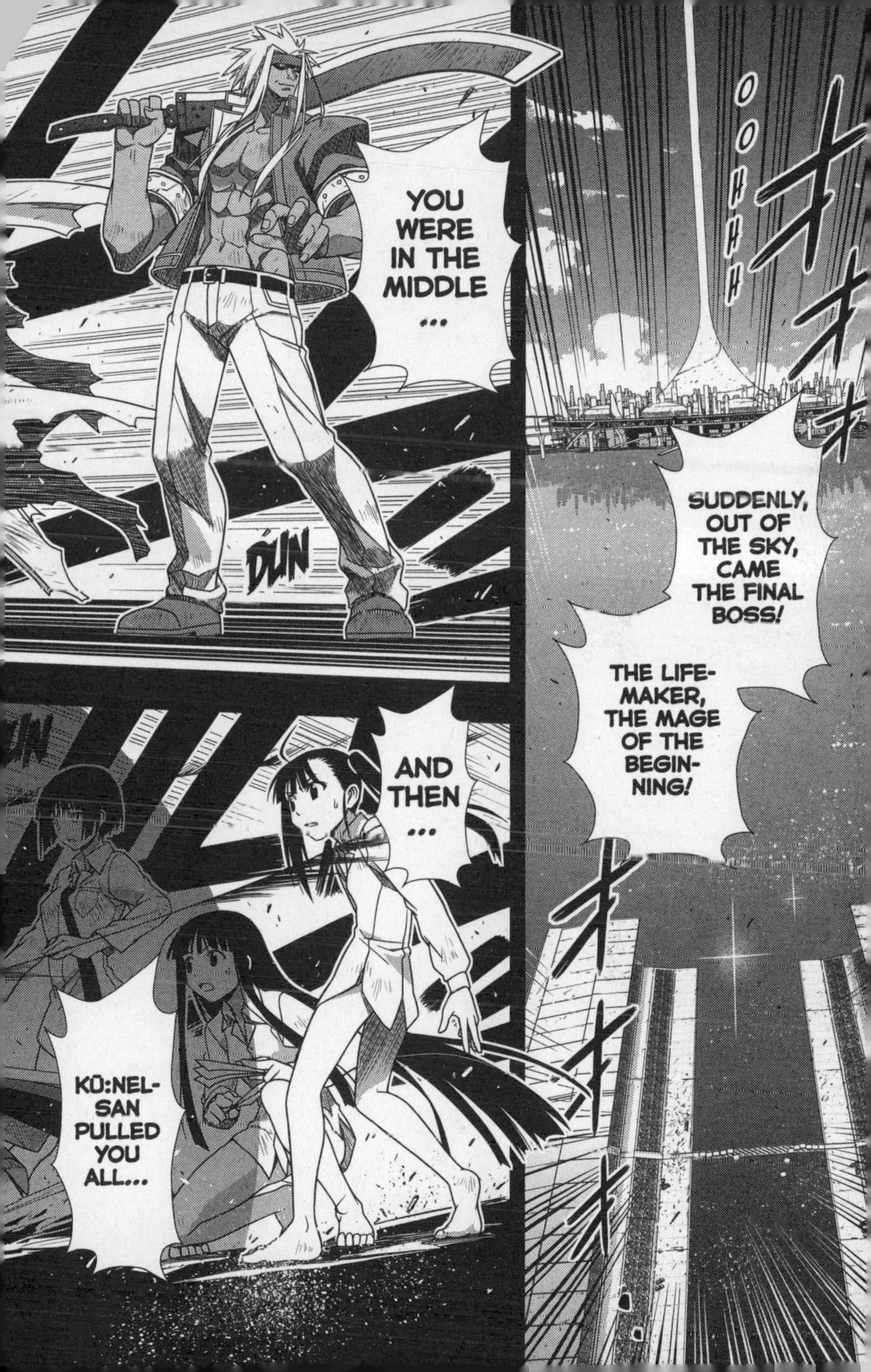
OOHHH
SUDDENLY, OUT OF THE SKY, CAME THE FINAL BOSS!
THE LIFE-MAKER, THE MAGE OF THE BEGINNING!
YOU WERE IN THE MIDDLE ...
DUN
AND THEN ...
KŪ:NEL-SAN PULLED YOU ALL...

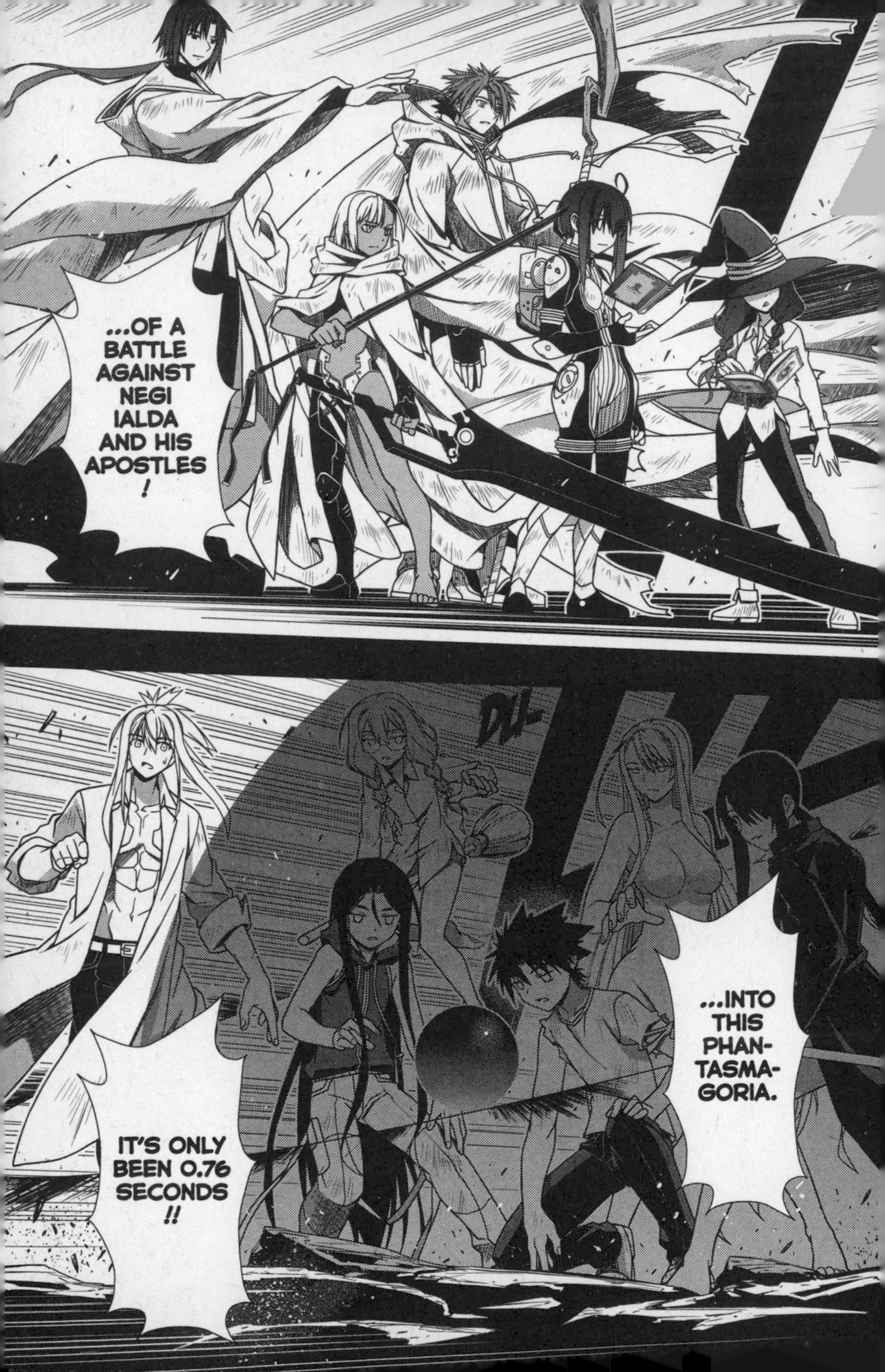
...OF A BATTLE AGAINST NEGI IALDA AND HIS APOSTLES!
...INTO THIS PHANTASMAGORIA.
IT'S ONLY BEEN 0.76 SECONDS!!

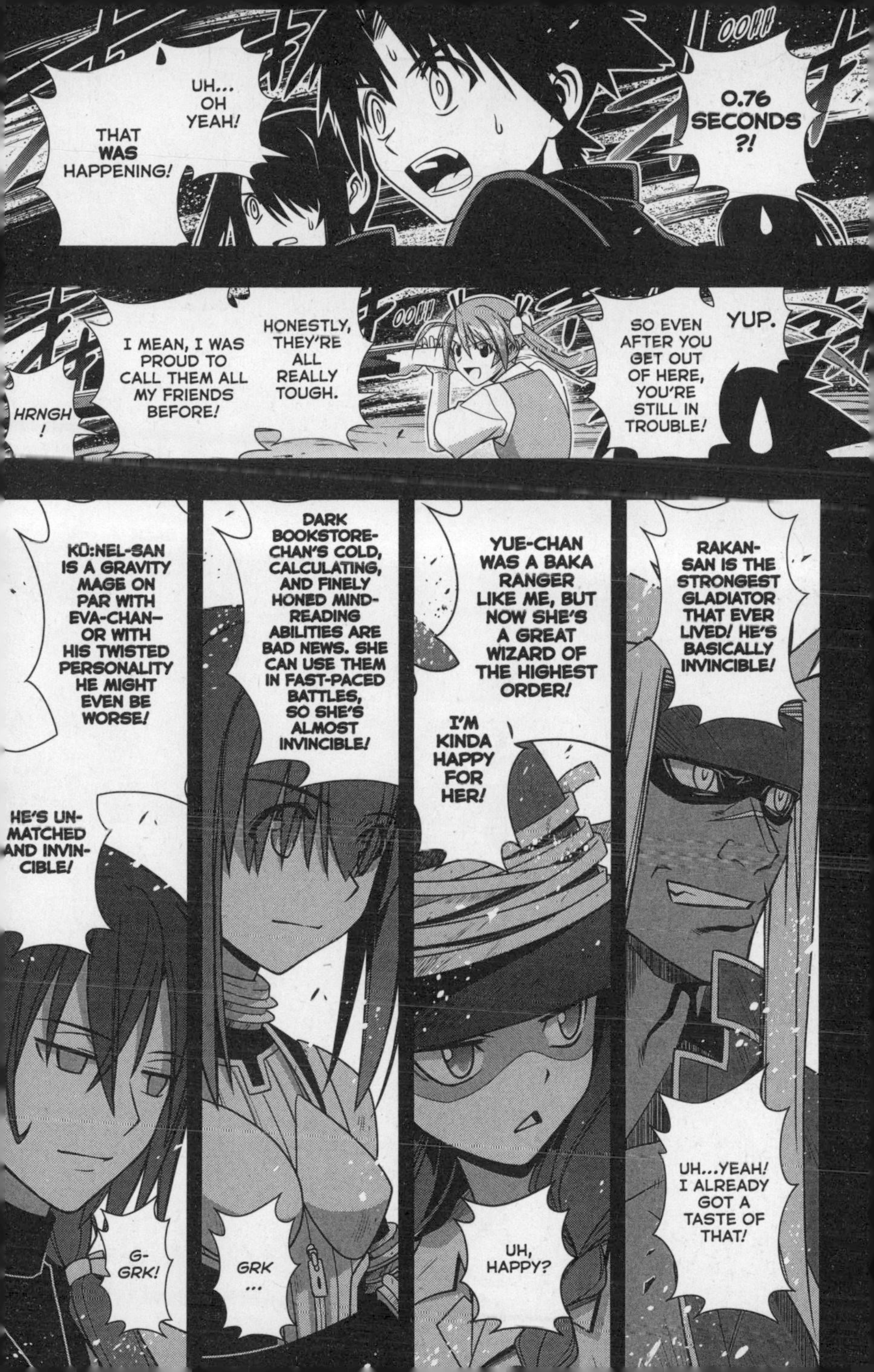
0.76 SECONDS ?!
UH... OH YEAH!
THAT WAS HAPPENING!
YUP.
SO EVEN AFTER YOU GET OUT OF HERE, YOU'RE STILL IN TROUBLE!
HONESTLY, THEY'RE ALL REALLY TOUGH.
I MEAN, I WAS PROUD TO CALL THEM ALL MY FRIENDS BEFORE!
HRNGH!
RAKAN-SAN IS THE STRONGEST GLADIATOR THAT EVER LIVED! HE'S BASICALLY INVINCIBLE!
UH...YEAH! I ALREADY GOT A TASTE OF THAT!
YUE-CHAN WAS A BAKA RANGER LIKE ME, BUT NOW SHE'S A GREAT WIZARD OF THE HIGHEST ORDER!
I'M KINDA HAPPY FOR HER!
UH, HAPPY?
DARK BOOKSTORE-CHAN'S COLD, CALCULATING, AND FINELY HONED MIND-READING ABILITIES ARE BAD NEWS. SHE CAN USE THEM IN FAST-PACED BATTLES, SO SHE'S ALMOST INVINCIBLE!
GRK...
KŪ:NEL-SAN IS A GRAVITY MAGE ON PAR WITH EVA-CHAN—OR WITH HIS TWISTED PERSONALITY HE MIGHT EVEN BE WORSE!
HE'S UN-MATCHED AND INVIN-CIBLE!
G-GRK!

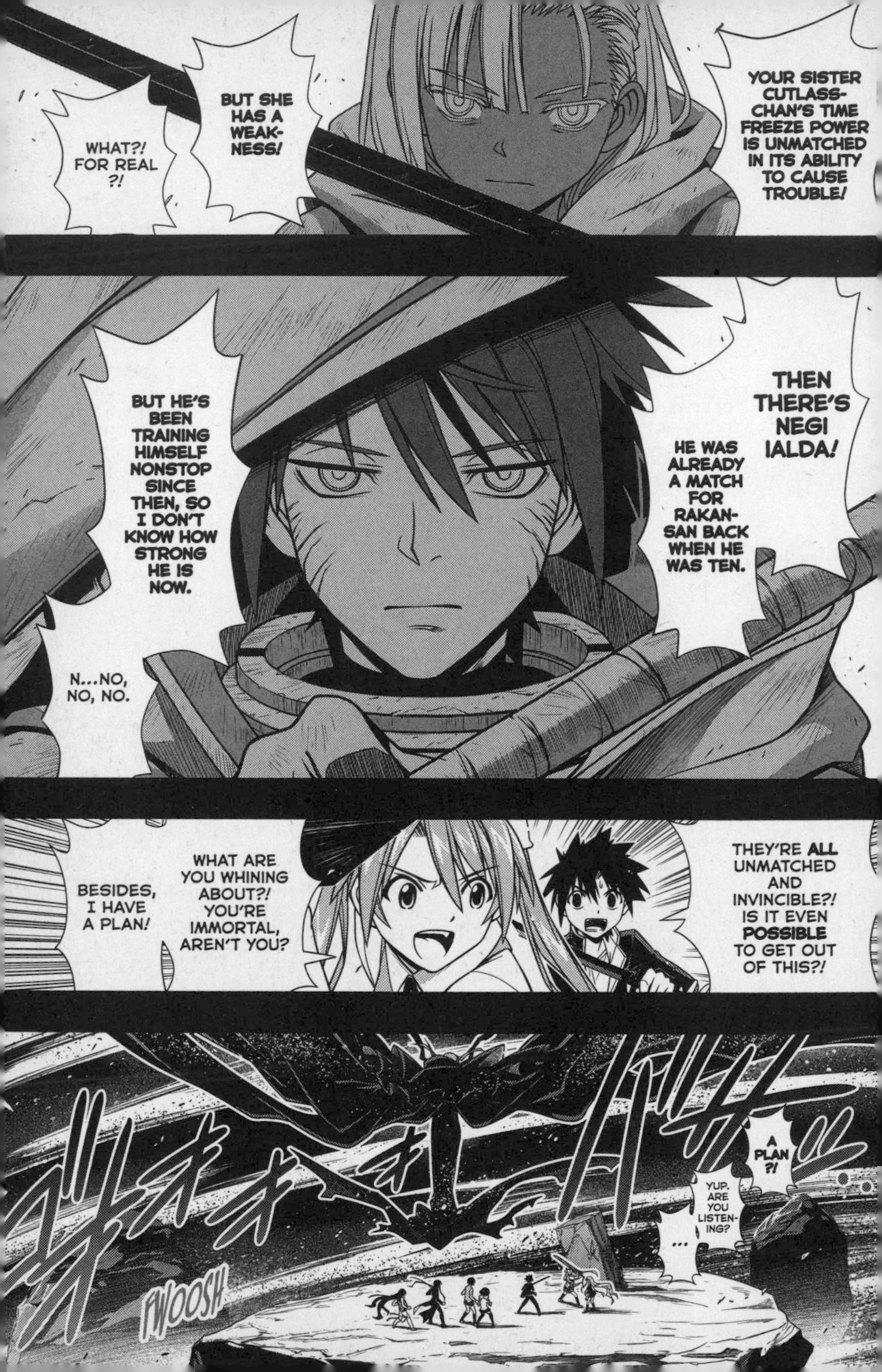
YOUR SISTER CUTLASS-CHAN'S TIME FREEZE POWER IS UNMATCHED IN ITS ABILITY TO CAUSE TROUBLE!
BUT SHE HAS A WEAK-NESS!
WHAT?! FOR REAL ?!
THEN THERE'S NEGI IALDA!
HE WAS ALREADY A MATCH FOR RAKAN-SAN BACK WHEN HE WAS TEN.
BUT HE'S BEEN TRAINING HIMSELF NONSTOP SINCE THEN, SO I DON'T KNOW HOW STRONG HE IS NOW.
N...NO, NO, NO.
THEY'RE ALL UNMATCHED AND INVINCIBLE?! IS IT EVEN POSSIBLE TO GET OUT OF THIS?!
WHAT ARE YOU WHINING ABOUT?! YOU'RE IMMORTAL, AREN'T YOU?
BESIDES, I HAVE A PLAN!
A PLAN ?!
YUP. ARE YOU LISTEN-ING?
...
FWOOSH

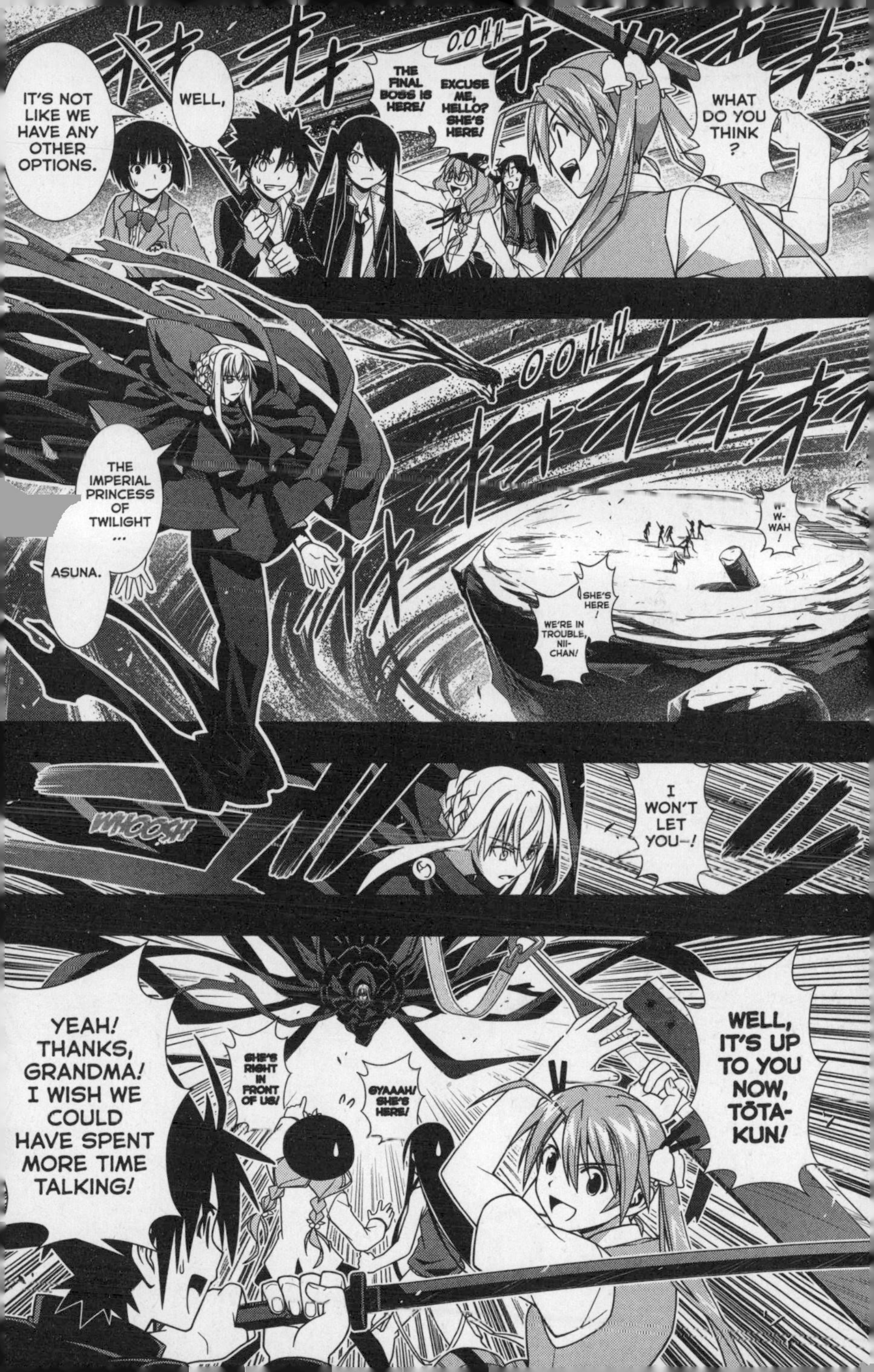
OOHH
WHAT DO YOU THINK?
EXCUSE ME, HELLO? SHE'S HERE!
THE FINAL BOSS IS HERE!
WELL,
IT'S NOT LIKE WE HAVE ANY OTHER OPTIONS.
W-W-WAH!
SHE'S HERE!
WE'RE IN TROUBLE, NII-CHAN!
OOHH
THE IMPERIAL PRINCESS OF TWILIGHT...
ASUNA.
I WON'T LET YOU—!
WHOOSH
WELL, IT'S UP TO YOU NOW, TŌTA-KUN!
GYAAAH! SHE'S HERE!
SHE'S RIGHT IN FRONT OF US!
YEAH! THANKS, GRANDMA! I WISH WE COULD HAVE SPENT MORE TIME TALKING!

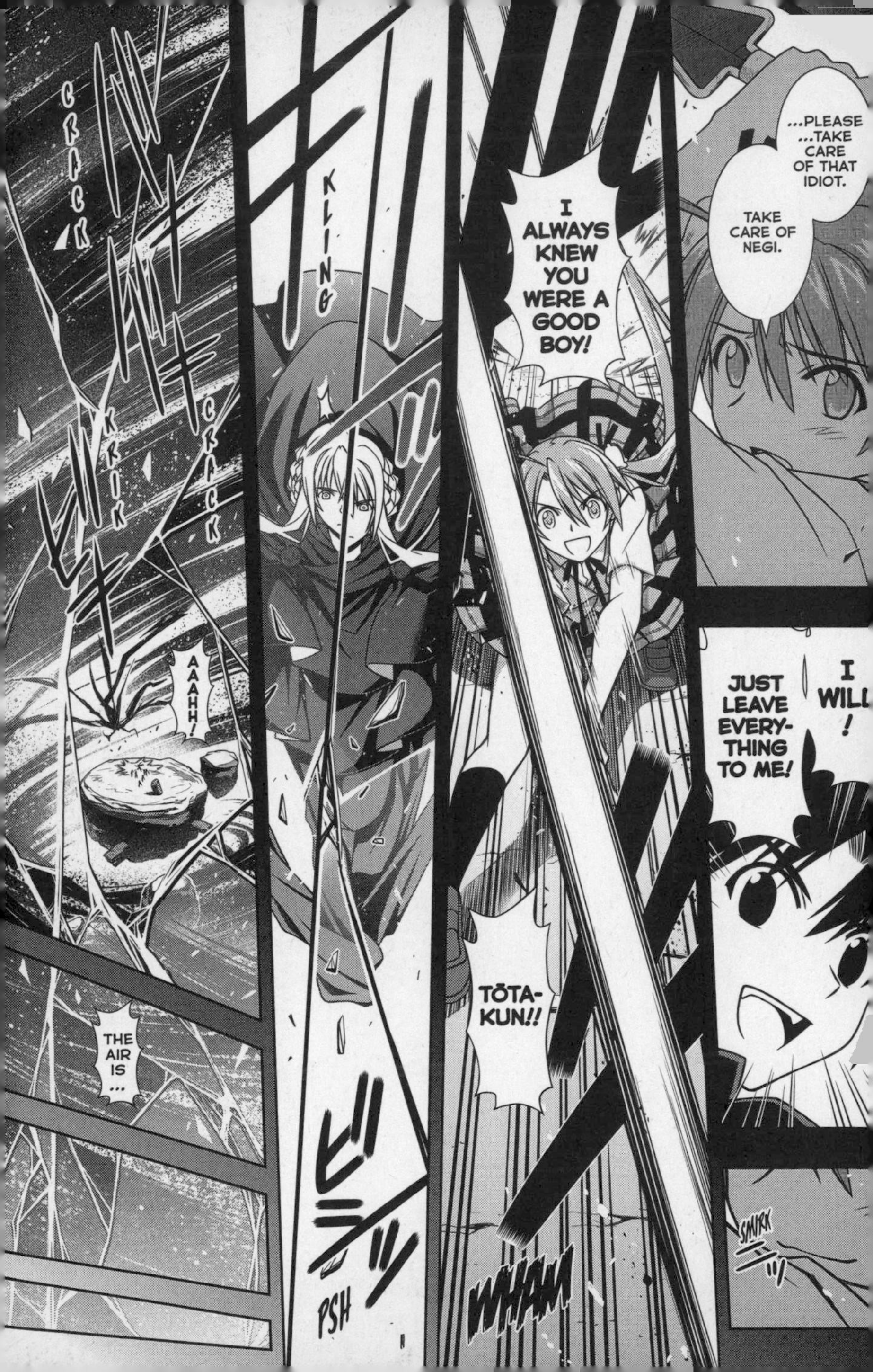
...PLEASE ...TAKE CARE OF THAT IDIOT.
TAKE CARE OF NEGI.
I WILL!
JUST LEAVE EVERY-THING TO ME!
SMIRK
I ALWAYS KNEW YOU WERE A GOOD BOY!
TŌTA-KUN!!
WHAM
KLING
PSH
CRACK
CRACK
KRIK
AAAHH!
THE AIR IS ...

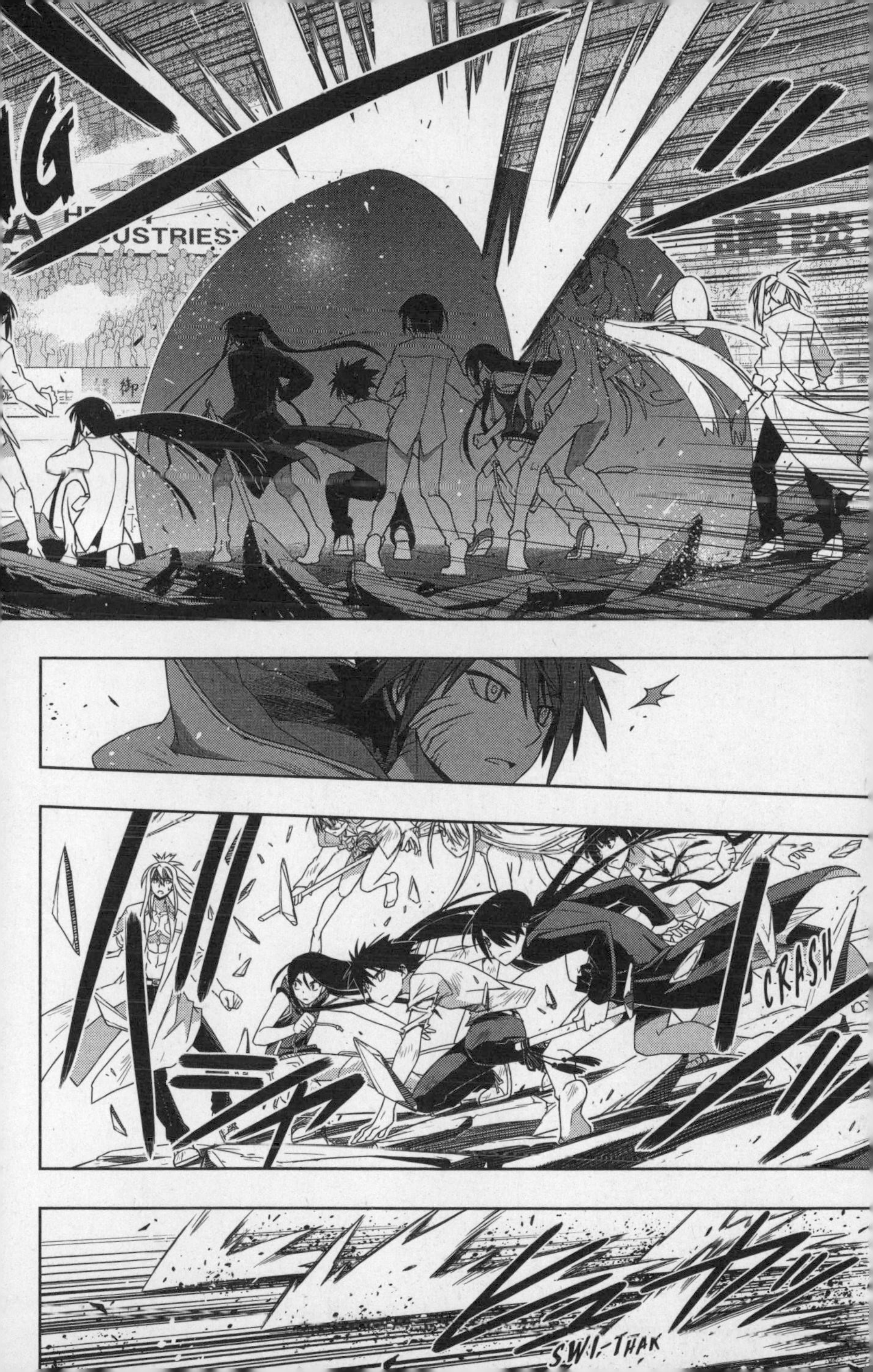

講談
CRASH
SWI-THAK

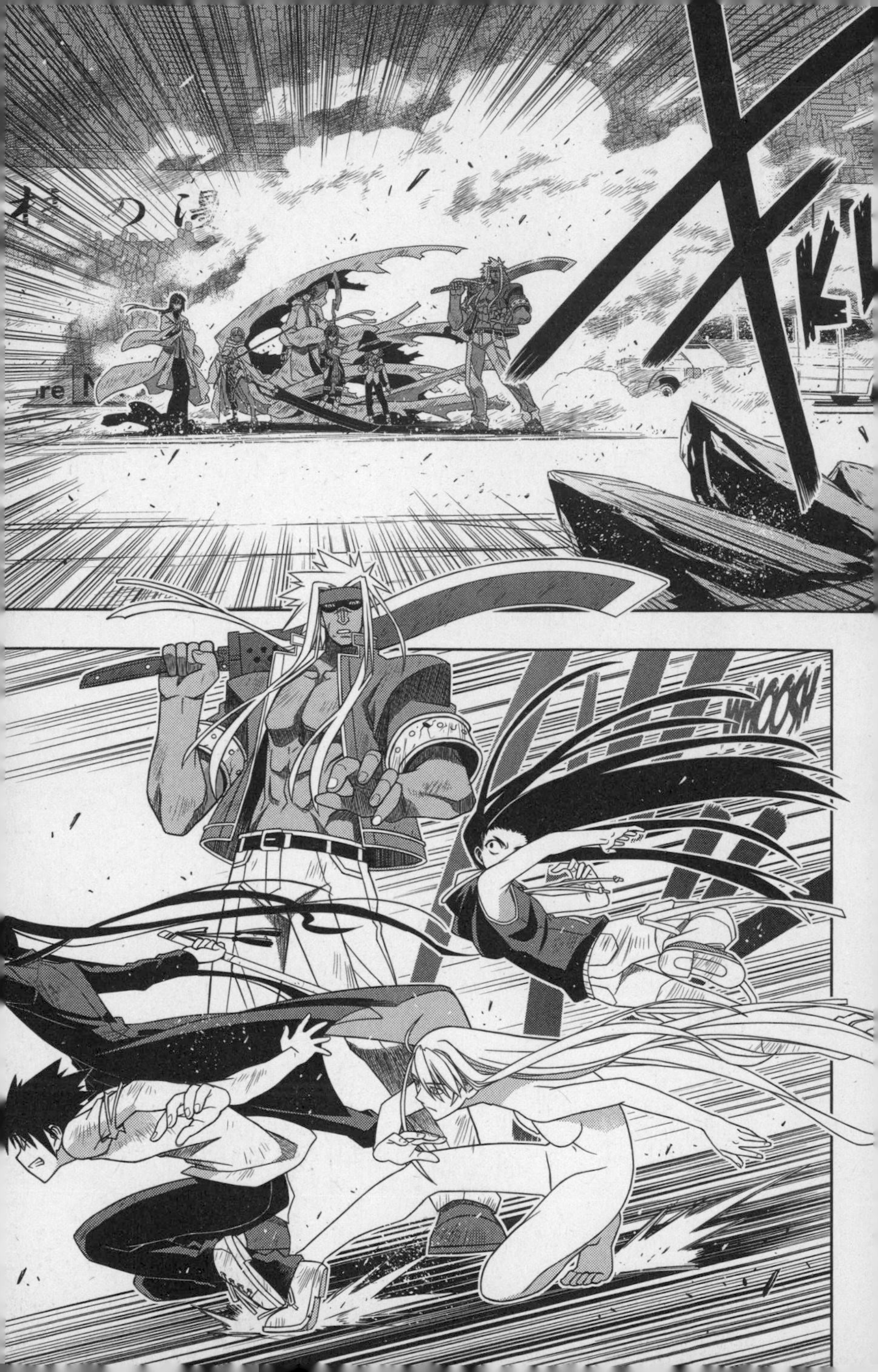
WHOOSH

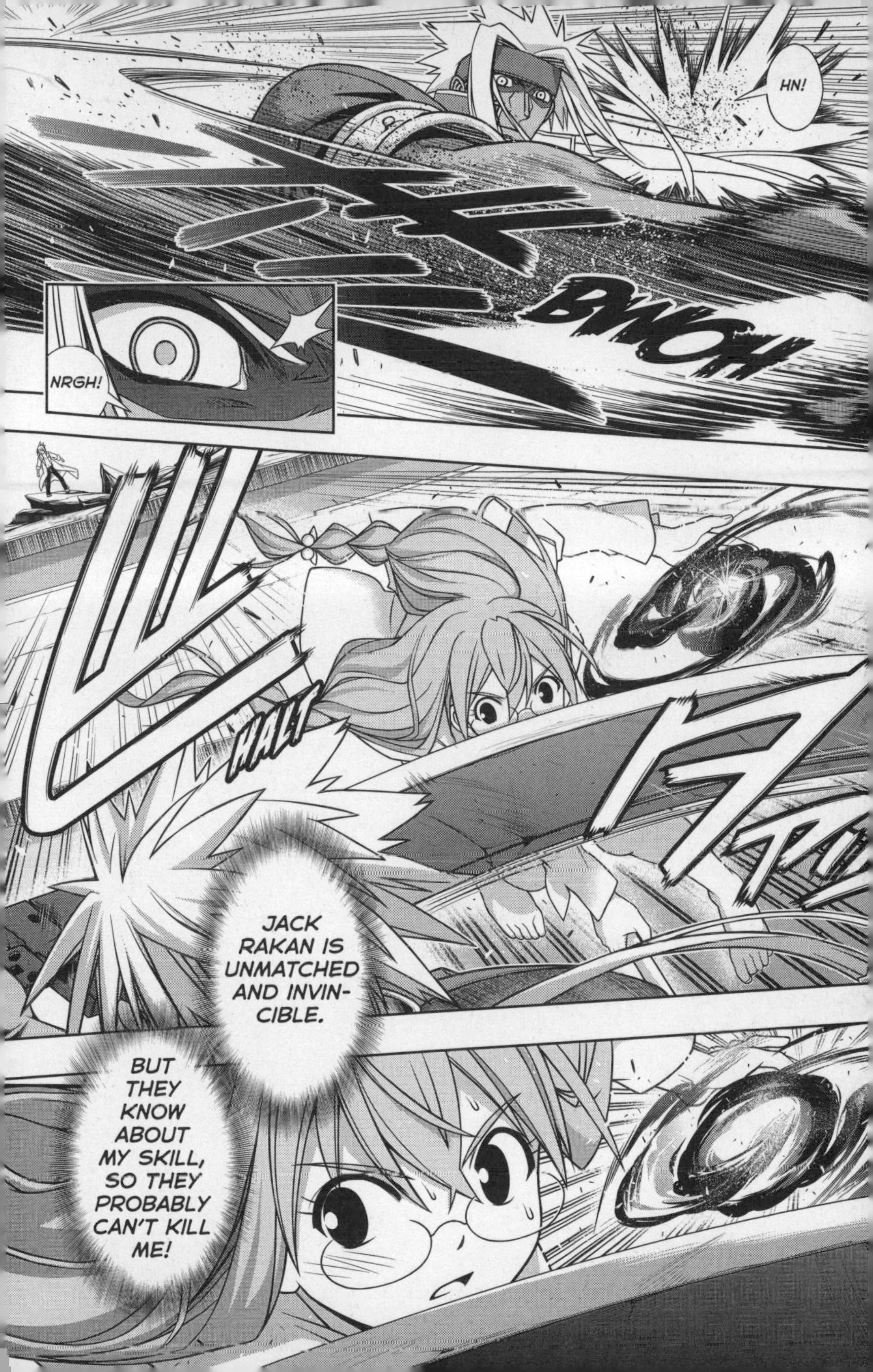
HN!
BWOH
NRGH!
HALT
JACK RAKAN IS UNMATCHED AND INVIN-CIBLE.
BUT THEY KNOW ABOUT MY SKILL, SO THEY PROBABLY CAN'T KILL ME!

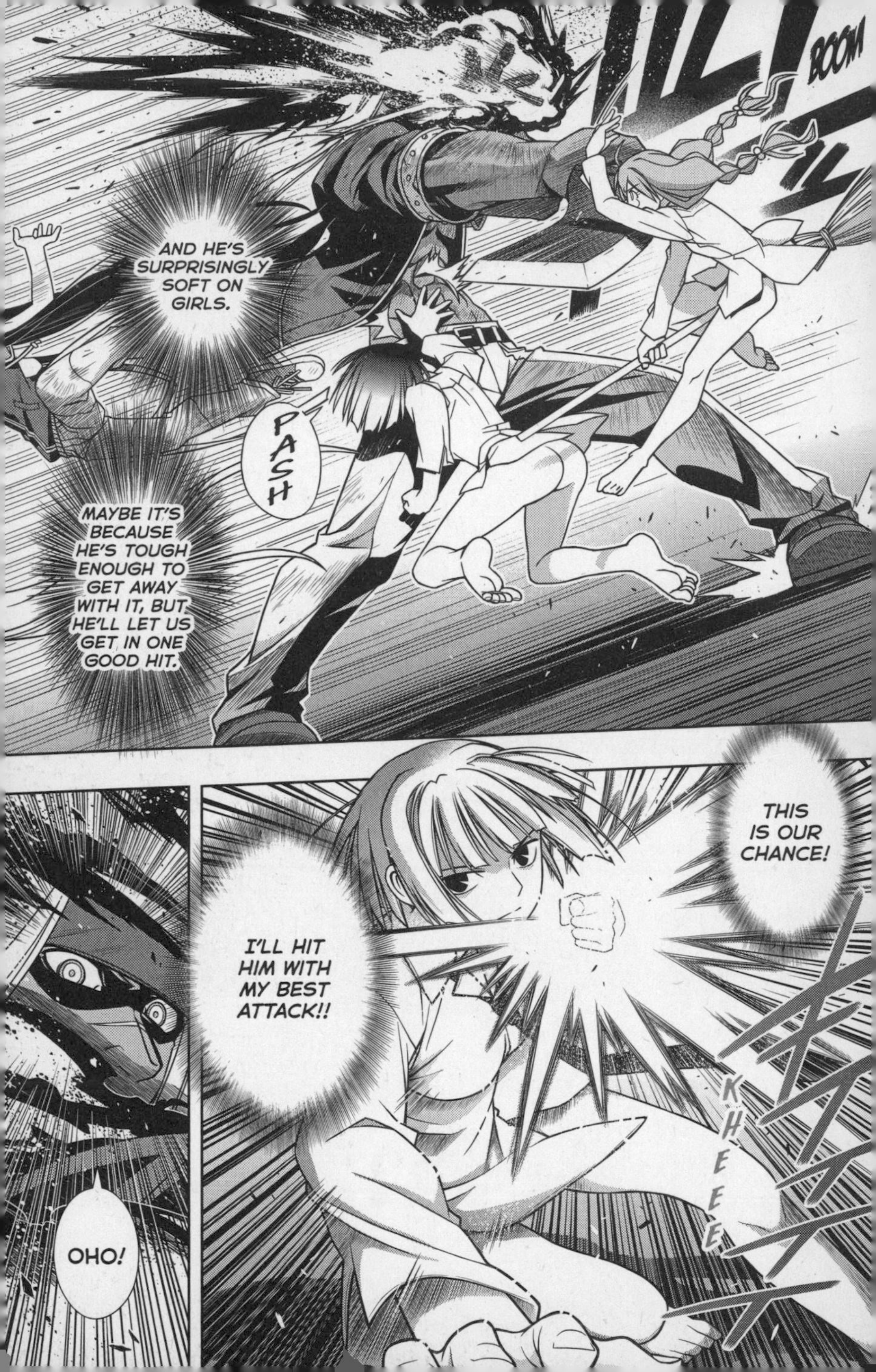
BOOM
AND HE'S SURPRISINGLY SOFT ON GIRLS.
PASH
MAYBE IT'S BECAUSE HE'S TOUGH ENOUGH TO GET AWAY WITH IT, BUT HE'LL LET US GET IN ONE GOOD HIT.
THIS IS OUR CHANCE!
I'LL HIT HIM WITH MY BEST ATTACK!!
KHEEEE
OHO!

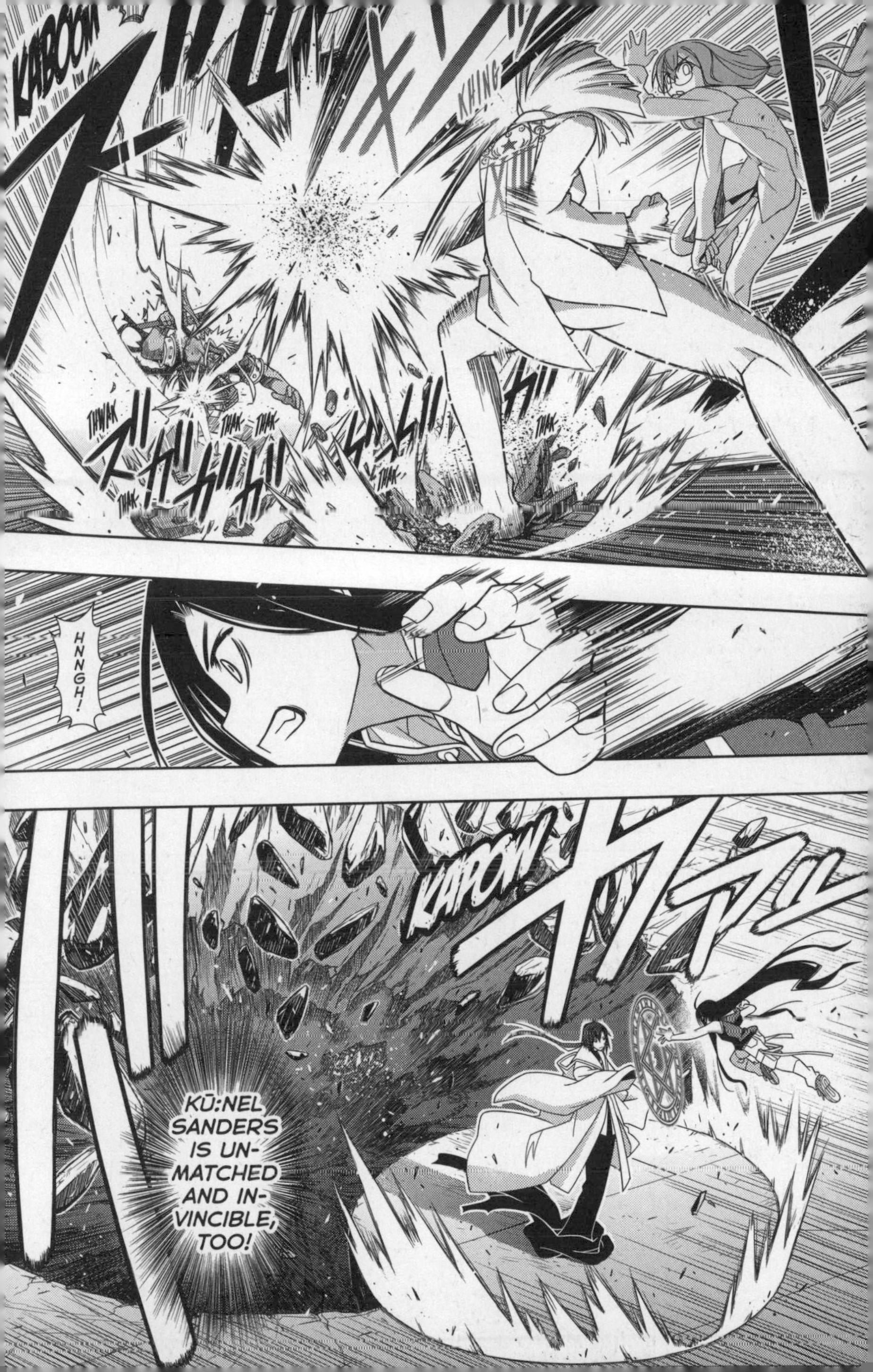
KHING
KABOOM
THAK
THAK
THAK
THAK
THWAK
THAK
HNNGH!
KAPOW
KŪ:NEL SANDERS IS UN-MATCHED AND IN-VINCIBLE, TOO!

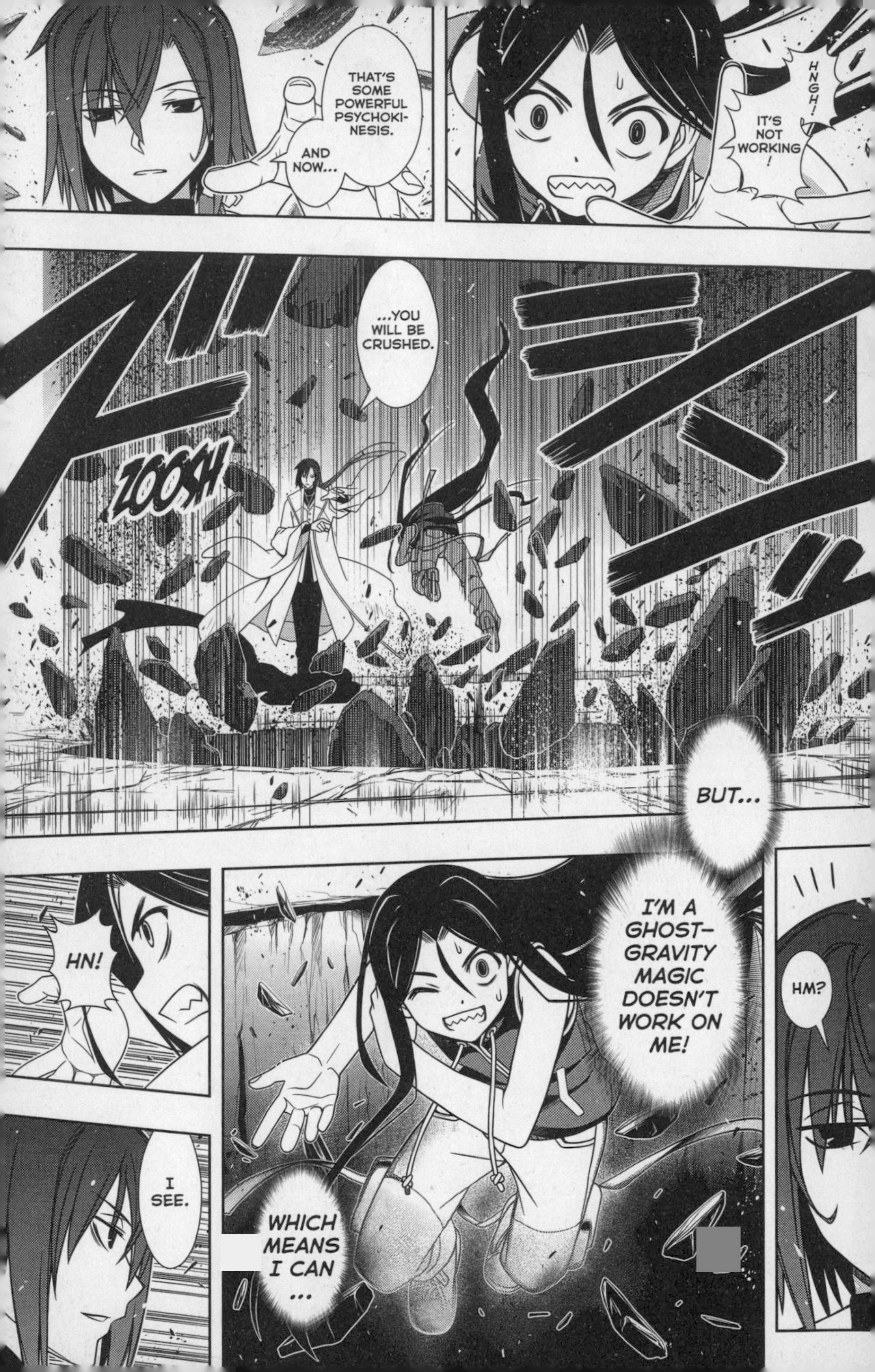
HNGH!
IT'S NOT WORKING!
THAT'S SOME POWERFUL PSYCHOKINESIS.
AND NOW...
...YOU WILL BE CRUSHED.
ZOOSH
BUT...
HM?
I'M A GHOST—GRAVITY MAGIC DOESN'T WORK ON ME!
WHICH MEANS I CAN ...
HN!
I SEE.

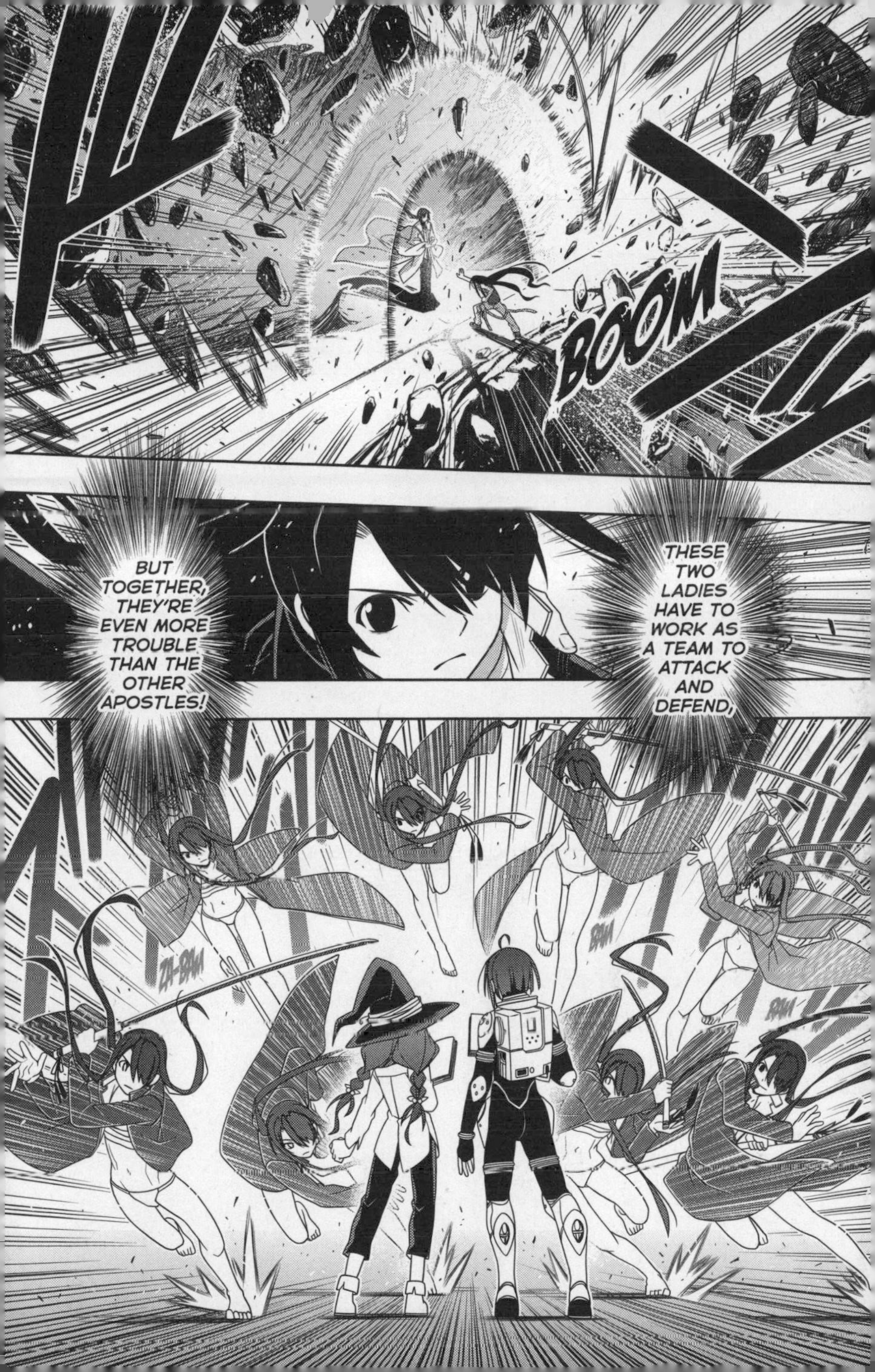
BOOM
THESE TWO LADIES HAVE TO WORK AS A TEAM TO ATTACK AND DEFEND,
BUT TOGETHER, THEY'RE EVEN MORE TROUBLE THAN THE OTHER APOSTLES!
ZA-BAM

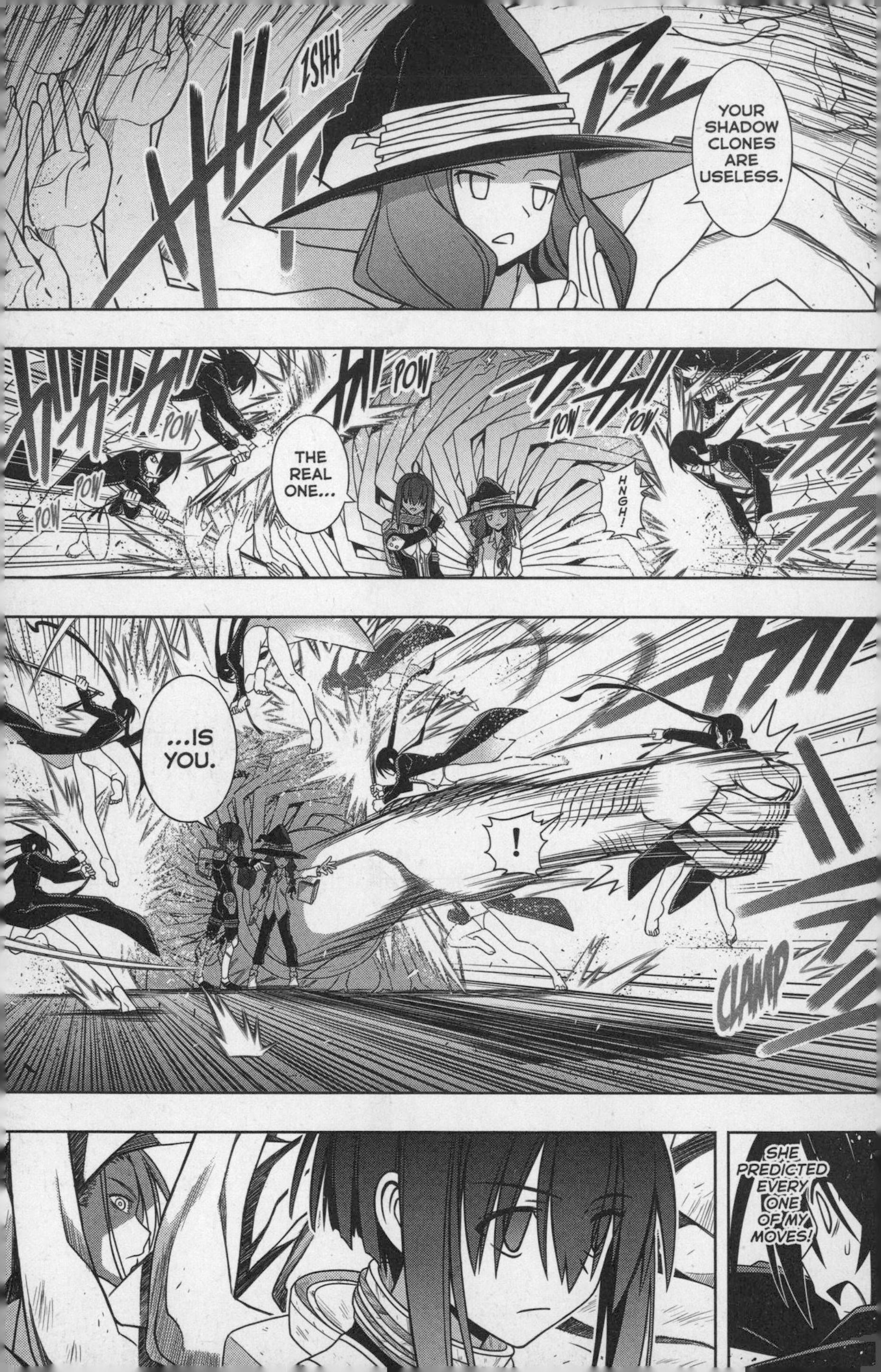
YOUR SHADOW CLONES ARE USELESS.
ZSHH
POW
POW
POW
HNGH!
THE REAL ONE...
POW
POW
POW
!
...IS YOU.
CLAMP
SHE PREDICTED EVERY ONE OF MY MOVES!

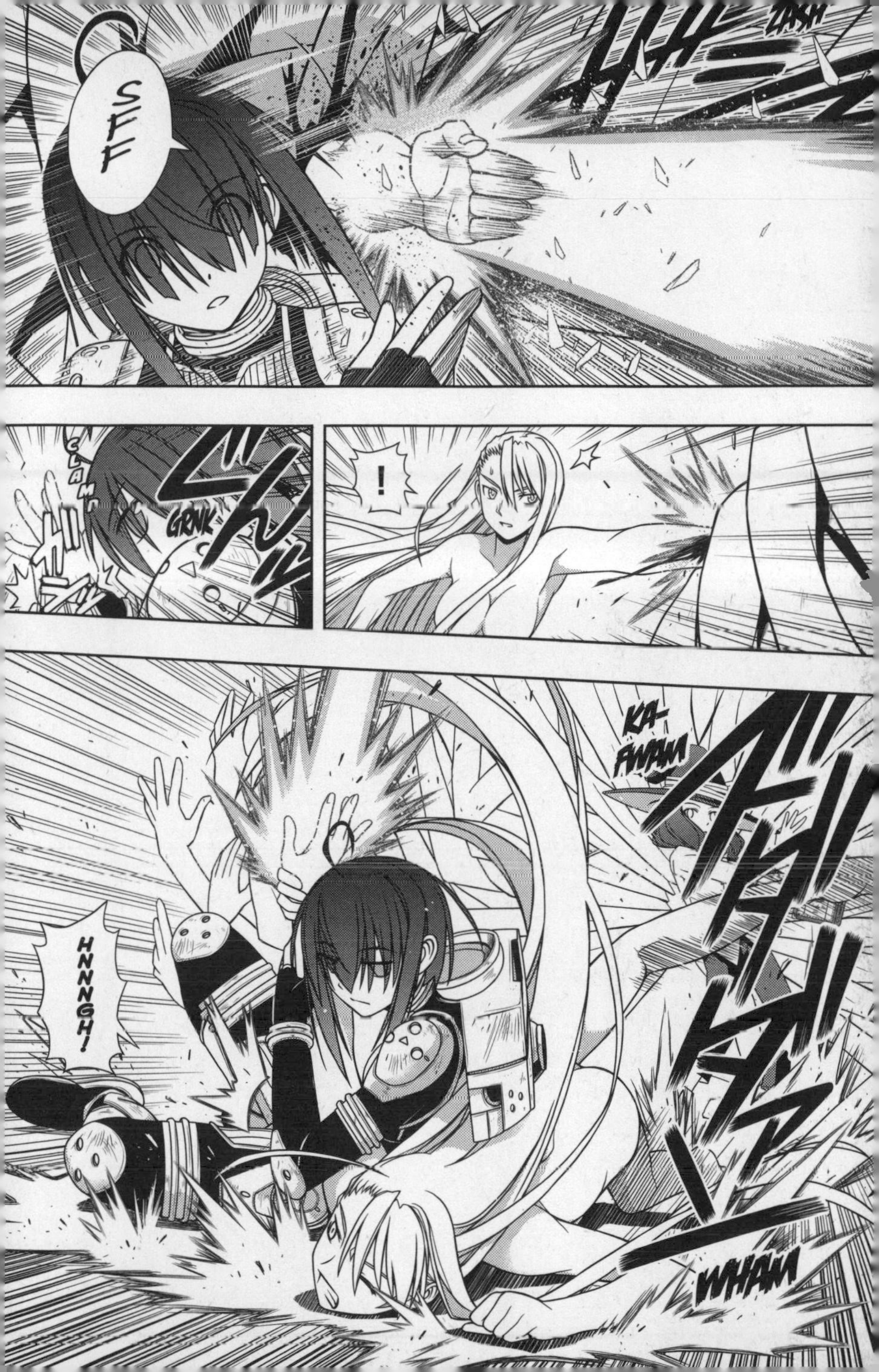
ZASH
SFF
!
CLAMP
GRNK
KA-FWAM
HNNNGH!
WHAM

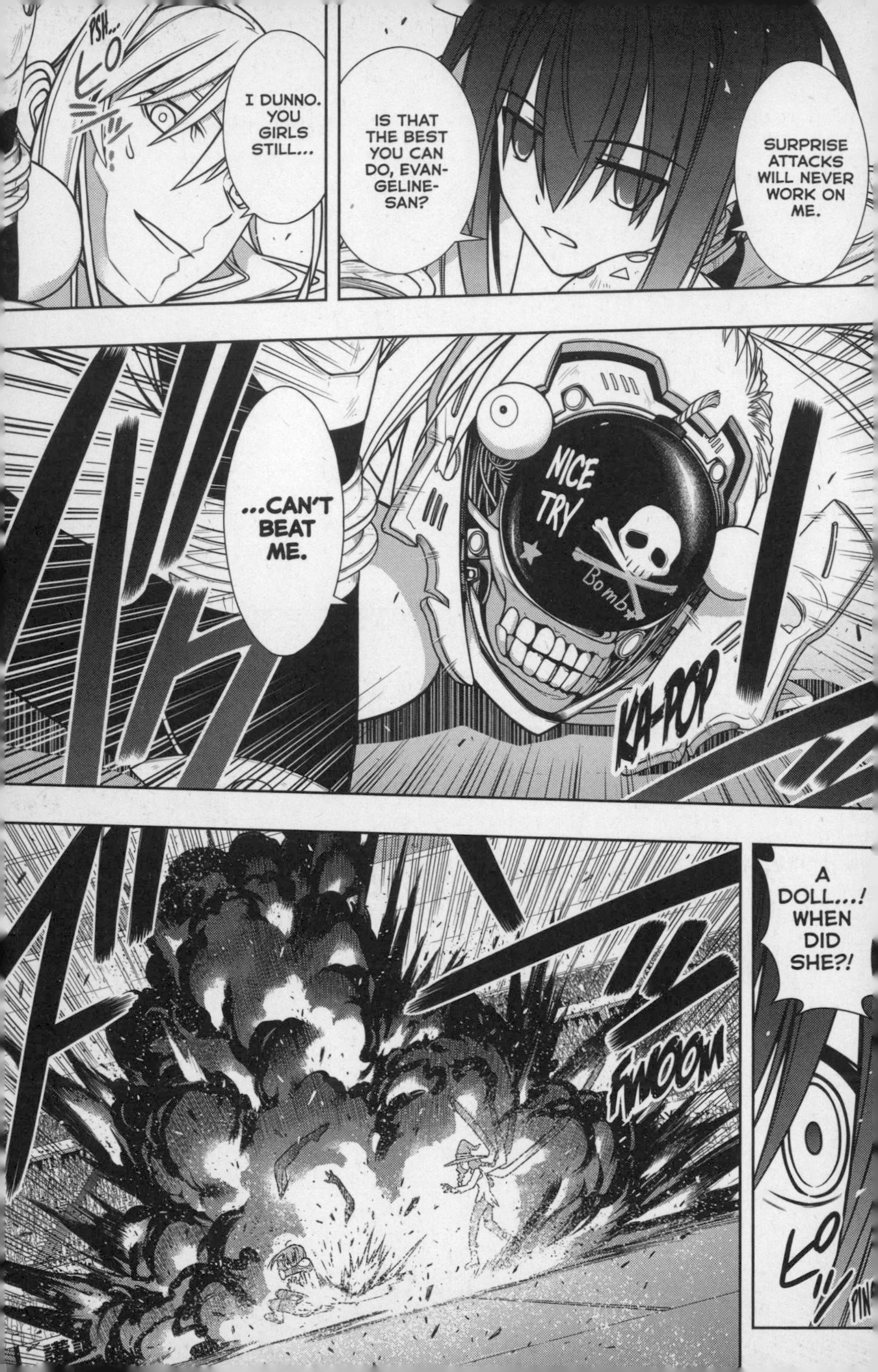
SURPRISE ATTACKS WILL NEVER WORK ON ME.
IS THAT THE BEST YOU CAN DO, EVANGELINE-SAN?
PSH...
I DUNNO. YOU GIRLS STILL...
...CAN'T BEAT ME.
NICE TRY
Bomb
KA-POP
A DOLL...! WHEN DID SHE?!
PIN
FWOOM

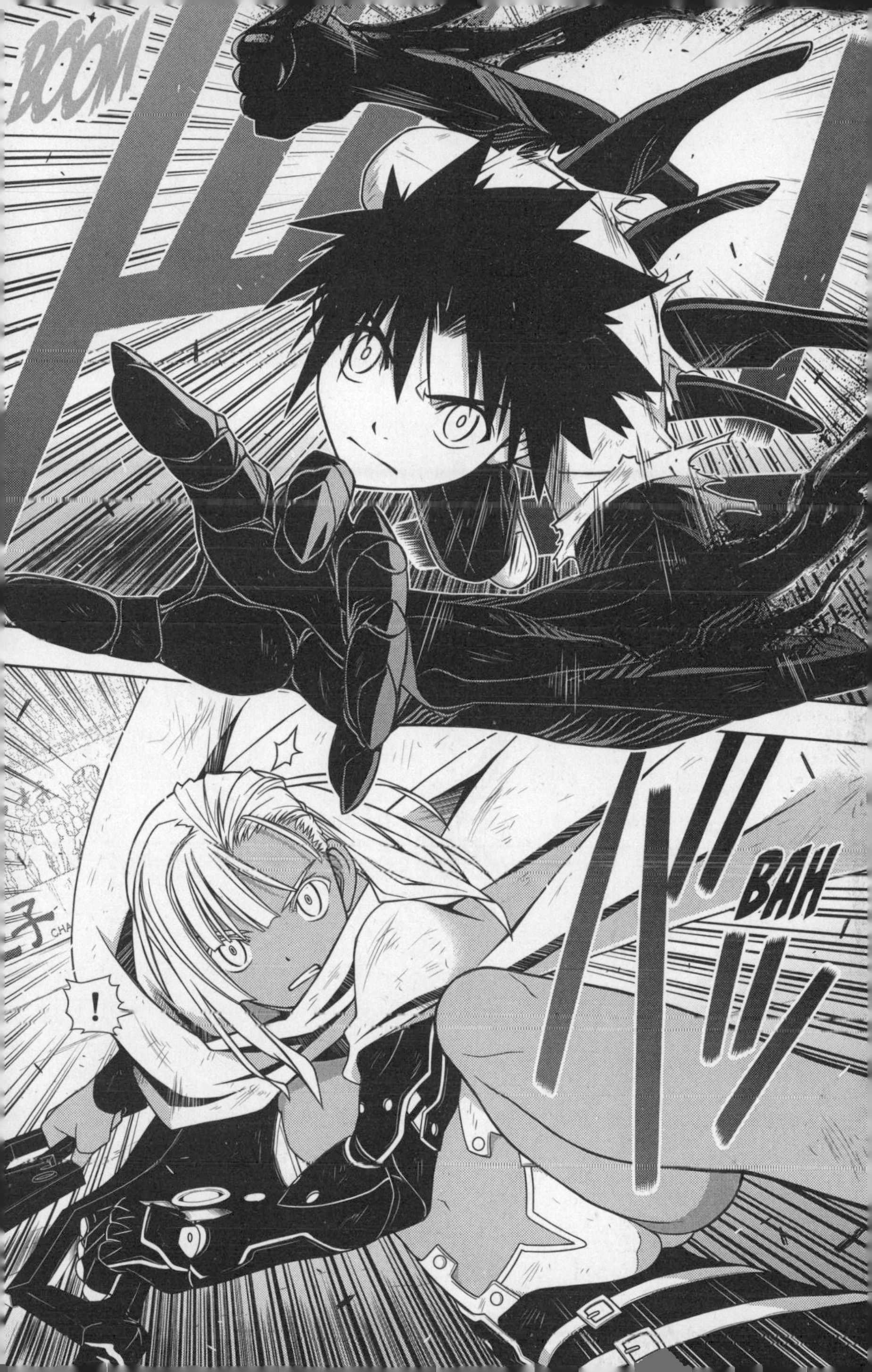
BOOM
BAH
CHA
!

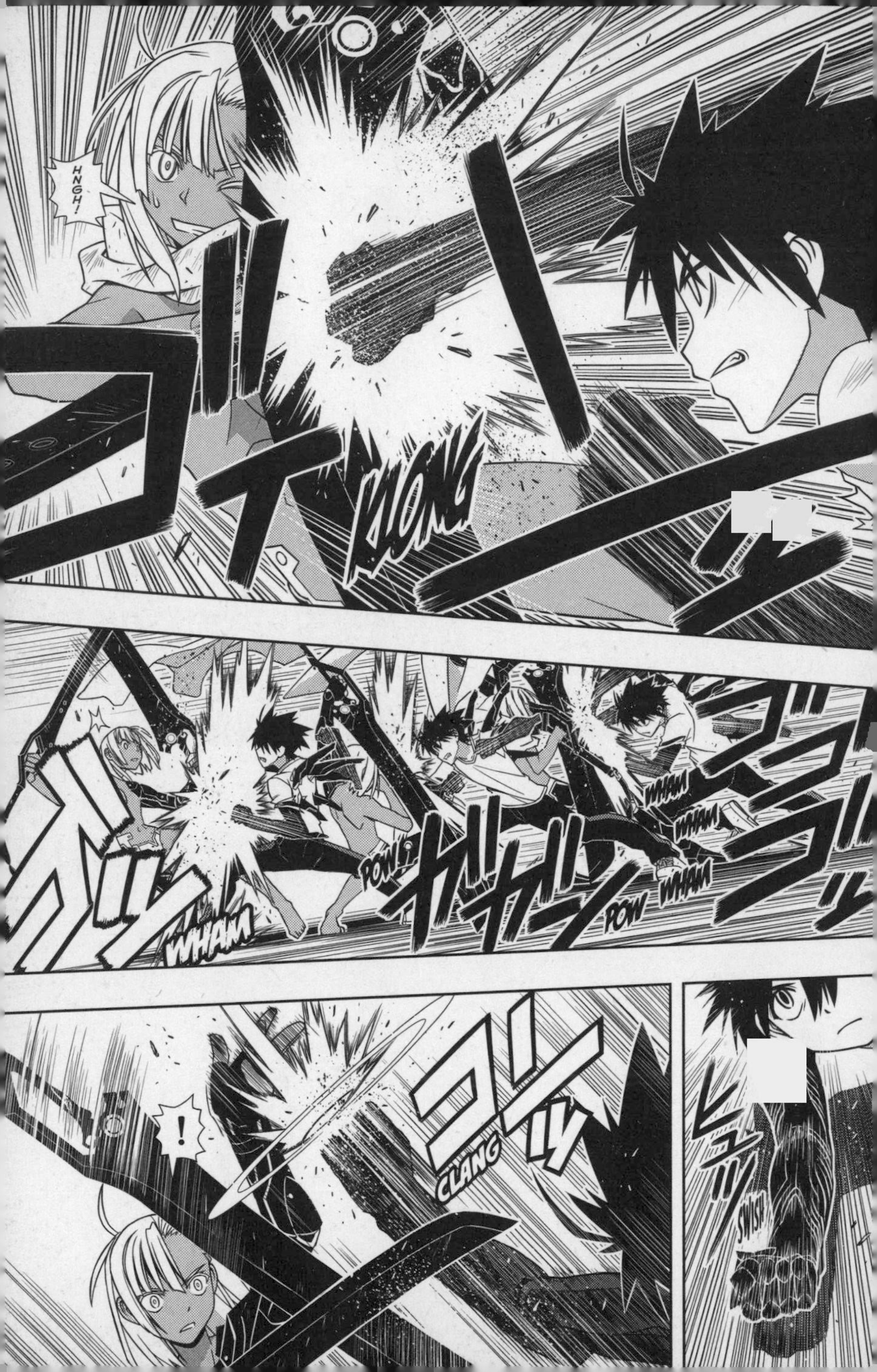
HNGH!
KLONG
WHAM
WHAM
WHAM
POW
POW!
WHAM
SWISH
!
CLANG

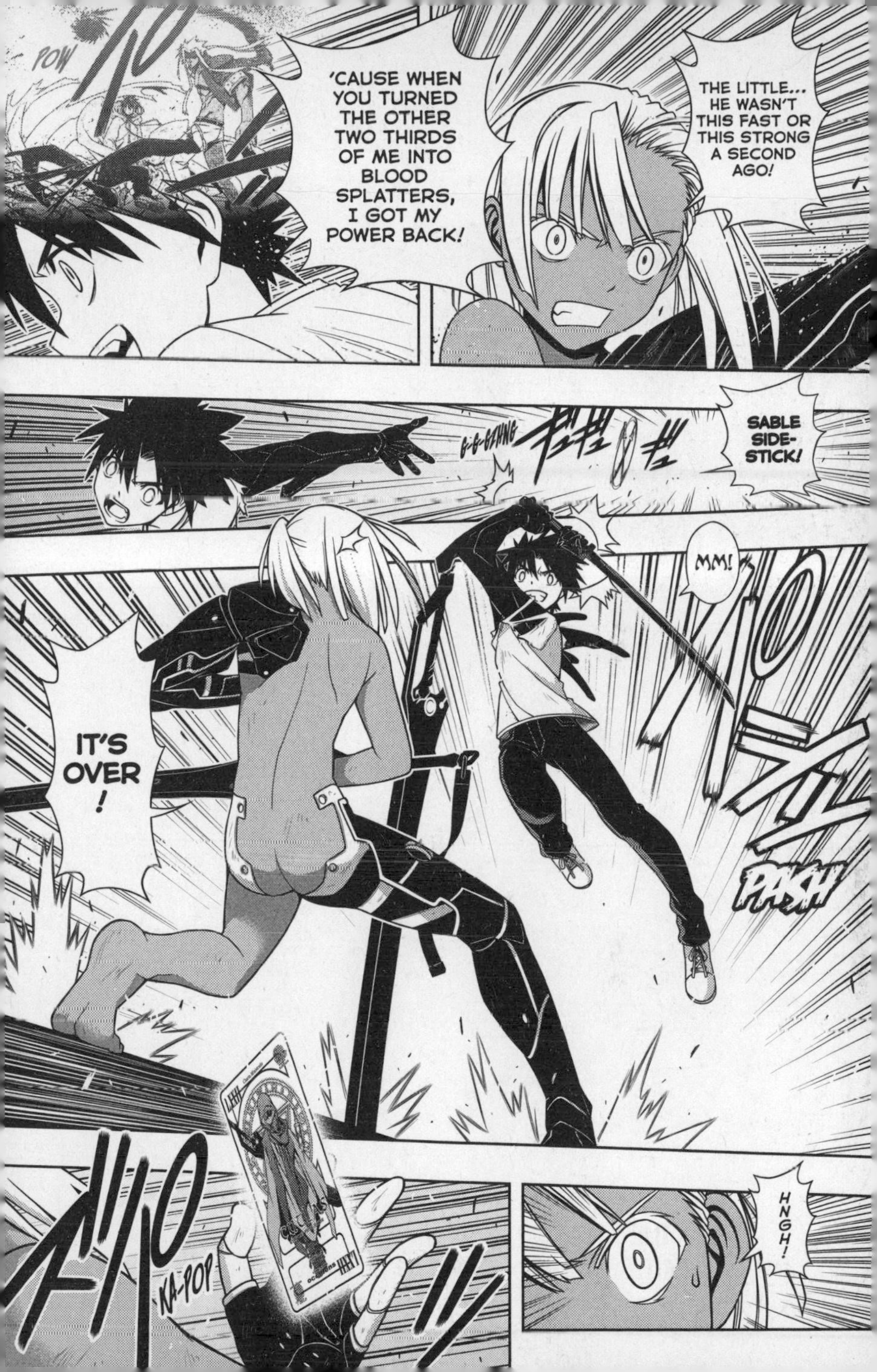
THE LITTLE... HE WASN'T THIS FAST OR THIS STRONG A SECOND AGO!
'CAUSE WHEN YOU TURNED THE OTHER TWO THIRDS OF ME INTO BLOOD SPLATTERS, I GOT MY POWER BACK!
POW
SABLE SIDE-STICK!
G-G-GZHNG
MM!
PASH
IT'S OVER!
HNGH!
KA-POP

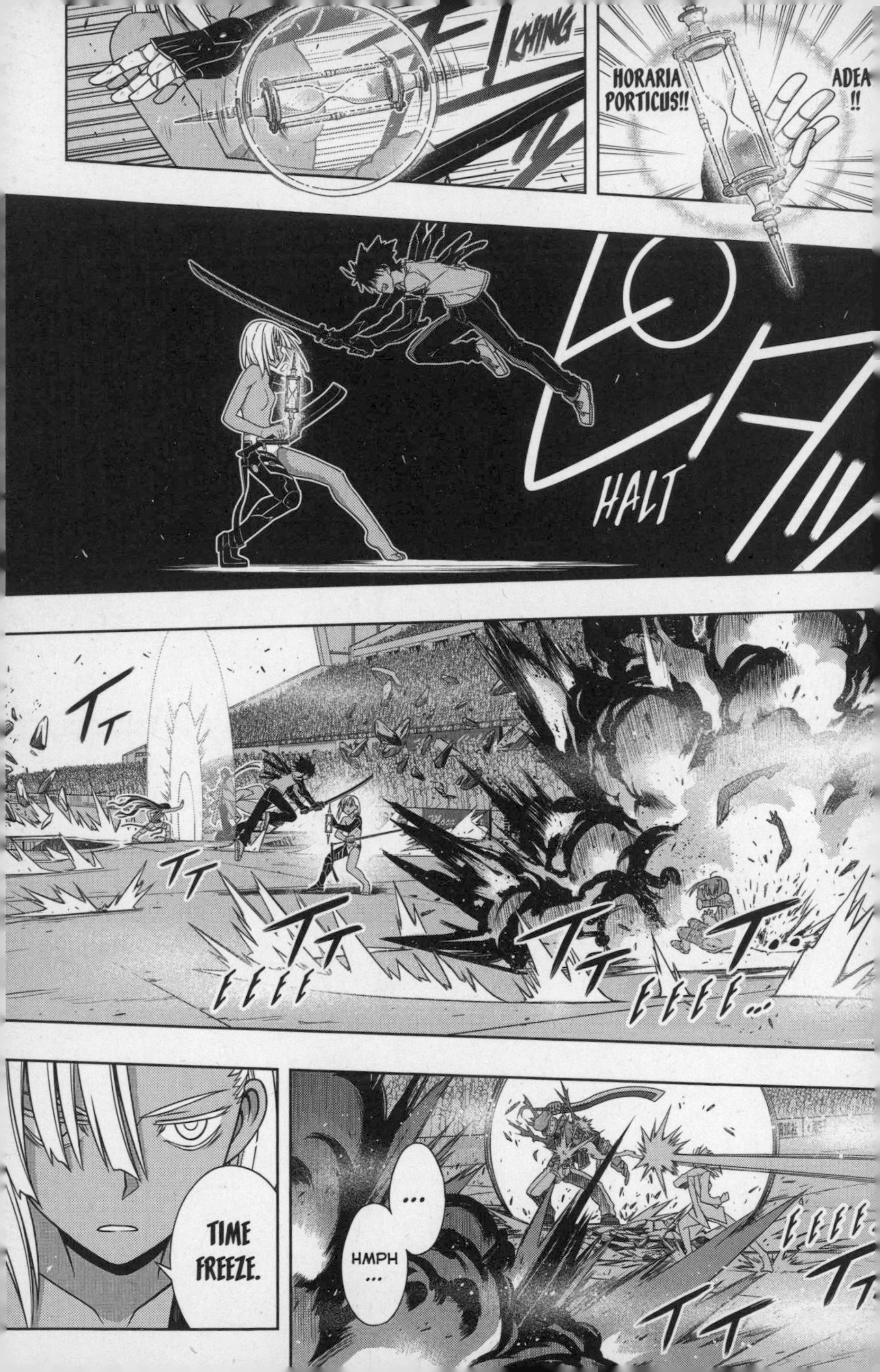
ADEA !!
HORARIA PORTICUS!!
KHING
HALT
TT
TT
TTEEEE
TTEEEE...
...
HMPH ...
EEEE.
TT
TIME FREEZE.

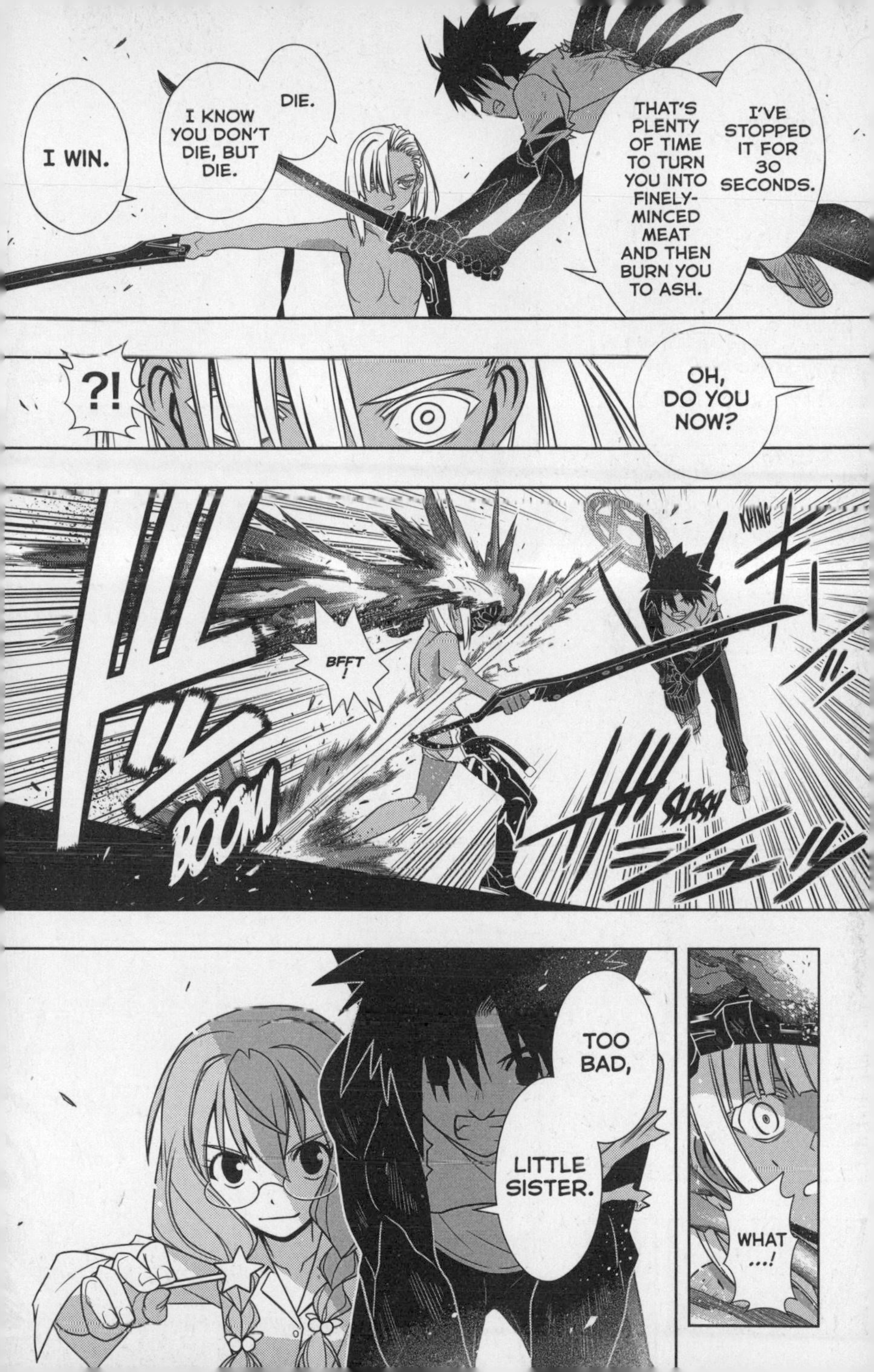
I'VE STOPPED IT FOR 30 SECONDS.
THAT'S PLENTY OF TIME TO TURN YOU INTO FINELY-MINCED MEAT AND THEN BURN YOU TO ASH.
DIE.
I KNOW YOU DON'T DIE, BUT DIE.
I WIN.
OH, DO YOU NOW?
?!
KHING
SLASH
BFFT!
BOOM
WHAT ...!
TOO BAD,
LITTLE SISTER.

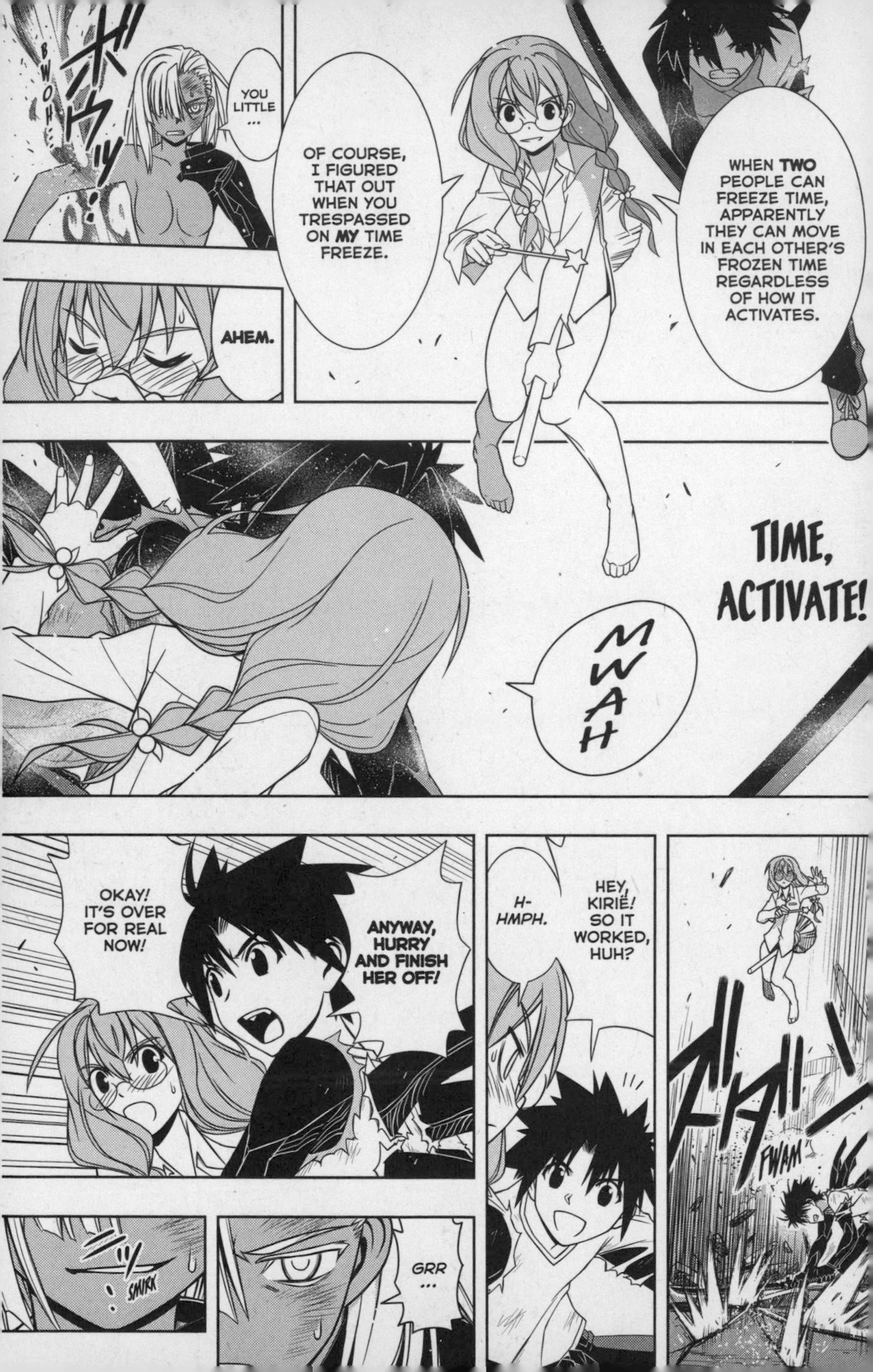
WHEN TWO PEOPLE CAN FREEZE TIME, APPARENTLY THEY CAN MOVE IN EACH OTHER'S FROZEN TIME REGARDLESS OF HOW IT ACTIVATES.
OF COURSE, I FIGURED THAT OUT WHEN YOU TRESPASSED ON MY TIME FREEZE.
BWOH
YOU LITTLE ...
AHEM.
TIME, ACTIVATE!
MWAH
FWAM
HEY, KIRIË! SO IT WORKED, HUH?
H-HMPH.
ANYWAY, HURRY AND FINISH HER OFF!
OKAY! IT'S OVER FOR REAL NOW!
GRR ...
SMIRK

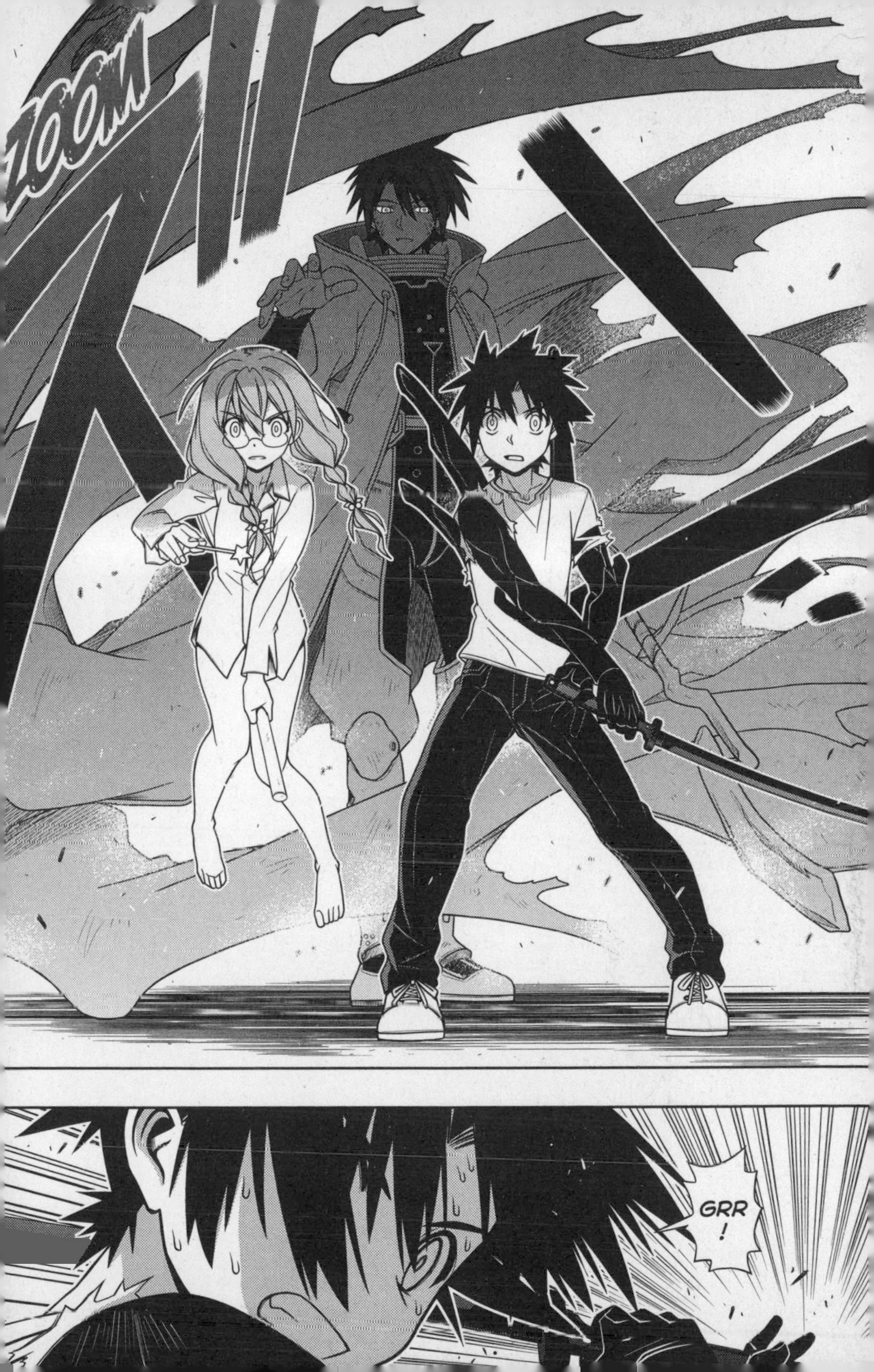
ZOOM
GRR
!

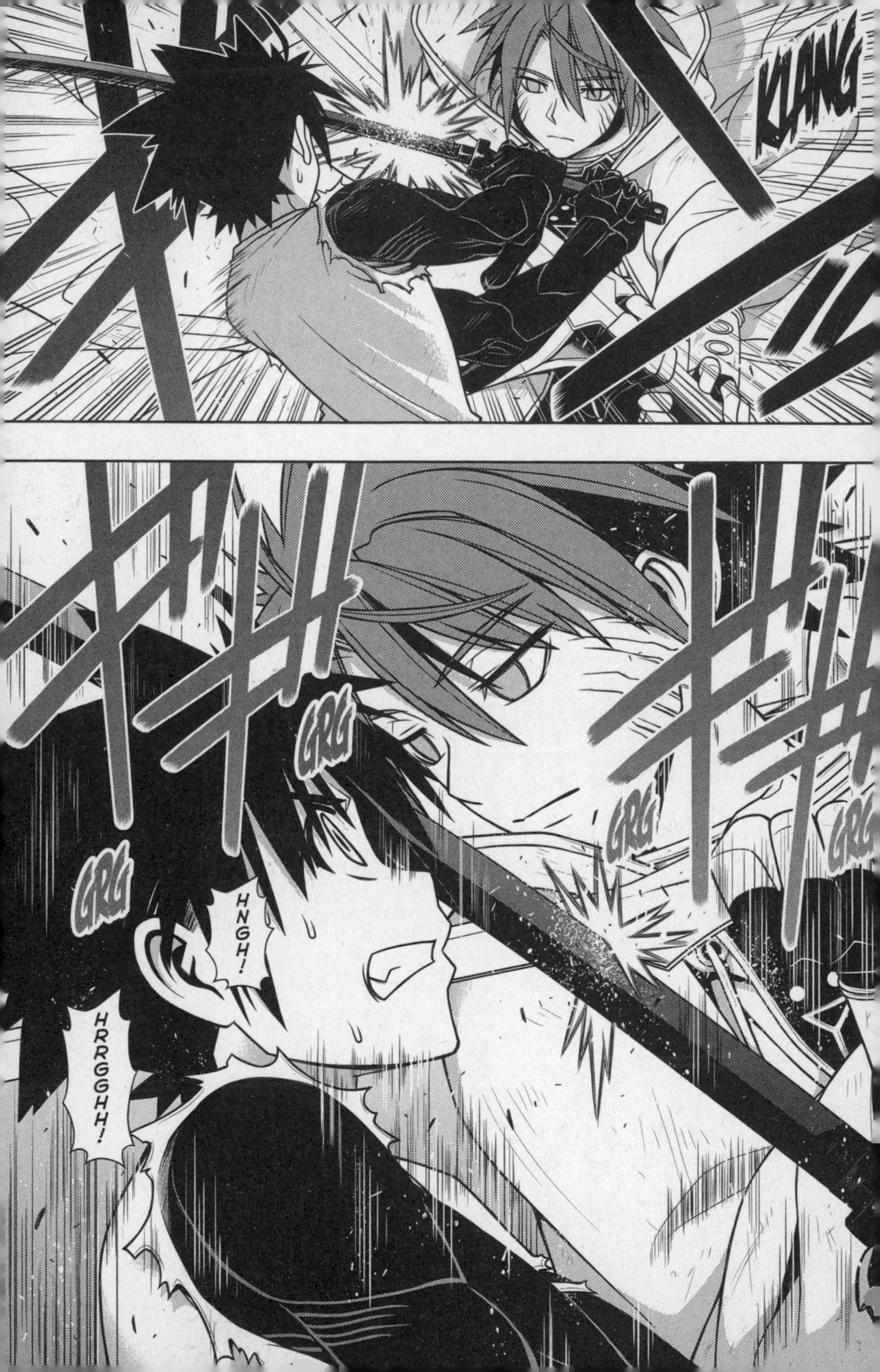
KLANG
GRG
GRG
GRG
GRG
HNGH!
HRRGGHH!

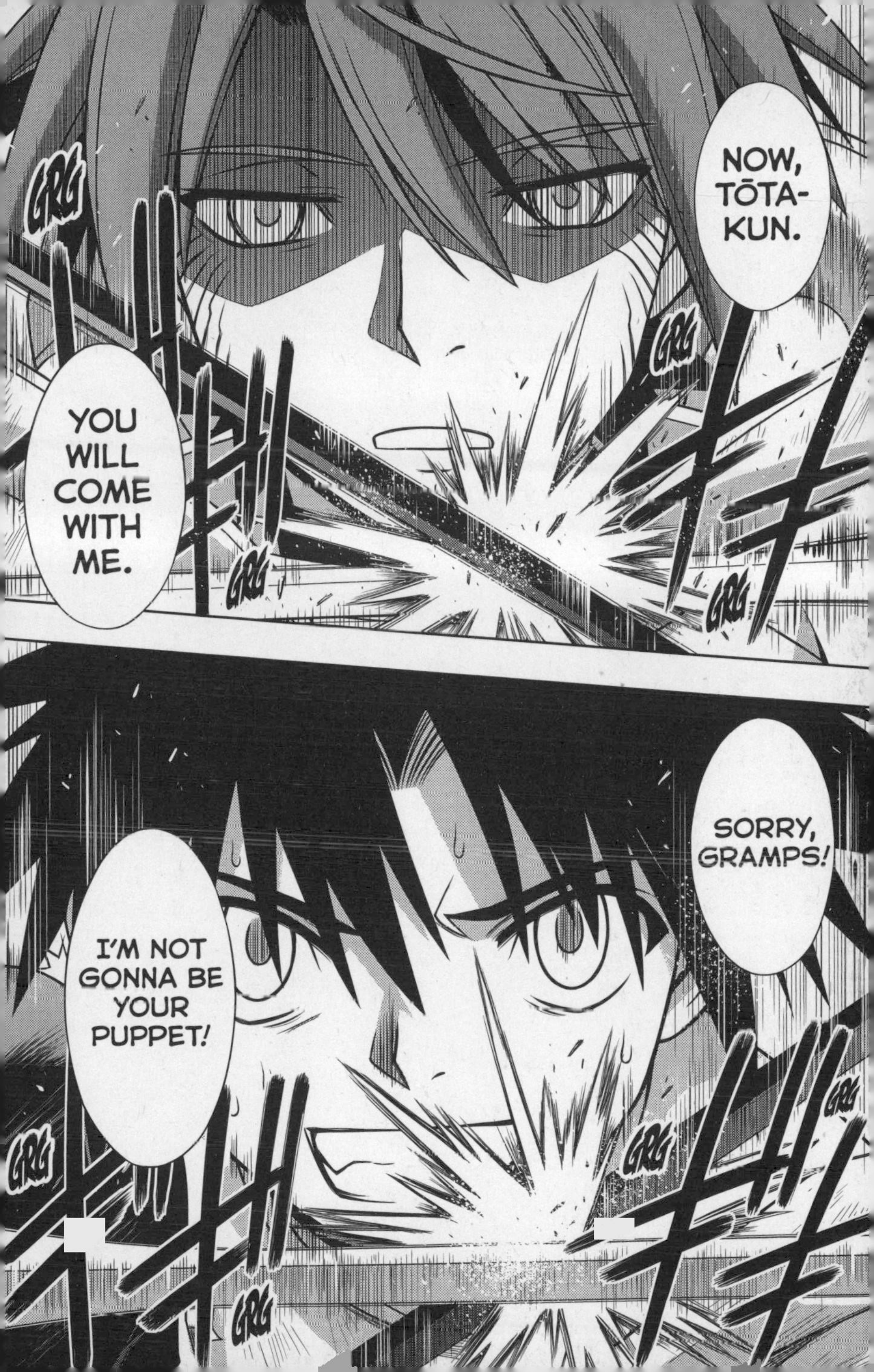
NOW, TŌTA-KUN.
YOU WILL COME WITH ME.
GRG
GRG
GRG
GRG
SORRY, GRAMPS!
I'M NOT GONNA BE YOUR PUPPET!
GRG
GRG
GRG
GRG

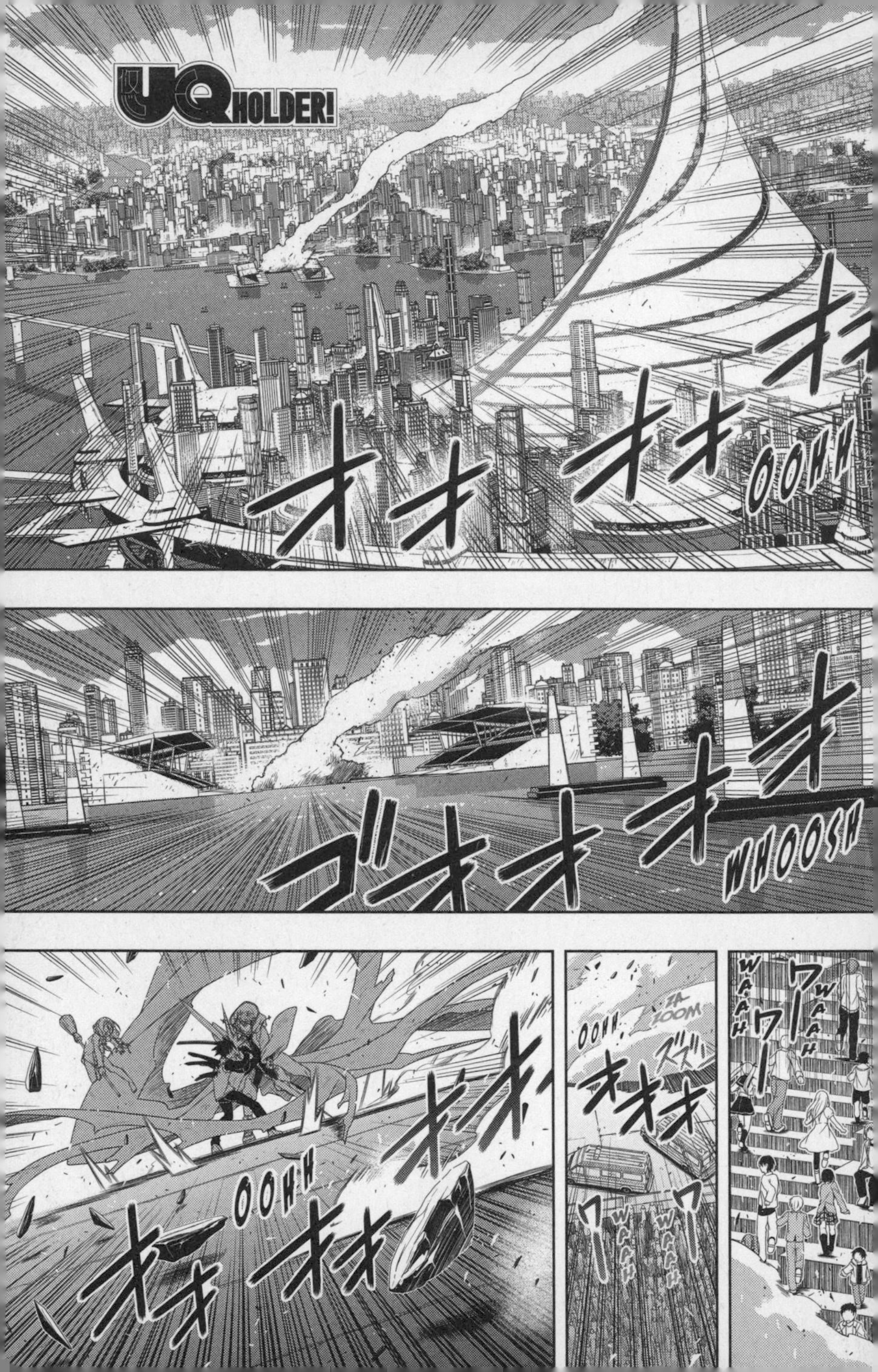
UQ HOLDER!
オオオオオ
OOHH
ゴオオオオ
WHOOSH
ワーワー
WAAH
WAAH
ZA
ZOOM
ズズ
OOHH
オオオ
ワーワー
WAAH
WAAH
オオオオオ
OOHH

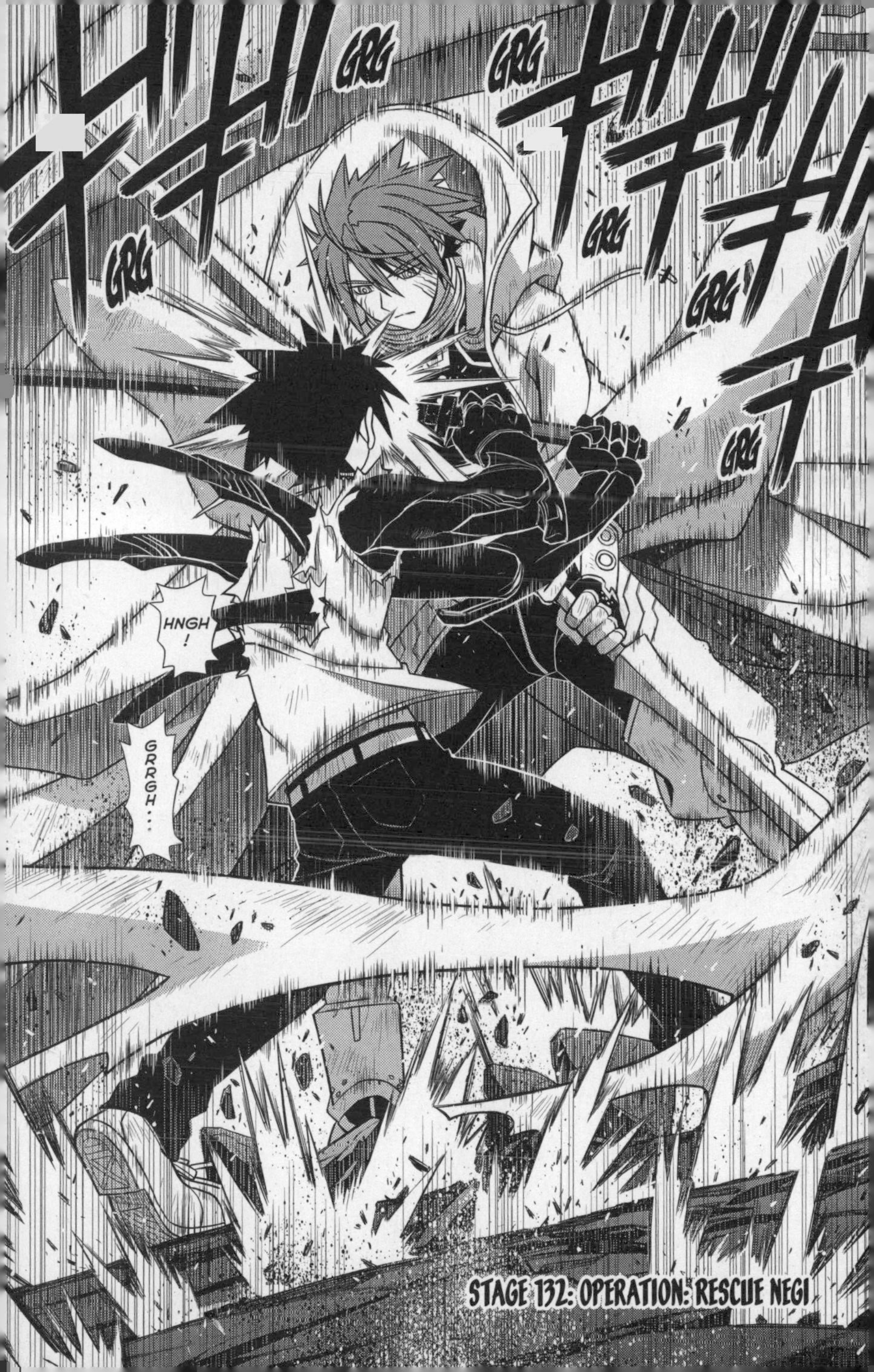
GRG
GRG
GRG
GRG
GRG
GRG
HNGH!
GRRGH...
STAGE 132: OPERATION: RESCUE NEGI

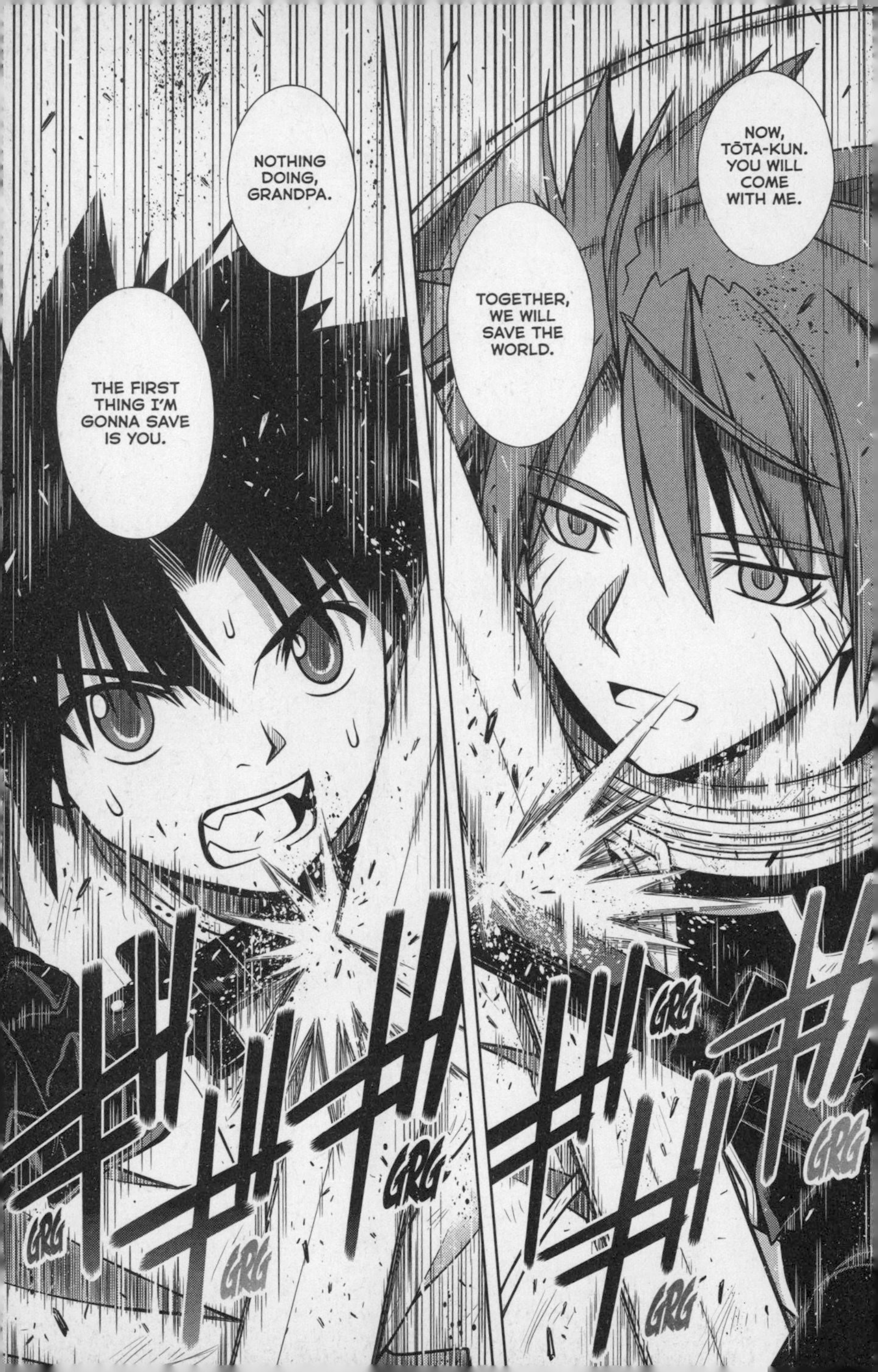
NOW, TŌTA-KUN. YOU WILL COME WITH ME.
TOGETHER, WE WILL SAVE THE WORLD.
GRG
GRG
GRG
NOTHING DOING, GRANDPA.
THE FIRST THING I'M GONNA SAVE IS YOU.
GRG
GRG
GRG

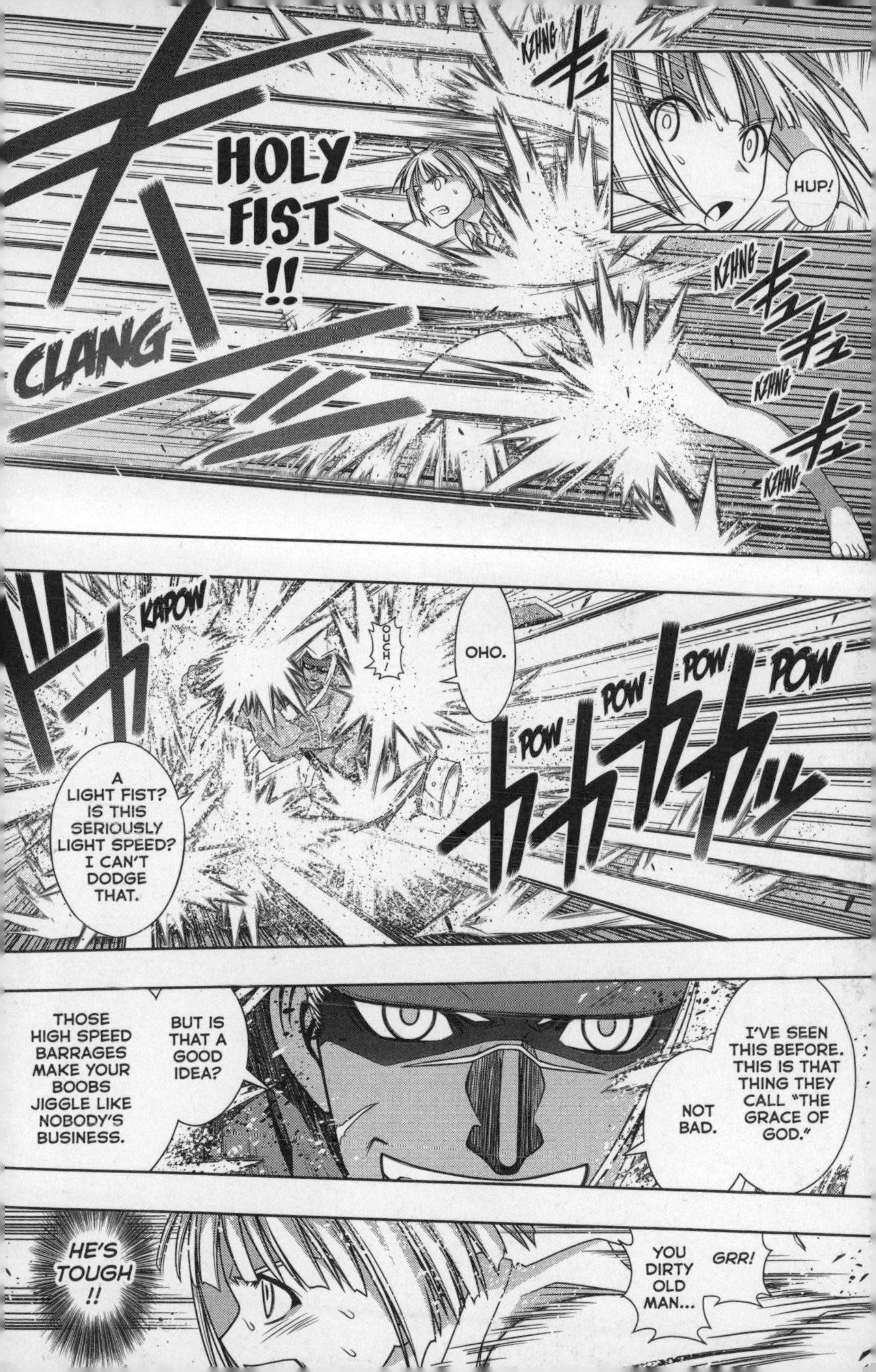
KZHNG
HUP!
KZHNG
KZHNG
KZHNG
HOLY FIST !!
CLANG
POW POW POW POW
OHO.
OUCH!
KAPOW
A LIGHT FIST? IS THIS SERIOUSLY LIGHT SPEED? I CAN'T DODGE THAT.
I'VE SEEN THIS BEFORE. THIS IS THAT THING THEY CALL "THE GRACE OF GOD."
NOT BAD.
BUT IS THAT A GOOD IDEA?
THOSE HIGH SPEED BARRAGES MAKE YOUR BOOBS JIGGLE LIKE NOBODY'S BUSINESS.
GRR!
YOU DIRTY OLD MAN...
HE'S TOUGH !!

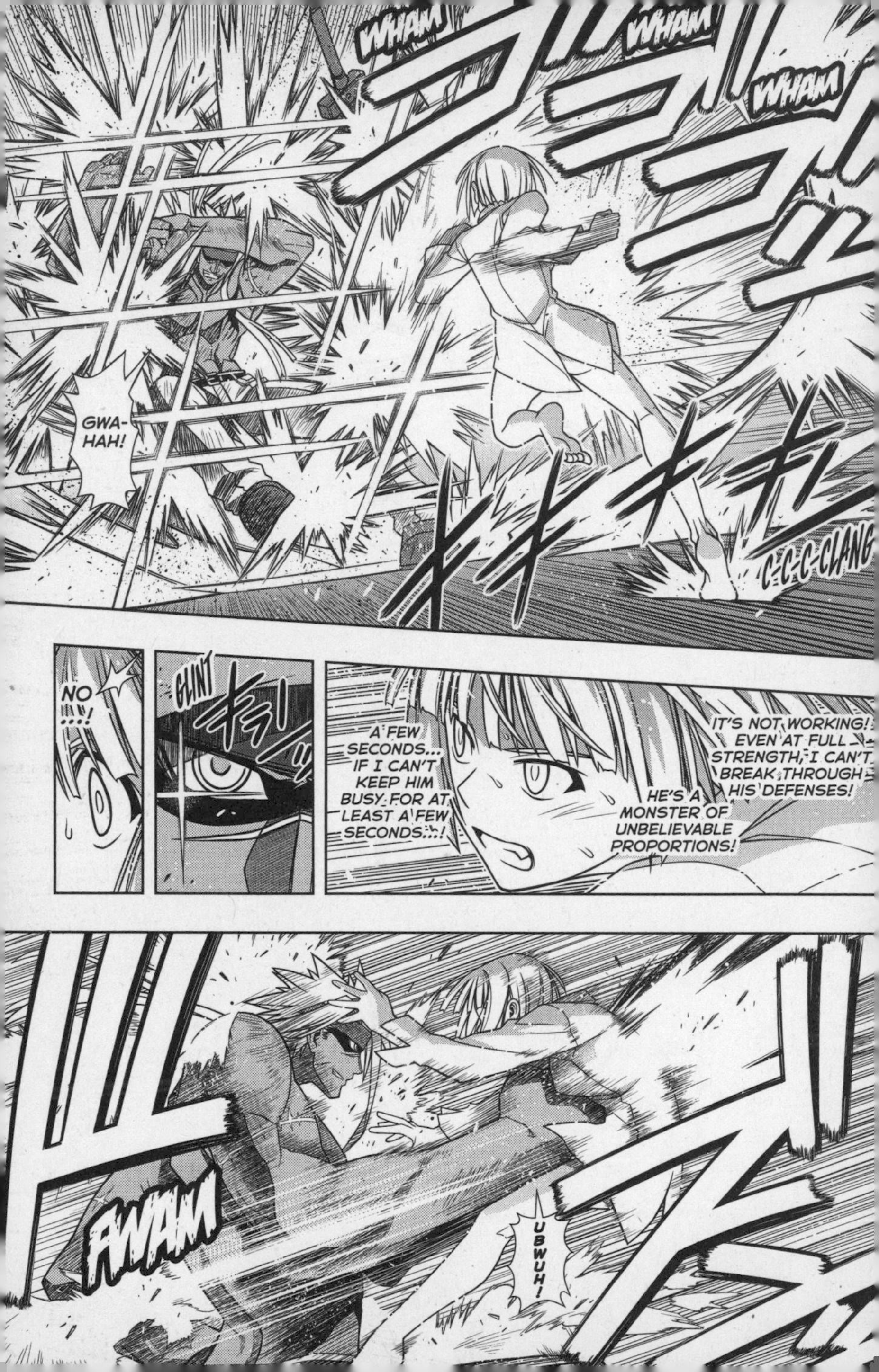
WHAM
WHAM
WHAM
GWA-HAH!
C-C-C-CLANG
IT'S NOT WORKING! EVEN AT FULL STRENGTH, I CAN'T BREAK THROUGH HIS DEFENSES!
HE'S A MONSTER OF UNBELIEVABLE PROPORTIONS!
A FEW SECONDS... IF I CAN'T KEEP HIM BUSY FOR AT LEAST A FEW SECONDS...!
GLINT
NO...!
UBWUH!
FWAM

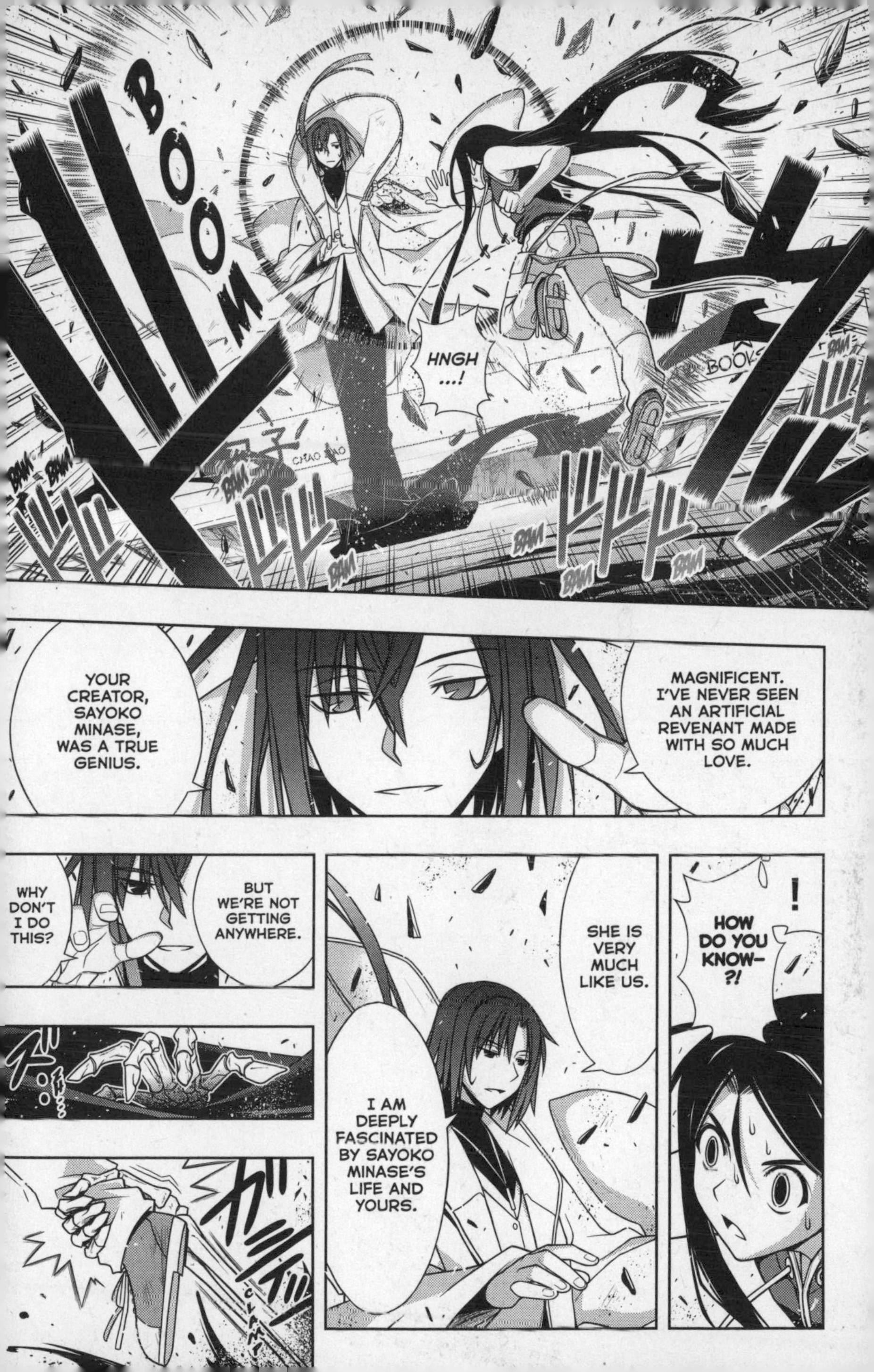
BOOM
HNGH ...!
BAM
MAGNIFICENT. I'VE NEVER SEEN AN ARTIFICIAL REVENANT MADE WITH SO MUCH LOVE.
YOUR CREATOR, SAYOKO MINASE, WAS A TRUE GENIUS.
!
HOW DO YOU KNOW-?!
SHE IS VERY MUCH LIKE US.
I AM DEEPLY FASCINATED BY SAYOKO MINASE'S LIFE AND YOURS.
BUT WE'RE NOT GETTING ANYWHERE.
WHY DON'T I DO THIS?
CLAMP

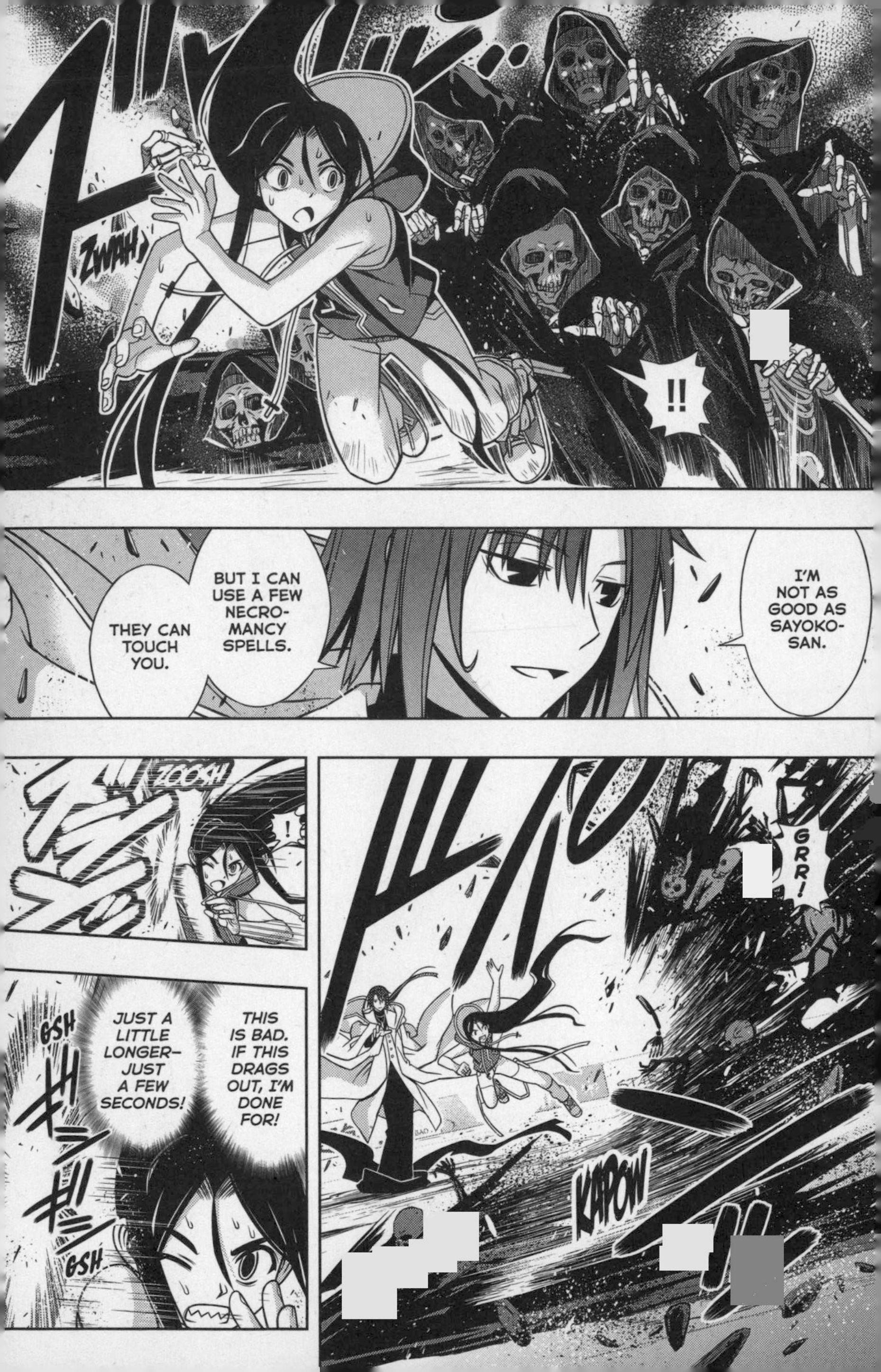
!!
ZWAH
I'M NOT AS GOOD AS SAYOKO-SAN.
BUT I CAN USE A FEW NECRO-MANCY SPELLS.
THEY CAN TOUCH YOU.
GRR!
KAPOW
ZOOSH
!
THIS IS BAD. IF THIS DRAGS OUT, I'M DONE FOR!
JUST A LITTLE LONGER—JUST A FEW SECONDS!
GSH
GSH

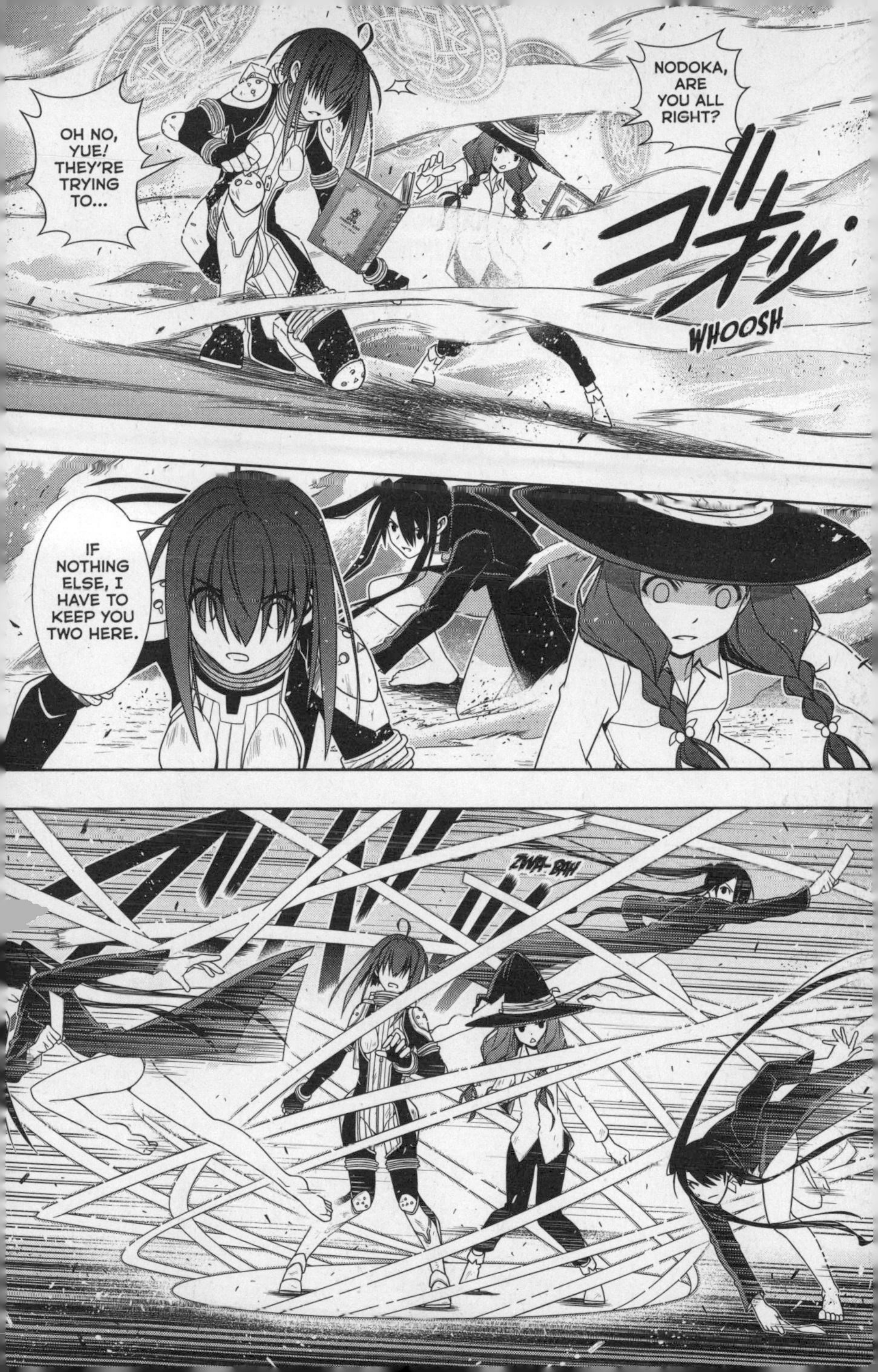
NODOKA, ARE YOU ALL RIGHT?
OH NO, YUE! THEY'RE TRYING TO...
ゴオッ
WHOOSH
IF NOTHING ELSE, I HAVE TO KEEP YOU TWO HERE.
ZWA-BAH

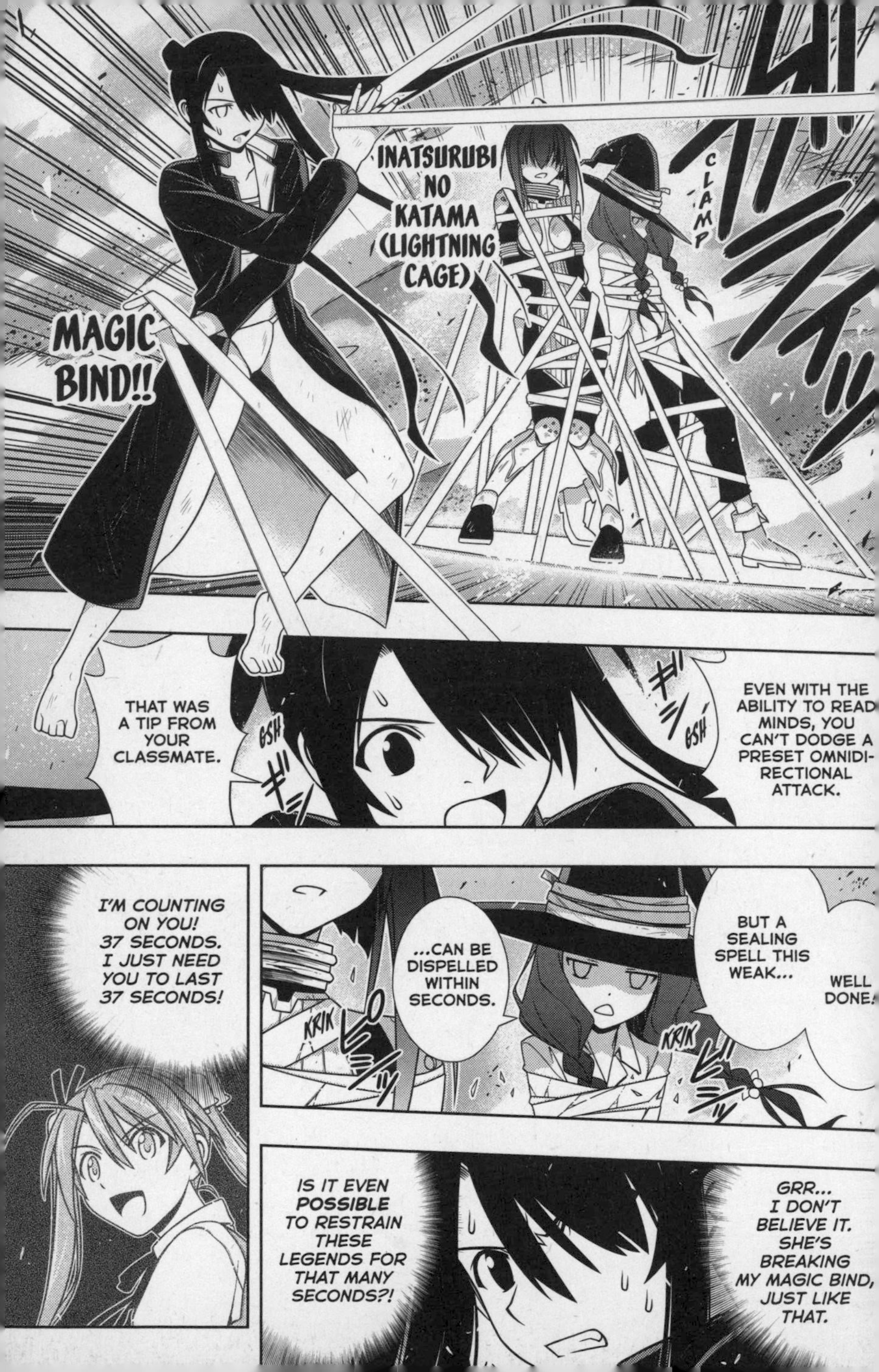

CLAMP
INATSURUBI NO KATAMA (LIGHTNING CAGE)
MAGIC BIND!!
EVEN WITH THE ABILITY TO READ MINDS, YOU CAN'T DODGE A PRESET OMNIDI-RECTIONAL ATTACK.
GSH
GSH
THAT WAS A TIP FROM YOUR CLASSMATE.
WELL DONE.
BUT A SEALING SPELL THIS WEAK...
KRIK
...CAN BE DISPELLED WITHIN SECONDS.
KRIK
GRR... I DON'T BELIEVE IT. SHE'S BREAKING MY MAGIC BIND, JUST LIKE THAT.
IS IT EVEN POSSIBLE TO RESTRAIN THESE LEGENDS FOR THAT MANY SECONDS?!
I'M COUNTING ON YOU! 37 SECONDS. I JUST NEED YOU TO LAST 37 SECONDS!

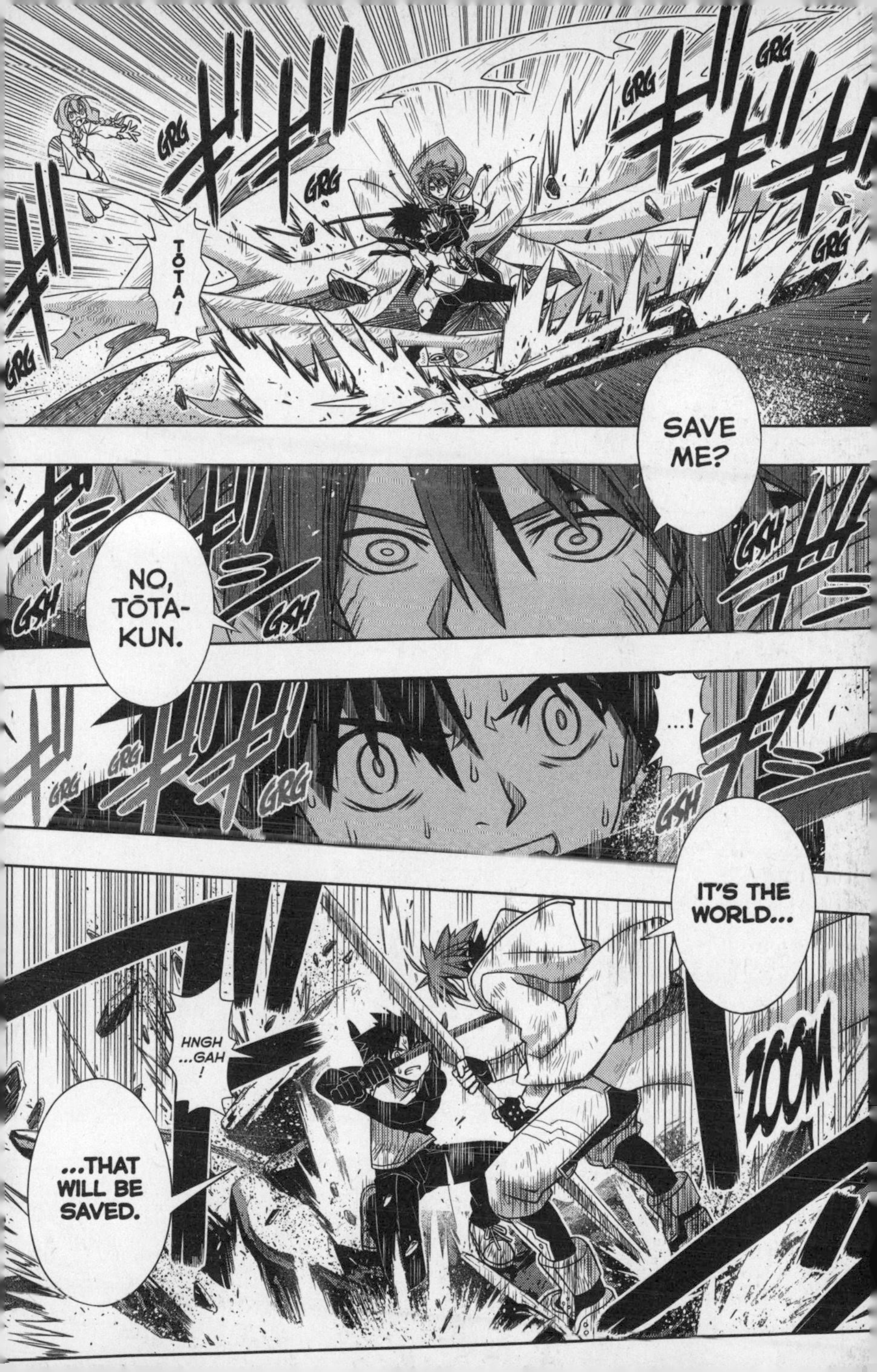
GRG
GRG
GRG
GRG
GRG
GRG
TŌTA!
SAVE ME?
GSH
NO, TŌTA-KUN.
GSH
GSH
...!
GSH
GRG
GRG
GRG
IT'S THE WORLD...
ZOOM
HNGH ...GAH!
...THAT WILL BE SAVED.

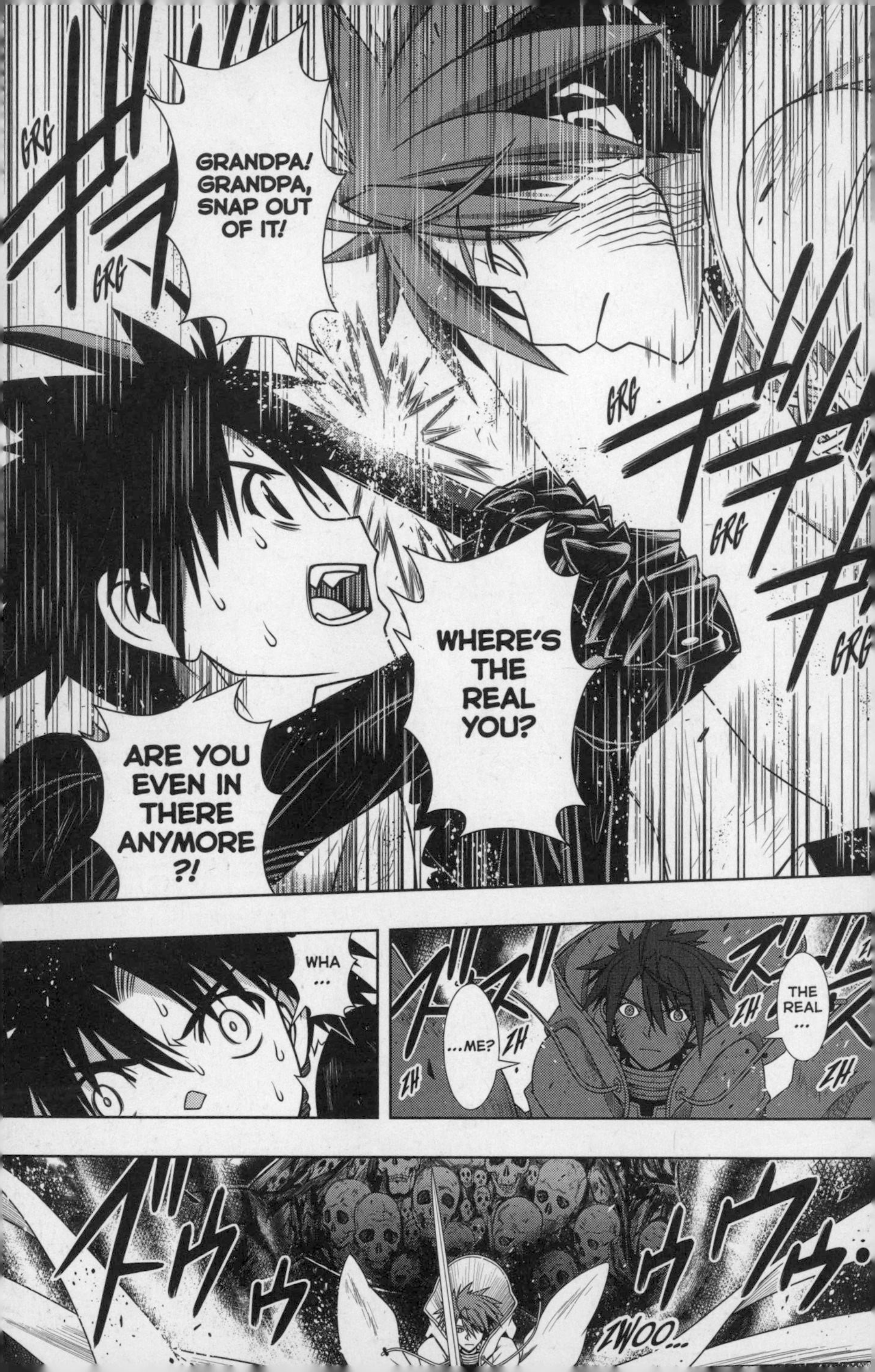
GRG
GRG
GRANDPA! GRANDPA, SNAP OUT OF IT!
GRG
GRG
GRG
WHERE'S THE REAL YOU?
ARE YOU EVEN IN THERE ANYMORE ?!
ZH
THE REAL ...
ZH
ZH
...ME?
ZH
WHA ...
ZWOO...

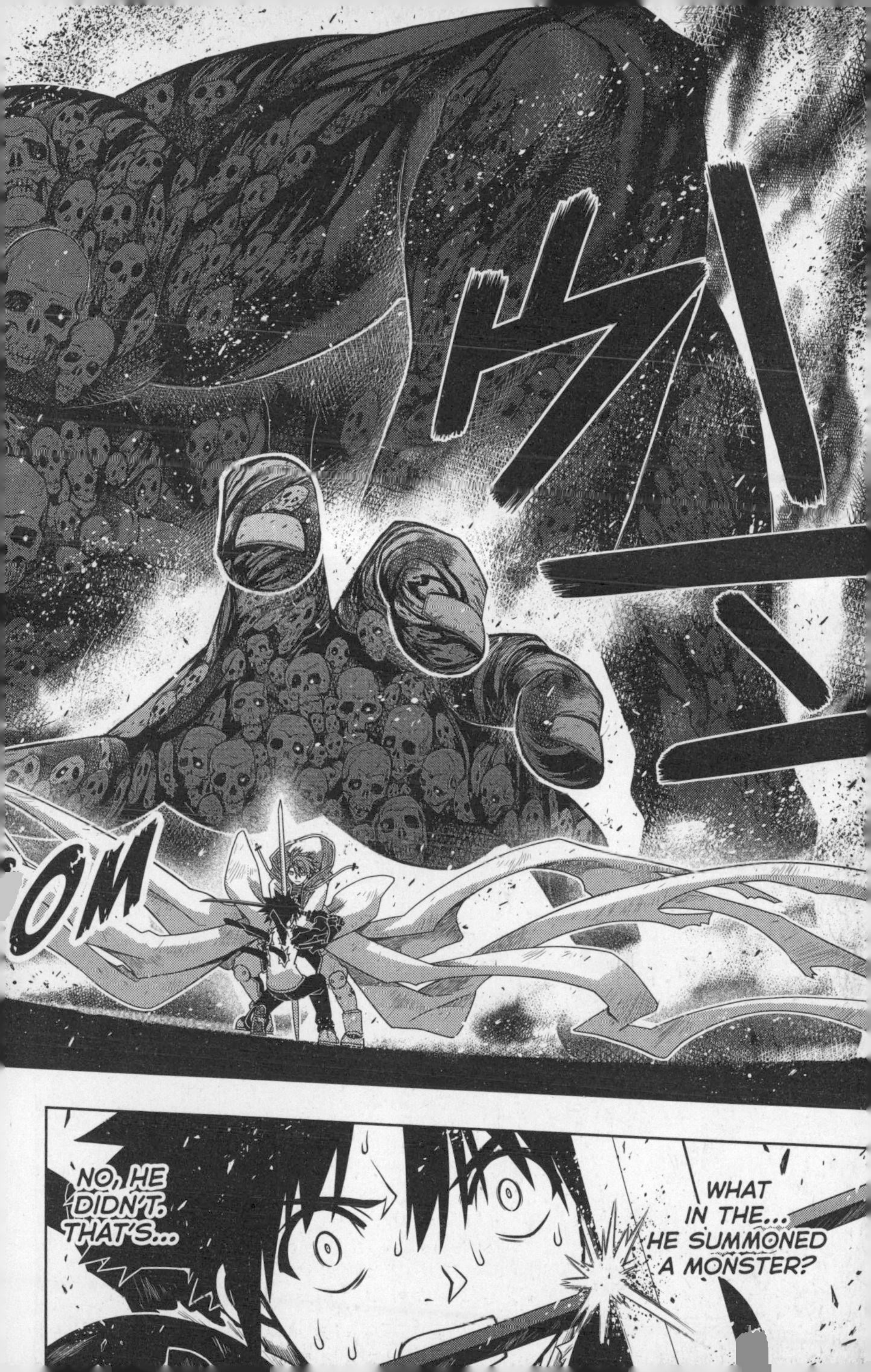
OM
WHAT IN THE... HE SUMMONED A MONSTER?
NO, HE DIDN'T. THAT'S...

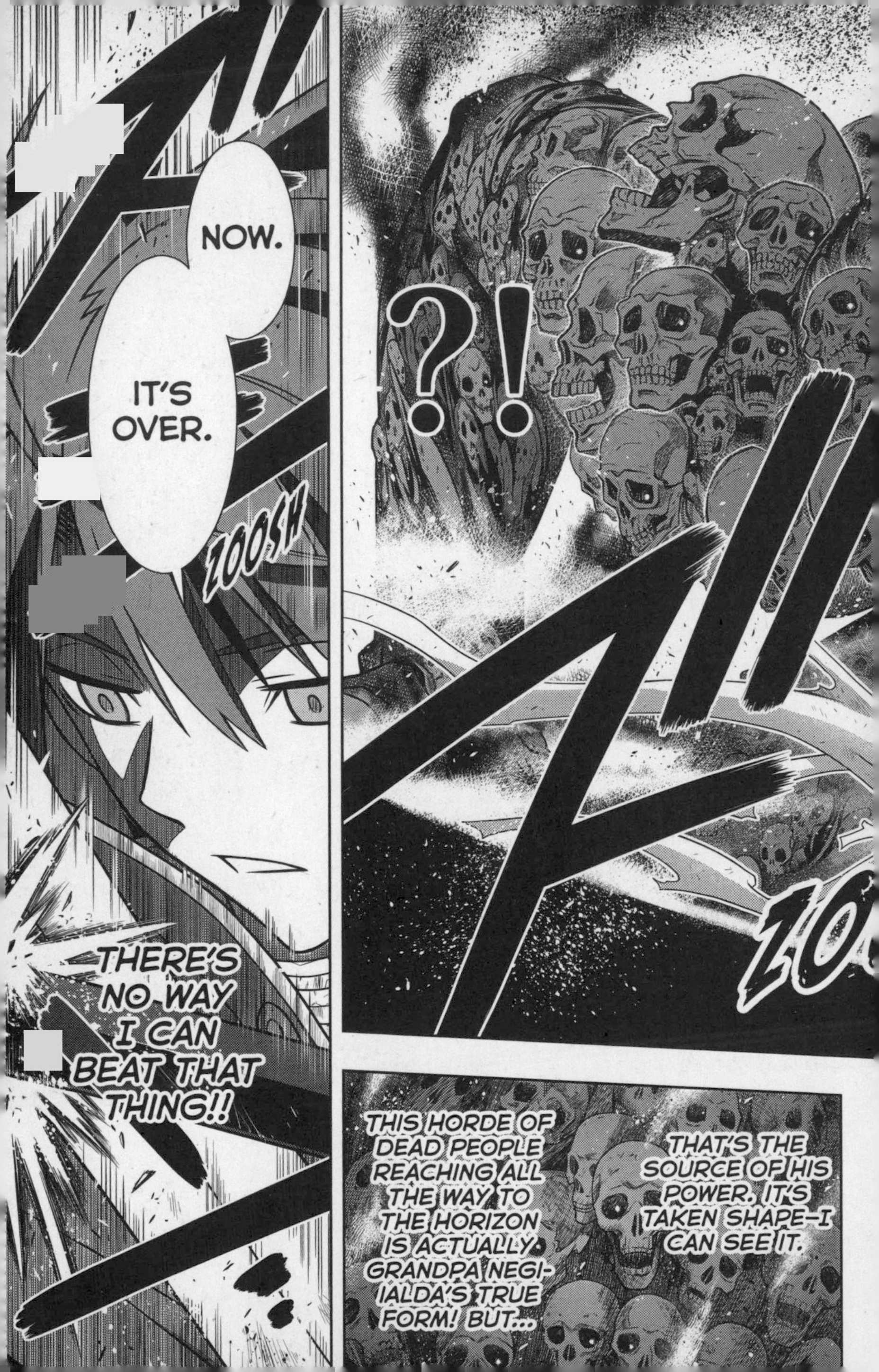
?!
ZOO
THAT'S THE SOURCE OF HIS POWER. IT'S TAKEN SHAPE—I CAN SEE IT.
THIS HORDE OF DEAD PEOPLE REACHING ALL THE WAY TO THE HORIZON IS ACTUALLY GRANDPA NEGI-IALDA'S TRUE FORM! BUT...
NOW.
IT'S OVER.
ZOOSH
THERE'S NO WAY I CAN BEAT THAT THING!!

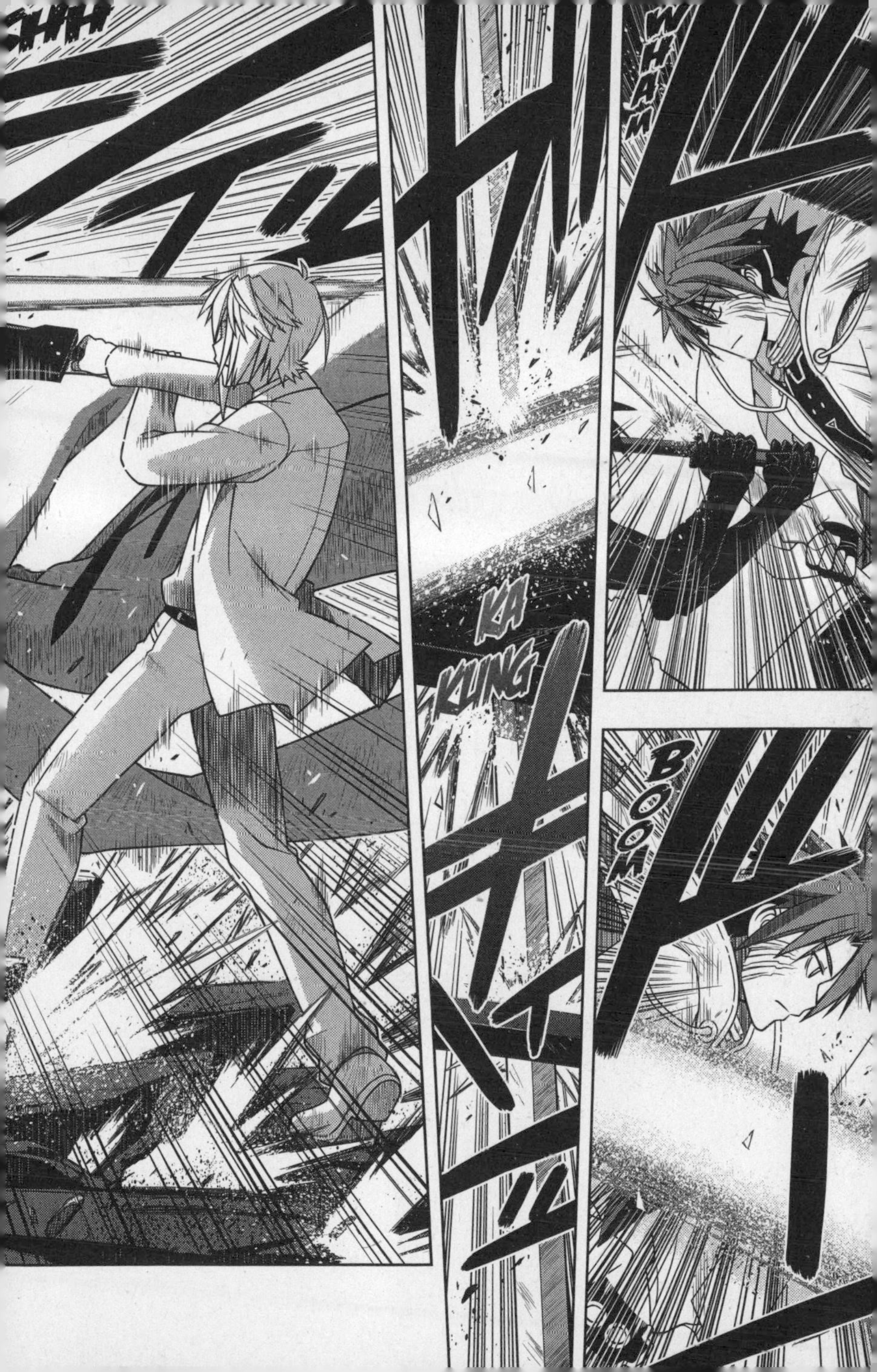
WHAM
BOOM
KA KLUNG

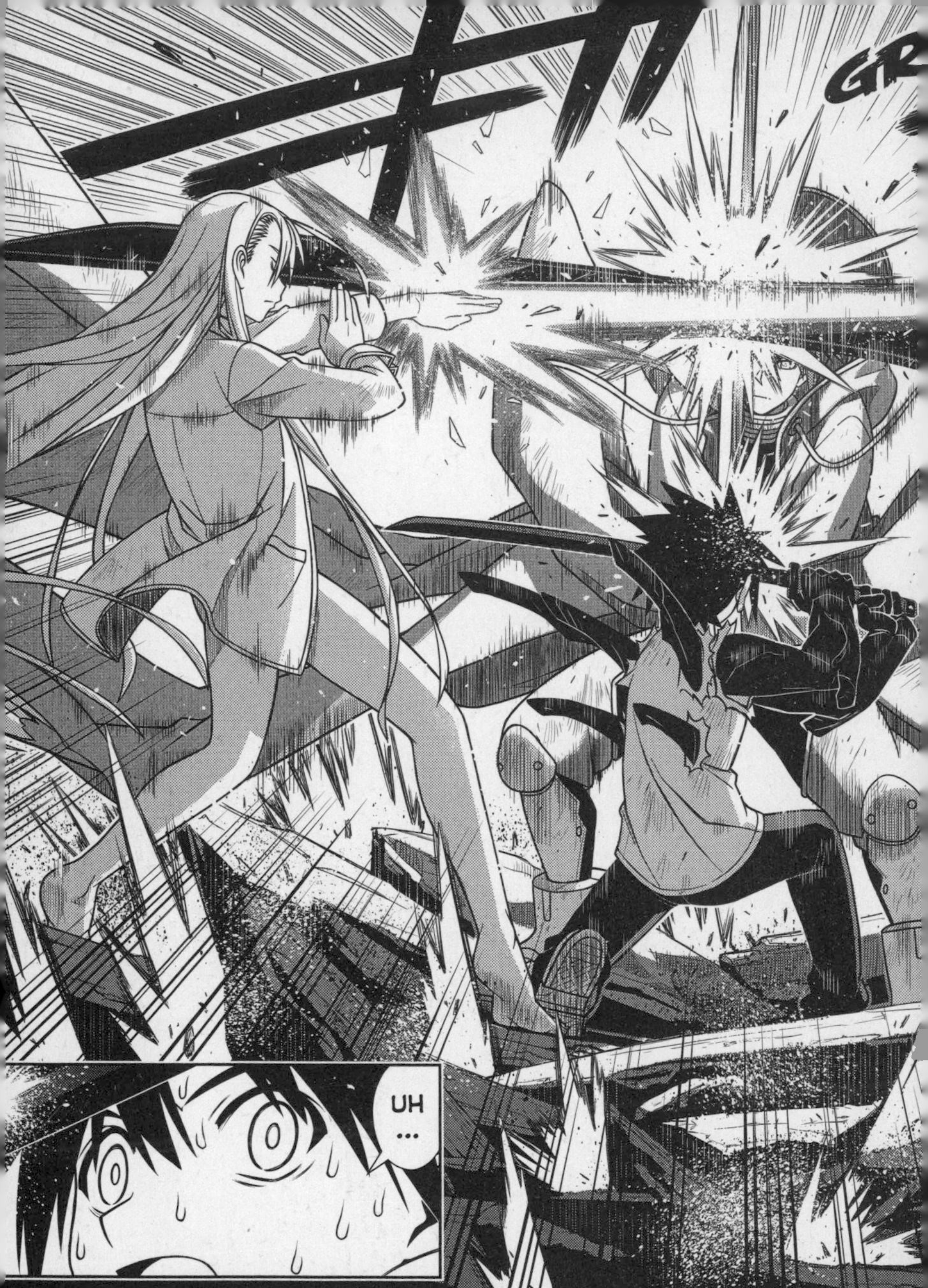
GR
UH
...

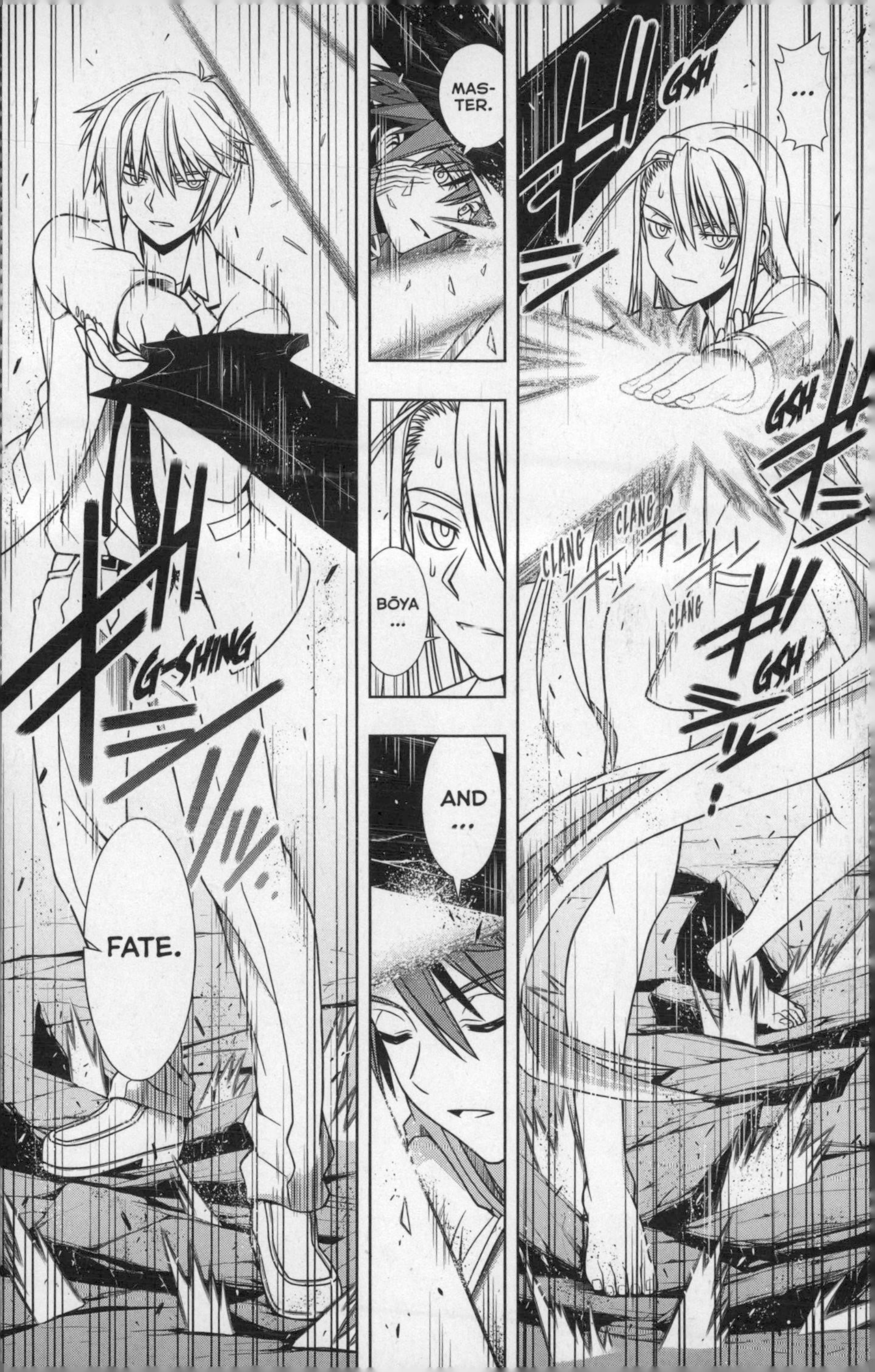
...
GSH
GSH
CLANG
CLANG
CLANG
GSH
MAS-TER.
BŌYA ...
AND ...
G-SHING
FATE.

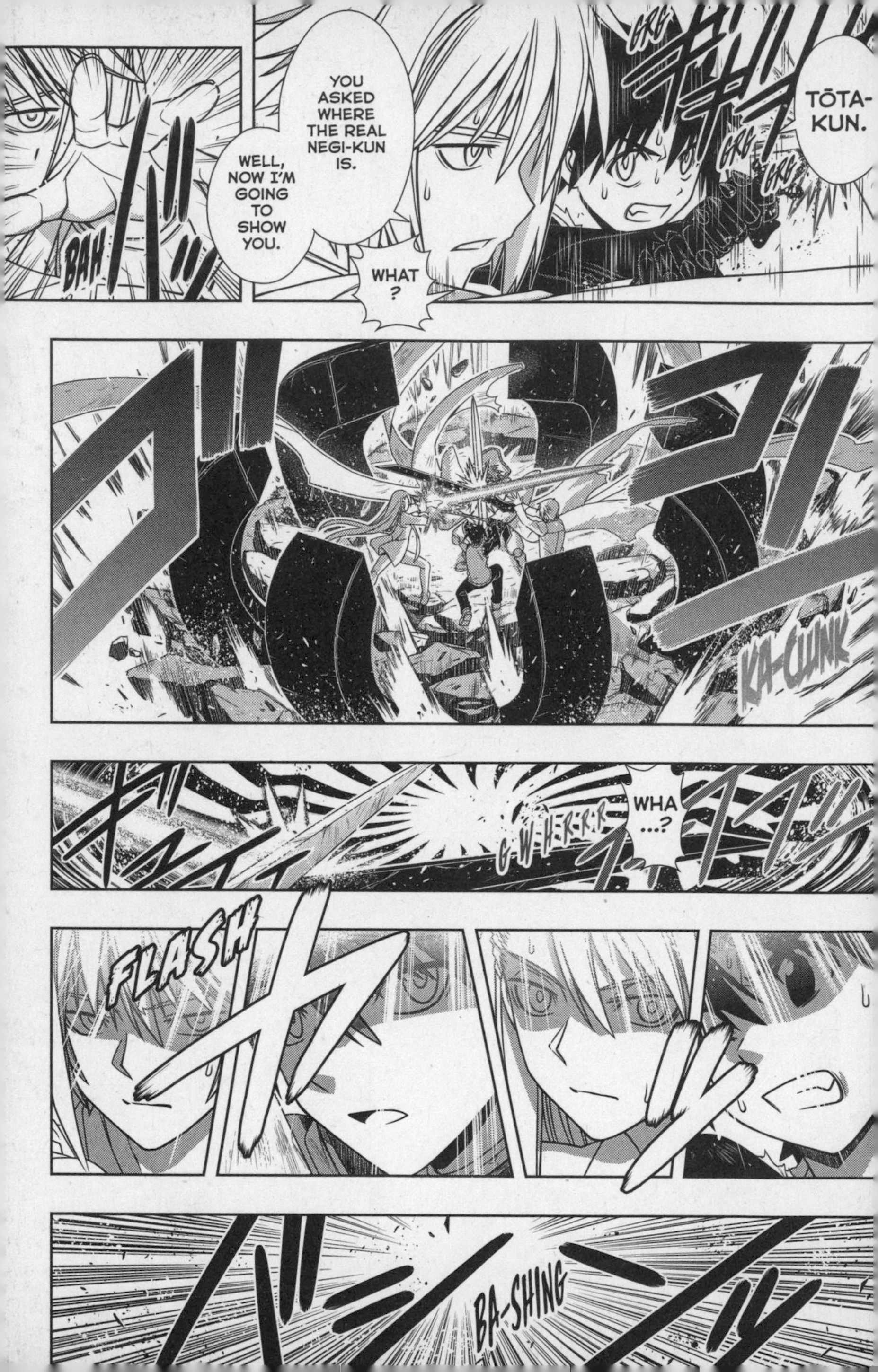
TŌTA-KUN.
GRR
GRR
GRR
YOU ASKED WHERE THE REAL NEGI-KUN IS.
WELL, NOW I'M GOING TO SHOW YOU.
WHAT?
BAH
KA-CLUNK
WHA...?
GWHRRR
FLASH
BA-SHING

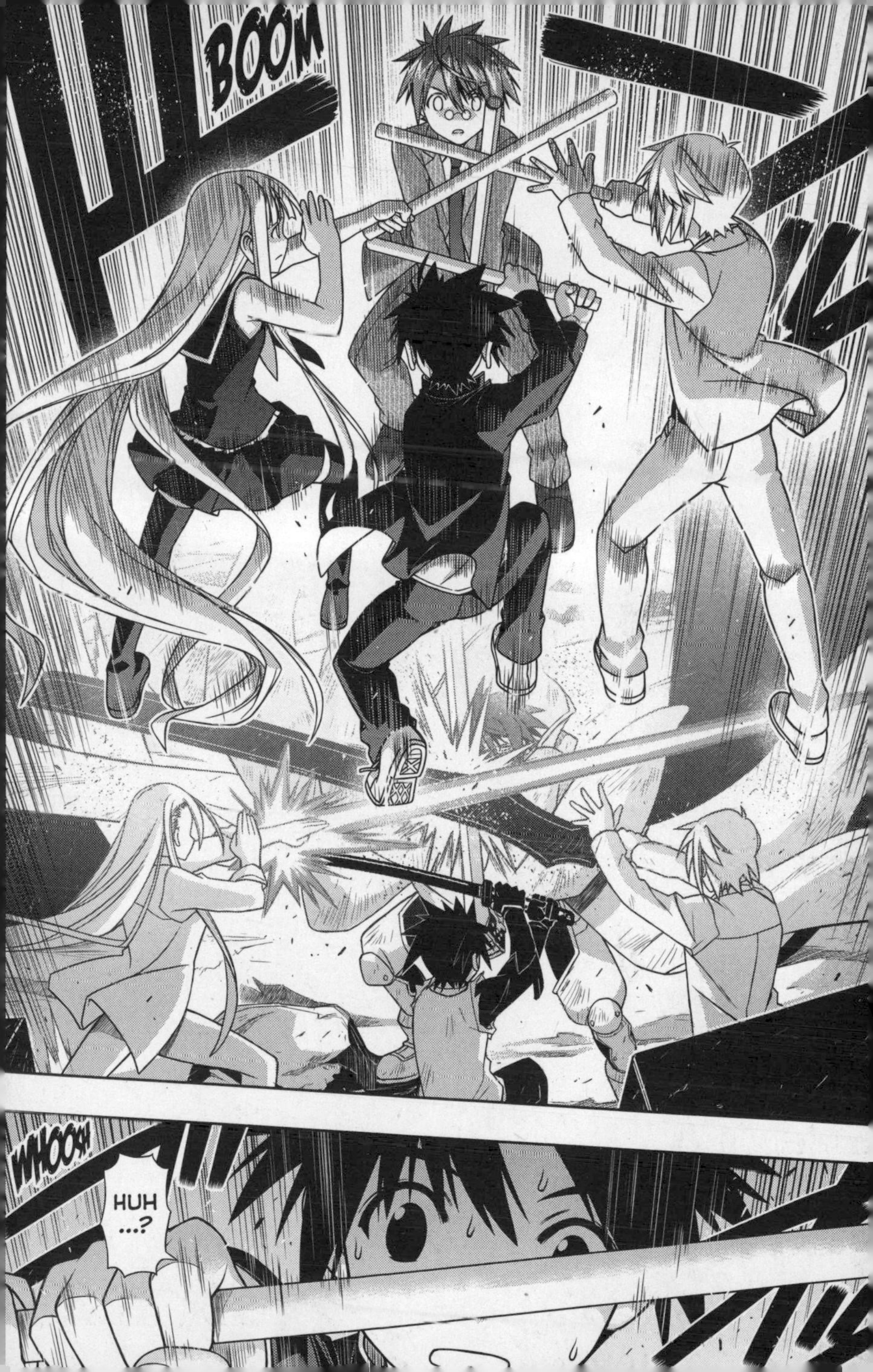
BOOM
WHOOSH
HUH ...?

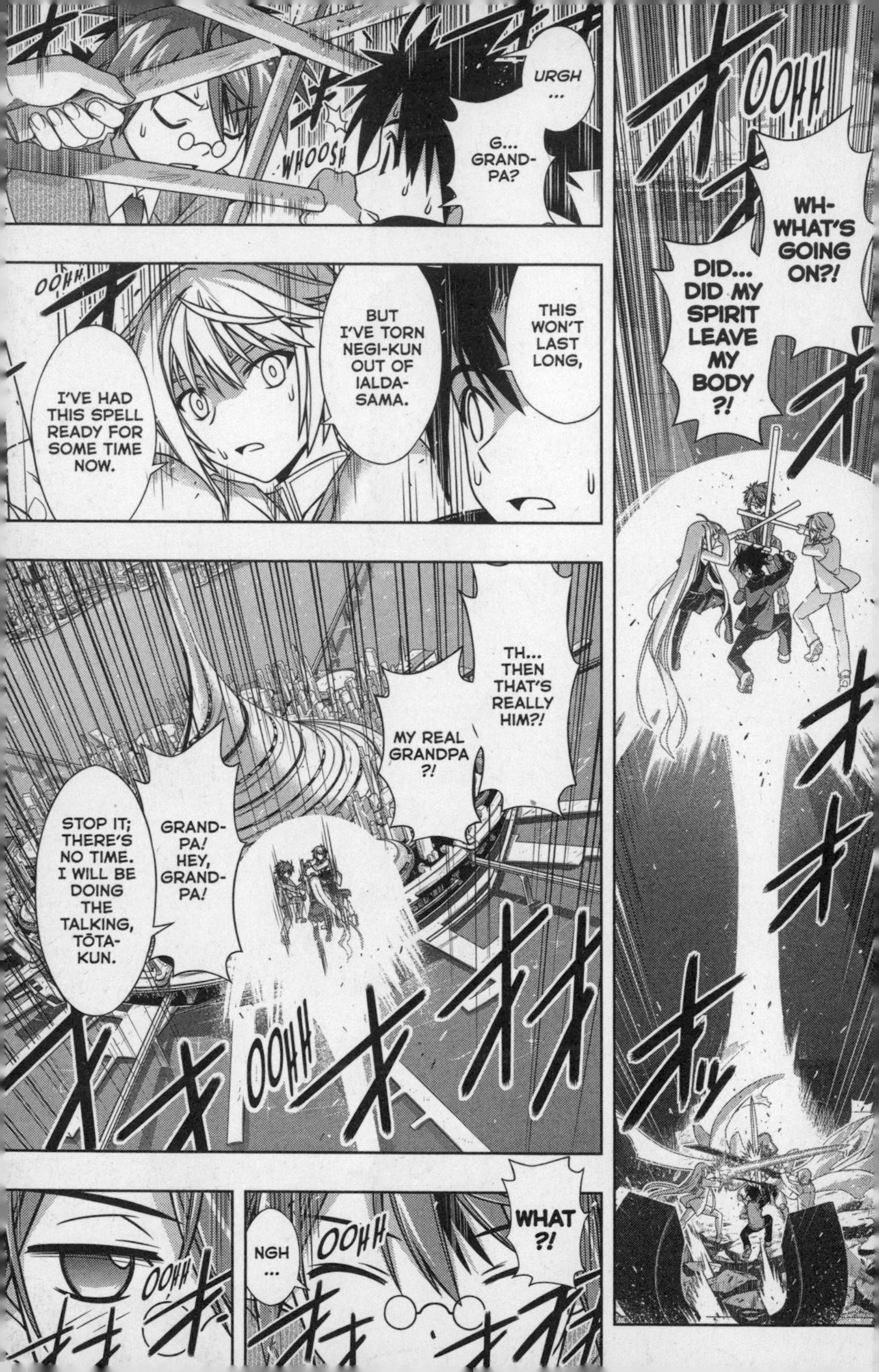
OOHH
WH- WHAT'S GOING ON?!
DID... DID MY SPIRIT LEAVE MY BODY ?!
URGH ...
G... GRAND-PA?
WHOOSH
THIS WON'T LAST LONG,
BUT I'VE TORN NEGI-KUN OUT OF IALDA-SAMA.
I'VE HAD THIS SPELL READY FOR SOME TIME NOW.
OOHH
TH... THEN THAT'S REALLY HIM?!
MY REAL GRANDPA ?!
GRAND-PA! HEY, GRAND-PA!
STOP IT; THERE'S NO TIME. I WILL BE DOING THE TALKING, TŌTA-KUN.
OOHH
WHAT ?!
NGH ...
OOHH
OOHH

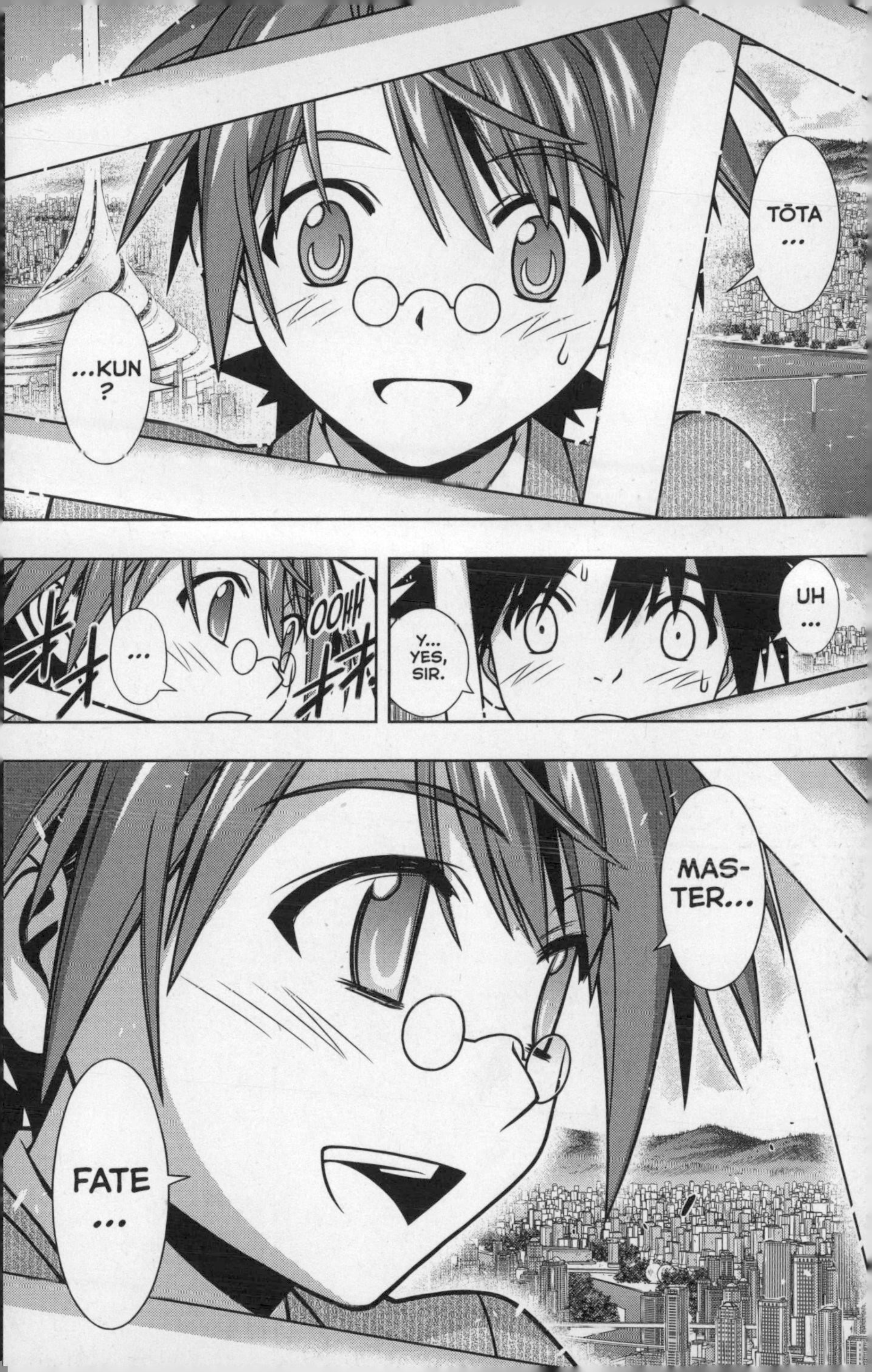
TŌTA ...
...KUN ?
UH ...
Y... YES, SIR.
...
MAS-TER...
FATE ...

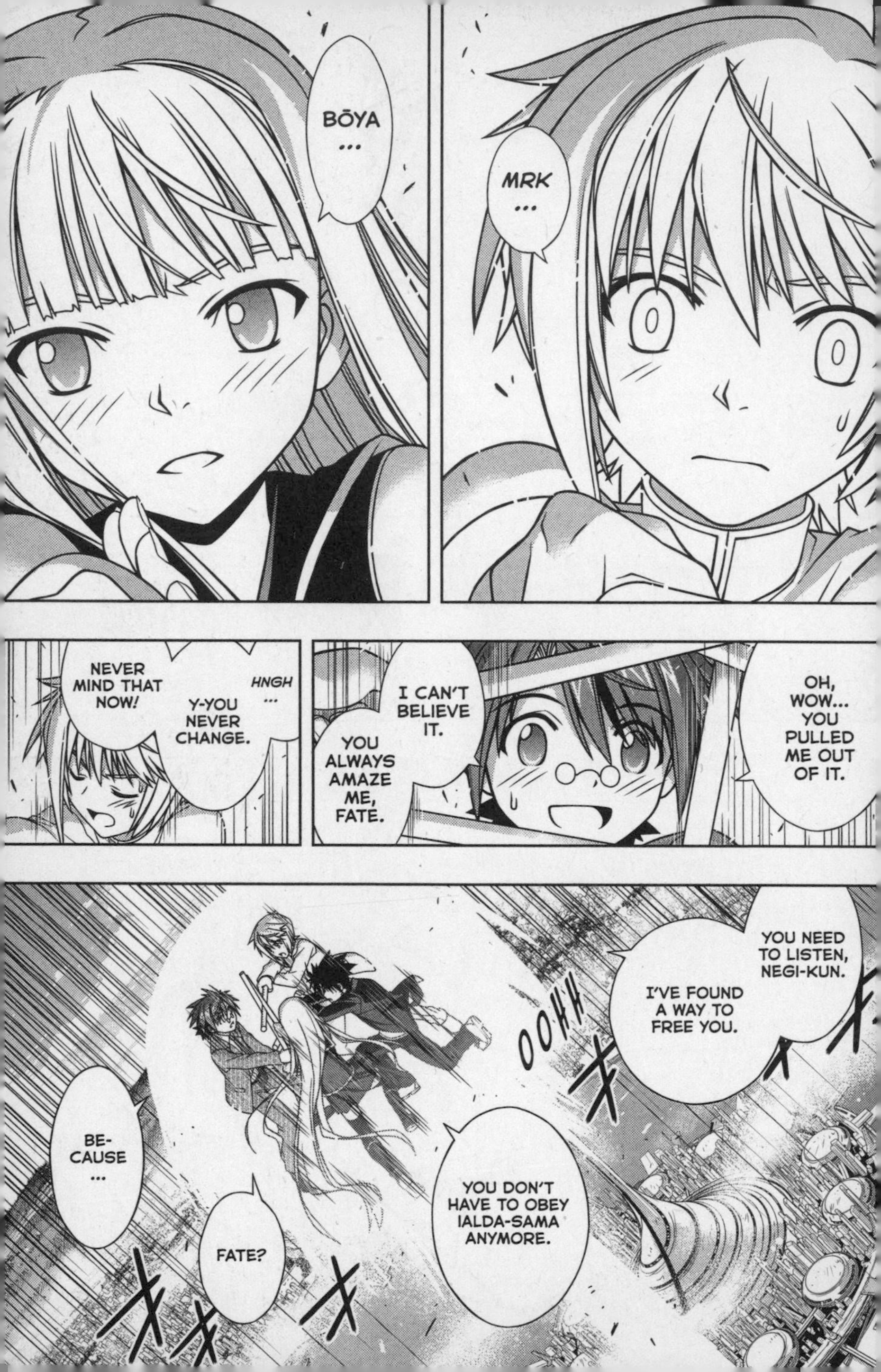
MRK ...
BŌYA ...
OH, WOW... YOU PULLED ME OUT OF IT.
I CAN'T BELIEVE IT.
YOU ALWAYS AMAZE ME, FATE.
HNGH ...
Y-YOU NEVER CHANGE.
NEVER MIND THAT NOW!
YOU NEED TO LISTEN, NEGI-KUN.
I'VE FOUND A WAY TO FREE YOU.
OOKK
YOU DON'T HAVE TO OBEY IALDA-SAMA ANYMORE.
BE-CAUSE ...
FATE?

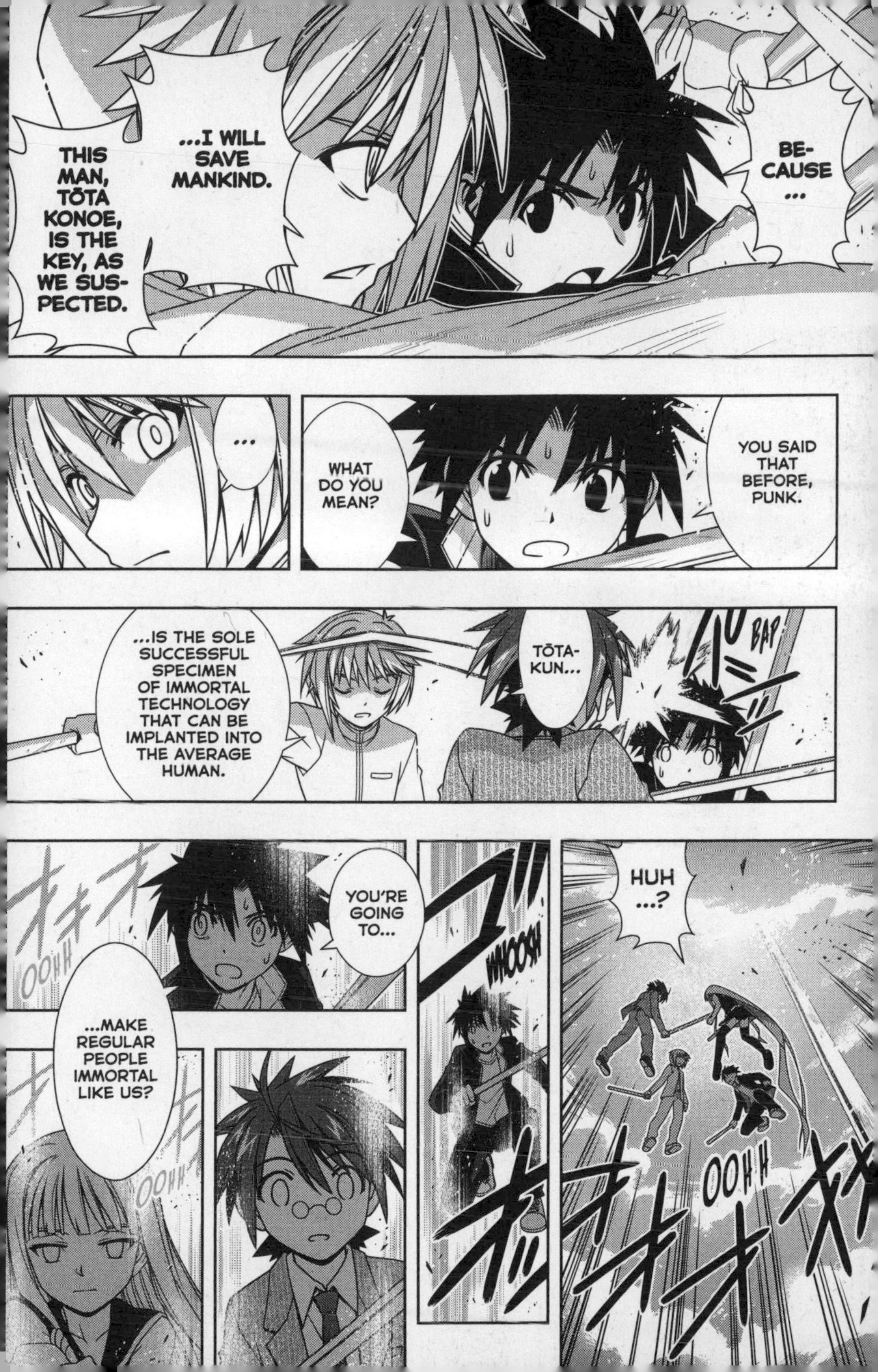
BE-CAUSE...
...I WILL SAVE MANKIND.
THIS MAN, TŌTA KONOE, IS THE KEY, AS WE SUSPECTED.
YOU SAID THAT BEFORE, PUNK.
WHAT DO YOU MEAN?
...
BAP
TŌTA-KUN...
...IS THE SOLE SUCCESSFUL SPECIMEN OF IMMORTAL TECHNOLOGY THAT CAN BE IMPLANTED INTO THE AVERAGE HUMAN.
HUH...?
OOHH
WHOOSH
YOU'RE GOING TO...
OOHH
...MAKE REGULAR PEOPLE IMMORTAL LIKE US?
OOHH

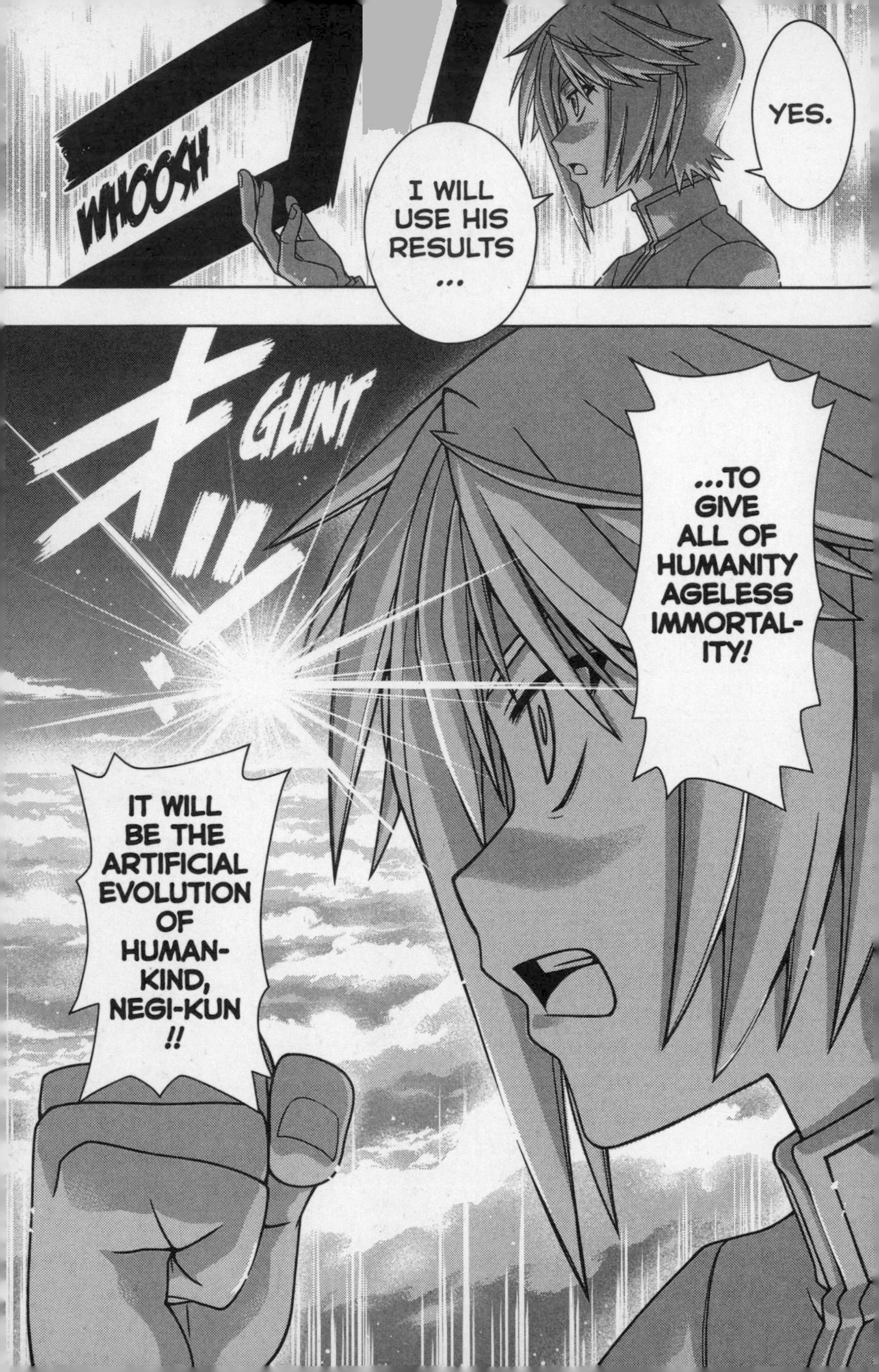
YES.
I WILL USE HIS RESULTS ...
WHOOSH
...TO GIVE ALL OF HUMANITY AGELESS IMMORTAL-ITY!
GLINT
IT WILL BE THE ARTIFICIAL EVOLUTION OF HUMAN-KIND, NEGI-KUN !!

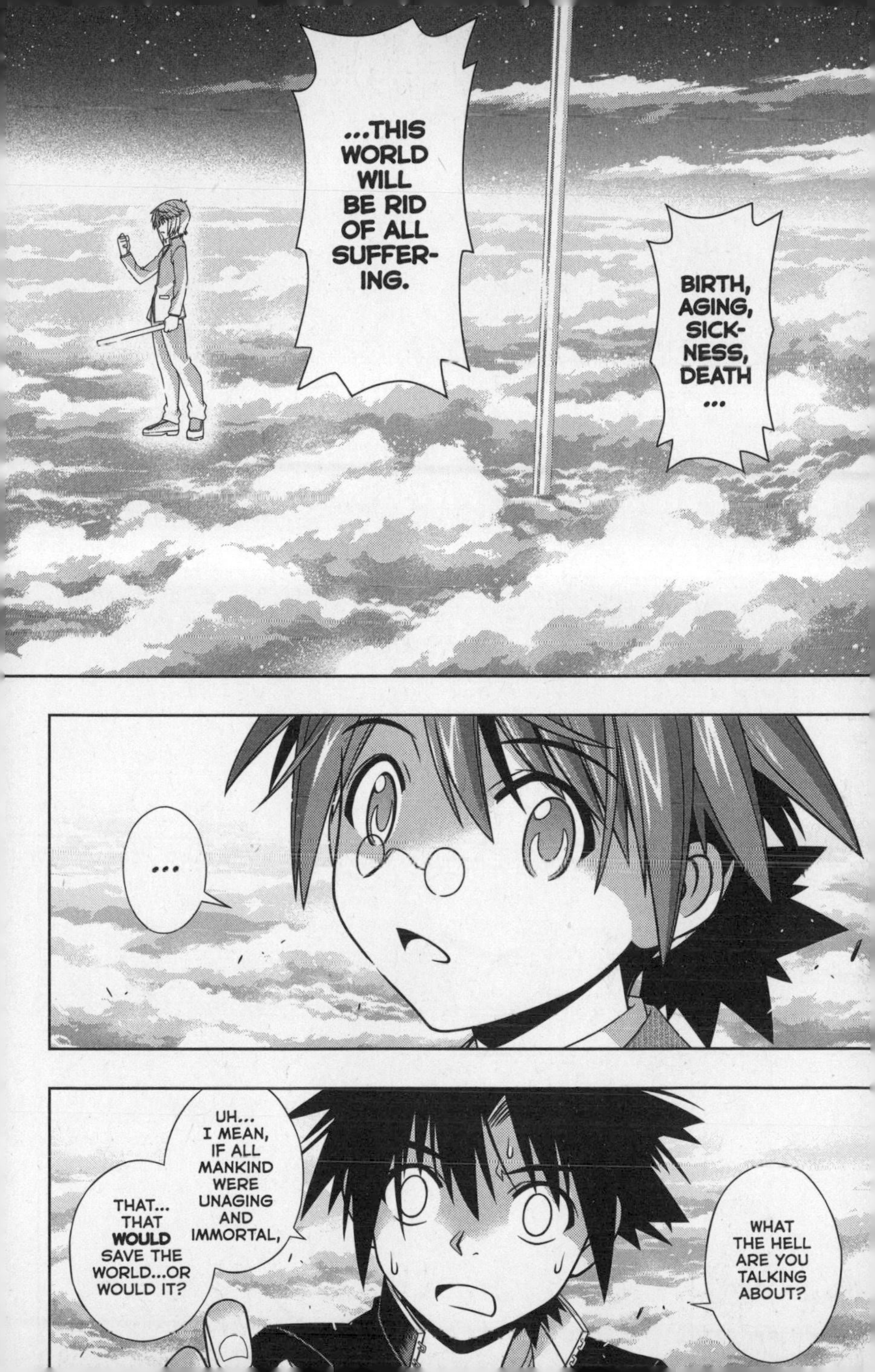
BIRTH, AGING, SICK-NESS, DEATH...
...THIS WORLD WILL BE RID OF ALL SUFFER-ING.
...
WHAT THE HELL ARE YOU TALKING ABOUT?
UH... I MEAN, IF ALL MANKIND WERE UNAGING AND IMMORTAL,
THAT... THAT **WOULD** SAVE THE WORLD...OR WOULD IT?

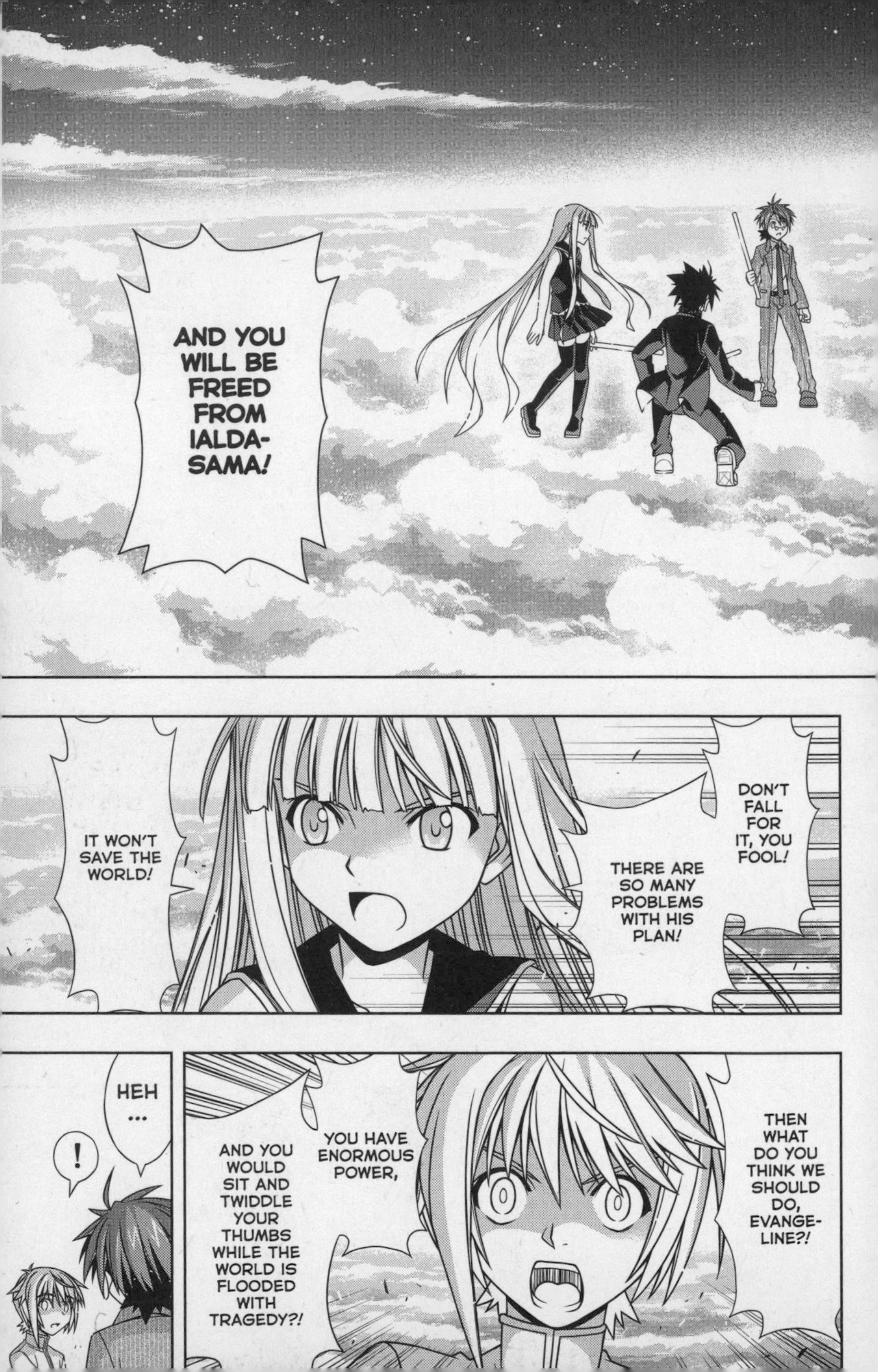
AND YOU WILL BE FREED FROM IALDA-SAMA!
DON'T FALL FOR IT, YOU FOOL!
THERE ARE SO MANY PROBLEMS WITH HIS PLAN!
IT WON'T SAVE THE WORLD!
THEN WHAT DO YOU THINK WE SHOULD DO, EVANGELINE?!
YOU HAVE ENORMOUS POWER,
AND YOU WOULD SIT AND TWIDDLE YOUR THUMBS WHILE THE WORLD IS FLOODED WITH TRAGEDY?!
HEH...
!

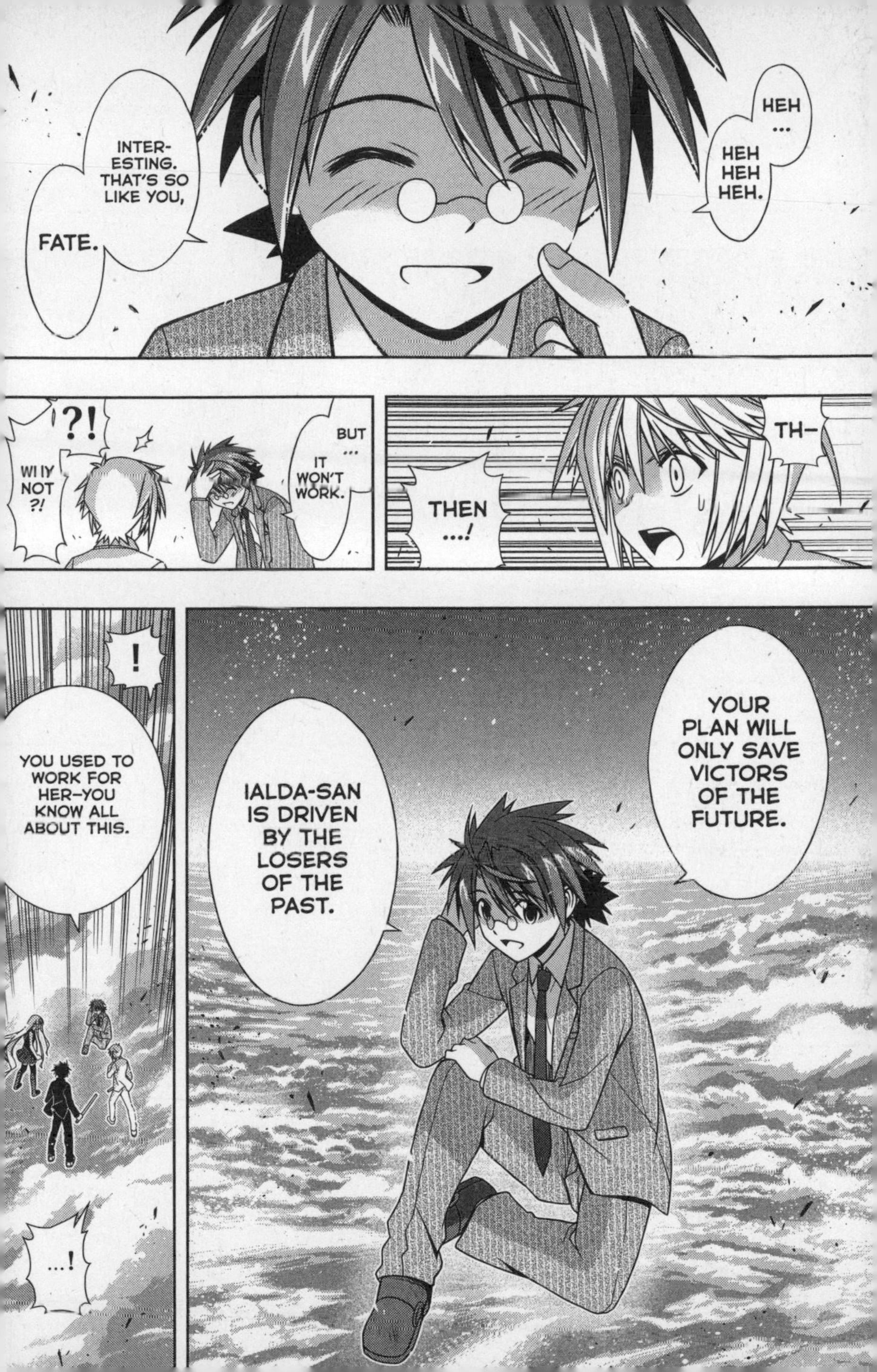
HEH ... HEH HEH HEH.
INTERESTING. THAT'S SO LIKE YOU, FATE.
TH-
THEN ...!
BUT ... IT WON'T WORK.
?!
WHY NOT?!
YOUR PLAN WILL ONLY SAVE VICTORS OF THE FUTURE.
IALDA-SAN IS DRIVEN BY THE LOSERS OF THE PAST.
!
YOU USED TO WORK FOR HER—YOU KNOW ALL ABOUT THIS.
...!

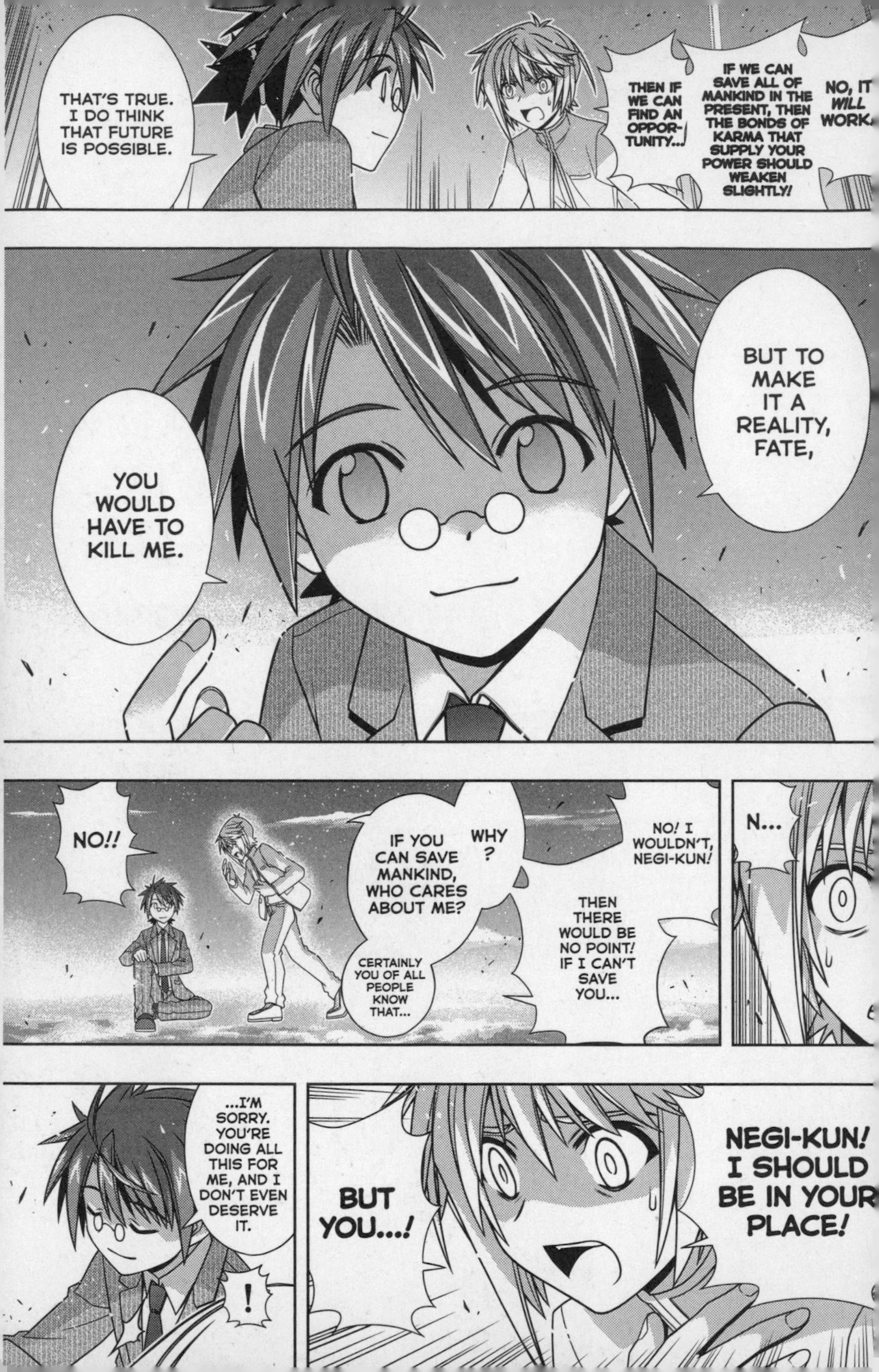
NO, IT WILL WORK.
IF WE CAN SAVE ALL OF MANKIND IN THE PRESENT, THEN THE BONDS OF KARMA THAT SUPPLY YOUR POWER SHOULD WEAKEN SLIGHTLY!
THEN IF WE CAN FIND AN OPPORTUNITY...!
THAT'S TRUE. I DO THINK THAT FUTURE IS POSSIBLE.
BUT TO MAKE IT A REALITY, FATE,
YOU WOULD HAVE TO KILL ME.
N...
NO! I WOULDN'T, NEGI-KUN!
THEN THERE WOULD BE NO POINT! IF I CAN'T SAVE YOU...
WHY?
IF YOU CAN SAVE MANKIND, WHO CARES ABOUT ME?
CERTAINLY YOU OF ALL PEOPLE KNOW THAT...
NO!!
NEGI-KUN! I SHOULD BE IN YOUR PLACE!
BUT YOU...!
...I'M SORRY. YOU'RE DOING ALL THIS FOR ME, AND I DON'T EVEN DESERVE IT.
!

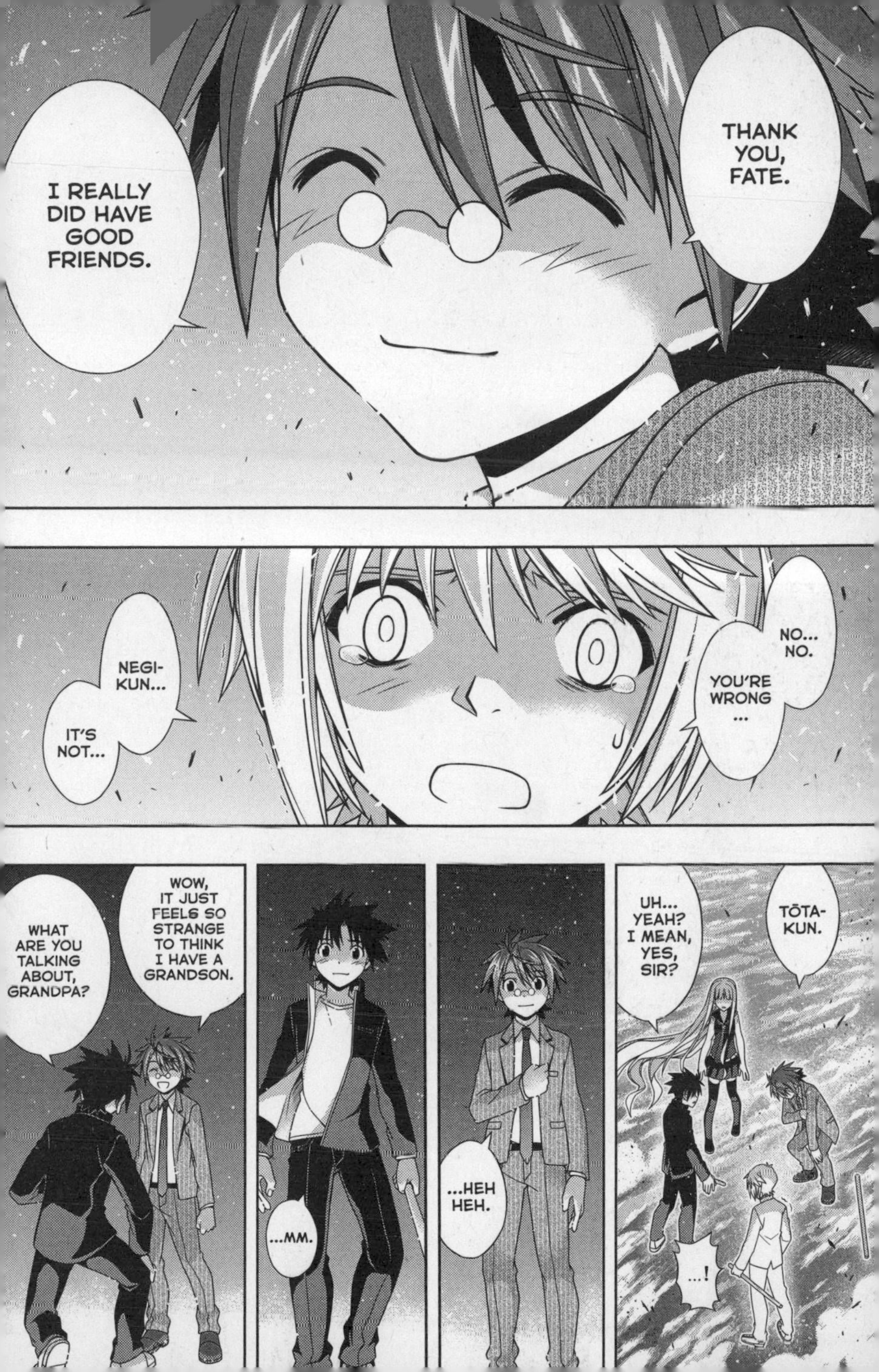
THANK YOU, FATE.
I REALLY DID HAVE GOOD FRIENDS.
NO... NO.
YOU'RE WRONG ...
NEGI-KUN...
IT'S NOT...
TŌTA-KUN.
UH... YEAH? I MEAN, YES, SIR?
...!
...HEH HEH.
...MM.
WOW, IT JUST FEELS SO STRANGE TO THINK I HAVE A GRANDSON.
WHAT ARE YOU TALKING ABOUT, GRANDPA?

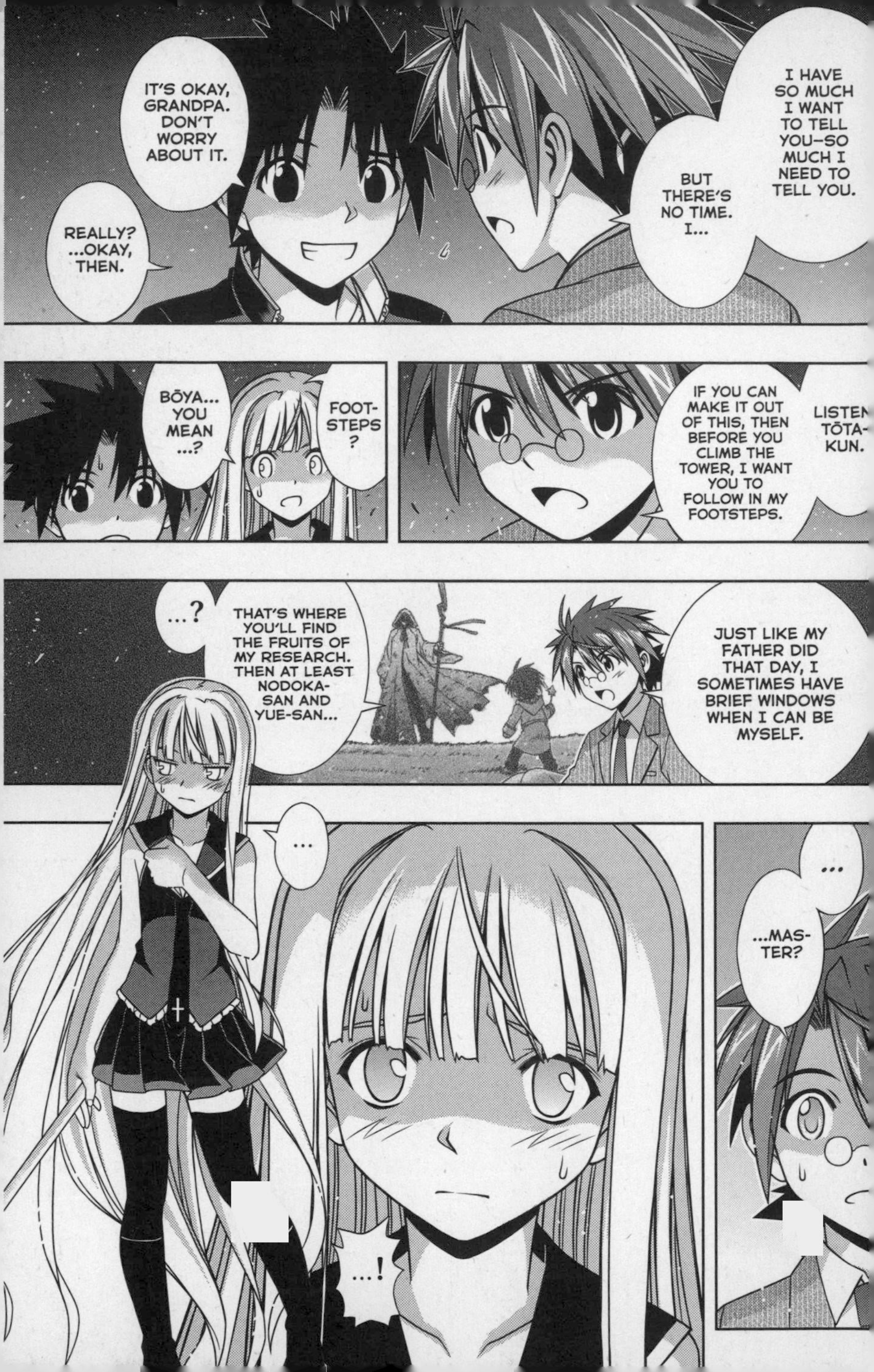
I HAVE SO MUCH I WANT TO TELL YOU—SO MUCH I NEED TO TELL YOU.
BUT THERE'S NO TIME. I...
IT'S OKAY, GRANDPA. DON'T WORRY ABOUT IT.
REALLY? ...OKAY, THEN.
LISTEN TŌTA-KUN.
IF YOU CAN MAKE IT OUT OF THIS, THEN BEFORE YOU CLIMB THE TOWER, I WANT YOU TO FOLLOW IN MY FOOTSTEPS.
FOOT-STEPS?
BŌYA... YOU MEAN ...?
JUST LIKE MY FATHER DID THAT DAY, I SOMETIMES HAVE BRIEF WINDOWS WHEN I CAN BE MYSELF.
THAT'S WHERE YOU'LL FIND THE FRUITS OF MY RESEARCH. THEN AT LEAST NODOKA-SAN AND YUE-SAN...
...?
...
...MAS-TER?
...
...!

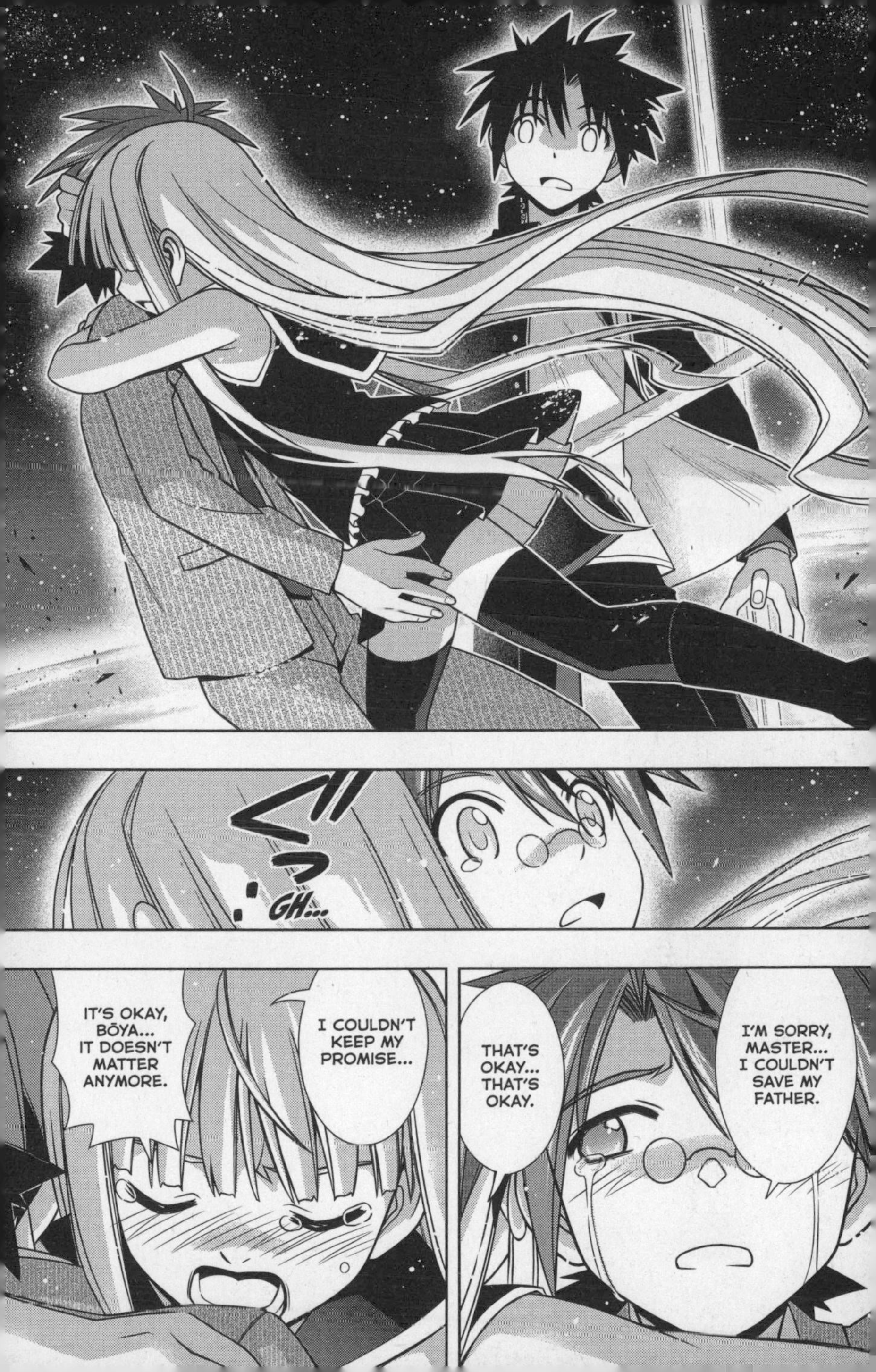
GH...
I'M SORRY, MASTER... I COULDN'T SAVE MY FATHER.
THAT'S OKAY... THAT'S OKAY.
I COULDN'T KEEP MY PROMISE...
IT'S OKAY, BŌYA... IT DOESN'T MATTER ANYMORE.

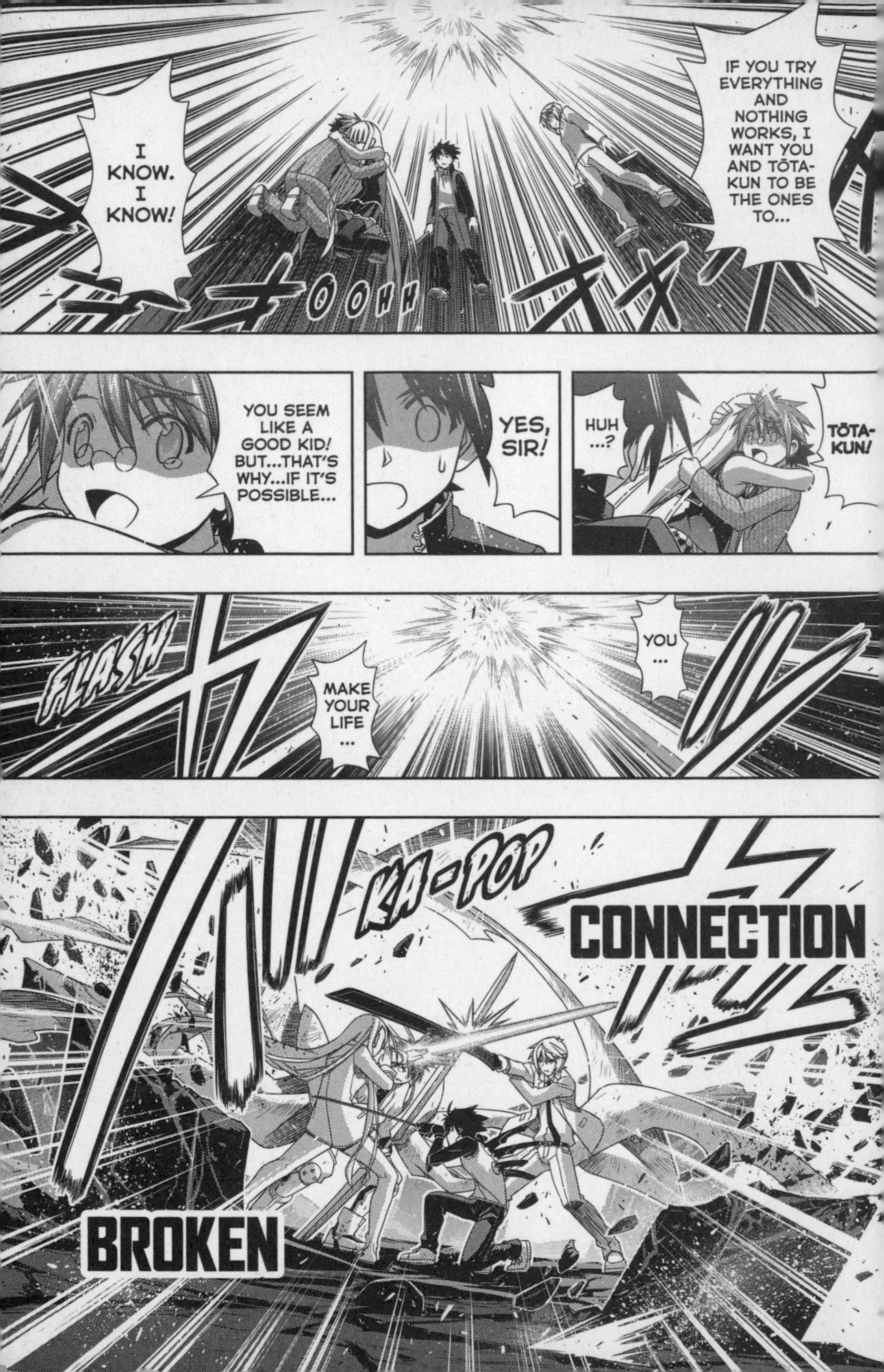
IF YOU TRY EVERYTHING AND NOTHING WORKS, I WANT YOU AND TŌTA-KUN TO BE THE ONES TO...
I KNOW. I KNOW!
TŌTA-KUN!
HUH ...?
YES, SIR!
YOU SEEM LIKE A GOOD KID! BUT...THAT'S WHY...IF IT'S POSSIBLE...
YOU ...
MAKE YOUR LIFE ...
FLASH
KA-POP
CONNECTION
BROKEN

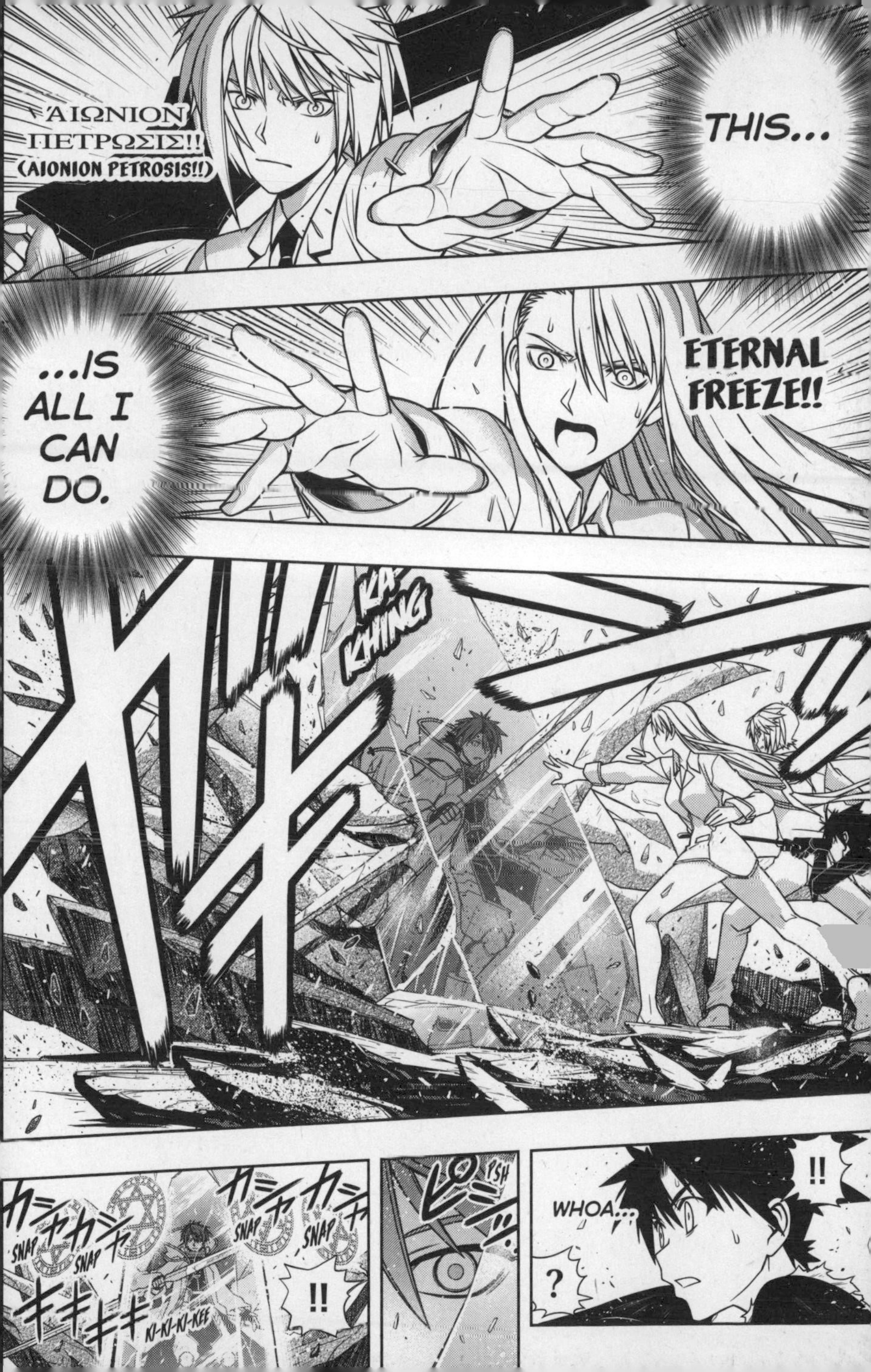
THIS...
ΆΙΩΝΙΟΝ ΠΕΤΡΩΣΙΣ!!
(AIONION PETROSIS!!)
ETERNAL FREEZE!!
...IS ALL I CAN DO.
KA-KHING
!!
WHOA...
?
PSH
!!
SNAP
SNAP
SNAP
SNAP
KI-KI-KI-KEE

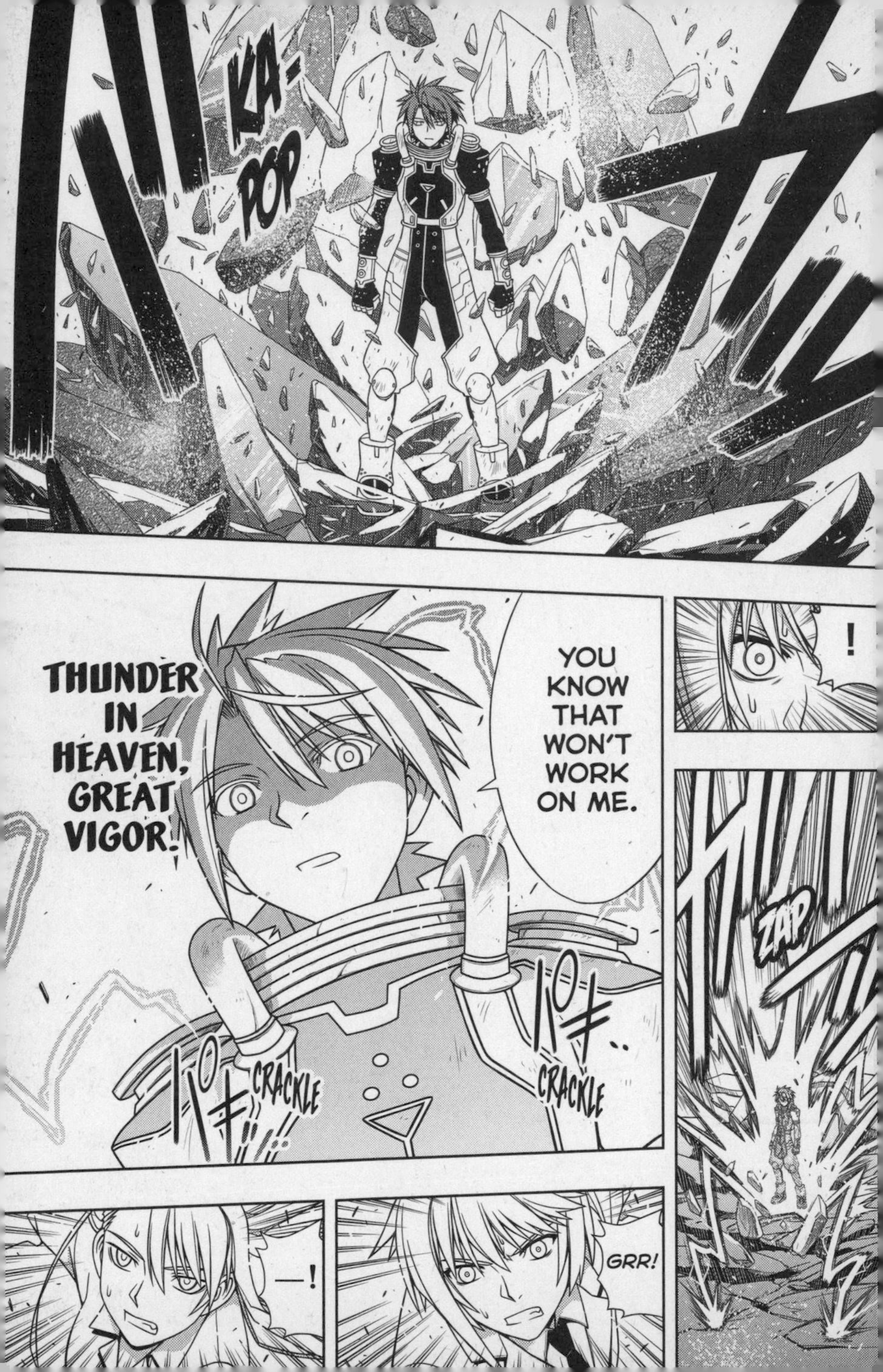
KA-POP
!
ZAP
YOU KNOW THAT WON'T WORK ON ME.
THUNDER IN HEAVEN, GREAT VIGOR!
CRACKLE
CRACKLE
GRR!
—!

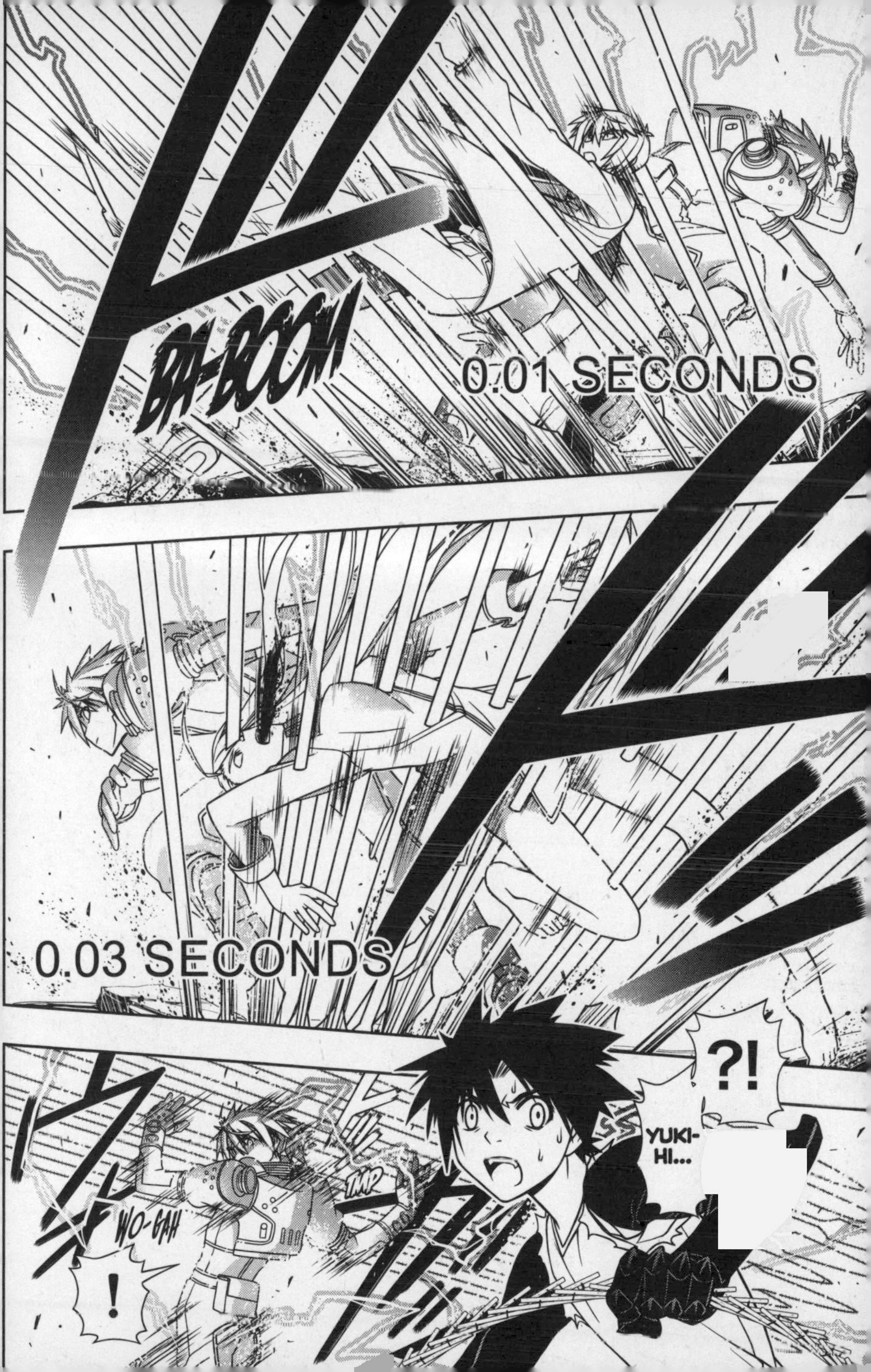
BA-BOOM
0.01 SECONDS
0.03 SECONDS
?!
YUKI-HI...
TMP
WO-GAH
!

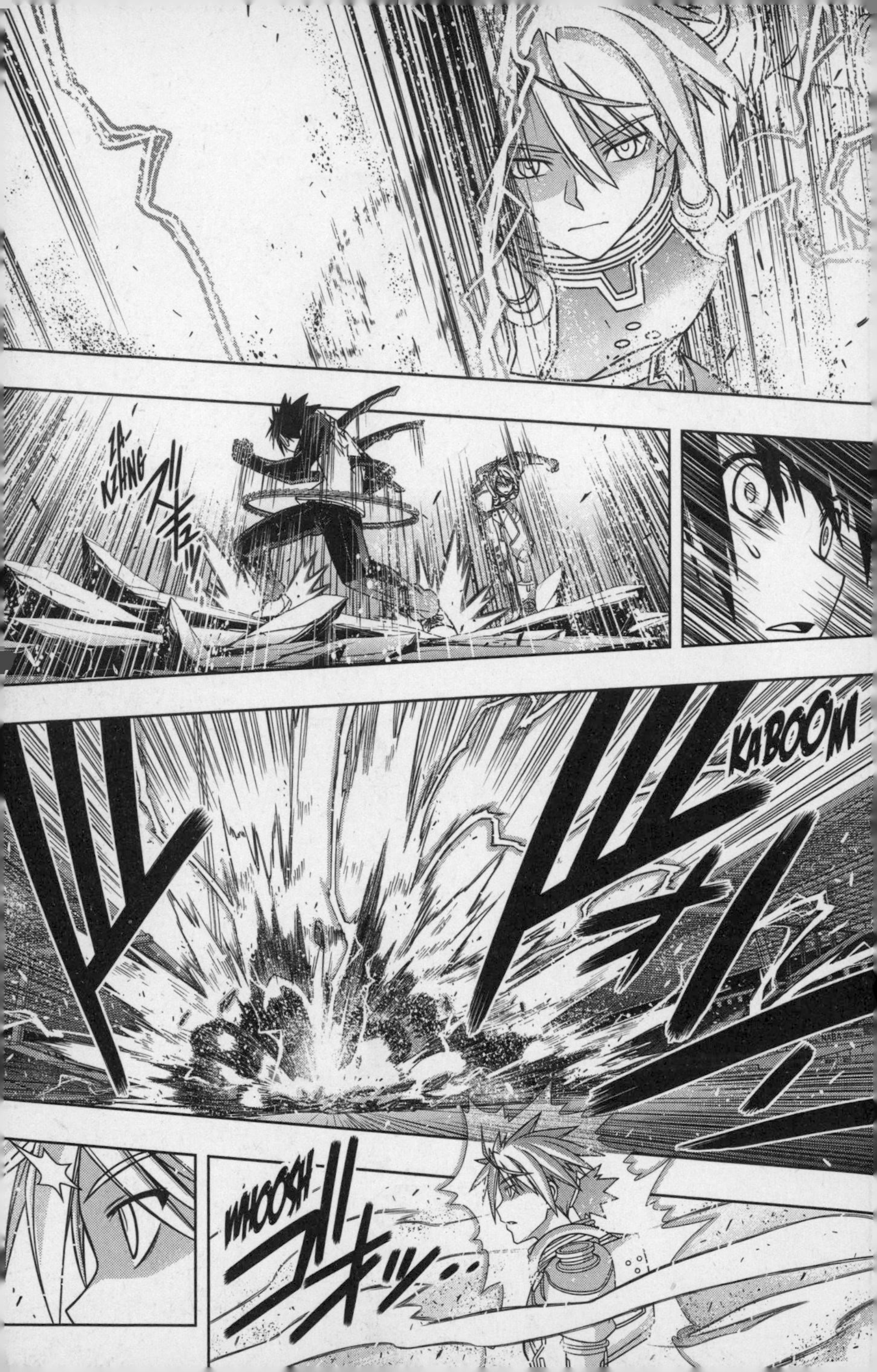
ZA-KZHNG
KABOOM
WHOOSH

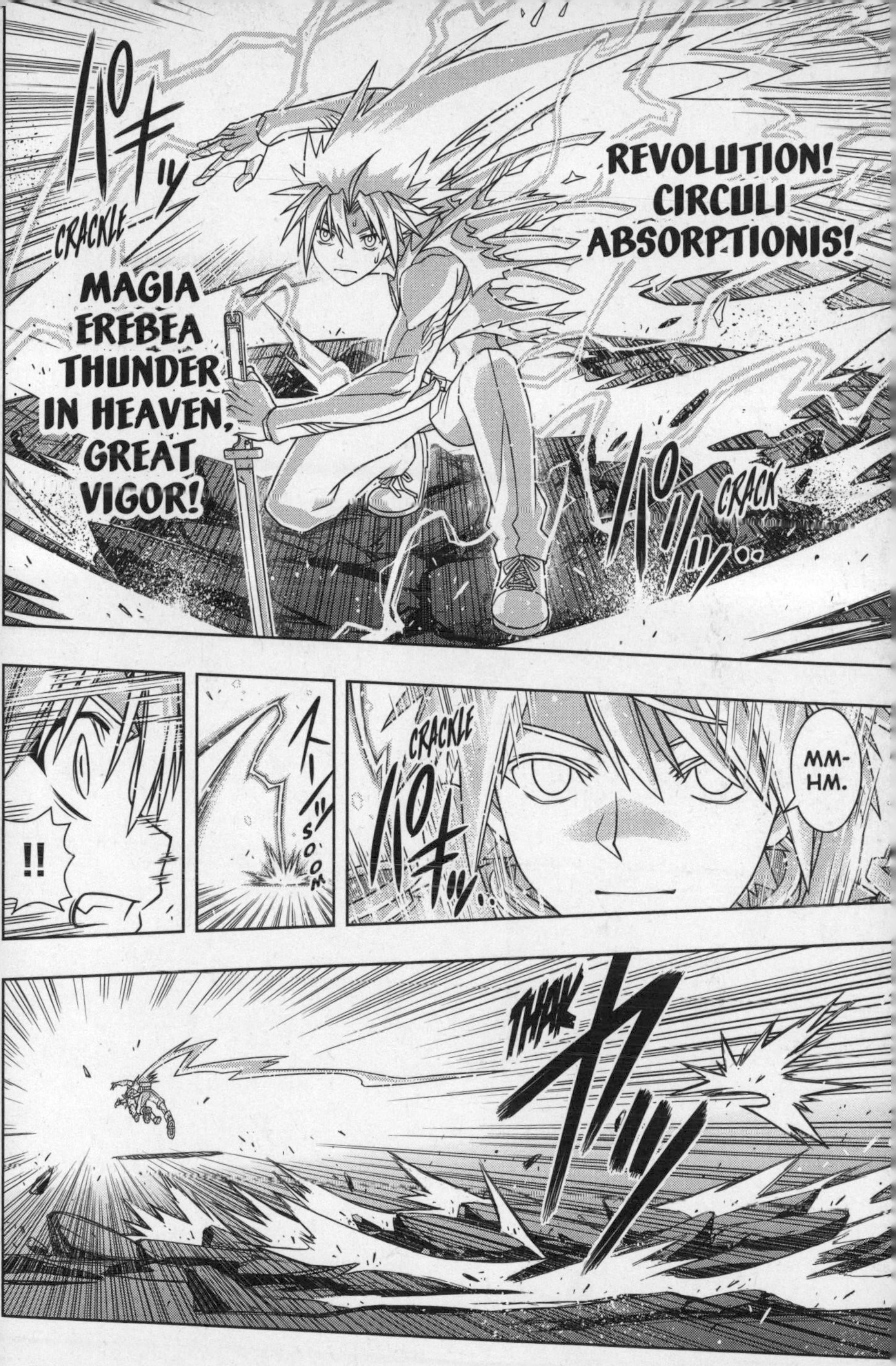
REVOLUTION! CIRCULI ABSORPTIONIS!
CRACKLE
MAGIA EREBEA THUNDER IN HEAVEN, GREAT VIGOR!
CRACK
MM-HM.
CRACKLE
SOOM
!!
THAK

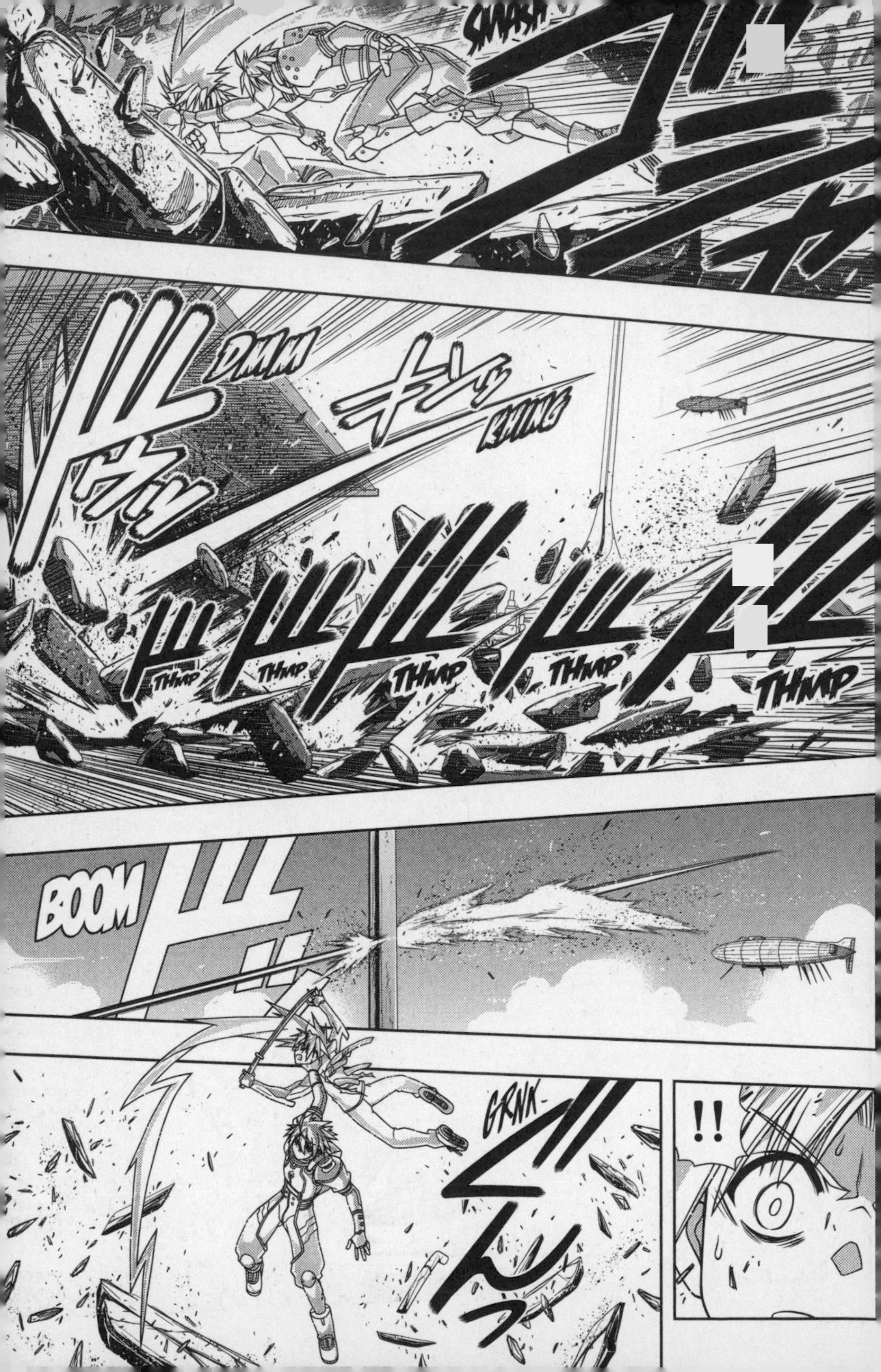
SMASH
DMMM
KHING
THMP
THMP
THMP
THMP
THMP
BOOM
!!
GRNK

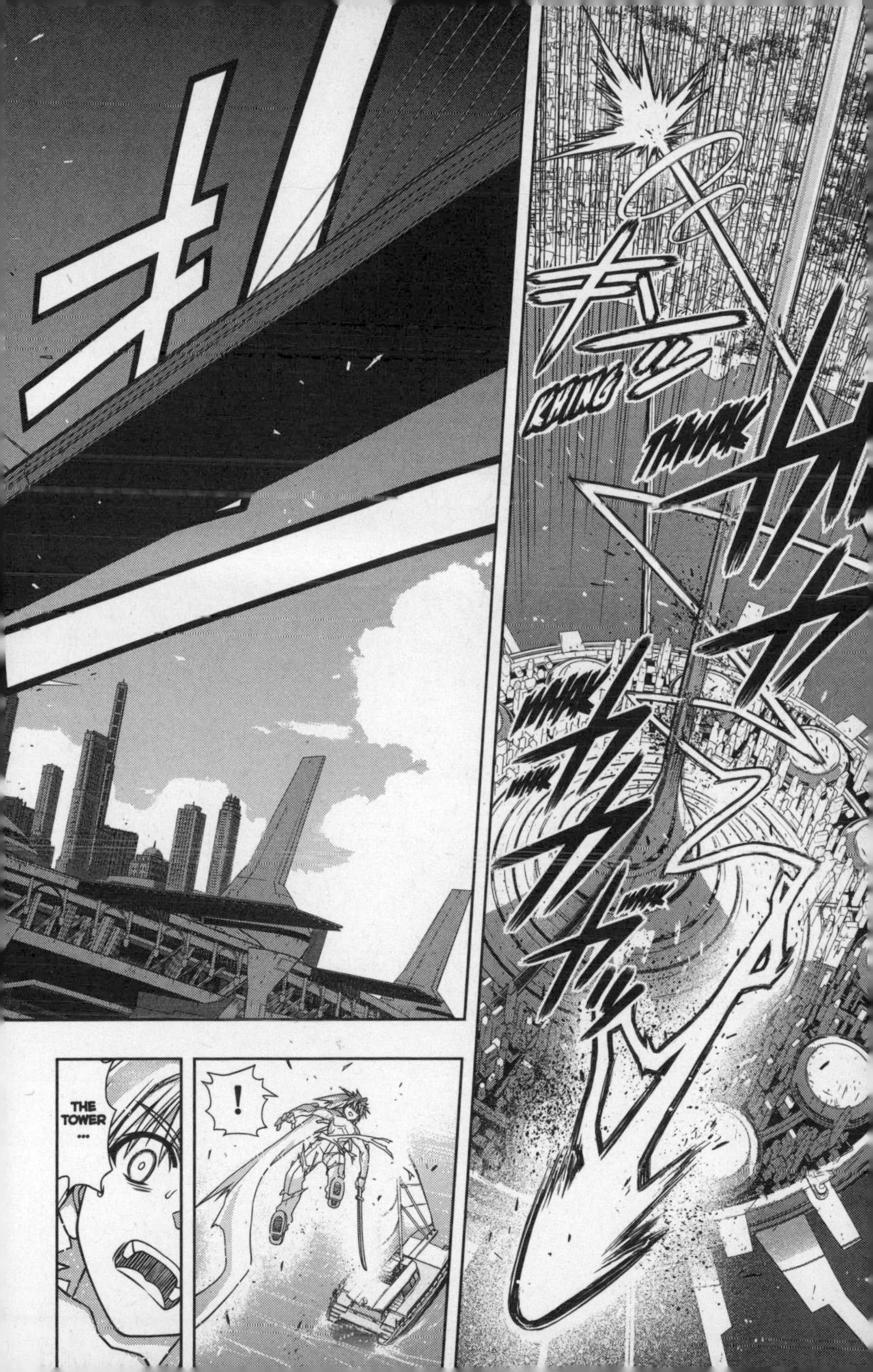
KHING
THWAK
WHAK
!
THE TOWER ...

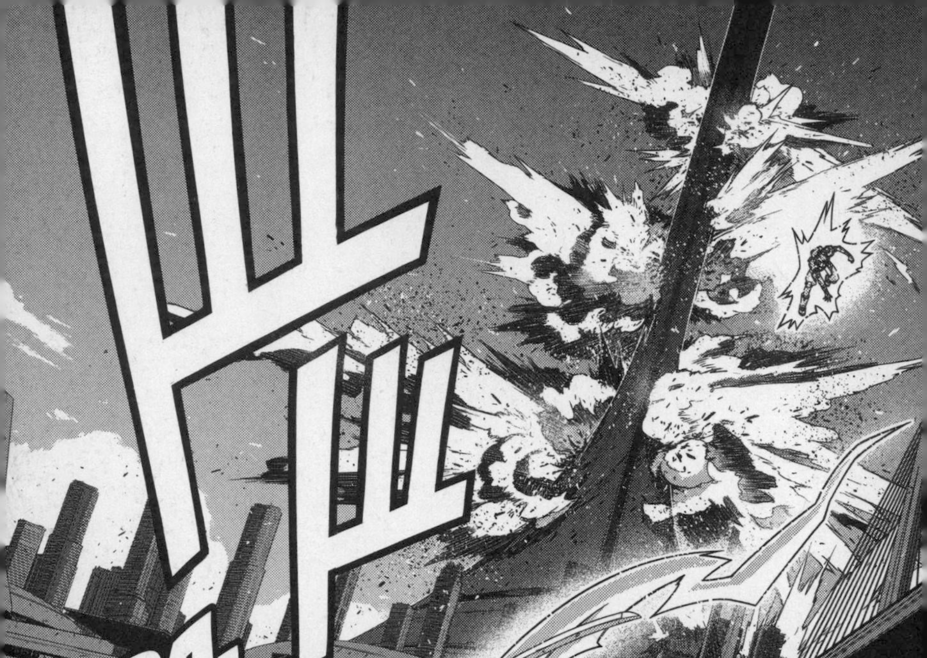
BA-
BOOM

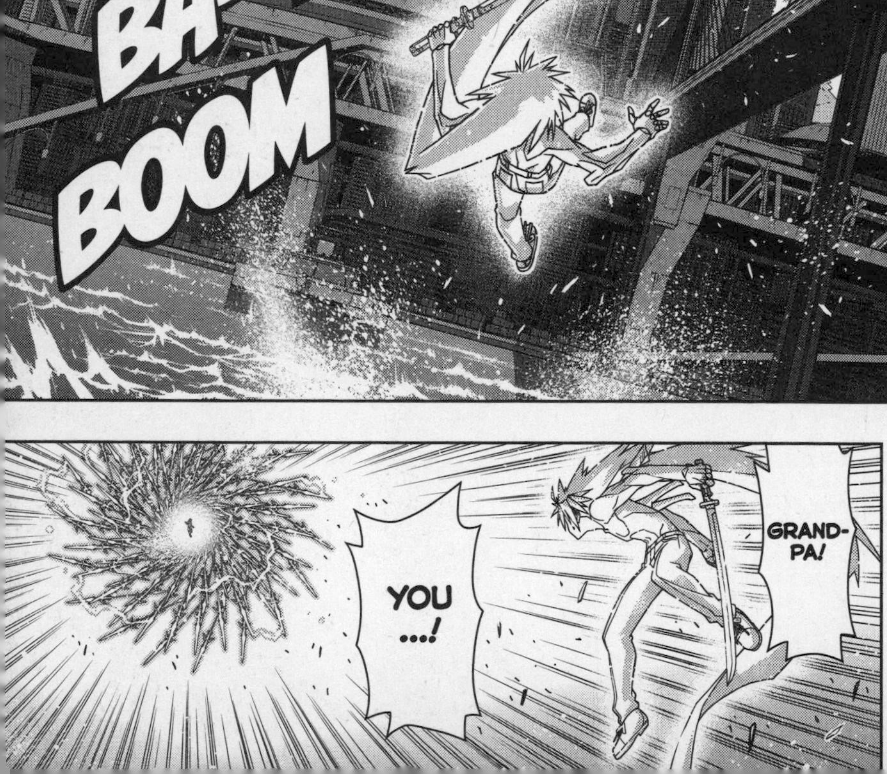
GRAND-
PA!
YOU
...!

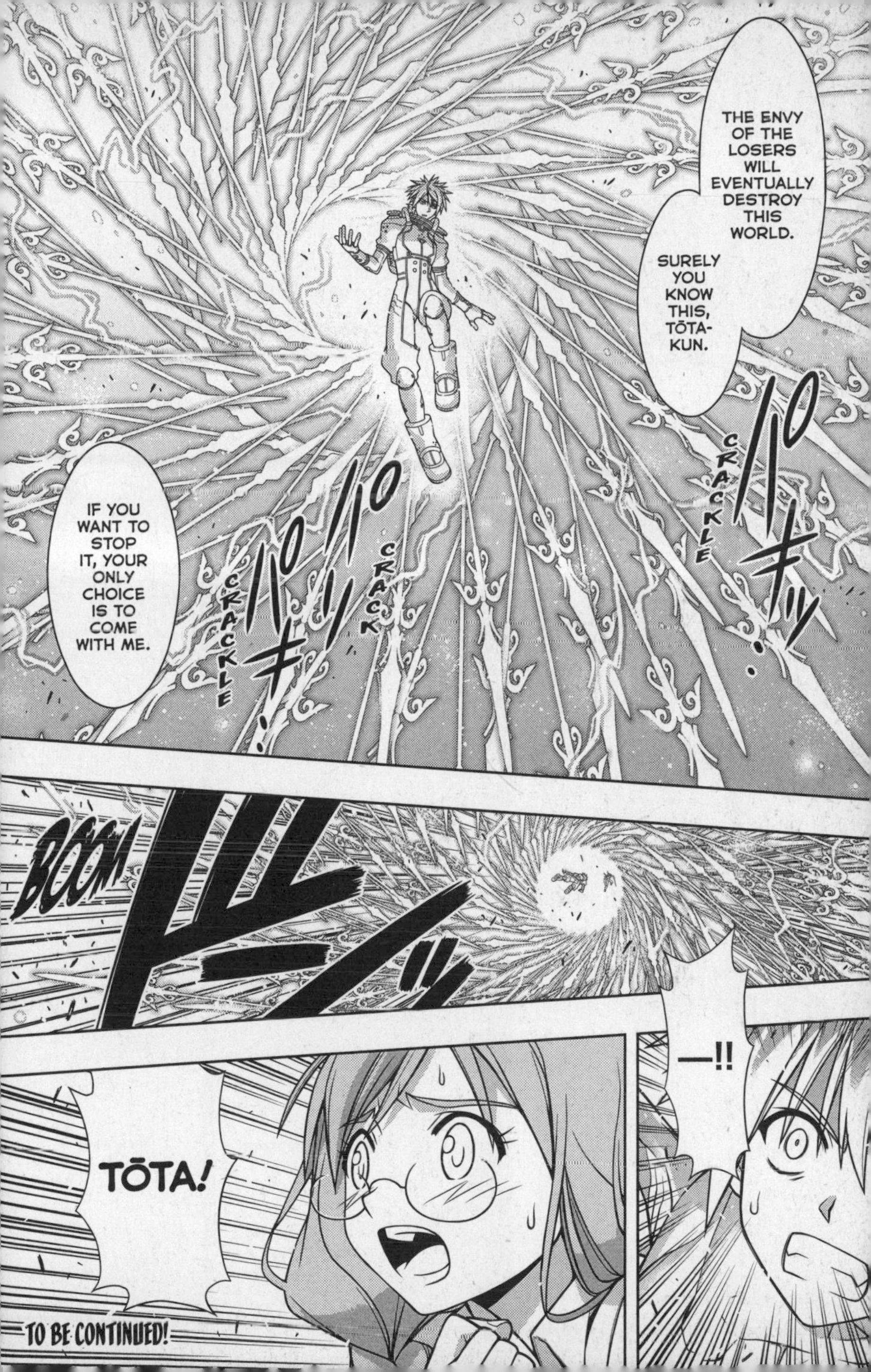
THE ENVY OF THE LOSERS WILL EVENTUALLY DESTROY THIS WORLD.
SURELY YOU KNOW THIS, TŌTA-KUN.
CRACKLE
CRACK
CRACKLE
IF YOU WANT TO STOP IT, YOUR ONLY CHOICE IS TO COME WITH ME.
BOOM
—!!
TŌTA!
TO BE CONTINUED!

UQ HOLDER!

STAFF

Ken Akamatsu

Takashi Takemoto

Kenichi Nakamura

Keiichi Yamashita

Yuri Sasaki

Madoka Akanuma

Thanks to Ran Ayanaga

KODANSHA COMICS x wacom

UQ HOLDER! DRAWING CONTEST

To celebrate the release of the *UQ HOLDER!* anime, Kodansha Comics teamed with up Wacom for a special drawing giveaway contest! Contestants described what kind of original character they would create in the *UQ HOLDER!* universe, and the top entries were selected by Ken Akamatsu.

Kodansha Comics and Wacom enjoyed all the great artwork submitted by the contestants, and offer our congratulations to the prize winners!

CONTEST GALLERY

GRAND PRIZE

DANILO BALEVA
BY JUNO LASTIMOSA

Akamatsu: He became immortal when microorganisms entered his body through injuries after an accident. That concept is outstanding and awesome. Plus, the parasite doesn't like high temperatures and is attracted to the ice-wielding Yukihime, so high points for the romantic comedy setup. And the character design is good, too.

spikes
Parasite's Defense Mechanism
UQ

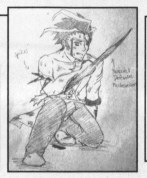

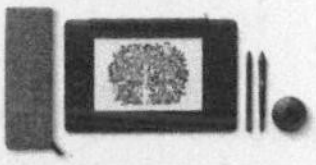

Wacom Intuos Pro Paper Edition

Enjoy the feel of drawing with the Finetip Pen on paper while your every stroke is captured, ready for further work in your favorite software.

SECOND PRIZE

CRIMSON FREYER
BY KAGETSU-13

Akamatsu: The "zombie" thing makes him sound more like an enemy character, but with his ability to control his body parts using string and trade out rotten parts, it's just begging to be made into a manga, which is fantastic. Story ideas are coming to me just from looking at your character illustration.

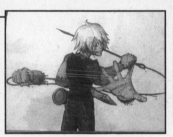

Wacom Intuos Pro

Designed to let you focus on what's important – your creativity.

THIRD PRIZE

HOSHIMIYA YUMEKO
BY NEIDA CABRERA

Akamatsu: Yumeko-chan gets third place because she's adorable (ha ha). Characters that take supportive roles because they aren't the strongest fighters are in high demand in manga, and are often more popular than those power players. Smart approach.

Name: Hoshimiya Yumeko
Age: 18
UQ Holder: 77
Abilities: Clairvoyance Immortality
Magic
Dream Restore
夢子

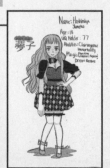

Intuos Comic Pen & Touch Tablet

If you want your characters to fly off the page, Intuos Comic is your perfect sidekick. Sketch, ink, and color frame after frame, and bring your story to life. It's never been easier to make your manga pop.

HONORABLE MENTIONS

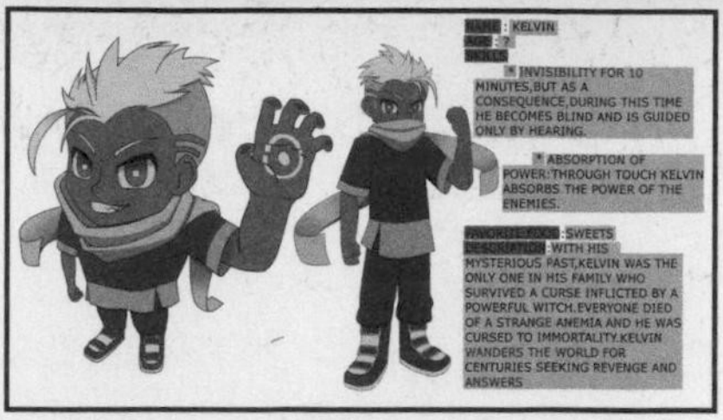
[redacted] : KELVIN
[redacted] : ?
[redacted]
* INVISIBILITY FOR 10 MINUTES,BUT AS A CONSEQUENCE,DURING THIS TIME HE BECOMES BLIND AND IS GUIDED ONLY BY HEARING.
* ABSORPTION OF POWER:THROUGH TOUCH KELVIN ABSORBS THE POWER OF THE ENEMIES.
[redacted] :SWEETS
[redacted] :WITH HIS MYSTERIOUS PAST,KELVIN WAS THE ONLY ONE IN HIS FAMILY WHO SURVIVED A CURSE INFLICTED BY A POWERFUL WITCH.EVERYONE DIED OF A STRANGE ANEMIA AND HE WAS CURSED TO IMMORTALITY.KELVIN WANDERS THE WORLD FOR CENTURIES SEEKING REVENGE AND ANSWERS

KELVIN BY CARLOS SANTOS

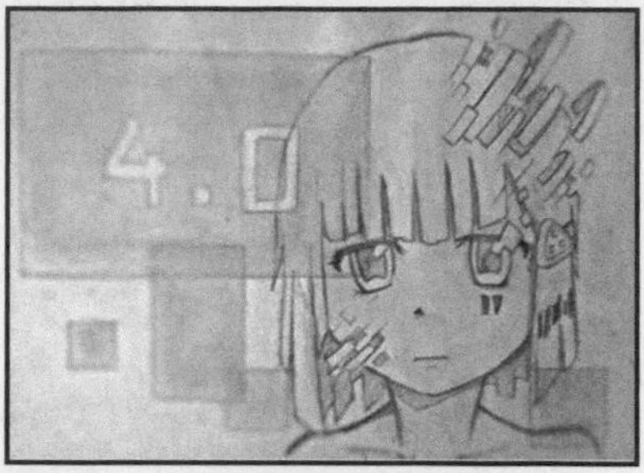
4.0

PROGRAM 4.0 BY ASAD AANAN KHAN

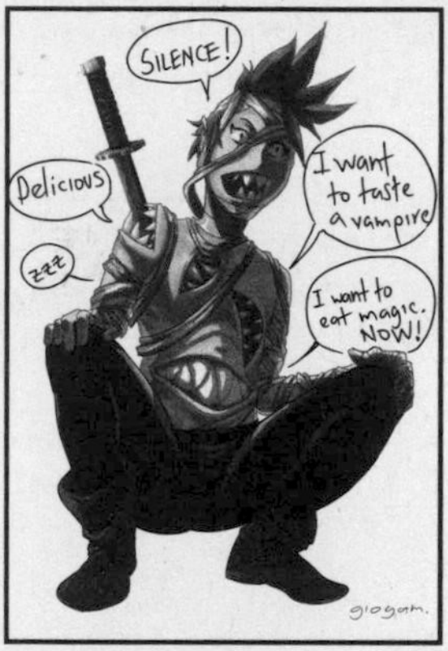
SILENCE!
I want to taste a vampire
Delicious
zzz
I want to eat magic. NOW!
giogam.

TIM BY GIOGAM8

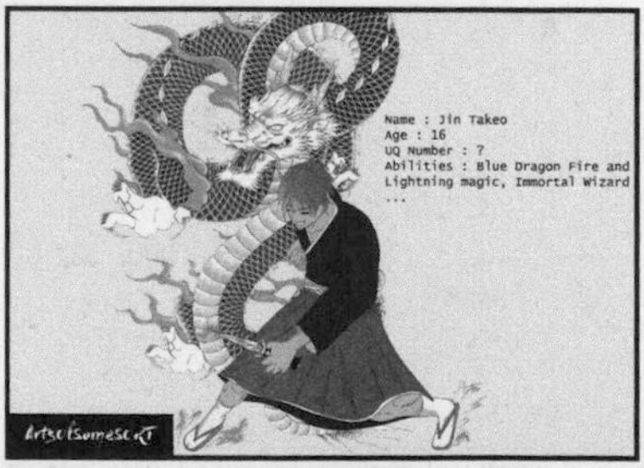
Name : Jin Takeo
Age : 16
UQ Number : ?
Abilities : Blue Dragon Fire and Lightning magic, Immortal Wizard
...

JIN TAKEO BY WANDILE ZWANE

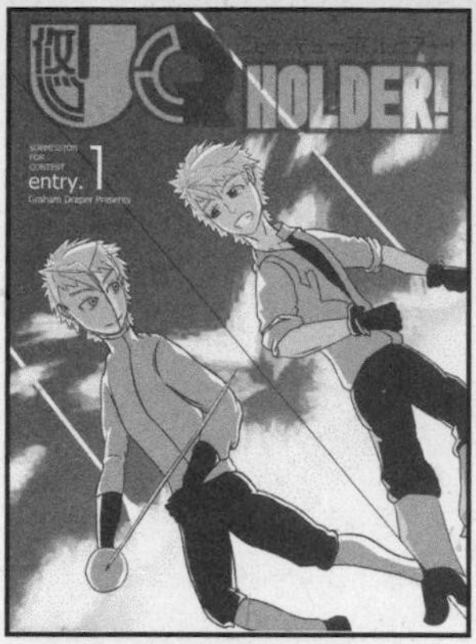
HOLDER!
entry. 1
Graham Draper Presents

GUILLAUME LA ESCRIMEUR BY GRAHAM DRAPER

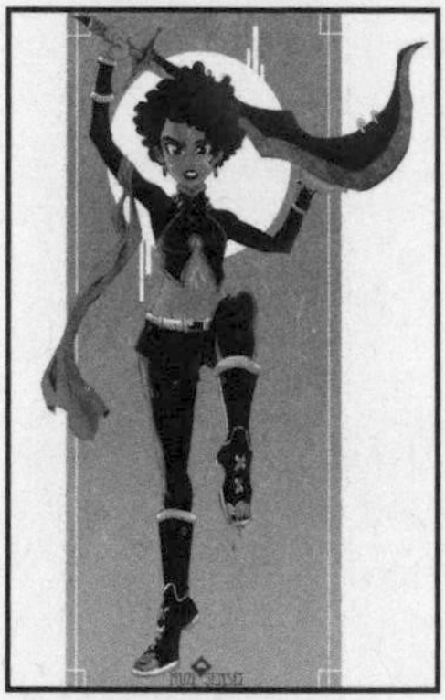

ZANDI NAKAMURA BY MUZI SENSEI

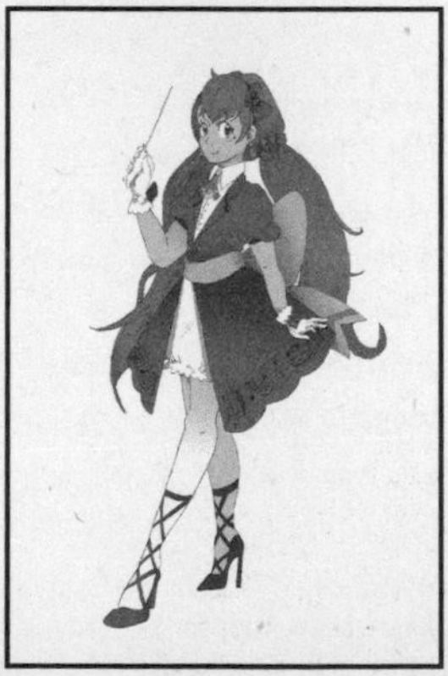

CHIYO GREEN BY PHILLIPA CARRINGTON

TOOLS OF THE TRADE

Ken Akamatsu shares a look into his process for creating and drawing *UQ HOLDER!*

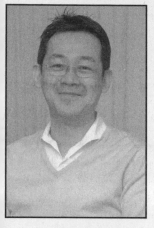

When designing a new character, the personality and abilities come first, and I think of their look from there. But when the character is animated, sometimes their personality starts to resemble their voice actor. (Like Setsuna from *Negima!*)

My manga drawing process is currently entirely digital. However, at the very end of the process, I will always print everything out on a laser printer and see what it looks like to the naked eye. There's a balance that's hard to gauge on a liquid crystal screen. As for color illustrations, I've done them all in digital since *Love Hina*.

On Using Digital Tools

The biggest change from paper to a digital process is that my assistants don't have to come to my studio; they can work from home. We use a private internet server to gather up all the completed individual panels, then put them together to finish each page. Also, it's gotten easier to work with the 3D polygon backgrounds.

There are many things that I can do only with digital tools. The one I use more than I thought I would is the function that lets me change the thickness of a line, to make it wider or narrower, after I've drawn a character. This was impossible in the days of pen and ink. And I can make explosions, magic effects, etc., more realistic with a computer than I can by shaving off screen tone to make them. And the Undo function is useful on color illustrations.

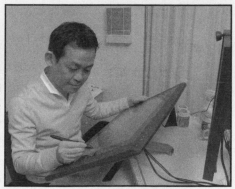

Ken Akamatsu uses a Wacom Cintiq Pen Display to draw his manga digitally.

I started using 3D polygon backgrounds back in the *Negima!* days, but I didn't start doing rough drafts and inking digitally until *UQ HOLDER!* I'm good with computers, and I wanted to go digital as soon as possible, so as soon as *Negima!* ended, I went all digital.

When you've been drawing for a long time, sometimes your sketches start to get wacky. In the days of paper, I would hold them up to the light and look at them backwards to make sure everything looked okay, but now I can just use the Flip tool to check them

instantly. It's very convenient. [Note: Apparently looking at the picture reversed helps you to see it with fresh eyes so you can see if something looks weird, because it's not the same picture you've been staring at.]

Any tips and advice for other artists?

If you use a Wacom product, like a Cintiq Pen Display or a Wacom Intuos Pro Tablet, and manga drawing app or software, you'll be using the exact same tools as professional Japanese manga artists. And we live in an age where you can publish instantly on the internet, so all you need after that is effort and talent.

Actually, the "effort" part goes for paper or digital, so anyway, all you can really do is just draw, draw, draw.

Ken Akamatsu revealed some of his techniques and secrets during a masterclass with his fans at the Japan Expo 2015 Wacom booth.

...JUST DRAW, DRAW, DRAW!

UQ HOLDER! VOLUME 13 IS A WORK OF FICTION. NAMES, CHARACTERS, PLACES, AND INCIDENTS ARE THE PRODUCTS OF THE AUTHOR'S IMAGINATION OR ARE USED FICTITIOUSLY. ANY RESEMBLANCE TO ACTUAL EVENTS, LOCALES, OR PERSONS, LIVING OR DEAD, IS ENTIRELY COINCIDENTAL.

A KODANSHA COMICS TRADE PAPERBACK ORIGINAL

PUBLISHED IN THE UNITED STATES BY KODANSHA COMICS, AN IMPRINT OF KODANSHA USA PUBLISHING, LLC, NEW YORK.

PUBLICATION RIGHTS FOR THIS ENGLISH EDITION ARRANGED THROUGH KODANSHA LTD., TOKYO.

FIRST PUBLISHED IN JAPAN IN 2017 BY KODANSHA LTD., TOKYO.

ISBN 978-1-63236-579-8

PRINTED IN THE UNITED STATES OF AMERICA.

WWW.KODANSHACOMICS.COM

9 8 7 6 5 4 3 2 1

TRANSLATION: ALETHEA NIBLEY AND ATHENA NIBLEY
LETTERING: JAMES DASHIELL
EDITING: LAUREN SCANLAN
KODANSHA COMICS EDITION COVER DESIGN: PHIL BALSMAN